Beware the Thunderbolt!
The 56th Fighter Group in World War II

BEWARE THE THUNDERBOLT!

THE 56TH FIGHTER GROUP IN WORLD WAR II

DAVID R. McLAREN

FOREWORD BY HUB ZEMKE
FORMER COMMANDER, 56TH FIGHTER GROUP

Schiffer Military/Aviation History
Atglen, PA

Dust jacket and color profile artwork by Steve Ferguson, Colorado Springs, CO

56th FIGHTER GROUP – WOLF ONE/ D-DAY PLUS ONE
June 7, 1944 finds Group Leader Col. Hub Zemke and three wingmen from his 63rd FS just south of Paris in mid-afternoon. They have spotted Fw 190 fighters, possibly from Jouvincourt based JG 54, and the "Wolfs" have jettisoned their belly tanks to engage. It will result in Zemke's last two kills with his Wolfpack, bringing his career victory count to fifteen. In July, his P-47 will be hit by enemy fire and it will be turned over for repairs. By years end, Zemke will move on to command the 479th Fighter Group only to fall victim to air turbulence and he became a prisoner-of-war.

Acknowledgements

Most of the primary research material utilized for this book came from two official sources. The Air Force Historical Research Agency at Maxwell Air Force Base, Montgomery, Alabama. I am indebted to Mrs. Judy Endicott for her support over many years from there, along with S/Mgt. Gary McDaniel and Archie Difante for recent help. Also, the staff of the library at the Air Force Museum, Wright-Patterson Air Force Base, Dayton, Ohio: Wes Henry and David Menard. Additional primary source material was furnished by Leo D. Lester, the 56th Fighter Group's historian. Leo has supported this effort over many years and provided invaluable help and material.

Particular acknowledgement goes to Larry Davis, an author of his own book on the 56th Fighter Group, among many others. Additional thanks go to Job Conger, Bob Esposito, Peter Hutting, Marty Isham, and Alexander "Stormy" Sadowski for their support and willingness to provide data and photographs.

Special thanks to Hub Zemke for writing the foreword.

Dedicated To
Kevin, Eric and Christa

Book Design by Robert Biondi.

Printed in the United States of America.
ISBN: 0-88740-660-2

We are interested in hearing from authors with book ideas on related topics.

Published by Schiffer Publishing Ltd.
77 Lower Valley Road
Atglen, PA 19310
Please write for a free catalog.
This book may be purchased from the publisher.
Please include $2.95 postage.
Try your bookstore first.

FOREWORD

The course of history carried the victory scores of the 56th Fighter Group to the forefront of the nations headlines for two years – from 13 April 1943 until 25 April 1945. During these dramatic years of World War II this intrepid group of young, energetic, fighter pilots set the pace for aerial victories for the U.S. Army Air Force Fighter Groups in the European theatre – a goal set for all other Fighter Groups to strive in the quest to down the Luftwaffe Fighter opposition.

Beginning with a diminutive cadre of five pre-war officers and a handfull of staunch enlisted men, the Group took up the crash action task to organize and train a combat qualified fighting unit in the United States. The 56th Fighter Group was allocated the very first, untried, combat designated P-47s. The units' ranks were filled with willing but mostly inexperienced 2nd Lieutenant pilots direct from U.S. Army flying schools. Undaunted they prevailed in overcoming the early aircraft bugs that cropped up, and logged precious basic flying experience in their assigned 2000 horsepower fighting machines.

Unwavered by some training losses – inflicted by self created errors of judgment or unfortunate mishaps associated with their dangerous life – they did report in mid-winter of 1943 at combat duty stations in England. Fully confident with youthful energy and aspiration, they chafed at the delays it took to get their aircraft and supportive logistics across a hazardous Atlantic Ocean. After three more months of bleak winter weather and orientation to living in a completely combat environment, the day came when combat missions were laid on. Two other American Fighter Groups, the 4th and the 78th, entered the fray, simultaneously with the 56th. In retrospect all stood at about the same degree of combat effectiveness.

All had studied and adopted diligently the venerable defensive tactic of the veteran Royal Air Force but they were destined to enter another phase of the war – The Offensive Phase. Faced with the testing of an untried Fighter aircraft that had been built to carry out an Interceptor role, it fell upon each Group to design their own new formations and tactics. All based on carrying the offensive to the enemy.

David McLaren takes up the scenario of the fledgling 56th Fighter Group where it begins its 450 combat missions against experienced and unrelenting Luftwaffe opposition. The 56th seldom wavered from offensive pressure being applied to the Germans. As the capabilities and limitations of their high flying "Thunderbolt" came to be better known, the ratio of wins to losses improved mission by mission. Licking their wounds after slashing encounters with the adroit Jagdgeschwader 26 tacticians, 56th commanders modified tactics to counter their adversaries. By mid-summer 1943 the pitiful range of the P-47 had been extended with external gasoline tanks and could now reach the German border. Formations had been changed from the RAF "string" formation to the German "Finger Four" offensive formation. Launching with a maximum of 36 aircraft in a Group formation, the squadron was beefed up to bring the Group mission strength to 48 aircraft.

The tactics of establishing an Assault, a Support and a Reserve Squadron prevailed for fighter sweeps. Herein developed the hit and recover tactic, wherein the Assault unit broke up the opposition with a vengeance to allow the follow on Support unit to attack and destroy. The Reserve Squadron maintained its high flying alert position to prevent intruding enemy from sneaking into combat.

Long before Major General James Doolittle arrived on the scene as Commanding General of the 8th Air Force, the 56th Fighter Group transitioned its Bomber escort tactics from the stereotype Close Escort duties, as dictated by a persuasive and predominated Bomber Command, to a loose "Free Attack" escort. Under new self established rules of engagement a fighter squadron was assigned to each flank of the bomber stream. The third squadron of the Group took a weaving position well ahead of the Bomber formation. In case of a withdrawal the third squadron fell a mile or two to the rear of the bomber stream. Concern in this case remained in driving the enemy away from battle damaged or straggling bombers.

Under these new tactical dispositions each Fighter Squadron commander retained the inherent flexibility of fighter units to launch attacks wherever the enemy was seen – high or low, or at a distance. In doing so, the squadron commander announced his intention to the Group and pressed his attack on the enemy. Thus the independent squadrons led in attacks, preventing the enemy from gaining positions of advantage before launching assaults.

Coverage to the vacant escort space was taken over by the lingering escort squadrons. After an engagement with the enemy the assaulting squadron returned to the Bomber Stream for reassembly and further escort. A veritable long standing axiom, wherein fighters were tied to bomber formations at all cost, had been broken. Protective Fighters carried the offensive to the enemy, wherever or whenever found. Long range Bomber escort philosophy changed to unburden protective fighters to go after the enemy fighters, before they could close their attacks against the Bombers.

By the early winter of 1943 the variants to the P-47 had added bombs, rockets and napalm to the arsenal of the "Thunderbolt." With added capability the 56th rapidly expanded its lethal potential to also take on the ground support role in addition to long range escort. Over half the missions flown after D-Day found a tried and tested Group doing interdiction work against locomotives, trains, armored convoys bridges, tunnels, barge lines, ships tugs, airfields and other military targets. The flexibility of the unit really unfolded. Even cameras were hung on the armor plate of a few P-47 Group and Squadron leaders to take reconnaissance photos of potential targets.

Somehow and somewhere David McLaren has dusted off 56th Fighter Group records that have lain buried these 50 years. His chronological mission by mission review gives a timeless portrayal of a Fighter Group's dedication to the relentless combat tasks at hand. For the student of aerial warfare, who wishes to trace the development of one of the most progressive Fighter Groups during World War II, recorded here is a resumé of their accomplishments. The evaluation of the 56th's plusses and minuses lays open for review.

The leader of the pack, Hub Zemke. His first P-47C was 41-6330, LM❂Z. The name translates to "May Tovarish, 'My Comrad.'" This particular Jug was moved around a bit and was later coded as UN❂U, UN❂S, and UN❂Z. It was destroyed in a crash landing by Lt. Adam Wisniewski on December 24, 1943. (via Davis)

HUB ZEMKE
Col. USAF (Retired),
Commander 56th Fighter Group, World War II.
(As this book was going to press we were saddened to learn of the death of Hub Zemke on August 30, 1994)

CONTENTS

INTRODUCTION

There are many things that the reader should consider while reading this book. To this point, each day's mission account is given a short background on what else was happening during the course of the particular day's effort by the 8th Air Force, and in some instances what else was occurring during the war at the moment.

Many of the missions described herein were termed "uneventful" by the squadron's historians which were documenting them at the time. Maybe they were mundane and boring – if going out to destroy an enemy force can be described as such. But "uneventful" still meant pre-mission jitters and anticipation of meeting the Luftwaffe in some form. It meant pre-flight briefings and pre-flighting aircraft. It meant getting a heavily laden fighter off the ground, forming into formation, and a friend said to me that "You have never been scared until you've flown formation." It meant penetrating clouds where the enemy was ice, turbulence and the unannounced arrival of another formation within the murk. It meant navigating for a long or short period over water, and then over hostile territory, circumventing known enemy antiaircraft positions – and hoping the intelligence officers were right in identifying their locations, and that the enemy had not relocated some of their AA guns somewhere along your track. It meant watching the gauges and praying that all the needles remained pointing where they should, all the while sweating out the gas and waiting for the time to turn for home and that the mission had not overextended your range. And then came the trek back over the water to home, and prayers that the base was not fogged-in.

Many of the pilots mentioned in this book flew "uneventful" missions for almost their entire combat tour. It was a matter of scheduling and timing and being in the right place at the right time. Others always seemed to be on the right mission at the right time. It was a matter of chance, although many, too, knew when a big show was on and made sure that they were going to be there. Some flew missions because they had to, others because it was expected of them that they be there, while others aggressively sought out each one they could, and came back for more, combat tour after tour.

During World War II many became national heroes: Erich Hartmann and Adolph Galland in Germany; Douglas Bader, Standford Tuck, and J.E. Johnson from England. American pilots were Dick Bong and Thomas McGuire in the Pacific Theater, and Donald Gentile and Robert Johnson in the European Theater.

Their names became household known through the power of the press. Others never have received the acknowledgement they deserved, either because their exploits were overshadowed by someone else's, or that the press was not there at the right time to cover the event, or that history and the historian has neglected them.

You will read here of some of the greatest fighter pilots and fighter missions in history. Many of the participants names will be familiar to the aficionado, while many more are not. Remember that their contribution to the war was equal, and remember the names of those that were lost.

Now, what made some of the great's really great? Desire, aggressiveness, "eye's of an eagle" and physical stamina were a big part of it. Also was the ability to endure, frankly, the bullshit that the fledgling Army Air Force pilot had to contend with in order to obtain his wings to begin with. Things that had to be tolerated to get him into the cockpit of an aircraft that had little bearing upon the knowledge required to pilot an airplane. There were those who did not desire enough. Another factor was the ability to control fear. No rational individual is without it in a life threatening situation, but the great fighter pilots knew how to place it aside and get on with what had to be done.

Regardless, as the more modern day expression goes, "If you don't know who the best fighter pilot is, you aren't one." By the same reasoning, the older expression covers it better: "There are fighter pilots, and pilots who fly fighters." To those who do not understand the difference, I suggest reading the autobiographies listed in the bibliography.

During the Korean War the Air Force dedicated fighter pilots to the role of either air-to-air or air-to-ground combat, a situation that continues today. During World War II a fighter pilot was expected to fulfill both roles, and often on the same combat mission. Early on, the mission might have been a fighter escort to protect the bombers from enemy fighters. The following day the mission might have been a tactical one, dropping bombs and strafing. As the war progressed, escort missions were flown, and then shifted to interdiction on the way home. Then came close air support to the front line troops. A fighter pilot wore many hats, then.

While this book is the story of the fighter pilots of the 56th Fighter Group from inception to the time when the Group was dispersed ten years later, I do not want to neglect the memory of those who were ground-bound. There just is not room to mention them here, and I wished to maintain focus upon the actual air war. For those who pushed paper, pulled guard duty, KP or fulfilled other roles you deserve better than omission. I too am aware that there is nothing colder in winter or hotter than the heat of Hades in summer than a flightline. So, this book is dedicated to all of those that made their own contribution to the success of the Wolfpack at the will of the Air Force. Those ground troops who by their own determination and dedication made the 56th Fighter Group the top unit that it was. Cheers to you all.

David R. McLaren

CHAPTER 1

IN THE BEGINNING

The 56th Fighter Group was created, on paper, on November 20, 1940. The new Group, officially designated as the 56th Pursuit Group (Interceptor), then was activated on January 15, 1941. The initial cadre, consisting of three officers and 150 enlisted men, came from the 15th and 17th Bombardment Squadrons, 27th Bombardment Group (Light), then stationed at Hunter Field, Savannah, Georgia. The fledgling fighter group was assigned to Savannah Field, some seven miles northwest of downtown Savannah and Hunter Field. The Pursuit Squadrons assigned were the 61st, 62nd and 63rd.

Unfortunately, due to circumstances of the time and the rapid movements of the units, few records were retained by anyone, and even fewer records exist today to indicate who either the initial Group or Squadron commanders may have been. The first commanding officer of the 62nd Pursuit Squadron was known to be Captain Dixon Allison, who formed the squadron with two Master Sergeants, a Technical Sergeant, eleven Staff Sergeants and twenty-two men of lower grades. On February 12, Allison was replaced by 1st Lt. Norton Van Sicklen.

In the beginning: A few notables of the future Wolfpack on the flightline at Charlotte. Left to Right: Capt.'s David Schilling, G. Gorrell, Sylvester Burke, Lucian Dade, Phillip Tukey and Samuel Blair. Blair would go to the 341st Fighter Squadron in the South Pacific and become an ace. (Dade via Davis)

On May 10, 1941, the 56th Pursuit Group relocated to Morris Field, Charlotte, North Carolina. At this time the Group was under their first permanent commanding officer, Major David Graves. While at Morris Field they received their first aircraft, "only three early Aircobras, five antiquated Warhawks and several very tired trainers." 2nd Lt. James Orr was named as the new Commanding Officer of the 62nd Pursuit Squadron. As an indicator of just how rapidly changes were made, Orr was replaced by 2nd Lt. Albert Waldon on May 26, and two days later he was replaced by 2nd Lt. John Davis, who lasted for three days before reassignment to the 40th Pursuit Squadron. (Where he had one accredited claim). 1st Lt. Ramond Worsham was Commanding Officer for three more days, and was replaced on June 6 by 1st Lt. David Terry.

By October, they received ten new P-39s and commenced to participate in the "Carolina Maneuvers." This 24 million dollar exercise was to evaluate Army Air Corps and US Army cooperation and was the largest peace time exercise of its sort in the pre-World War II period. For the 56th PG's activities, pilots and support personnel were sent to Myrtle Beach, South Carolina for their interceptor role (This Air Force Base was closed in April 1993). On October 24 they flew an exercise encompassing two hundred fighters against an attacking force of 175 bombers, and successfully repelled the bomber's attacks, at least according to the exercise's judges interpretation of the rules of engagement.

Immediately after December 7, 1941 the 56th Pursuit Group moved again. The new Headquarters Squadron and the 61st Pursuit Squadron were assigned to Charleston Municipal Airport, Charleston, South Carolina. The 62nd PS went to Wilmington, North Carolina on December 10, and the 63rd PS to Myrtle Beach. At this time the P-39s were supplemented by antiquated P-36 Hawks.

On January 14, 1942, their first anniversary, the 56th PG was assigned to the 1st Interceptor Command, Headquartered at Mitchel Field, Long Island, under the command of B/General John Cannon, and assigned the role of defending the Northeastern seaboard. On the 15th the 61st PS moved to Bridgeport, Connecticut: the 62nd PS to Bendix Airfield, 2 1/2 miles southwest of Hackensack, New Jersey on the 17th; and the 63rd PS to co-locate with the Republic Aviation Corporation factory airport at Farmingdale, New York. Group Headquarters was established in the National Guard armory at Teaneck, New Jersey. Across the Hudson River from New York City.

Facilities at all these airfields were spartan. At Farmingdale the Air Corps leased the land required for the military installation from Republic Aviation and spent $2.5 million constructing taxiways and hardstands, having eleven revetments built by the time 63rd Pursuit Squadron arrived. Farmingdale had three runways, all less than a mile long. At Bridgeport

"Miss Mary Jane" with an unidentified pilot of the 61st Fighter Squadron at Mitchell Field. The early P-47Bs were left behind when the 56th Fighter Group went overseas. (via Davis)

there were no barracks, so everyone had to live wherever they could find accommodations in town. Their runways were only 3,000 feet long and the airfield was surrounded by obstacles. Bendix was similar, as construction had not yet caught up with expansion and need.

On May 15 "Pursuit" was dropped in favor of "Fighter" and all such units were redesignated as Fighter Group/Squadron.

As it was, the Group was still equipped with leftovers, some P-40s, and P-400s (Lend-Lease P-39s), rejected by the Royal Air Force, and Army Air Corps P-39s, along with an AT-6 for each squadron.

In mid-May the 63rd Fighter Squadron received the first P-47Bs off the Republic production line. It would be a long and glorious period, for they would fly the rugged Thunderbolt longer than any other unit in history. The first "to be outfitted with these seven-ton monsters, the largest single-engine fighters in the world, and it was largely up to us to put them into every conceivable test before they could be released from the 'secret' list and pronounced ready for combat." As it developed, however, the P-47 was not without its "teething" problems. Group commanding officer Colonel David Graves being the first to bailout of one after a turbocharger explosion.

The original Headquarters Squadron was deactivated in July and Headquarters 56th Fighter Group was formed with thirteen officers and forty-nine enlisted men. At this time a new Group Commander was also named, Colonel John C. Crosswaithe, who transferred in from the 80th Fighter Group. Colonel Graves then became the first Commanding Officer of the newly activated New York Fighter Wing. In an exchange, surplus personnel in the 56th FG were transferred to the 80th Fighter Group that had just moved to Farmingdale from Selfridge Field, Michigan.

On July 23 the 62nd Fighter Squadron moved to Bradley Field, Winsor Locks, Connecticut. Allocation of duties placed the 56th Fighter Group in control of all fighter aircraft within the New York Fighter Wing. The 80th

Fighter Group was assigned air defense in support of the 56th FG, except for their 88th Fighter Squadron that was given a tactical role.

On September 2, the 63rd Fighter Squadron, now versed in P-47s, moved to join the 61st FS at Bridgeport to assist in training the 61st in the idiosyncrasies of the Thunderbolt. Headquarters 56th FG made the move along with them.

Two weeks later a new Group commanding officer was assigned in the form of Major Hubert Zemke. Zemke had joined the Group three months previously as a 1st Lieutenant after returning to the United States from Russia where he had served as a liaison officer establishing the new Lend Lease program to Russia, and also while he was there he also had to convince them that the hand me down P-40s that the Royal Air Force had given them was a good airplane. Colonel Crosswaithe was transferred to the San Francisco Fighter Wing. (Actually, Zemke had been assigned to the 56th Fighter Group, and then transferred out to command the 89th Fighter Squadron, 80th FG, and then reassigned. In the interim he had been promoted twice!).

At this time the squadron commanders were Captain Loren McCollom for the 61st Fighter Squadron, having assumed command in June. Capt. David Schilling now had the 62nd FS after transferring in from Langley Field. Capt. Phillip Tukey also came from Langley and took over the 63rd FS. In a year's time the squadron commanders grade had been jumped from 2nd Lt. to Captain. Such was the exigencies of war, as prior to the war many officers spent four years in grade, now they were promoted in months, if not within weeks. As it was, Zemke would be promoted yet again before the Group went overseas, making the jump from 1st Lieutenant to Lieutenant Colonel in six months! (These promotions did not meet the approval of many of the Regular Army personnel who had spent the depression years eking out a living on low salaries and amassing many years in grade with the carrot of promotion still far in front of them. When

"Betty" was assigned to a Flight Commander of the 61st Fighter Squadron at Mitchell Field, hence the single red band around the aft fuselage. It too was left behind when the Group went overseas. (Air Force Museum)

the Air Force promoted a twenty-one year old to the rank of full Colonel, the resentment went through the roof).

As the 56th Fighter Group was the first to receive the P-47 they not only considered themselves a rather elite unit, but, as mentioned, had to "de bug" the many problems associated with a new airplane. Coupled with many of the pilots lack of experience, yet "hotshot" attitude, the tendency was to push it and themselves beyond rational limits. This caused an abysmal attrition record. Eighteen P-47 pilots from the 56th Fighter Group lost their lives in the six months they flew the aircraft prior to departing for overseas. This amounts to almost a quarter of those pilots assigned to the unit. At this time the Luftwaffe was not as much of an enemy as they were to themselves.

There are really too many losses to cite them all, so some examples will have to do. The first loss was when 2nd Lt. John Vogt had to make a forced landing in a potato patch on May 17 when his engine quit. A month later, in mid-June, the accidents were almost back to back. On the 16th two got too close together while landing and collided. On the 17th 2nd Lt. Earle Coneaux overshot the field and crashed. On the 20th 2nd Lt. Robert Knowle dove into a swamp. Colonel Grave's turbocharger blew on the 24th. 2nd Lt. Henry Plabet spun-in at Bridgeport on the 30th. On September 17 a pilot was buzzing and crashed into a house and was killed. This was the second such incident, only when Lt. Robill Roberts did it, he was able to get back to Bridgeport. Another got too low over long Island Sound and disappeared into the water. Lt. Milton Anderson's engine "blew" on takeoff and he went into the Sound inverted, only he survived. Another midair collision took two lives on October 2.

A factor that may have contributed to one or more other accidents was the heretofore unknown compressibility factor. On November 13 Lt.'s Harold Comstock and Roger Dyar were calibrating P-47 indicated airspeeds at 35,000 feet. After finishing their run, they dove to the next lower assigned altitude, and attained an indicated 725 mph in the process. At this time no one but aircraft engineers knew that the terminal velocity of a P-47 was just over 500 mph. Regardless, their aircraft's controls stiffened to the point where they had great difficulty in pulling out of their dives and regaining control and recovering from what they were sure was a new speed

record. Possibly other pilots had encountered this phenomenon and not lived to tell about it?

On Thanksgiving Day 1942 the 56th Fighter Group was given a Warning Order to prepare for an overseas movement. They marched off in slush three days after Christmas to board a train for Camp Kilmer, New Brunswick, New Jersey and spent almost ten days there waiting time to board ship. "Kilmer combined practicality with no mean portion of psychology." Inspections, shots, inspections, lectures, inspections, physicals, more inspections, and then at 3:00 A.M. on January 6 they were permitted to board the "Queen Elizabeth." It had taken them five hours to move from

Upon arrival in England, the 56th Fighter Group was initially assigned numerals for their aircraft's identification. #201 was 41-6322, and it was assigned to Loren McCollom. It later became identified as HV❂W, and was named "Little Butch." (Air Force Museum)

Camp Kilmer to the docks, and it would take five days to Gourock, Scotland, but it went like overnight compared to the hell of Kilmer.

They disembarked on the afternoon of January 12, 1943 and the Group and two squadrons moved to King's Cliffe. (Spelled variously as either one or two words). King's Cliffe, actually was a satellite for RAF Wittering which was an operational Mosquito night-fighter field with permanent facilities, and became the temporary home of the 63rd Fighter Squadron. Because of the lack of facilities for all at King's Cliffe. King's Cliffe, (was) "In a bleak setting of thick, yielding mud, swept by an incessant and determined wind, its multi-shaded grayish green huts and brown cement buildings were loosely scattered about the surrounding acreage of small farms, pastures and hedge growth; semifused into an ironical picture of rustic innocence." Living quarters were Nissen and Lang huts. It was the home of Hitler's "secret weapon, the common cold." And when the first P-47Cs began to arrive ten days later, fifty percent of the pilots were grounded with sinus and cold symptoms.

Flying training commenced as soon as the aircraft could be checked for any faults that might have occurred during reassembly. It concentrated upon foul weather flying, radio procedures and navigation. Some gunnery training was accomplished at Llanbedr, Wales by the 61st Fighter Squadron and at Matlask, England by the others, starting on March 10 but they did not have the time to get in as much as everyone would have liked. It was hardly even realistic, as it was against a target towed by a sluggish Lysander. During the course of this training the 56th Fighter Group suffered its first aircraft loss in Europe when Lt. Winston Garth, 62nd Fighter Squadron, had a mid-air collision with a Lysander that turned into him while he was concentrating on the target sleeve. Garth bailed out successfully over Llanbedr.

Between winter weather and the lack of aircraft, they just could not get in all of the flying time they desired. Each squadron averaged only twenty P-47s at the time.

CHAPTER 2

COMBAT CHRONOLOGY

On April 4, 1943 the air echelon flew down to Horsham St. Faith, Station F-123, in a group formation of forty-eight P-47s. King's Cliffe and Wittering would return to RAF control until August, when portions of the 20th Fighter Group moved in. Post War, it was sold as surplus by the RAF in January 1959 and is now basically farmland.

By the next day the entire Group had finished the move from Kings Cliffe, Northants, and Wittering to the new field near Norwich, Norfolk. Although the runways were sod, the base, itself, had been a permanent RAF base and had all the desired amenities. Brick barracks, including showers with warm water, hangers and maintenance shops.

April 8: Lt. Colonel Hub Zemke, Major David Schilling, Capt. John McClure and Capt. Eugene O'Neill flew with the 4th Fighter Group on a pre-operational, "Circus," orientation mission. The 4th Fighter Group put up seven P-47s on this mission, only their second one with the Thunderbolt, and the 78th Fighter Group added four more. It was just a sweep over the Pas-de-Calais area of France at 30,000 led by Lt. Col. Chesley Peterson of the 4th FG that swept in ten or fifteen miles beyond Dunkirk before turning back to England.

April 13: Another sweep over Abbeville-St. Omer area by the same four pilots. This mission was identified as Ramrod 50 and included a total of thirty-six P-47s marking the first official operational mission for the 78th Fighter Group in what the 4th FG was already calling the "Seven ton milk bottles." The 56th FG added to the high squadron on this mission, and did not see anything, while the low squadron reported seeing a few bandits that were not encountered.

That afternoon the 56th Fighter Group flew its first operational mission: Rodeo 202. They put up 12 P-47s, four from each squadron with the mission led by Lt. Col. Chesley Peterson and the 56th FG by Lt. Col. Zemke. Eight P-47s took off from Horsham at 1810 with Major Loren McCollom leading the 61st Fighter Squadron and Major Phillip Tukey the 63rd FS. They rendezvoused (RV'd) over Debden where they were met by Zemke and his wingmen, along with twelve P-47s from the 78th FG and sixteen from the 4th FG, and then proceeded over Hastings where Zemke aborted because of an oxygen regulator failure and returned to Debden. Major David Schilling, Deputy Lead, then took over command of 56th FG.

Landfall in was at Le Touquet at 1855, again at 30,000. They proceeded northeast to St. Omer, and then west to Dunkirk, where some heavy (large millimeter), flak was observed. At this point Capt. Roger Dyar, 63rd FS, had to leave the formation because of engine trouble. He glided to England and made a forced landing at Deal at 1930. An English antiair-

craft battery crew then stated that they had shot the P-47 down as it passed over them at 300 feet, believing it to have belonged to the 12th Fighter Group. (There was no such unit). On the way back the 78th FG lost one of their P-47s over the English Channel when its engine quit. Its pilot, Joseph Dickman, was rescued. The remainder of the formation crossed the English coast near Clacton-on-Sea at 7000 feet and landed Horsham at 1955.

April 15: Lt. Colonel Zemke again led the 56th Fighter Group, this time composed of twenty-four Wolfpack P-47s, along with an additional thirty-five from the 4th and 78th FG's, on Rodeo 204 over the Furnes-St. Omer and Gravesline areas.

The 62nd Fighter Squadron put up twelve fighters, the 61st FS seven, and the 63rd FS five. Off at 1707, the first abort occurred when Major McCollom, leading the 61st FS, had to turn back when his tachometer failed, being escorted home by 1st Lt. Kirby Tracy to land at 1730. The mission made landfall in on the French Coast at 1740 and then confusion reigned, as they had been briefed to expect to see German aircraft approaching from the east, but encountered P-47s of the 4th FG that had preceded them into the area and had encountered the Luftwaffe. (The 4th FG lost 3 P-47s, with two pilots MIA, and claimed 3-0-1). On leaving the French Coast on the way home Lt. Paul Conger of the 61st FS encountered three Fw 190s that passed directly in front of him, and he fired, but without result. The Group returned to Horsham at 1810.

April 17: Rodeo 205: The 56th Fighter Group put up twenty-one P-47s, six from the 61st Fighter squadron, led by Major McCollom that were airborne from Horsham at 1232, followed by eleven from the 62nd FS and four from the 63rd FS, with the mission led by Lt. Col. Zemke. The mission was an intended sweep of the Blankenberghe-Bruges-Flushing area and included both the 4th and 78th FG's. The intentions were to divert the Luftwaffe from a 1st Bomb Wing B-17 mission to Bremen. Major Tukey, leading the 63rd had to abort mid-channel because of engine trouble and was escorted home by his wingman. Capt. Lyle Adrianse, also from the 63rd, had to abort, and diverted to Ipswich, leaving but one pilot from the squadron to fly the mission. Landfall in was made on the French Coast at 1320 and only ten minutes was spent on the sweep before turning for home and crossing out over the Coast at 1330, where "slight inaccurate flak" came up behind them.

April 21: Rodeo 208 was a high altitude sweep over the Westhoofd, Noordwijk and The Hague areas of Holland. A total of eighty-two P-47s were dispatched from the 4th, 78th and 56th Fighter Groups. The 56th FG got airborne from Horsham at 1113, with Lt. Col. Zemke leading. The

Preparing for takeoff on one of the Group's first missions. HV⦿E was "Fracy Ann." She was lost on July 30, 1943 over Holland with Lt. Jack Horton being killed. "Little Butch" was Loren McCollom's personal "ship" (as the aircraft were often called). (USAF)

mission was plagued with mechanical problems. Lt. Robert Steel, 62nd Fighter Squadron, couldn't get his landing gear to retract and returned to land after the last fighter was airborne on the mission. 1st Lt. Joseph Egan, 63rd FS, had oxygen problems and turned back as the Group was climbing through 19,000 feet, accompanied by his wingman, Lt. Pat Williams. Just after landfall-in at the Dutch Coast Capt. Robert Weatherbee, 61st FS, engine started cutting out and he aborted, accompanied by Lt. Norman Brooks. No enemy aircraft or flak was encountered, however, and the Group returned at 1243.

April 29: One hundred twelve P-47s were dispatched on Rodeo 211, which was a high altitude sweep of the Pas de Calais and The Hague by the 4th, 56th and 78th Fighter Groups. The 56th Fighter Group, itself, was tasked to sweep Blankenberge-Woensdrecht and The Hague. Each squadron dispatched twelve P-47s and the mission was led by Major Schilling.

Shortly after making a turn over Holland, with the 61st Fighter Squadron led by Major Loren McCollom, flying as the high squadron, two Fw 190s were spotted diving on the two lower squadrons from 31,000 feet. Schilling saw them coming, but his radio quit and there was nothing he could do to warn the others. Between six and fifteen Me 109s and Fw 190s were involved, and they made a head-on attack on the 62nd and 63rd squadrons at 28,000, breaking under, and then zooming to 30,000 to repeat their attacks. Lt. Winston "Bill" Garth, 62nd FS, and Schilling's wingman, was hit early in the attack by 20mm rounds. He was seen to bailout at 600 feet over water. He was picked up by a German ship and became a prisoner of war. Capt. John McClure, 62nd FS, also went down, north of Breskens, and he also became a POW.

Yet the Group's troubles were still not over as the aggressive Luftwaffe pressed their attacks. Schilling, unable to call for help, had his P-47 hit by machinegun fire. Lt. Charles Harrison, 62nd FS, P-47 was "riddled by machine gun bullets and his left wing was hit by a 20mm cannon shell" while he was attempting to cover McClure's bailout. Major Philip Tukey and Capt. Lyle Adrianse were attacked at long range, but evaded damage. Lt. Gorden Batdorf, 63rd FS, also evaded enemy fire, by diving to 1,000 feet. The Group returned to Horshem at 1410.

The results of the mission were sobering as the pilots discovered that they, indeed, were in a real war. The initial exuberance, as evidenced by an incident where Lt.'s Tracy, Curtis, Johnson, Brown, Conger and Nilsson (a 61st FS Staff Officer) were all confined to the airfield for two weeks for firing their handguns inside of their barracks, would never be repeated. Likewise, Zemke came down on pilots that transgressed air discipline.

Schilling got "reamed" for not transferring command to another squadron commander and returning from the mission when his radio quit. Lt. Dick Mudge became Officer of the Day for three days for making an unauthorized landing at a Royal Air Force Base, and then taking off on a closed runway.

The first 56th Fighter Group mission for May 1943 was on May 3, a Rodeo under VIII Fighter Command's Field Order 8. (The VIII Fighter Command commenced redesignating their Field Order numbers on May 1, hence the new lower series of numbers). The VIII FC command put up 118 P-47s on this mission, with the 56th FG trailing the 4th and 78th Fighter Groups. They RV'd over Felixstone, England and set course for a sweep over Walcheren Island-Knocke-Ostend and Nieuport areas. Lt. Col. Zemke, with 12 P-47s of the 62nd FS led his group and they were airborne at 1710. They crossed the coast above Blankenburgh at 30,000 where 1st Lt. Jack Brown's, 63rd Fighter Squadron, engine quit. But he got it running again satisfactorily and rejoined the formation. Over Ostend the Group was recalled because of bad weather moving in, and they landed at 1832.

May 4: VIII FC FO 10 dispatched 117 P-47s of the three P-47 Fighter Groups on the first Ramrod mission for the 56th and 78th Fighter Groups, with the 56th FG providing withdrawal escort for fifty-four 1st Bomb Wing B-17s on a mission to bomb the Ford Motor Company plant at Antwerp. Lt. Colonel Zemke was first off with twelve Thunderbolts of the 62nd Fighter Squadron, followed by twelve from the 63rd and thirteen from the 61st FS's. Again the mission was plagued by mechanical problems. Zemke had to abort while approaching the Dutch Coast, Lt. Lucian Dade, 63rd Fighter Squadron, returned because of radio problems. Capt. Adrinanse's, 63rd FS, and Capt. Walter Cook's, 62nd FS, radio's both quit also, and 1st Lt. Williams', 63rd FS, guns wouldn't fire.

RV was made ten miles North of Flushing with forty B-17s that could be found and they were escorted back to Oxford. Since Zemke had aborted, command of the operation had passed to Major McCollom, 61st FS, and for the 62nd the mission was uneventful. However, Lt. Joseph Curtis, 61st FS, did believe that he saw three Fw 190s and went down to 15,000 to investigate, but had no encounter. The squadron also observed three Me 109s off the Dutch Coast. The 63rd FS did encounter some Luftwaffe fighters, though. Lt. Walker "Bud" Mahurin spotted a Spitfire IX from the RAF fighter group that was bringing up the rear on the mission come under attack by three Fw 190s and dove to its assistance. His P-47 was hit in the wing by enemy 20mm fire for his troubles. 1st Lt. John Vogt engaged another Fw 190, but made no claim of hitting it. One P-47 from the 4th FG was seen to be chased over the sea by two Fw 190s and then crash into the water. The pilot was lost. The 56th FG returned to Horshem at 1925.

May 6: Lt. General Frank Andrews was killed in an aircraft accident in Iceland. He had been named by General Eisenhower in January to lead the American troops in England. He was replaced by Lt. General Devers.

May 7: VIII Fighter Command Field Order 12 sent 104 P-47s from the three groups on a Rodeo over Flushing-Ostend-Knocke. Lt. Col. Zemke again led the mission, with the 56th FG getting thirty-eight Thunderbolts up. Off Horshem at 1500, they arrived over Felixstone five minutes early, and then proceeded to sweep Walcheren Island and Graveline at 30,000 feet at 1545. The 62nd and 63rd Fighter Squadrons spotted ten or eleven Fw 190s, but did not engage them, while the 61st FS was followed out over Dunkirk by four more Fw 190s. They returned to base, RTB, at 1925.

May 8: Lt. Col. Zemke was promoted to full, "Bird" Colonel.

May 11: VIII FC FO 16 called for a Rodeo over Dunkirk and Knocke with 128 P-47s from the three groups, but the mission was recalled shortly after becoming airborne at 1239, and they were all back down by 1304. Continuing bad weather causing the cancellation.

May 13: VIII FC FO 17 was to be the second Ramrod for the 56th Fighter Group. The 56th FG was tasked with providing high cover for thirty-one B-17s attacking airdromes at St. Omer, and also to provide a diversion for eighty-eight B-17s attacking the Potez aircraft factory at Meaulte. They crossed the coast at 1627 at 30,000 feet, being led by Col. Zemke. Although 63rd FS pilots, led by Major Philip Tukey, saw ten enemy aircraft, none were encountered and the mission was down at 1720.

May 14: VIII FC FO 18 was to send up 118 P-47s from the three fighter groups as escort for B-17s of the 94th and 95th Bomb Groups to bomb the ship building docks at Antwerp. This would prove to test the mettle of both the P-47 and the pilots of the 78th and 56th Fighter Groups's that had not as yet truly met the Luftwaffe. Airborne at 1228, landfall-in was over Knocke at 29,000 feet, with the 63rd Fighter Squadron flying as top cover for the forty Flying Fortress.

Col. Zemke, flying a 62nd FS P-47 while leading the 61st FS and the Group, saw the German fighters as they approached the bombers from 2 o'clock at 24,000 feet near Antwerp. About thirty-five Fw 190s, with the first group containing fifteen aircraft. Zemke took his White Flight into a diving 180 degree turn after four of them, fired without apparent result, and then climbed to meet two more, firing at the later pair again. Col. Zemke was sure that he had a "kill," but re-evaluated his thinking and decided it was maybe a "probable" and then, after looking at the gun camera film it was officially scored as a "damaged." Then, low on fuel, they headed for Flushing and home, missing Lt. Robert Johnson who had separated from the flight.

Meanwhile, Red Flight, Led by Capt Merle Eby, 61st FS, saw four German fighters coming in on the bombers and took his four Thunderbolts down after them. Eby fired on one, chasing it down to 15,000 feet. Lt. Milton Anderson fired on another, and did see red flashes about three feet behind the cockpit. He chased it down to 15,000 feet, but had to leave it as he too was being followed, being warned off by his wingman, Lt. Gerald Johnson. Lt. Albert Bailes chased this one and fired, claiming it as a probable. Lt. Gerald Johnson, breaking off, found another and fired at it, witnessing pieces fall off. For the mission, the 56th FG scored one probable and one damaged, while the 78th FG claimed three destroyed. (For the loss of three of their own P-47s). The 4th FG claimed two destroyed.

May 15: VIII FC FO 19. A high altitude Rodeo over Amsterdam and Rotterdam prior to a bombing mission. Major Tukey and the 63rd Fighter Squadron led the 56th Fighter Group's portion of the mission, with the 63rd FS putting up fourteen P-47s and the 62nd FS twelve. For these two squadrons the mission would be uneventful, except for encountering heavy flak over Rotterdam. The 61st FS, led by Major McCollom with fourteen Thunderbolts, was airborne at 0851. They locked on four Fw 190s out of a flight of twelve over Schoonham, and Capt. Francis Gabreski fired on three in succession, seeing hits on one that dove away. Lt. Dick Mudge fired on the last one in the flight, and saw strikes behind the cockpit. They landed at 1026, claiming two Fw 190s damaged.

May 16: VIII FC FO 20 was a combination Rodeo and diversionary sweep over Cayeux, Abbeville and Gravelines. The 4th, 56th and 78th Fighter Groups's sent 113 Thunderbolts, with the 56th FG specifically tasked to sweep Flushing-Bruges-Gravelines with twenty-five P-47s of the 61st and 63rd Fighter Squadron's, led by Col. Zemke. Up at 1205, they were back at 1333, and although the 61st FS spotted a dozen Fw 190s over Bruges at 1245, the mission was uneventful.

That afternoon's mission was VIII FC FO 21, and it was the first time that the 56th FG would fly two missions in one day, this time including the 62nd FS. The 61st FS was off at 1650 on a sweep of the Dunkirk-Dixmude-Flushing area with fourteen P-47s led by Major McCollom. A half hour later Col. Zemke took twenty-six P-47s from the other two squadrons along the same route, but no one saw anything and the mission was back by 1850. (The 78th FG flying a similar route would claim three enemy aircraft downed for the loss of one of their own).

May 17: VIII FC FO 22. A Rodeo over Brest and Cherbourg with 113 P-47s of the three groups. Each 56th Fighter Group squadron dispatched twelve P-47s, and the mission, led by Col. Zemke, was airborne from Horshem at 1345 where all but one flew to Exeter to top off their fuel tanks for the extended range mission. Lt. Joseph Egan, 63rd FS, having to make a forced landing near Grandsdon Lodge because his engine failed. From Exeter, they were to fly as a diversion for bombers striking Bordeaux and L'Orient, and they were airborne from Exeter at 1640.

At 1730 in the vicinity of Charbourg, about twenty unidentified German aircraft were seen, but not encountered. After an uneventful sweep, the 56th FG returned to Exeter at 1825 to refuel, and returned home at 2104.

May 18: VIII FC FO 23 put up 113 P-47s on fighter sweeps. The 56th Fighter Group flew their Rodeo over Noordwal-Flushing with the 61st Fighter Squadron taking off twenty minutes ahead of the other two squadrons at 1533. The 62nd and 63rd FS's became airborne at 1554, with this portion being led by Col. Zemke. 1st Lt. George Hall, 63rd FS, had to abort and was shepherded home by 1st Lt. Vance Ludwig. The 61st FS spotted gaggles of enemy fighters over the continent: Twelve Fw 190s over Rotterdam at 17,000 feet, three Me 109s over Flushing at 35,000 feet, and twelve Fw 190s over Ghent at 24,000 but combat was not joined with any of them. The other two squadrons spotted eight to ten Luftwaffe fighters, also, but had no encounters. The mission was back on the ground by 1725.

May 19: VIII FC FO 24 was a diversionary escort for B-17s of the 379th Bomb Group. This was the first Circus where the 56th Fighter Group would be on their own. Again led by Col. Zemke from the front of the 62nd Fighter Squadron, they were up at 1128 with forty Thunderbolts. Forty B-17s were to simulate a raid on Holland, while the main bomber mission went against Keil and Flensburg. As the B-17s of the 379th BG changed their route, they were never located, and so the 56th Fighter Group swept into Ijmuiden, and then out over The Hague.

At 1210 four Me 109s were spotted by the 61st FS, and four of the German fighters dove on their Blue Flight from dead astern, with two of them pressing their attacks, and then the rest followed, but the Blue Flight dove away and out distanced them. Zemke's White Flight had to land at Coltishall, while the rest RTB between 1250 and 1310.

Above left: "Princess Pat" formates with a B-17 over Europe for the long trip home. It belonged to Lt. Charles Reed, who joined the 63rd FS on March 12, 1943 and completed his missions in May 1944. He then returned to the United States and was assigned to the 507th FG. (USAF) Right: Another view of "Princess Pat" showing the paper, glue-impregnated belly tank. "Pat" was coded UN◆X, 42-75196. (Reed via Davis)

May 20: VIII FC FO 25 was another Rodeo, to Amsterdam, with the 56th Fighter Group contributing thirty-six of the 115 P-47s on the mission. Up at 1123 with Col. Zemke in charge. 1st Lt. Gorden Batdorf, 63rd Fighter Squadron, had to abort when he became sick, being replaced by 1st Lt. George Compton, who was flying as the squadron's spare. Other than Lt. Vance Ludwig having to make an early landing at Coltishall because he was low on fuel, the mission was totally uneventful.

May 21: VIII FC FO 26 sent 105 P-47s of the three groups on a Rodeo over Ostend and Ghent, "The old bus run." The 56th Fighter Group put up thirty-eight with Major McCollom leading from the 61st Fighter Squadron. The 62nd FS had 1st Lt. Charles Harrison and 2nd Lt. Richard Altshuler abort with mechanical problems. A dozen enemy fighters were seen to engage the 4th FG over the North Sea and Ostend at 1350 where they claimed one Fw 190 downed, but they lost two pilots as POWs and had one killed for their efforts. The 56th FG returned to Horsham at 1428.

May 25: VIII FC FO 28 provided another high-altitude sweep over Mardyck-Ypres-Knocke with 116 P-47s. The 56th Fighter Group's portion of the Rodeo was airborne from Horsham St. Faith at 1040 with Major David Schilling leading the 62nd Fighter Squadron and the Group. The 63rd FS had two aborts; 1st Lt. Joseph Egan, who had smoke and oil com-

"The Wolf" belonged to Lt. Wayne O'Connor. It was wrecked on takeoff on September 28, 1943 by another pilot. O'Connor, from Aberdeen, SD was killed at Coesfeld, Belgium on Nov. 11, 1943. His pet dog, "Slipstream," was to be impounded, but evaded and disappeared. (USAF)

ing out of the left side of his engine. 1st Lt. Pat Williams accompanied him home, since his supercharger regulator had failed. Due to odd climatic conditions, the vertical visibility over the continent was nil, although the horizontal visibility was good. But it did not matter, as no enemy aircraft or flak was seen. They returned at 1205.

May 26: VIII FC FO 29 was another Rodeo over Egmond-Amsterdam-The Hague with 122 Thunderbolts of the three groups. The 56th Fighter Group, led by Major McCollom and the 61st Fighter Squadron, put up a dozen P-47s from each squadron and were airborne at 1424. Other than spotting some German fighters that were too low and too far away to chase, and encountering heavy flak over Amsterdam, the mission was uneventful and they were home by 1543.

May 27: VIII FC FO 30 called for a Rodeo over Knocke-Roulers-Gravelines by the three P-47 groups. Led by Col. Zemke, each squadron of the 56th Fighter Group got up a dozen P-47s. 1st Lt. George Hall, 63rd Fighter Squadron, had his oxygen regulator fail and was escorted home by his Blue Flight, which was the only occurrence of note on the otherwise uneventful mission. They RTB'd at 1746.

May 28: VIII FC FO 32 took the three P-47s groups back over Walcheren Island-Eecloo-Dixmude-Dunkirk. Off at 1720 and led by Col. Zemke with the 62nd Fighter Squadron, they climbed to 31,000 feet and made landfall in over Eekloo, operating as a diversion for a Ventura attack on Zeebrugge. They crossed out over Dunkirk at 1820 and were back on the ground at 1859 after another uneventful mission. These Rodeo's were becoming old hat and boring.

May 29: VIII FC FO 33 brought a change, as finely they were assigned a Ramrod mission. Also, for the first time the squadron strength was increased from twelve to sixteen P-47s, and the three P-47 groups put up a total of 131 aircraft. The 56th Fighter Group was off at 1039 from Horsham, to land at Exeter at 1145 for fuel. Airborne again at 1507, led by Col. Zemke with the 62nd Fighter Squadron leading the 56th FG's portion of the mission. They were to escort seventy-two B-17s to Reenes, and over Reenes the 63rd FS spotted eight Fw 190s, but had no encounter with them. But, the 61st FS, led by Major McCollom, did, when they encountered thirty Me 109s carrying belly tanks. McCollom claimed 1 Me 109 as a probable, and Lt. Joseph Curtis another as damaged. Zemke's 62nd FS spotted twenty more Me 109s, but these avoided combat, so he dispatched eight of the squadron's P-47s to escort home a B-17 that was having engine trouble over the French Coast. The Group landed Exeter for fuel at 1650 and were back to Horsham at 1930.

May 31: VIII FC FO 34 put the three groups back on another Rodeo over Knocke-Courtrai-Dunkirk. Col. Zemke led the 56th Fighter Group's portion from the 63rd Fighter Squadron. The 63rd FS, was sorely hurt on this mission. First, 1st Lt. Jack Brown had to return because of a gas leak, being replaced by 1st Lt. Harold Comstock who was up as the spare. Then, 1st Lt. George Compton had to land at Hornchurch with mechanical problems. He was accompanied by 1st Lt. Arthur Sugas.

Landfall in was over Knocke at 1145, and they "swept deep around Countrai," only for the 63rd FS to loose 1st Lt. Pat Williams when his P-47s was seen to make a half-roll at 30,000 feet and enter a steep dive. Despite repeated calls by Zemke and others, no response was heard or observed and Williams was last seen descending through 10,000 feet. He was later determined to have been killed, with the failure of his oxygen regulator being the suspected cause for fatal ensuing anoxia. The Group returned to Horsham at 1240.

June 5: 1st Lt. Richard Allison, 63rd Fighter Squadron was, killed on a navigational training flight while enroute to visit a friend at another base. Apparently he suffered from vertigo while descending through a cloud layer on instruments. The wreckage was found the next day.

June 7: VIII FC FO 38. The 61st Fighter Squadron put up sixteen P-47s, the 62nd FS seventeen, including that of Col. Zemke's, the mission leader, and the 63rd FS sixteen on a Rodeo to the Nieuport-Dunkirk area. Landfall in was the vicinity of Ostend at 28,000 feet at 1229, whereupon they were recalled because of bad weather. The 61st FS returned to Horsham, landing at 1321. The 62nd and 63rd FS's were forced divert to Bradwell Bay because of fuel shortages, where they landed at 1315, refueled, and returned to Horsham at 1450.

June 9: Major McCollom was transferred to Hq. 56th Fighter Group as Deputy Commanding Officer and Flying Executive Officer. He was replaced by Captain Francis Gabreski as the 61st Fighter Squadron Commander. This resulted in a quandary for Col. Zemke, as when Gabreski had joined the Group in March he had already combat experience with the Polish Air Force in England, yet was lacking time in grade behind Capt. Eby and others. In the protocol of the military, seniority should have mandated the position to one of the others, but Gabreski got the job because of his experience.

June 10: VIII FC FO 40. The first large scale P-47 mission that did not include the 4th Fighter Group's participation; the 56th and 78th FG's put up ninety-two Thunderbolts on their own as an escort for six B-25s. The 56th FG's portion of the Order called for a sweep over Westhoofd-Ghent-Dunkirk, and they were airborne at 1710 with forty-nine P-47s, although three soon aborted with various mechanical difficulties. Col. Zemke led the mission as planned, and it turned out to be another uneventful one. They returned at 1945.

"Holy Joe" was the personal P-47 of Lt. Joe Egan. Egan was assigned to "C" Flight, 63rd FS in March 1943 and eventually commanded that flight. He finished his first missions in March 1944 and returned for another tour in April. He was killed on July 19, 1944. This ace was from New York, NY. (USAF)

The Thunderbolt was rugged enough to bring a pilot home with this kind of battle damage. Courage and confidence in both yourself and your aircraft made a big difference in the air war over Europe. (via Davis)

June 11: VIII FC FO 37 called for a high-altitude Rodeo over Ostend-Eecloo with 136 P-47s from the three Fighter Group's. (Apparently someone missed that FO #37 should have been in effect during the first week of the month, and decided to place the number this date, instead of not using it). The 56th FG, under Major McCollom, was off Horsham at 1207 with fifty Thunderbolts. Four, including McCollom, had to abort because of diverse problems.

Command of the mission was given to Major Phillip Tukey, 63rd Fighter Squadron, who took them over the continent at 28,000 feet at 1245. They spotted two gaggles of unidentified type enemy aircraft, but they were not engaged, and returned to Horsham at 1336.

The day's second mission was VIII FC FO 41, another Rodeo, this time over Graveslines-Courtrai-Ostend with 139 P-47s of the three groups. The 56th Fighter Group, led by Col. Zemke, was airborne at 1609 with fifty-one P-47s. The 61st Fighter Squadron had two aborts, and the 63rd FS one. Again the mission was uneventful, and unremarkable, with the exception that it was noted that the German's were attempting to block radio transmissions by placing a high-frequency tone on the radio channels. (As if they were not having enough problems with the radios, themselves). They RTB'd at 1738.

June 12: VIII FC FO 43. A high altitude Rodeo over Blankenburghe-Calais with ninety-six Thunderbolts of the 4th and 56th Fighter Group's. Led by Major McCollom, now the 56th FG's Operations Officer. The 56th FG was airborne at 1909 with forty-eight Thunderbolts, and for the first time in many missions they had no aborts. Arriving over Blankenburghe at 1945, they swept over Roulers, and while over Belgium Major Schilling saw twelve Fw 190s at five thousand feet and climbing. He took his White Flight down to attack, but overshot as eight Fw 190s dove away from the Thunderbolts, and four made a 180 degree turn, which threw Schilling's aim off, and he fired without effect.

Red Flight, led by Capt. Walter Cook, then dove out of the sun, Cook firing on his target from 300 yards and getting hits on the nose of his target. The Fw 190 then lost a large portion of its left wing when it ammunition compartment exploded and it went into an uncontrolled spin. It was last seen falling into a low cloud deck with the pilot believed to have been killed. This became the first "kill" credited to a member of the 56th FG. The 61st, and 63rd FS's, remaining as top cover for the 62nd FS had an uneventful mission, and the Group landed at 2032.

June 13: VIII FC FO 44. One more Rodeo, this time to Gravelines-Bailleul-Aeltre-Knocke with ninety-six P-47s of the 4th and 56th Fighter Group's.

The 56th FG, led by Col. Zemke, was off Horsham at 0900 with forty-nine aircraft. Two 62nd Fighter Squadron P-47s had to abort, one to Hartlesham, and the other back to Horsham, with mechanical problems.

The 56th FG made landfall in over Gravelines at 0937, sweeping east of Bruges. While providing high cover for the 4th FG, they were northeast of Ypres, and twenty Fw 190s were seen by Col. Zemke as they were climbing through 20,000 feet. Zemke took his White and Red Flight's from the 61st FS down to make the interception. All of the practice, training, years and work put into becoming a fighter pilot paid off as Zemke closed in on the tail of the number four man in the German formation. He fired from 200 yards and the Fw 190 burst into flame. Zemke then fishtailed his Thunderbolt and slid behind the number three Fw 190, observing strikes on its wingtip before he found himself in a more advantageous position to cut in directly behind the number two Fw 190. Upon this one he fired a long burst and it torched into a sheet of flame. 2nd Lt. Robert Johnson, 61st, swung in behind another and fired a two-three second burst of .50 caliber fire into it. The Fw 190 exploded and then fell away trailing a stream of heavy black smoke. 2nd Lt. Joseph R. Curtis "attacked the outside man, opening fire at about 300 yards and closing at 175 yards." Zemke was credited with two Fw 190s destroyed and one damaged, Johnson with one destroyed, and Curtis with one damaged. During this incident the 62nd and 63rd squadrons provided top cover and did not encounter any enemy aircraft. They headed for home over Durkirk at 0945 and were home at 1015. After they landed, Lt. Robert Johnson got himself "reamed" again by Col. Zemke for "lone-wolfing" it and breaking formation. When Zemke finished, Capt. Gerald Johnson, his flight leader, added a few words.

June 15: VIII FC FO 46. The 4th and 56th Fighter Group's were to have provided withdrawal support for a Ramrod mission. The 63rd Fighter Squadron, led by Major McCollom with sixteen P-47s took off from Horsham at 0425 to stage out of Thorney Island, landing there at 0520. Off there on the actual mission at 0820, they received a recall immediately thereafter, the mission being canceled because of weather. They returned to Horsham, landing at 0930.

June 17: VIII FC FO 47. Another Rodeo scheduled for the three 8th Air Force P-47s Fighter Groups. The sweeps, intended to draw forth the Luftwaffe into battle with fighters instead of allowing them to be available to attack the bomber formations was getting to be boring and frustrating for the Thunderbolt pilots, as the Germans were not adhering to the scheme. The 56th Fighter Group put up forty-eight P-47s for this sweep of Westhoofd-Eecloo-Ypres-Gravesline, and had three aborts. Led by Major

Capt. James McClure demonstrates a "wheel landing" for the troops. McClure, one of three pilots with the same surname assigned to the 56th FG, was assigned to the 62nd FS. He finished his missions in August 1944. (USAF)

1st Lt. Albert Knafeltz had one kill with the 62nd FS. His P-47 was coded LM✪A (bar), with the underlining bar signifying that there was more than one aircraft assigned to the particular squadron with the code letter A. (USAF)

Quirk banks away from the camera ship. This aircraft was passed on to Lt. Herbert Holtmeier when Quirk was killed while flying another aircraft. (USAF)

McCollom, they were in over Westhoofd at 0943 at 30,000 feet, made their sweep and were out over Knocke, RTB'ing Horsham at 1026.

June 20: VIII FC FO 50. The first independent Rodeo for the 56th Fighter Group,. A sweep of The Hague-Rotterdam area with forty-seven P-47s (after three aborts), led by Major McCollom. Off Horsham at 1546, they were back at 1722 after an uneventful mission.

June 22: VIII FC FO 52 was to provide fighter escort for the 1st Bomb Wing's B-17s to Antwerp by the three P-47 groups. However, missed communications resulted in the bombers being early, and instead of making the RV over Lochern as intended, the 56th Fighter Group RV'd with them at Flushing. Led by Col. Zemke and the 62nd Fighter Squadron, the mission was considered uneventful, although the Group records mention that Colonel Zemke engaged an Fw 190 over Walcheren Island without making a claim, the 62nd FS made no comment. (At the time of RV the B-17s were under Luftwaffe attack and several were seen going down with their crews

bailing out. The 4th FG claimed three Fw 190s destroyed, and the 78th FG claimed four).

This mission included the YB-40 version of the B-17 that carried heavier armament. Successful until the B-17s dropped their bombs, the YB-40 could not keep up with the lighter Flying Forts afterwards, and the program was soon dropped. As many experiments were still being carried out by Bomber Command, and the best tactics to be used by Fighter Command were also in the experimental stage, few successful escort missions were being flown at the time. The fighters just did not have sufficient range to be truly worthwhile as escorts, and most fighter missions were still to a point just within the enemy coastlines. Mission durations for the fighters ran only 1:30 to 1:45 minutes. Bomber missions, thus, were usually of short duration, in comparison to those in the future when the fighters became "long legged" enough to cover them. Also, at this time, the few B-24s were off to North Africa for an exceptional mission of their own. The B-17 missions usually consisted of two hundred aircraft, or less.

LM✪K was the personal "Jug" of Lt. Mike Quirk, who was one of the original pilots assigned to the 62nd FS. He finished his first tour in March 1944, and returned for a second on August 3. By now promoted to Captain, he became first the squadron's Operations Officer, and then, on August 14, the Squadron Commander. He was killed on September 10, 1944. (via Davis)

UN◉C was assigned to Lt. Raymond Petty. Note the position of the underwing landing light. (via Davis)

June 24: VIII FC FO 54 provided for a Rodeo over The Hague and St. Omer by eighty Thunderbolts of the 56th and 78th Fighter Groups. Led by Major McCollom, the 56th FG's forty-eight P-47s were up at 0813, made landfall-in over Westhoofd at 0846 at 24,000 feet and then swept Dordecht. Just southeast of The Hague, on the way out, Major Tukey, leading the 63rd FS, sighted ten enemy fighters trailing their formation at 28,000 feet, but as he prepaired to turn his squadron around to attack, they turned away. They RTB'd at 0951.

June 25: VIII FC FO 56. Another Rodeo mission, this time sweeping Ijmuiden-Amsterdam-Rotterdam. The 8th AF dispatched 130 P-47s from

42-7975, UN◉C, which had also been coded as UN*I, was lost on November 6, 1943 over Son-Breugel, Holland. Its pilot, 1st Lt. Robert Sheehan, evaded capture to return in January 1944. (via Davis)

the three groups, with the 4th Fighter Group moving to Horsham to operate in conjunction with the 56th FG. The 56th FG, led by Col. Zemke, was airborne at 0840. 1st Lt. Donald Goodfeisch, 63rd FS, had to abort because of an oxygen system failure. This was followed by Capt. Sylvester Burke, 63rd FS, aborting with his entire flight diverting to Martlesham Heath. One pair of 61st FS P-47s got separated from the rest of the formation on climb-out and never did catch up with the mission. Due to 10/10 (Solid cloud cover.) clouds over Holland, the mission only penetrated the continent a short distance before being recalled. As the weather had also deteriorated over England, the squadrons split, with the fighters landing at Martlesham Heath, and Bradwell Bay. The later being a primary RAF air-sea rescue base.

June 26: VIII FC FO 57 was a welcome Ramrod, or so it was first thought. The three Fighter Groups's would put up a maximum effort for this bomber escort mission, 130 P-47s, with the 56th FG contributing forty-nine. To extend their range, the 56th FG staged from Manston, Kent, on the Southeast tip of England, and were airborne from there at 1812, Led by Major McCollom. 1st Lt. Edgar Whitley, 63rd Fighter Squadron, aborted early because of a radio failure. Just after landfall-in at Dieppe, Lt. Mahurin's supercharger regulator failed, followed by his propeller governor, and then his engine quit. He got things sorted out and restarted at 5,000 feet and turned back to land at Horsham, accompanied by Lt. Frank Peppers.

One hundred B-17s had bombed Villecoublay, near Paris, and they were RV'd with between Gisore and Rouen and were undergoing a heavy attack by between forty to sixty German fighters that were coming in on them in waves from various altitudes, mostly headon. The 61st FS, led by

Gabreski, encountered twenty-two Fw 190s and eight Me 109s near Foucarmont, and later four Me 109s near Le Tres. Gabreski led his White Flight on these and Lt. Gerald Johnson claimed one Fw 190 that he raked with .50 caliber fire from its nose to just behind the cockpit before it exploded. Lt.'s Donavon Smith, Robill Roberts and Robert Johnson all fired, and had claims pending awaiting gun camera film assessment. Near Forges, Lt. Justus Foster's Yellow Flight was attacked by a dozen Fw 190s and he had to belly land at Hawkings with his hydraulic system shot out. Lt. Robert Johnson's P-47 also received "Catagory B" damage, a total write-off.

The 62nd FS, led by Major David Schilling entered the fray with Capt. Ray Dauphin claiming one Fw 190 destroyed and one damaged, while Major Schilling claimed a probable. 2nd Lt. Byron Morrill and 2nd Lt. Charles Harrison each claimed one damaged. Thirteen 62nd FS P-47s returned to Manston, while Capt. Dauphin put down at Mailing, Kent. 2nd Lt. Ralph Johnson came home, accompanied by Lt. Wayne Brainard, with one wheel hanging down after being hit by 20mm fire. Col. Zemke took off to provide assistance and suggestions to alleviate the wayward landing gear, but when nothing worked and with Johnson almost out of fuel, Zemke ordered him to bailout. He came down in the North Sea five miles north of Great Yarmouth and four hundred yards off shore. He was picked up by air-sea rescue. Four other 62nd FS Thunderbolts were slightly damaged.

The 63rd FS got into the battle and 1st Lt. Goodfleisch fired at one German fighter without apparent result, but on the way home he got another opportunity "and saw his shots strike the fuselage . . . (and) There was a puff of smoke, the Fw 190 went into a spin." 2nd Lt. William Janson claimed a probable. In all, the 56th FG claimed two Fw 190s destroyed, two as probably destroyed, and six damaged.

On the negative side, the losses were not only high, but traumatic. Five 56th FG P-47s were destroyed, and one later determined to be beyond repair. Six were battle damaged. Headquarters 56th FG lost their Assistant Operations Officer, Captain Robert Weatherbee, the 61st FS lost Capt. Merle Eby, their Operations Officer, and 2nd Lt. Louis Barron. Capt. Roger Dyar, 63rd FS, and Commander of their "A" Flight, was last seen commencing an attack and diving through clouds at 6,000 feet. Lt. Charles Clamp, 63rd, heard and felt three explosions in the turbo area in his aft fuselage and a 20mm fragment hit him in the left arm just below the elbow. He returned to Manston to discover that his P-47 had been hit by five 20mm shells and between ten and twenty .30 caliber rounds. He became the first 56th FG pilot to receive the Purple Heart. If there had ever been any doubt of the seriousness of the war it was now clear to everyone that it was a "for real" event. Of the four pilots that were killed this day, three were experienced Captains. There would be no more exultant incidents like the one Lt. Dick Mudge had been involved in, harassing barrage balloons. (After which Zemke prevented him from flying alone and restricted him to the base for a week). This mission would be the secondmost costly for the Group during their entire operational history in terms of human life.

June 28: VIII FC FO 58, a Ramrod to provide forward support for the 1st Bomb Wing to the limit of the P-47s range as the B-17s went to St. Nazaire. All three P-47s groups were involved, with the 56th Fighter Group taking off at 1150 to refuel at Exeter. Departing Exeter at 1603, the 56th FG was led by Col. Zemke with forty-nine Thunderbolts. Major Tukey had to abort, being escorted home by Lt. Batdorf. 2nd Lt. Caleb Reeder, 62nd Fighter Squadron, was flying as their spare, but didn't hear the order to return, so he flew the mission and got credit for it.

The rear of the first box of bombers was sighted approximately fifty miles off the French Coast, and the second box at landfall-in at St. Brieue at 1634. Escort was continued to Londene, and except for seeing a pair of Fw 190s and very heavy, intense flak, the mission was uneventful. Lt. Reeder did have to land at Tredinnick, Cornwall, and 2nd Lt. Robert Steele at Roborough, Deven, because of low fuel upon return.

June 29: VIII FC FO 59. Ramrod to Villacoublay, southwest of Paris, by 126 P-47s of the three groups. The 56th Fighter Group was airborne from

A young Lieutenant from Oklahoma by the name of Robert Johnson was the first Army Air Force pilot to break the record established by Eddie Rickenbacker in World War I. Johnson used five Thunderbolts in the process. One of which was "Lucky," HV❂P 42-8461. (via Davis)

Manston at 1956 to provide withdrawal support for the B-17s returning from this mission. The B-17s were met at Neufchatel at 2026 with the P-47s at 27,000. They were escorted until 2045 when relieved by the 4th FG and then the 56th FG broke away for Manston to refuel before returning to Horsham. Uneventful.

July 1: VIII FC FO 60. All three 8th AF P-47 groups were up on Rodeos. The 56th Fighter Group, led by Col. Zemke, was airborne at 1502 on a sweep of The Hague-Rotterdam. Capt. Gabreski's 61st Fighter Squadron had two aborts: Lt. Eugene Barnum and Lt. Leslie Smith, both with fuel problems. Lt. Wayne Peterson, 62nd FS, also had to abort, with mechanical difficulties, being escorted home by Lt. James Quirk.

Landfall-in was made over The Hague at 1548 at 27,500, and twenty Fw 190s were seen there, heading north, but were not engaged because the Thunderbolts already were short on fuel.. Apparently the Fw's were heading for their own home, as the 78th FG, on the earliest part of the sweep

OPPOSITE: Robert Johnson, Hub Zemke and Bud Mahurin. The victory swastika's are barely visible under the aircraft's name. (via Davis)

Johnson had a narrow escape in his first P-47, 41-6235, HV❂P, "Half Pint." He was trapped in the fighter's cockpit after an enemy's fire jammed his canopy so he could not bailout, and had to bring it home to be rescued. (via Davis)

Capt. Horace Craig and wingmen of the 62nd FS hang on the wing of a B-24 for the photographer. LM◆X was lost in a fatal mid-air collision on August 22, 1943. (USAF)

Captain Eugene O'Neil's personal Jug carried several names – "Lil Abner," "Jessie O," and "Torchy." O'Neil carried back to England several feet of aircraft cable from a destroyed Me 110 on November 26, 1943 with this Thunderbolt. (via Davis)

had claimed 4-1-5 (4 kills, 1 probable, 5 damaged), for the loss of their Group Commander, Col. Arman Peterson. The 56th FG RTB'd at 1640.

July 2: VIII FC FO 62 called for a Rodeo to Le Touquet with eighty P-47s of the 56th and 78th Fighter Groups. Major Loren McCollom led forty-eight P-47s as the 56th FG's contribution to the mission off Horsham at 1550. Only Capt. Sylvester Burke, 63rd Fighter Squadron, aborted, because of a radio failure. Major Schilling's 62nd FS, already staging from Halesworth, was late at the RV point and had to play catch-up behind the other two squadrons for the entire uneventful mission which RTB at 1716, except for the 62nd FS that landed fifteen minutes later.

July 6: VIII FC FO 65 put up 124 P-47s of the three 8th AF P-47 groups on a Rodeo over Holland. The 56th Fighter Group only contributed thirty-two Thunderbolts, with the 61st Fighter Squadron not participating on this mission. They were led by Col. Zemke and the 62nd FS. They swept The Hague and Westhoofd area, making landfall-in over The Hague at 1053 stacked between 26,000 and 28,000 feet. Landfall-out was between Westhoofd and Noorderhoofd at 1105 and the only reportable topic was heavy but inaccurate flak over Rotterdam at their altitude.

July 8: The 56th Fighter Group started to move from Horsham St. Faith to Halesworth, near Ipswich, and only eight miles from the North Sea. The

Thunderbolts in a step-down formation over England. The classic milk bottle shape is obvious. (USAF)

Strung-out nicely while overtaking a B-24 over England. (via Davis)

BELOW: LM◉R, 42-7870 belonged to Captain Horace Craig and was named "Happy." 42-7866, LM◉G was lost September 5, 1943 due to a faulty propeller control. 42-7979, LM◉C, was flown by Lt. Byron Morrill when he became a POW at Huizen, Holland on November 26, 1943. (via Davis)

new airfield was all mud, including in the food. Nieson, aka. Quonset huts, and no hot water. Originally intended as a bomber base, the main runway was 6,000 feet long, while the two shorter runways were 4,200 feet in length. Fifty hardstands were built for the P-47s. Most of the living quarters were on the south end of the base, in or near the encompassed village of Holton, a long distance from the other required facilities.

July 9: The invasion of Sicily got underway. VIII FC FO 67 took the three P-47s groups back on another uneventful Rodeo, this time over the Ghent area. The three groups put up 128 Thunderbolts, but the 56th Fighter Group only dispatched thirty-two, as once again the 61st Fighter Squadron stood down.

Led by Major McCollom, they were airborne from Horsham at 0725 on the last mission from this base. 1st Lt. Vance Ludwig, had to abort because of radio problems. He was replaced by 1st Lt. Wayne O'Connor, who was up as a spare. Landfall-in was west of Schouwen Island at 0814. 1st Lt. Gorden Batdorf, 63rd, had to turn back over Ghent with cramps and radio problems, being shepherded home by his Yellow Flight. The mission returned at 0848.

July 10: VIII FC FO 68 sent the three fighter groups back on a Ramrod type mission, with the 56th Fighter Group providing penetration support for B-17s to the Abbeville-Poix areas. The primary target being an airdrome some fifteen miles southeast of Abbeville. Again only the 62nd and 63rd Fighter Squadron's dispatched fighters, a total of thirty-three, being

UN⊙A (bar) was assigned to the 63rd FS on November 18, 1943 and given to FO Archie Robey. Robey, one of the first replacement pilots, was killed while on a training flight on April 22, 1944 near Oxfordness. By then he had become a 1st Lt. (USAF)

Wolfpack Thunderbolt maintenance. Note that the ammunition doors hinge from the rear. The aircraft is jacked up for boresighting the machineguns. (USAF)

led by Col. Zemke. Capt. Ray Dauphin, 62nd FS, had to abort with supercharger trouble. They were airborne on the first official mission from Halesworth, Station F-365, at 0640. (The earliest morning mission to date). RV was made with the Flying Forts twenty miles northwest of the mouth of the Somme River at 28,000 feet with the 63rd FS taking the right side escort position. The bombers were escorted over the targets, with bomb hits seen on the airdrome at Abbeville. They were relieved for withdrawal escort by the 4th FG. No enemy fighters were seen and no flak was reported, either. They returned to Halesworth at 0820.

July 14: VIII FC FO 71 called for the three fighter groups to send out 128 P-47s on a Ramrod for the 1st Bomb Wing's B-17s to strike Amiens-Glisy. The 56th Fighter Group, to provide general support for the mission, dispatched thirty-three P-47s of the 62nd and 63rd Fighter Squadron's at 0644 and were led by Major McCollom. Lt. Don Goodfleisch, 63rd FS, had to abort with engine trouble, being replaced by the spare. Lt. Glenn Schlitz, 63rd FS, was late getting off, and not making RV with his squadron after the spare filled in Goodfleisch's spot, had to RTB.

RV with the bombers was made fifteen miles northwest of Le Treport at 0730 at 27,000. Just after the sixty B-17s bombed the airdrome at Amines,

Boresighting one of the Group's early P-47Cs into the pits at Kings Cliffe. If the machine guns were not properly harmonized and the pilot missed his target, the mission might as well have not been flown. (USAF)

Major McCollom sighted fifteen Fw 190s attacking a straggling B-17 over Doullens and led his White Flight of the 63rd FS down on a pair of them. He had one boresighted, but his guns wouldn't fire. 2nd Lt. Robert Hall, White Two, engaged the other, claiming a damaged. The 63rd FS was now scattered and short on fuel, thus Lt.'s Hannigan and Comstock landed at Wattisham, Lt. Dugas at Framlingham, and Lt.'s Compton and Janson at Manston. The remainder of the Group was down at Halesworth at 0825. (The 4th FG, on this mission claimed one damaged, for the loss of one. The 78th FG claimed one destroyed for the loss of two P-47s).

July 16: VIII FC FO 72. Col. Zemke led the 56th Fighter Group's portion of a diversionary Rodeo over Dunkirk-Roulers-Ostend. The 61st Fighter Squadron returned to operations on this mission, while the 62nd FS stood down. The 56th FG put up thirty-two of the scheduled 127 P-47s from the three groups, and they made landfall-in five miles northeast of Dunkirk at 29,000 feet at 2001, penetrated to Roulers, turned left and went out over Blankenburghe at 2010, landing Halesworth at 2040.

Although sighting the bombers they were providing the diversion for, nothing else was observed. No enemy aircraft were encountered, although the German's continued to place an unpleasant sidetone on their radio frequencies.

July 17: VIII FC FO 74 (Wing Ramrod #6); Was a Ramrod with the 56th Fighter Group ordered to provide close escort for withdrawing B-17s of the 4th Bomb Wing that had attacked Amsterdam. Preceded by the 4th FG, they were airborne at 0821, and led by Col. Zemke. They RV'd the bombers fifteen miles northeast of The Hague and made landfall-out over The Hague with the bombers below them. Twenty miles west of The Hague they were relieved by the 78th FG. Although Luftwaffe fighters were seen over the Zuider Zee, they were no threat to either the bombers or the fighters, and the 56th FG chalked up another uneventful mission.

July 19: Rome, Italy was bombed for the first time. The 12th and 15th Air Forces were getting stronger. Col. Hubert Zemke was awarded the Distinguished Flying Cross, being the first pilot within the Group to receive an award. The following day the rest of the awards were passed out to pilots, almost of the original ones receiving Air Medals with clusters.

July 25: VIII FC FO 78. The 56th Fighter Group put up thirty-three P-47s for their part of a Ramrod to provide withdrawal support for B-17s of the 1st Bomb Division. Major McCollom led the 61st Fighter Squadron and

Captain Eddie Rickenbaker visits the Wolfpack on July 28, 1943. He is flanked by Col. Zemke and General Hunter. Three months later Rickenbacker would head for the Pacific Theater and be lost at sea for weeks. (via Davis)

the mission, while Major Tukey led the 63rd FS. (The 62nd FS did not participate, being on rotational duty to VIII Fighter Command to learn air defense duties in the East Anglia area). Landfall-in was between Ostend and Blankenburge after taking off at 1429. Lt. Robill Roberts, 61st FS, having to abort with mechanical problems. Penetration was to Courtrai, where the Group turned left to Ghent.

Over Hulst, Lt. Frank McCauley, 61st FS, dove on the lead Fw 190 in a flight of seven that had been seen approaching from the east between 22,000 and 25,000 feet. He fired on the leader, but made no claim. Landfall-out was over Walcheren Island at 1515 and they were back on the ground at Halesworth at 1551.

The two squadrons were airborne on their second mission of the day at 1931, this time led by Col. Zemke and the 63rd FS. Capt. Donald Renwick led the 61st FS. Zemke was forced to abort with engine trouble, and was accompanied home by Major Tukey, who also had to abort, because of electrical problems. Thus Capt. Renwick became the mission leader. Landfall-in was over Zandvoort at 2008, at 28,000 feet with the 63rd FS crossing in two minutes later after the two squadrons became separated while penetrating clouds during the climbout. Southwest of Schipot a mixed formation of an Me 109 and an Fw 190 were bounced by Lt. Gerald Johnson and Lt. McCauley, but they made no claims. While this encounter took place, the remainder of the Group orbited Amsterdam, where they encountered intense flak. Landfall-out was made at 2022 and they were back on the ground at 2056.

July 26: VIII FC FO 80 was to be a diversionary Rodeo to Rotterdam prior to a B-17 mission that would pass nearby on its way to Hannover. All three groups were up, with Major McCollom leading the 56th Fighter Group, composed of the 61st and 63rd Fighter Squadrons's and thirty-two P-47s out of a mission total of 123. Landfall-in was over Walcheren Island at 26,000 feet at 1030, and over Rotterdam the squadrons split up to sweep over the city. Although three to five unidentified aircraft were spotted, the 56th FG had no encounters. (The 4th FG claimed one probable Fw 190). They were back to Halesworth at 1118.

VIII FC FO 81 was another Rodeo that afternoon, to Gravelines-St. Omer-Armentiers and out over Nieuport. Again, all three P-47 groups were on the mission, with the 56th Fighter Group utilizing only the 61st and 63rd Fighter Squadrons. Led by Major McCollom, they took off at 1659 and were back at 1819 after an uneventful sweep that was only marred by the constant carrierwave the Germans were placing on their radio frequencies.

July 27: VIII FC FO 82 was to put up 119 P-47s of the three groups. The

56th Fighter Group's portion of the mission, Ramrod FO 13, called for an escort for B-26s of the 323rd Bomb Group to Tricqeville. Airborne at 1729 with twenty-five P-47s of the 61st and 63rd Fighter Squadrons, and led by Col. Zemke, RV was made at 1757 at 18,000 feet. The bombers were circled twice before landfall-in five miles northeast of Dieppe at 1814. Due to fuel constraints and the length of the mission, the 63rd FS landed at Bradwell Bay, while the 61st FS landed at Manston. They were all back at Halesworth at 2054.

July 28: VIII FC FO 83 was the first mission of the day for the three Thunderbolt groups, a long-range Ramrod for B-17s. The 4th Fighter Group carried 200 gallon unpressurized belly tanks for the first time. Although only being able to use half of the contents as usable fuel, the extended range surprised the Luftwaffe and permitted the 4th FG to hit them unexpectedly near Leerdam, where they claimed 9-1-6.

The 56th FG only put up twenty-three P-47s on this mission, from the 61st and 62nd Fighter Squadrons. Led by Col. Zemke, they provided withdrawal support for the B-17s. Meeting the Forts over Dordrecht, they made protective turns over the formation until landfall-out at 1220. Lt. John Eaves, 62nd FS, flying as a spare, picked up a disabled B-17 over the North Sea and escorted it back to Aldeburgh where it made a forced landing on the beach. Thus, Eaves was credited with a mission. Time home was 1253.

The second mission for the day was VIII FC FO 84 that called for all three P-47s groups to assist a 323rd BG B-26 mission to Tricqueville Airdrome. The 56th FG's portion of the mission was to provide initial escort. Led by Col. Zemke, they were airborne from Halesworth at 1813 with twenty-four Thunderbolts of the 61st and 63rd FS's. RV was made over England, and the B-26s were escorted to mid-channel, whereupon the 56th FG went on an uneventful diversionary sweep. Time home was 1922.

July 29: VIII FC FO 85 provided for Rodeos for the three groups over Holland. Again, the 56th Fighter Group only had the 61st and 62nd Fighter Squadrons participating with twenty-five P-47s, led by Major McCollom. Landfall-in was over The Hague at 1046 at 26,000 feet.

Blue Flight of the 62nd FS, led by Lt. Voorhis Day, with Lt. Robert Steele as his wingman, and Lt's Anthony Carcione and Caleb Reeder making up the rest of the flight, spotted some unidentified aircraft at 15,000 feet on the way to Amsterdam and dove down to take a look. Finding Spitfires, they started to climb back up to rejoin the rest of their formation, and during the process, Blue Three and Four were jumped by two Me 109s while Lt. Day spotted three Fw 190s which he proceeded to bounce. Lt. Carcione, Blue Three, went after those Messerschmitts chasing him, and claimed one Me 109 probably destroyed. Lt. Day reported that as he went down on the Fw 190s, his flight was bounced by a pair of Me 109s that came on them out of the sun. He told Lt. Steele to break left, as he did, but Steele didn't turn sharply enough. an Me 109 got behind him and Steele's P-47 was hit in the engine and wings. Steele bailed out and landed two miles off shore of The Hague and became a POW. The other Me 109 continued its attack on Day and set his left wing on fire and caused his Thunderbolt to roll, so Day continued the roll around to straight and level and after about four minutes the fire went out. He joined up with Carcione and headed home on the deck. (Reeder joined up with the 61st FS). Upon landing at Halesworth, Day's landing gear collapsed and his P-47 wound up on its nose.

The second mission was off at 1722 on a diversionary Ramrod for 386th Bomb Group B-26s on a feint to the coast of Belgium. Led by Major McCollom with twenty-four P-47s from the 61st and 62nd FS's, they swept Noorderhoof-Ostend-Nieuport and were back at 1912 after an uneventful mission.

A rather distinguished visitor gave a motivational speech to the Group between missions. Captain Eddie Rickenbacker, America's highest scoring WWI pilot. At least a couple pilots took his speech to heart and set goals for themselves to surpass his record of twenty-six kills.

July 30: VIII FC FO 87. A Ramrod for a large B-17 mission to Kassel with the 78th Fighter Group providing penetration support, while the 4th and 56th FG's provided withdrawal support. The 56th FG put up twenty-five P-47s from the 61st and 62nd Fighter Squadrons, and were led by Major McCollom. Airborne at 0925, they made RV with the three boxes of the "Big Friends" about seven miles west of Arnhem after making one orbit awaiting them. They escorted the Forts out over the Scheldt estuary. In the vicinity of Arnhem they also met the Luftwaffe.

At this point, 2nd Lt. Jack Horton, 61st Fighter Squadron, was last seen, and later determined as killed. In the ensuing combat, the 61st FS bore the brunt of it. Lt.'s Robert Lamb and Joe Powers shared an Fw 190, and Powers was credited with an Me 109 by himself. Lt. Donavon Smith claimed an Me 109. Capt. Leroy Schreiber claimed an Me 109 destroyed and another as a probable. Lt. Leslie Smith claimed a probable Fw 190. Major McCollom damaged one Me 109. Lt. Jones, 62nd FS, claimed some hits on either an Me 109 or an Fw 190, in the excitement he just wasn't sure. On the way out over the Scheldt estuary, Lt. Robert Stover, 62nd FS, dropped out of formation with the intention of attacking a pair of Fw 190s he had spotted. He was not seen again by any members of the 56th FG, but a pilot of the 4th FG reported watching a P-47 coded "LM" going down smoking off Walcheren Island. It was later discovered that Stover had got as far as twenty miles from Felixstone before he bailed out, but he was drowned.

As it turned out, Schreiber's probable was credited as a kill, so he became the first 56th FG pilot to score a "double" in one mission. Schreiber: "As I started down the three Me 109s were still in a rather close V formation and taking no evasive action. I opened fire on the number three Me 109 after the other two started a break to the right and down. My Me 109 then broke down and to the right. I followed him, firing continuously, from about 350 to 250 yards range. I observed pieces fly off the e/a from the right side of the fuselage and wing root. Then a cloud of while glycol smoke poured out . . ." Meanwhile three Me 109s were maneuvering for a stern attack on Lieutenant Anderson . . . I dove on these Me 109s. One broke off his attack immediately and the second shortly after . . . I followed the third Me 109 which was following Lieutenant Anderson. The Me 109 was firing constantly out of range. Lieutenant Anderson was skidding to avoid the fire. I closed to about 150 yards and fired all the rest of my ammunition from dead astern (altitude-3,000 feet). The Me 109 blew up in a splash of oil and flame. I flew through the debris, drew up alongside of Lieutenant Anderson, and together we came home on the deck." (Major Eugene Roberts, 84th FS, 78th FG, became the first Thunderbolt pilot to score a "tripple," on this same Ramrod). The Group returned to England in elements, and Lt. Milton Anderson's, 61st FS, P-47 was written-off through battle damage after he brought it back.

All three fighter Groups received letters of commendation for their efforts during "Blitz Week," the last week in July when the 8th Air Force mounted their heaviest attacks against German targets thus far in the war. Their efforts on July 30 were singled out in particular, for between them, the three groups claimed twenty-five German aircraft shot down, four probably shot down, and eight damaged. Luftwaffe fighters that surly would have inflicted casualties on the bomber crews had they not been intercepted and destroyed beforehand.

July 31: VIII FC FO 88 dispatched the three P-47s groups on a diversionary escort mission for B-26s of the 387th Bomb Group. The 61st and 62nd Fighter Squadrons each put up fifteen Thunderbolts, with Col. Zemke leading the mission off Halesworth at 1524. RV with the Marauders was over Clacton, going to Doullens-St. Ingelvert. Except for the aggravating radio tones the mission was uneventful and they were home at 1709.

August 1: Ploesti was bombed for the first time. Many of the participants were 8th Air Force crews TDY to North Africa.

August 2: VIII FC FO 91 was to provide a fighter escort for B-26s of the 387th Bomb Group. However, the 56th Fighter Group was tasked to provide penetration escort for B-17s into Europe. Off at 1721, led by Major McCollom, the 61st and 62nd Fighter Squadrons dispatched thirty-three P-47s. At 1755 the mission was scrubbed, due to fog and clouds rising to 18,000 feet. The bombers were escorted back to England, and then the 56th FG returned to Halesworth, landing at 1826.

August 4: An orientation mission for the 305th FS! This seems to be a mythical mission that is recorded in the 56th Fighter Group history to include the 61st and 63rd Fighter Squadrons, but it is not mentioned in either squadron's history's. No VIII Fighter Command Field Order was cut, and the 305th FS was an Air Training Command squadron in Flordia.

August 9: VIII FC FO 95. Rodeo #28, a sweep of the Abbeville area with 139 P-47s of the 4th, 56th, 78th and the 353rd Fighter Groups. This was the first combat mission for the 353rd FG, led by Col. Joseph Morris. The three 56th Fighter Group squadrons put up thirty-two Thunderbolts, with the mission being led by Col. Zemke and the 63rd Fighter Squadron. Landfall-in was over Knocke at 1645 at 25,000 feet, turning to Rotterdam, and out over The Hague. The Group was down at 1739.

August 11: Wake turbulence was an unknown factor during WWII, although an aircraft being tossed about behind another was often attributed to "prop wash." (And how many airmen have been sent off on the fool's errand of a bucket of prop wash to the amusement of others?) Capt. Walker Mahurin, 63rd FS, was formatting on a B-24 as a lark when his P-47 was sucked into the vacuum created by the Liberator's wings. The aircraft collided, and although the B-24 landed okay, Mahurin had to bailout of his damaged Thunderbolt. He could have been Court Martialed, but instead was fined $100.00. Less than a week later he would be put in for a Distinguished Flying Cross!

August 12: VIII FC FO 98. A Ramrod with Col. Zemke leading the Group with the 61st Fighter Squadron. Airborne at 0720, the squadrons climbed to 15,000 feet over Halesworth, then climbed on course to 22,000, making landfall-in south of Flushing. This was the first mission for the 56th Fighter Group with unpressurized two hundred gallon belly tanks, which were dropped over Walcheren Island. The tanks were more of a detriment than a help, as the P-47s were unstable with them hanging underneath the fuselages and they could barely make it to 22,000 feet with them. Most of the fuel could not be sucked into the engines, so they had to be dropped when only half used. Thus, their range was only extended by a total of forty-five minutes.

RV with the B-17s heading for Gelsenkirchen, in the Ruhr industrial area, was made over Antwerp where there was intense and accurate flak. At that time they climbed to 33-34,000 feet. Two groups of German fighters were sighted over Dienst and Herennthals, twenty-four fighters in all. About ten Fw 190s were seen attacking the bombers, and Lt. Jones, White Four in Major Schilling's flight from the 62nd FS damaged one near Turnhout. The 63rd FS, on the way home escorted out a crippled B-17, and the mission was down at 0940.

August 14: VIII FC FO 102. The 56th Fighter Group put up forty-eight Thunderbolts to act as an escort for thirty-four B-17s that were making a feint against the Dutch Coast, thus their part of the mission was covered as a Circus under FO 34. Off at 1647, RV was made at 1725 near The Hague with three separate boxes of bombers, with each squadron covering a box, which were then escorted back to twenty-five miles from England. They were back on the ground at 1800 after an uneventful mission.

August 15: VIII FC FO 103 included all four P-47 groups on a Rodeo. The three 56th Fighter Group squadrons were airborne at 0725 and were led by

August 12, 1943 a young and slightly brash fighter pilot decided to give a B-24 a good look at a P-47 and this was the demise of UN☉M, 41-6334. "Bud" Mahurin's first Jug. He was embarrassed, but uninjured. (USAF)

Col. Zemke. RV was made with the 353rd FG at 0828 near Noordwall, they flew to east of Rotterdam, and then turned south to Antwerp, but passing Woensdrecht a dozen bogies were sighted below them.

Col. Zemke took White and Red Flights from the 61st Fighter Squadron down on the bounce, but the enemy aircraft evaded by diving away. Only Zemke and Capt. Schreiber being able to fire, each without apparent effect. Approaching Flushing, another dozen e/a were sighted, and the 62nd FS attempted to bounce these, but again the e/a evaded by diving away and no encounter ensued. A third contact was made with the Luftwaffe, over Ghent, by the 63rd FS, when they spotted three single-engine and three twin-engine fighters, but they were too distant to be identified as to type or engaged. The 56th FG was back at 0923.

VIII FC FO 13/104 called for a Ramrod as general escort for B-17s to an airdrome at Poix. The 56th Fighter Group became airborne from Halesworth at 1811, led by Major McCollom. Due to a scheduling mixup caused by confusing control times with GMT, the 56th FG arrived over the RV point, Calis, a half hour early. They made four orbits, and then spotted the B-17s at mid-channel on their way in as the 56th FG was already making their way home. Other than Lt. Morrill, 62nd FS, developing an oil leak over Calis and having to be escorted to Manston by Lt. Charles Ginn, the mission was uneventful for the 56th.

August 16: VIII FC FO 37/105. Dispatched were 180 P-47s from the four groups, with the 56th Fighter Group launching forty-eight. Major McCollom led the 63rd Fighter Squadron off at 0825. Escort was for 180 B-17s on a raid to Le Bourget airdrome, and landfall-in and RV was made at St. Valery at 0916, where their belly tanks were dropped. Capt. Goodfleisch, 63rd FS, couldn't get his to drop, so he had to be escorted home by Lt. Batdorf. 1st Lt. Frank Peppers, 63rd FS, then developed electrical problems and was escorted to Marthesham Heath by 2nd Lt. Walter Hannigan.

Over Paris, Lt. George Spaleny, 62nd FS, engine quit and he went into a long, slow descent, being escorted down by 2nd Lt. John Bryant with Lt.'s Voorhis Day and Calab Reeder providing top cover. He bailed out near Chaumont, but his parachute was not seen to open and Spaleny was feared lost when his P-47 struck the ground and exploded. However, he did survive as a POW.

Several encounters took place over France. Lt. Gerald Johnson, 61st FS, fired on one German fighter, but made no claim. The 63rd FS's 2nd Lt. Raymond Petty engaged an Me 109 and then an Fw 190 at 0945 at 23,000 feet northeast of downtown Paris. 1st Lt. Vance Ludwig, Yellow Four, fired on an Fw 190 near Everux at 0955. 1st Lt. Walker Mahurin, Yellow Lead, fired on another Fw 190, but missed. So, 1st Lt. John Vogt, Yellow Three, fired and damaged it. The squadrons were now scattered and low on fuel

and flights had to return to various airfields scattered across southeastern England, primarily landing at Ford, Sussex at 1035.

The 4th FG, having arrived over Paris within minutes of the 56th FG, cost the Luftwaffe eighteen fighters for the loss of one pilot who became a POW on this Ramrod). The 353rd FG lost their first pilot and their Group Commander, Joseph Morris.

To replace the missing Morris, Major Loren McCollom was promoted to Lt. Colonel and transferred to the 353rd Fighter Group as their new commander. (He would be shot down on November 25 and became a POW for the duration of the war. He would not be lonely in the POW camp, however, as he was soon joined by many of his old friends from the Wolfpack).

McCollom, in turn, was replaced by Major David Schilling as Deputy Group Commander, Schilling's place in leading the 62nd Fighter Squadron now being taken by Captain Horace Craig.

August 17: VIII FC FO 38/106. Ramrod and bomber missions on this day became known to the 8th Air Force and airmen everywhere for its heroism and courage. Sixty B-17s were downed and 168 were battle damaged on a dual mission to Schweinfurt and Regensburg. 562 bomber crewmen were missing in action, seven were initially known to have been killed, and twenty-one more wounded. The missions to Schweinfurt and Regensburg had been well planned, but the initiation of the plans was thrown off by weather and some screw-ups in timing, for which this heavy price was paid.

The Field Order called for a maximum effort by the four 8th Air Force P-47 fighter groups. Two hundred-forty Thunderbolts to provide penetration and general support for the bombers on their way to their targets, and withdrawal support for those returning to England. (Half the force would be making a shuttle mission to North Africa).

The first mission was off Halesworth at 0922 with fifty P-47s, and was led by Col. Zemke, leading the 62nd Fighter Squadron. Landfall-in was west of Schouwen Island at 1010, and they dropped their belly tanks in the estuary off Woensdrecht and started a climb to 26,000 feet. RV was made with the rear box of bombers ten miles north of Antwerp, and the front box near Bilsen. Escort was provided to just beyond Eupen, Belgium and this was the first time where the 56th Fighter Group had actually penetrated the German border.

The Group had to turn for home at this point, leaving the bombers enroute to the Messerschmitt factory's at Regensburg and on to Africa, as they had reached the limit of their range. On the way home, approaching Eupen, near Hasselet at 1030, fifteen to thirty German fighters were seen. Major Tukey's 63rd FS attempted to break them up, and in the vicinity of Hasselet 1st Lt.'s Arthur Sugas and Edgar Whitley dove down and fired on two Fw 190s in an attempt to break up their attack on the bombers. Although no hits were claimed, the enemy fighters were driven away. Over Eupen, 1st Lt. Jack Brown fired on an Me 109, again with inconclusive results. The Group made landfall-out over Walcheren Island at 1058 and were back to Halesworth to refuel at 1140.

The second Ramrod was made up by the 56th and 353rd FG's on a withdrawal support mission for the B-17s that had gone to Schweinfurt. The 56th FG was up from Halesworth at 1520, again led by Col. Zemke and the 62nd FS. They put up fifty-one P-47s, with Capt. Francis Gabreski leading the 61st FS and Major Tukey the 63rd. Inbound to Germany they flew the reverse of the earlier mission, making landfall-in over Walcheren at 1555 climbing through 20,000 feet. Belly tanks were dropped near Antwerp at 1605 and the climb was continued to 26,000 feet. RV was made some fifteen miles east of Eupen, where the bombers were still under attack by the Luftwaffe. Some fifty-five Fw 190s and Me 109s were involved, as well as a half dozen Me 110s.

To the P-47s advantage, the Germans had revised their tactics. Instead of flying alongside and some three thousand feet above the bombers to a point just in front of them, before they made a 180 degree turn and

UN◉Y, 41-6236 was one of the first P-47s assigned to the 56th FG when they went to England, receiving it on January 28. In turn it was assigned to "Bunny" Comstock. (via Davis)

dove back upon them in a head-on attack, they were now flying a parallel course to a point some five miles in front of the B-17s before reversing their course for the head-on interception. This revision permitted the P-47s to dive between them and the bombers and break up the German attacks between their turn point and the actual interception of the bombers. The 56th FG, swinging in over the beleaguered B-17s as top cover, joined combat with the Luftwaffe over Liege, some fifteen miles west of Eupen, and it continued to Antwerp, where the 56th FG had to break off for home after being relieved by Spitfires.

(Now) Capt. Gerald Johnson, 61st FS, was firing on an Me 110 when he saw another P-47s shooting at it, too. It was Lt. Frank McCauley, and the Messerschmitt could not withstand the blast of sixteen .50 caliber machine guns and it exploded. Johnson: "There, in front of our eyes, was an enormous pillar of fire. It must have been one thousand feet high and 150 feet across. Just a big pillar of fire suspended in space-right in front of us. It was one of the brightest lights I have ever seen, and I was so surprised that I pulled back on the stick and gave her the gun."

Johnson, now climbing up-sun, then looked down, and saw an Me 109 that he quickly dove upon. He hit it between the engine and the cockpit from 200 yards and the pilot bailed out before it too exploded. He then saw another Me 109 positioning itself for a stern attack on a B-17. With speed and altitude to his advantage, Johnson dove on it and gave it a two second burst of fire from the length of a football field away. It rolled over and dove to the ground and exploded.

Lt. McCauley continued looking for the Luftwaffe and soon spotted three Fw 190s in a V formation to the north of the B-17s. He dove down to

The "Top Guns" of the 56th FG. Zemke, Schilling, Gabreski and Christensen saunter down the perimeter track at Halesworth. When the photograph was taken they had over sixty German aircraft destroyed between them. (USAF)

A gaggle of pros. Left to right: Francis Gabreski, Robert Johnson, "Bud" Mahurin and Robert Landry. On the wing are Walter Cook and David Schilling. Cook was "C" Flight leader and the first 62nd FS pilot to be rotated home, in August 1943, to become a combat instructor. (USAF)

Two more young pros, from the 63rd FS. On the left is Major Philip Tukey, Elizabeth, ME. He was the squadron commander between June 1942 and October 1943 and then after a stint with Hq. VIII Fighter Command, took over the 356th FG. On the right is Capt. Sylvester Burke, Operations Officer. Burke replaced Tukey as squadron commander, was promoted to Major in December, and also went to VIII FC, in February 1944. He then went to Harding Field, LA to take a training command position. (USAF)

Lt. Samuel Stamps, 63rd FS and his ground crew pose with their P-47 "Tinkle." Stamps, from Tuscon, AZ was a replacement pilot, assigned in December 1943, and he finished his tour in June 1944. He had .5 credits. (USAF)

1st Lt. George Bostwick, 62nd FS, made Captain in September 1944, rotated home in October, and returned to the 63rd FS on January 8, 1945. He became their operations officer, and then there last wartime squadron commander, on March 19. (USAF)

Colonel Robert Landry was Operations Officer of the 56th FG and took over command of the Group in Zemke's absence during the fall winter 1943-44. Although a capable combat leader, he verified the axiom of being in right place at the right time, as in all his combat missions he was only credited with one claim. (USAF)

Flight Officer Walter Frederick was assigned to the 63rd FS as a replacement pilot in November 1943. Awarded a Purple Heart for wounds on a combat mission, he finished his tour in July 1944. Opting for a second combat tour, he went to the South Pacific Theater and was killed while flying with the 507th FG. (USAF)

Capt. Ray Dauphin was assigned to the 62nd FS in April 1944. Although not scoring in air combat, he flew with the 56th FG almost as long as Dave Schilling, including the Post War years. (USAF)

Major Donald Renwick and his P-47, "Doc." Renwick was moved up the line from the 61st FS to become the last Deputy Group Commander of the Wolfpack during the war years. (USAF)

Lt. Samuel Stamps and the "nose art" on "Tinkle." Artwork on aircraft was an important way to personalize the war effort, add a little character and enhance the morale factor. The aircraft was UN⦿S, 43-25307. (USAF)

1st Lt. Glen Schlitz, from North Canton, OH. He was assigned to "A" Flight, 63rd FS in March 1943 and took over as leader of that flight in January 1944. He had played semi-pro baseball before the war, and had the proverbial "good eye." He scored the Group's first "triple kill" on August 17, 1944. (USAF)

attack the northern most of these and gave it a short burst, seeing pieces fly off of both wings and smoke from its engine. Yet it held its position in the formation, so he gave it another burst, and its pilot bailed out. McCauley also damaged another before turning for home.

Capt. Donald Renwick's Blue Flight was bounced by another German fighter, believed to be an Fw 190, but the German pilot lost control of his aircraft and crashed, so Renwick was credited with its downing. The 61st FS claimed 5-0-1.

The 62nd FS had a different story. They took on the Me 110s, with Col. Zemke destroying one near Maastricht. Lt. Charles Harrison got another between Maastricht and Hasselt. 2nd Lt. Caleb Reeder got another, and damaged one identified as an Me 210. Lt.'s Vorris Day and Robert Stultz were last seen chasing two more Me 110s near Hasselt. Radio communications indicated that Lt. Day shot both of them down, but both Day and Stultz were killed during this mission so their downing of the enemy aircraft could not be confirmed. All of these Me 110s were painted white, so it was believed that they had just been transferred into the area from the Eastern Front.

The 63rd FS made their interceptions over Liege. Lt. Harold Comstock spotted two Me 109s just below him and heading for the B-17s. Comstock did a half roll and started after them, with the number two Me 109 breaking away. The leader, intent on the bombers, did not break, so Comstock closed to 100 yards and fired a one second burst, but missed. He fired again with a two second burst, and the eight .50 caliber machine gun bullets cut the wing right off the German fighter.

Capt. Mahurin also cut off an Fw 190 that was too intent on getting at the B-17s. He closed on it to 150 yards and opened fire. It exploded, leaving nothing in the air but a ring of smoke. Mahurin then looked around and saw another heading for his wingman, 2nd Lt. George Hall. Mahurin turned on it and hit it in its wingroots and sent it down spinning out of control. Hall, being occupied by the Fw 190 he was intercepting, didn't see Mahurin's efforts. He had another Fw 190 boresighted and fired on it from a hundred yards. The Focke-Wulf flipped off to its right and went down in a spin for a probable. 1st Lt. Glenn Schlitz was having his best day after flying thirty-seven missions without firing his guns. He bounced thirty Fw 190s. Two of them saw him coming and turned to meet him head-on. Schlitz started firing at one of them and just let him fly through his .50's, but made no claim on this one. He then turned up-sun to see four more in a string. He closed to 400 yards on the number two man and opened fire. At 200 yards range he saw strikes on its engine and cockpit and assumed that he killed its pilot. Schlitz then concentrated on the leader, giving it a four second burst from 300 yards. Its right wing snapped off and it started down. He then started a turn to pick up the B-17s again and found himself looking at two more Fw 190s that were chasing the Forts. Schlitz selected the number two man and fired at its wingroot, walking his gunfire along its fuselage up to its nose, whereupon it burst into flame. This was the 56th FG's first "triple kill."

Schlitz: "I peeled down through the formation and sprayed two Fw 190s, but nothing happened. Then I peeled up again to find two more Focke-

Wulfs dead ahead and turning. I gave the first one a two-second burst. The bullets knocked pieces off his wing root and went into the cockpit. I guess it killed the pilot, for he nosed over into a spin. The second one was like a pigeon-after a five second burst his canopy fell off and he began falling. The third one was just like the first, except that the engine caught fire and he began spinning in." 2nd Lt. John Truluck also got an Me 210 as a probable, which had been previously damaged by 1st Lt. Edgar Whitley. 1st Lt. Don Goodfleisch was credited with a damaged Me 110.

On the negative side, the 63rd FS lost 1st Lt. Arthur Sugas over Ans, Belgium. Sugas, White 3, and 2nd Lt. George Compton, White 4, encountered thirty Fw 190s preparing to attack the B-17s. Two of these Fw's elected to take on the two Thunderbolts at 28,000 feet, and when they started firing, Compton told Sugas to break, and dove away, himself. He didn't believe that Sugas heard him. Sugas was killed in action.

In all, the 56th FG claimed fifteen destroyed, three probably destroyed and four damaged. Not a record, as the 4th FG had destroyed eighteen the day before, but they served notice that they were on the way to become the top scoring air-to-air fighter group in the American Air Force.

August 19: VIII FC FO 40/108 called for Ramrod missions, with the 4th and 78th Fighter Groups providing penetration support, while the 56th and 353rd FG's provided withdrawal support. Col. Zemke led the 56th's FG's portion of the mission, escorting back from Gilse/Rijen airdrome forty B-17s. Airborne at 1715, RV with the bombers was made east of Woensdrecht at 25,000 feet at 1757.

White and Red Flights of the 62nd Fighter Squadron had immediate contact with German fighters and Lt. Michael Quirk took on a pair of Fw

190s, one split away and headed for Germany, the other headed towards the sea, but reversed his course to quickly and Quirk was able to stay behind him, firing until it exploded. Col. Zemke damaged an Fw 190 in White Flight's encounter. Red Flight then rejoined its squadron over the target. For some reason unknown to the fighter pilots, the bombers circled the target twice, which created some consternation for the fighters, as it was placing them at their minimum fuel limitations while the bombers orbited. Lt. Glen Hodges, Red Four of the 63rd FS, had to leave the area as his engine started loosing power. He was only able to pull 26" of mercury (Turbocharger pressure.) at 27,000 feet. Under escort by Lt. Harold Comstock, they headed for Halesworth. Over Breda, Germany Hodges started a rapid descent at 220 mph down to only two hundred feet, they crossed the coastline, and got as far as Thoen Island, off the Dutch coast. Flak boats in the estuary opened fire, and Comstock directed his attention upon them by both strafing and placing himself as a target to draw their fire away from Hodges. Then Hodges pulled up his nose to bleed off his airspeed and stalled his P-47 into the water. As he ditched, the flak boats were firing on the spray thrown up by the hydroplaning Thunderbolt. Hodges became a POW. Comstock had done all he could do. As this was taking place, the Luftwaffe arrived in force. Some thirty-five to forty-five enemy fighters, mostly Me 109s and Fw 190s, with at least a pair of Me 210s thrown in. Major Tukey's 63rd FS continued to score with Lt. Joseph Egan getting an Fw 190 and Lt. John Vogt an Me 109. Lt. Edgar Whitley got an Me 109, also.

Major Gabreski's 61st FS enjoyed most of the action from the interception over Glise/Rijen that lasted to Schoonhoven. Capt. Gerald Johnson destroyed an Me 109, along with damaging another. (And erroneously be-

Lt. Norman Brooks, 61st FS, and "Slugger." This aircraft was the usual mount of Lt. Joe Popplewell. (USAF)

Captain Fred Christensen and "Miss Fire" with one of the better pieces of artwork found on a Wolfpack aircraft. (via Davis)

Promoted to 1st Lt. April 9, 1944, Lt. Stamps went to Marana Field, FL when he finished his tour in June. (USAF)

Major Gerald Johnson, from Owensboro, KY. This Johnson was the second AAF ETO ace while flying with the 61st FS. He became the squadron commander of the 63rd FS on Feb. 22, 1944, and became a POW on May 27. Post War he commanded the 62nd FS. (USAF)

Cold winter maintenance on Lt. Samuel Stamps UN❂S. Exposed on both aircraft are the oil cooler filters. (via Davis)

came credited as the 56th FG's first ace on this date, but his actual score was now 4.5.) Lt. Robert Johnson got his second kill, an Me 109. Lt. Frank McCauley got a pair of Me 109s, which brought his total score up to 3.5. Capt. Robert Lamb got an Fw 190 and damaged another, and Lt. James Carter got a probable Me 109.

Escort was broken with the bombers over Zevenbergen at 1824 and the Group landed at Halesworth at 1906. (The 78th FG had scored one kill on their early part of the mission, the 4th FG got skunked).

August 22: Combat missions were not the only way to loose pilots. At 1000 1st Lt. Conaway Saux and 2nd Lt. Don Tettemer, 62nd Fighter Squadron, took off from Halesworth on a training flight. Shortly after becoming airborne and during the flight join-up, their P-47s collided at too low of an altitude for either of them to bailout. Both were killed. They were interned with honors at the US Cemetery at Broockwood, Surrey.

August 23: VIII FC FO 111. A Rodeo by the four 8th AF P-47 Fighter Groups over Bruges-Woensdrecht-Schippol areas, with the 353rd Fighter Group simulating a bomber formation in an attempt to lure up the Luftwaffe. Major Schilling, now the Deputy Group Commander, led the mission from the 62nd Fighter Squadron.

Landfall-in and RV with the pseudo-bombers was at Haamstede at 1528. They swept to east of Gilzn-Rijan, sighted twenty enemy fighters, and the 62nd FS attempted to intercept them, but they dove into cloud cover and evaded. Later an Me 109 was sighted, wearing old RAF roundel style markings, but it too escaped. Landfall-out was made north of Ijmuiden at high altitude, and they made a slow descent across the sea to land at 1630.

August 24: VIII FC FO 44/112. The 56th Fighter Group was to provide escort and target support for seven Bomb Groups of the 1st Bomb Wing's B-17 force to bomb the Luftwaffe base at Villacoublay, near Paris. For this mission, Col. Zemke led the 63rd Fighter Squadron, and the Group dispatched fifty-two Thunderbolts. Landfall-in was Dieppe at 1730 and they RV'd the eighty-six effective Forts (Out of 110 dispatched.) southwest of Rouen at 1741 after dropping their belly tanks.

About fifty German fighters were encountered, mostly Fw 190s. From the 63rd FS, only Lt. Vance Ludwig had success, damaging an Fw 190 over Paris. Due to favorable weather conditions, the Luftwaffe revised their tactics during the ensuing encounters. There was a solid overcast at 29,000 feet, and the Fw's formed up just under the cloud cover and dove on the Thunderbolts, ignoring the B-17s.

Capt. Horace Craig, was flying his first mission as squadron commander of the 62nd FS, although Major Schilling was leading the squadron and White Flight on this mission. Craig took his Red Flight into the melee and damaged an Fw 190, and Lt. James Jones finished it off. Capt. Leroy Schreiber, on loan from the 61st FS on this mission, got another. Although cautioned, ordered if you will, to stay at high altitudes and with the bombers, the combats got down to as low as 5,000 feet and encountered heavy flak, but none of the 62nd FS P-47s were damaged. But they still had to sweat out their fuel, as the mission encompassed 560 miles, their longest ranged sorties so far. Thirteen had to land at Thorney Island, and only three had enough gas left to get back to Halesworth.

The 61st FS's portion of the mission was led by Major. Francis Gabreski with fifteen P-47s. Encountering the Fw 190s between Evereux and Breiupont, Gabreski scored his first kill with the P-47, while Lt. Robert Johnson damaged another. 2nd Lt. Frank McCauley's P-47 was pretty well shotup, but he got it back and he squadron was back at 2018.

August 25: VIII FC FO 46/114. The 56th and 353rd Fighter Groups put up ninety Thunderbolts on a Rodeo intended as a diversionary mission for B-26 raids to Rouen and Triqueville. Major Schilling led from the 63rd Fighter Squadron and the Group off Halesworth at 1752. 1st Lt. John Vogt had to

ABOVE & TWO BELOW: 2nd Lt. Don Tettemer and 1st Lt. Conway Saux, 62nd FS, tookoff at 1000 hours on the morning of August 22, 1943 on a training mission. As they joined-up they collided and both were killed. (USAF)

turn back when his engine quit, but he got his T-Bolt back down safely. Landfall-in was over Gravelines at 1833 at 24,000 feet, sweeping over Bethune-Doullens, Breck-sur-Mer, north along the coast, and out over St. Inglevert at 1902. Other than encountering heavy flak at their altitude over Dunkirk the mission was totally uneventful.

August 27: VIII FC FO 48/116 Col. Zemke led the 63rd Fighter Squadron and the mission, while Capt. Gabreski led the 61st FS on this Ramrod that was airborne at 1731. (The 62nd FS was in the process of having B-7 bomb/fuel tank shackles installed on their aircraft and did not participate on this mission). Escort was provided to the 1st and 4th Bomb Wings B-17s returning from Watten where they made the first attack on V-1 launching sites.

After sweeping Lille, RV with the bombers was made at St. Poi, and the Forts were escorted to just off the French Coast on the way home. Enroute home the 63rd FS was bounced by a flight of Spitfires and scattered, along with having one of their P-47s damaged by .303 gunfire by an overzealous Spit pilot. Col. Zemke, 1st Lt. Frank Peppers and 2nd Lt. John Wilson landed at Bradwell Bay. Lt.'s George Compton and Harold Comstock at Manston, 2nd Lt. Raymond Petty at Eastchurch. The remaining ten fighters from the squadron got back to Halesworth at 1925.

August 31: VIII FC FO 119 dispatched the four P-47 groups on a Ramrod for the General LeMay's 4th Bomb Wing. Major David Schilling led the 61st Fighter Squadron and the mission off Halesworth at 1612. RV was made with the bombers at Fecamp and they were escorted to Les Andelye, where the bombers turned back, aborting the mission some twenty miles short of the target. There was heavy cloud cover obscuring the ground at this point. On the way out, Capt. Horace Craig's 62nd FS saw an unescorted box of B-17s coming back from another mission, and flew over to escort them out. The mission returned at 1852.

September 2: VIII FC FO 50/120 was for an intended Ramrod, but wound up as a Rodeo. The Field Order called for 182 P-47s from the four groups, but, because of the installation of the belly tank shackles not being completed, the 56th Fighter Group was only able to send out thirty-six aircraft. Led by Col. Zemke, the 56th FG was airborne at 1751.

Landfall-in was over Ostend at 1836 at 24,000 feet and two minutes later the belly tanks, "babies," were dropped. RV with the bombers was accomplished at Deynze, with the 56th FG flying as top cover. To the concern of the fighter pilots, the bombers had to make a second pass on the targets and then did not bomb at all. The cloud cover being so heavy that they did not want to endanger friendly Belgians by bombing indiscriminately. This extra time over the target area stretched the fighters fuel to the limit once again. At 1920, near Ghent, the 56th FG was bounced by a mix of Me 109s, Fw 190s and some unidentified twin-engine types. Under a high overcast, the Group was at a disadvantage, as the Luftwaffe dropped down from above this cloud cover to make their initial attack, and then repeatedly zoomed back up into it to evade and position themselves for repeated attacks on the P-47s, upon which they concentrated, instead of the B-17s.

The 63rd FS, led by Col. Zemke received the brunt of these attacks. His White Flight, composed of himself, 1st Lt.'s Edgar Whitley and Wilfred Van Able (White Three), and 2nd Lt. Walter Hannigen (White Four), received the German's first bounce at 1921 at 25,000 feet and paid dearly. Van Able and Hannigan both were hit by cannon fire from Fw 190s, and 2nd Lt. Justus Foster, 61st, saw one of them at 22,000 feet spinning down in flames near Armentieres. Van Able ditched in the Dutch Islands and was shot at by shore batteries and believed surely killed, but he survived as a POW. Hannigan was killed. Lt. John Vogt's P-47 was well and truly clobbered. He was hit in the aft fuselage by 20mm fire which holed his supercharger ducts and caused a corresponding loss of manifold pressure and power. His guns were knocked out of commission, as well as his elevators and trim tabs. Due to the lack of supercharger boost, the Fw 190 was able to stay with him with ease as Vogt dove, slipping and sliding towards the ground while attempting to escape. They hit the deck ten miles southeast of Ghent, and the Fw 190 stayed a hundred yards behind him until north of Dunkirk, firing its machine guns after it ran out of 20mm cannon shells. It was another miracle story for Republic Aviation, as Vogt was able to get back to Eastchurch to make a gear-down, no-flap landing in spite of being wounded in the left leg by 20mm shards. No matter that he nosed-up at the end of the runway.

Lt. Norman Brooks, 61st FS, had "Catagory A" damage to his P-47 due to flak, and so did Lt. Donald Goodfleisch's, 63rd FS, Thunderbolt,

Lt. Wilfred Van Able was assigned to "B" Flight, 63rd FS when they went to England in 1943. He was downed over Armentieres, France on September 2, 1943 and became a prisoner of war. UN✪Q, 41-6537 was his personal P-47 and he was downed in this aircraft. (USAF)

but they got back home okay. (The German pilot chasing Vogt, a Lt. Kehl from II/JG26, claimed Vogt's P-47 as destroyed, which it was, but not exactly under the circumstances that he thought. The 4th FG also lost a pilot on this Ramrod, which meant a loss of four P-47s and two pilots killed, one POW and one wounded for the mission. No known damage was inflicted on enemy fighters).

September 3: VIII FC FO 51/121, all fighter groups on Ramrods, with the 56th Fighter Group tasked to escort 180 1st Bomb Wing B-17s to Romilly airdrome. Col. Zemke led the 63rd Fighter Squadron and the Group, while Capt. Craig led the 62nd FS and Major Gabreski led the 61st. Airborne at 0737, belly tanks were dropped at 0816 and landfall-in was made over Pointe Haut Blano at 26,000 feet one minute later.

Near Romilly, and just prior to the point where they were due to break escort, Zemke's "Postgate" (The squadron's radio callsign at the time), White Flight dove from 29,000 feet down to 20,000 feet to intercept four Fw 190s that were in a line abreast formation. Zemke and Capt. Don Goodfleisch each claiming one. Immediately thereafter, Red Flight, Capt. Lyle Adriense, 2nd Lt.'s John Truluck, Harold Comstock and George Compton bounced four more Fw 190s in a box formation, with Adriense getting one.

2nd Lt. William Janson, out of Blue Flight fired at two more, and they fired back. Janson's P-47s being hit in the cowl, right flap and right elevator. He struggled home okay, and made no claim on his own shooting prowess. The 62nd FS, "Woodfire," made no claims.

The 61st FS, "Keyworth," however, was in on the fray. Major Gabreski got one Fw 190, while Lt.'s Albert Biales and Robill Roberts fired on two more, without claims. The 61st FS lost Lt. Hiram Bevins in the vicinity of Meaux, outside of Paris. The last they heard of him was when he reported that he was on the deck and heading out. He became a POW. Two 62nd FS P-47s landed at Manston on the way home. The remainder were back to Halesworth at 0958.

VIII FC FO 52/122, the second mission for the day was a Rodeo over Dunkirk by ninety-five P-47s of the 56th and 78th Fighter Groups. Airborne at 1420, Col. Zemke again leading with the 63rd Fighter Squadron. 2nd Lt. Robert Hall, 63rd FS, had to abort, being escorted home by the spares; Lt.'s Pat Wilson and Truluck. The 62nd FS, again led by Craig, included two P-47s from the 355th FG that were making their first orientation mission. The 61st FS was led by Major Gabreski. They swept Noordwal-Tholen-Dunkirk uneventfully, seeing no enemy fighters and only encountering some light flak and were back home again at 1555.

The Invasion of Italy also commenced this day.

On September 3, 1943 Lt. Hiram Bevins was forced down in France in HV❂E, 41-6232. He spent the rest of the war as a POW. Here German troops inspect his aircraft. (via Davis)

Lending your personal aircraft to another pilot can be venturesome. UN❂F, 42-22534 "The Wolf" was wrecked by another pilot who failed to unlock the rudder before takeoff on a Ramrod to Leeuworden on Sept. 7, 1943. (USAF)

September 4: VIII FC FO 54/124 once again sent ninety-five Thunderbolts of the 56th and 78th Fighter Groups on a Rodeo. The 56th FG was airborne at 1646 with Col. Zemke leading the 63rd Fighter Squadron. Capt. Craig the 62nd FS, and Major Gabreski the 61st. Col. Zemke had to abort with engine problems, so Major Gabreski took over his place. They swept in over Westhoofd at 1720 at 25,000 feet. Between Ostend and Ghent they were advised of possible enemy aircraft, but they could not find them, and made landfall-out between Zeebrugge and Knocke. They landed at 1832 after an uneventful sweep.

September 6: VIII FC FO 55/125. 176 P-47s from the four groups on a Ramrod to Guigincourt. Major Schilling led with the 63rd Fighter Squadron, making landfall-in at Calais after a 0709 takeoff. Just prior to Calais, Schilling had to abort with a radio failure, passing the mission lead to Major Gabreski and command of the 63rd FS to Capt. Mahurin. 2nd Lt. Joseph Walker, 62nd, had to abort with belly tank problems. 1st Lt. Michael Quirk, 62nd, aborted with supercharger difficulties. RV with the bombers was accomplished at 0805 over Doullens, escorting the 320 B-17s to north of Reims, on their way to Stuttgart, and then turning back over the bomber formation in order to continue the top cover as long as possible.

They left the last box of bombers over Peronne. Radio jamming was again encountered, this time with a voice-over that sounded like "Goering,

Goering, Goering," or "You can't get home, you can't get home." In some respects it was prophetic, as thirty-five B-17s went down on this mission. Only one kill was claimed, by a 4th FG pilot, and the 353rd FG lost one P-47 in exchange. The 56th FG RTB'd at 0937.

September 7: VIII FC FO 56/126 was a Ramrod for B-17s of the 1st Bomb Division and B-24s of the 2nd BD with 178 P-47s from the four groups. The 56th Fighter Group, airborne from Halesworth at 0743, with forty-six Thunderbolts was led by Capt. Sylvester Burke, Operations Officer of the 63rd FS. Their part of the Ramrod was to support twenty-five B-24s to Leeuworden.

The Group approached enemy territory near Kijkduin, where they turned left along the coast to make landfall-in at 27,000 feet over Vieland at 0833, making RV with the B-24s at this point. The target at Leeuwrden was obscured by 10/10 (solid clouds) undercast, so the B-24s proceeded to their secondary objective, Alkmear, which was also covered by clouds. The Liberators then turned to bomb two convoys, totalling 22 ships off the Tessel Islands.

While over the North Sea, Lt's Ralph Johnson and Anthony Carcione flight, 62nd FS, spotted three Me 109s and dove on them. Carcione positioned himself to attack one, but another came in on his tail, which Johnson dispatched from up-sun, seeing strikes on its wing ammo bay which then

2nd Lt. John Truluck started out as a "brown bar" and eventually earned his "railroad tracks." During this time he also destroyed seven German aircraft. He started his combat tour on May 7, 1943 and was assigned to the 495th Fighter Training Group in England on May 13, 1944. (USAF)

"Category 'E'" was a war weary P-47 that was converted to a two-seater by S/Sgt.'s Thurman Schreel and Charles Taylor. It took them 550 man-hours, and earned each a Bronze Star. It was returned to combat in April 1945 and was flown on several of the Group's last combat missions. (USAF)

"Lady Jane" belonged to John Truluck. It was 42-74750, UN◉L. (via Davis)

exploded and tore off a chunk of its wing, whereupon its pilot bailed out. Carcione continued his own attack, and fired until the Me 109 dove into the sea. The mission returned at 0954.

September 8: VIII FC FO 57/127 a Rodeo sweeping Neipourt-Flushing-Courtrai-Ghent with ninety-three P-47s of the 56th and 78th Fighter Groups. Capt. Sylvester Burke again leading the Group with fifty Thunderbolts. The diversionary sweep for 140 B-26s and A-20s attacking Vitry en Francois was totally uneventful. Off at 0840, they were back at 1025.

September 9: VIII FC FO 58/128 sent out 215 P-47s on a Ramrod for the 1st and 3rd Bomb Division's B-17s. This mission was the first for the 352nd Fighter Group, whose part of the mission was to provide withdrawal support for the return of the 56th and 353rd FG's from Europe. The 56th FG was off Halesworth at 0650, led by Col. Zemke and the 63rd FS. Landfall-in and RV with 120 B-17s heading for an airdrome at Beauvais was made at Dieppe with Major Craig's 62nd FS providing top cover for the Group. Approaching the target thirty Fw 190s were waiting for them and attempted to make head-on attacks on the bombers, but the 56th FG dove in between them and forced the Fw's to break off the majority of the attacks.

Capt. "Bud" Mahurin: "I sighted two Fw 190s flying line abreast about 1,000 below me and in front of me. I went after them and closed to about 600 yards and the one on the left saw me. He split out while the other one started a turn to the right. I tried to get a deflection, but was unable to. I straightened out and let him fly right through my fire at about 100 yards. I broke off to the right, and when I saw him, he was falling like a leaf; with very large objects coming off the plane. I think the canopy came off, part of his wing, and the pilot came out too . . ." Both Lt. Robert Johnson and Capt. Gerald Johnson from the 61st FS went after Fw 190s and fired, but neither made claims of hitting them. Landfall-out was made at 0839 with the bombers remaining under escort and they continued to be covered until mid-channel, when the Group broke off to RTB Halesworth at 0940.

VIII FC FO 59/129 sent out the 355th Fighter Group on a practice sweep and the 56th FG on a Ramrod for 80 B-17s the evening of September 9. The 56th FG put up forty-nine P-47s under Major Schilling, who led the mission with the 62nd Fighter Squadron. Briefed to go to Cambrai, they were off at 1745, but were recalled just after landfall-in at Dunkirk because of 10/10 clouds and the inability to find the bombers. They RTB'd at 1906.

September 14: VIII FC FO 60/130 was a Rodeo after almost a week's worth of inactivity, due to the weather. This Field Order marked the first combat mission for the 355th Fighter Group, and included the 4th, 56th

and 353rd FG's with 176 Thunderbolts. The 78th FG standing down for this one. Major Schilling led from the 63rd Fighter Squadron and brought the 61st FS along on this Rodeo that was off Halesworth at 1110. The 62nd FS did not participate in this mission. They made RV with the 352nd FG over Aldburgh at 13,000 feet, climbed to 27,000 feet to make landfall-in at Knocke at 1154.

Climbing to 32,000 feet they turned north to sweep over Neuzen, and then out over Westhoofd. They RTB'd at 1238 after another uneventful sweep.

September 15: VIII FC FO 62/132 201. Thunderbolts from five 8th Air Force fighter groups up on this mission. The first with over two hundred P-47s in action on Ramrods. The 56th Fighter Group put up fifty-four, and led by Col. Zemke and 61st Fighter Squadron, they were airborne at 1720. Their portion of the mission being general support the bombers penetration.

Landfall was made at Cayeux, and RV with the bombers at Poix, where intense flak was encountered. Lt.'s Carcione and Charles Harrison, 62nd FS, aborted because of engine problems. Lt. Adam Wisniewski, 63rd FS, couldn't drop his belly tank and had to turn back at 1809. The Thunderbolts went over the top of the bombers at 28,000 feet, and upon meeting the first box, dropped down to 26,000 feet. They were escorted to beyond Crepy, where the Group turned right and picked up a second box of bombers, which were escorted to just short of Paris, and then the Group returned to their origional charges near the WWI battle site of Chateau Thierry. They broke escort at Cayeux. Other than seeing ten Fw 190s near Paris that did not interfere with the mission, and observing exceptionally heavy flak coming up from Paris, itself, the mission was uneventful for the 56th FG that RTB'd at 1954.

September 16: VIII FC FO 63/133. The 56th and 353rd Fighter Groups dispatched seventy-nine P-47s as escort for the 1st Bomb Division. Major Schilling led forty-nine fighters of the 56th FG off the forward refueling base at Tangmere at 1310. Capt. Leroy Schreiber and Lt. Ralph Johnson, 62nd Fighter Squadron, had to abort because their belly tanks would not feed. Flight Officer Robert Walker 62nd FS, oxygen system failed. The 63rd FS had even more difficulties: squadron commander Major Burke had propeller problems, 2nd Lt. Frederick Windmayer went back to Halesworth with an oxygen system failure. Lt.'s Charles Clamp and Gordon Batdorf went back to Halesworth because of the delays incurred in taking off put them so late that they could not catch up with the rest of the squadron. This took Blue Flight entirely out of the mission. Then, Lt. Harry Dugas headed back to Halesworth with prop and generator problems. 2nd Lt. Bernard Smith and 1st Lt. Frank Peppers aborted enroute with mechanical difficulties. Belly tanks were dropped just prior to entering enemy territory at Cayeux and they proceed to St. Lo to RV with the 150 B-17s, which were eleven minutes late, requiring the Group to orbit St. Lo twice. At 1420, ten minutes after RV, forty to fifty Fw 190s and Me 109s were seen approaching the bombers from the northwest, with half of them at 19,000 feet and the other half at 20,000 feet. The lower bunch, upon sighting the Thunderbolts, dove away, and then turned to attack the bombers head-on. The higher group turned back northwest and passed behind the bombers, to return ten minutes later to attack the bombers from the rear.

Yellow Flight of the 63rd FS dove on them from out of the sun to break up the attack, but made no claims. The 62nd FS had better luck. Blue Three, 1st Lt. George Goldstein dove down to 8,000 feet to knock down an Me 109. He was followed by Lt. Robert Taylor, Yellow Three, who got an Fw 190. Blue Leader, Capt. Walter Cook, damaged an Fw 190. Separated by the encounter, Goldstein and his wingman, 2nd Lt. Felix Williamson, returned to Halesworth. The rest of the Group continued the escort to Chateau Briand, the limit of their range, and returned to Tangmere at 1540. Oddly enough, pilots of the 61st FS saw a P-47 explode in the air after going through several violent evasive maneuvers, but none were reported as lost on this mission by either fighter group.

September 22: VIII FC FO 67/138. After six days of being forced to stay on the ground by Mother Nature, the VIII Fighter Command ordered two missions this day. The first was a Rodeo by the six operational P-47 groups. The 56th Fighter Group, led by Col. Zemke tookoff from Halesworth at 1048 to sweep Lille-Ghent, making landfall-in at Mardyck at 1126. They swept to east of St. Omer, turned left to Armentieres, then to Lille. Over Lille ten to twelve all silver colored Fw 190s circled over the Zemke's 63rd Fighter Squadron, then dove down through Major Craig's 62nd FS and Capt. Renwick's 61st FS's formation. The Fw's hit the deck and kept on going, so there was no ensuing action. The Group RTB'd out over Blankenberghe at 1147 and were back on the ground at 1223.

VIII FC FO 139 that afternoon was another Rodeo with the 56th, 352nd, 353rd and 355th Fighter Groups. The mission was intended to be an orientation sweep for new 56th FG pilots and a practice sweep for the 355th Fighter Group that was going on its first mission. Major Schilling led the 61st Fighter Squadron and the 56th FG off Halesworth at 1432, whereupon they swept Lille-Ghent and were back at 1618 after a milkrun.

September 23: VIII FC FO 140. The 4th, 56th, 78th and 353rd Fighter Groups to provide support for the 1st Task Force. During the evening of September 22, the 56th FG flew to the Thorney Island staging base in preparation for this mission. Because of the austere conditions there, the pilots had to pre-flight their own aircraft, as well as contend with a lot of mud. Scheduled for a 0640 takeoff, they were twenty minutes late getting airborne and twenty minutes late at the RV point. They finally caught the rear box of bombers over Rannes just as the B-17s were coming under attack by an estimated thirty Fw 190s. Capt. Mahurin led the 63rd Fighter Squadron down on them, but just as the interception of the Forts by the Luftwaffe, and the Fw's by the P-47s was about to take place, the Forts and the Fw 190s entered a massive cloud bank that went up from 17,000 to 32,000 feet, and that was the last that was seen of them. Now at the limit of their range, the 56th FG had to turn back at this point. They made landfall-out at Pointe de Barfleur, and landed at Thorney island to refuel at 0915.

VIII FC FO 142 was a second Ramrod that afternoon. Major Schilling led forty-three Thunderbolts off Thorney Island at 1635 on a general support mission for B-17s. Capt. Eugene O'Neill and 2nd Lt. Charles Ginn, 62nd Fighter Squadron, had to abort with radio and belly tank problems, respectively.

Landfall-in was made over St. Brieno at 1732 at 26,000 feet. They escorted ninety-seven B-17s to a point twenty miles northeast of Nantes. Just southwest of Reenes a dozen silver-grey Fw 190s came in on the B-17s head-on, exploding one. Blue Flight of the 63rd FS was bounced by one of the Fw 190s, but he was in and out of the haze so quickly that he could not be chased. Another attempted an attack on Blue Flight of the 61st FS, but changed his mind and dove away. Bomber escort continued on the way out until relieved by the 4th FG, and the Group returned to Thorney Island at 1848, refueled, and went home to Halesworth.

September 26: VIII FC FO 145 sent all six P-47s groups on a Ramrod for the heavy bombers. Major Schilling led the 56th Fighter Group off from Halesworth at 1628. They went in on the deck to Orfordness, then climbed to 9,000 feet, leveled off for awhile, and then climbed to 25,000 feet over Berok-sur-mer, where they dropped their belly tanks.

Over Amines, RV with two boxes of B-17s was accomplished at 1739. Approaching the target, Major Schilling developed an oil leak and turned back, being replaced by Major Burke as mission leader. The 120 B-17s were escorted to their target of Reims, and escort was broken off over St. Poi on the way out. No German aircraft were encountered, but flak was reported as accurate as high at 31,000 feet. RTB was at 1903.

September 27: VIII FC FO 146. The six Thunderbolt groups put up 262 fighters on the largest Ramrod to date. The 56th Fighter Group sent out fifty-one, and for the first time in a long time, had no aborts. This was also their first mission with the new 108 gallon paper drop tanks, of which almost all of the fuel was usable. Withdrawal escort was provided for a mission to the submarine base at Emden for 340 B-17s, the largest force the Group was tasked with escorting thus far in the war.

Major Schilling led the 61st Fighter Squadron and the Group off at 0910, making landfall-in over Ameland at 1005 at 27,000 feet. Arriving five minutes early over the RV point, they orbited between the East Frisian Islands and Germany for twenty minutes before Major Burke, leading the 63rd FS, spotted the lead box of bombers coming out over Borkum, the western island of the chain. The bombers were just coming under attack by Fw 190s carrying rockets and long range fuel tanks, as well as Me 109s with unusual bulges under their wings.

While the 61st and 62nd FS's took up escort positions over the bombers, Major Burke led his 63rd in to break up the enemy fighter attacks. This was the last anyone saw of 1st Lt. Harry Dugas, Red Four, as he was going down in a dive over Juist Island. He was killed in action. 2nd Lt. John Truluck knocked down an Fw 190 and an Me 109. 1st Lt. John Coenen, Assistant Squadron Operations Officer, got two Fw 190s, and 1st Lt. Wayne O'Connor an Me 109. 1st Lt.s Jack Brown and John Vogt also fired their machine guns, but made no claims. On return, the 63rd FS came back in pairs and flights, while the 62nd FS got a bad vector from the Direction Finding station in England and their fighters wound up scattered to airbases all over the country with only six getting back to Halesworth as planned.

September 30: Major Phillip Tukey was transferred to VIII Fighter Command as their Operations Officer. His replacement as Squadron Commander of the 63rd Fighter Squadron was Capt. Sylvester Burke. Although Tukey flew combat missions for all but the six months he was at VIII FC, and when he was on leave became the commander of the 356th Fighter Group, he never would score an air-to-air kill. As always, it remained a matter of being in the right place at the right time.

October 2: VIII FC FO 148. Five P-47s fighter groups on a Ramrod to escort the heavies. The 56th Fighter Group was tasked to provide general support from Zootkamp to the target, and then withdrawal support until fuel considerations mandated they break off for home. Led by Col. Zemke and the 61st Fighter Squadron, they were airborne at 1449 with forty-nine Thunderbolts. The belly tanks continued to create difficulties and two 62nd FS P-47s had to abort because of them, as well as one more with an oil leak.

Landfall-in was accomplished over Hoorn, in the Tassel Islands, at 1534 at 23,000 feet. In the vicinity of Zootkamp RV was made with the first box of 360 B-17s enroute to Emden. At the RV point a pair of unidentified German fighters were spotted, but not encountered. Then, over Emden between thirty and fifty more were seen down between 10,000 and 15,000 feet, operating just above the solid undercast.

They made little attempt to intercept the bombers, but Major Schilling, leading the 63rd FS, and his wingman, Flight Officer Robert Sheehan, went down to break up their formations. They bounced five Fw 190s and a single Me 109 at 17,000 feet east of Groningen, with Schilling destroying one Fw 190. Sheehan fired, but made no claim. Col. Zemke went after an Fw 190 that was positioning himself for an attack on a straggling B-17 west of Terschelling Island, and shot it down. This feat made Colonel Hub Zemke the first 56th FG "ace." Escort was broken off at this point and the fighters returned home at 1733.

October 4: VIII FC FO 150 sent 223 P-57s from the 4th, 56th, 78th, 353rd and 355th Fighter Groups on a Ramrod. It was a wondrous day for the 56th FG, as the 4th FG couldn't find the bombers they were supposed to escort, nor could they find the Luftwaffe. The 56th FG, on the other hand, had their best day so far, destroying sixteen German fighters. Their mission was to escort 220 B-17s to Frankfurt via Haamstede and Koblenz and was off Halesworth at 1019, being led by Major Schilling and the 63rd Fighter Squadron.

Landfall-in was accomplished south of Flushing and RV made between Voglesanq and Duren at 27,000 feet. The B-17s were formated into three wings in box formations, and the 353rd FG covered the first two boxes, while the 56th FG the later.

At 1132 near Duren a mixed gaggle of Fw 190s, Me 109s, Ju 88s and Me 110s were seen, with the heaviest number of German fighters being the "easy meat" twin-engine Me 110s. They were preparing to attack the Flying Fortresses from the rear, but the 56th FG dove in on them from their own rear and broke up the attack before it got started. Schilling led the 63rd FS down on the initial interception, and the squadron claimed fourteen Me 110s destroyed and one damaged. The 61st FS claimed three destroyed, and one probable, but one of these claims was downgraded to a probable. Those awarded claims were: Lt.'s William Marangello and Frank McCauley from the 61st FS, with McCauley and Lt. James Carter also credited with probables. Major Schilling, Headquarters 56th FG got one.

The 63rd FS, having the best of times, confirmed three each by Capt. Mahurin and Lt. Vance Ludwig, while Lt.'s Jack Brown, Harold Comstock, Bernard Smith, Glen Schlitz, John Vogt and John Wilson each got one, as well as Capt. Don Goodfleisch. The 62nd FS, remaining as top cover for the Group, never got off a shot. Escort was continued to Westerschelde, and landfall-out was made at 1223. The elated pilots landed thirty-five minutes later.

It is noted that the claims made by the 63rd FS were the highest recorded by any single fighter squadron in the ETO to this point. This was also the longest mission flown so far by P-47 pilots, 750 miles.

Excitement continued when a crew bailed out of a B-17 over the field. Four members of the crew from the 355th (sic) BG had to be hospitalized. The pilot had a broken leg and pelvis. "Training should be given to these people in how to land in a parachute!"

October 8: VIII FC FO 151. After four days of weather-enforced inactivity, the six P-47 groups were sent on a Ramrod for the 1st and 3rd Bomb Divisions. A new record, 274 P-47s were sent out on this mission. The 56th Fighter Group was tasked with providing withdrawal support for 300 B-17s coming back from Breman. Major Schilling led the 62nd FS and the Group on this mission, off Halesworth at 1421 with fifty Thunderbolts.

Landfall-in was over Ijumiden at 1508 at 28,000 feet, with RV accomplished near Hasselunne at 1533. They provided close escort until Meppel, where the bomber formation split, but they were still able to weave above both boxes of B-17s to provide a loose top cover for the remainder of the mission.

After making RV with the main formation, the straggling B-17s became the main concern, as they were under constant attack by German fighters, approximately a dozen, mostly Fw 190s. The 61st and 62nd FS's took them on, and the 62nd FS made up for being shut out on the previous mission. Major Schilling, leading, got one Fw 190. Also scoring were Capt. Leroy Schreiber, Lt's Michael Quirk and Harry Coronios, with Coronios also claiming a damaged. Capt. Ray Dauphin claimed a probable, and he was slightly wounded in the hands and legs by fragments of a 20mm shell that exploded in his cockpit in the process. Lt. Joseph Walker claimed a damaged. From the 61st FS, Lt. Robert Johnson knocked down one, and Capt. Donald Renwick damaged another. All of these were Fw 190s.

Under somewhat strange circumstances the 63rd FS lost Lt. Dover C. Flemming. He had gone up as their spare, with the intention of replacing Lt. Frank Peppers that had to abort. Flemming was last seen over the Zuider Zee by Lt. Charles Clamp at 1600, well into the mission, when he had tacked himself on to Yellow Flight, and then he tried to catch up with Blue Flight to replace Peppers, but never made the RV with the flight. Flemming was declared as killed in action, but the details were never ascertained. A

HV◉L, 41-6311, was flown by Lt. Dick Mudge on a Ramrod, escorting B-17s back from Bremen, on October 8, 1943. After suffering battle damage to both wings, Mudge made an emergency landing at Tibenham. (USAF)

few minutes later landfall-out was made over Edmond, and the Group landed at 1649. On return, Lt. Dick Mudge, 61st FS, had to make a forced landing at Tibenham, but his P-47 was repaired.

October 10: VIII FC FO 153. Five P-47s groups active on Ramrod missions. Major Schilling leading the 62nd Fighter Squadron and the Group with a total of forty-nine Thunderbolts to provide withdrawal support for 360 B-17s returning from bombing the marshalling yards at Munster. At RV with the rear boxes of B-17 just west of Munster, the lead bombers were already dropping their bombs and were under heavy attack by an estimated 250 enemy fighters of all their types.

With the B-17s at 27,000 feet, the Luftwaffe was making their attacks from astern, and Schilling led his fighters on a gaggle of about thirty Fw 190s, Me 109s and Me 210s. Schilling got one Fw 190, his fifth victory in four consecutive missions, and joined the ranks of aces. Capt. Walter Cook got an Me 210, and Lt. Walter Brainard damaged another. Lt.'s Robert Taylor and James Jones each got Fw 190s. Lt.'s Anthony Carcione and John Eaves got an Me 109 apiece.

From the 61st FS, Capt. Gerald Johnson got an Me 110 and an Me 210 and became an ace. Lt. Robert Johnson got an Me 109 and an Me 210. He was then fired at by an Me 110 carrying rockets in a head-on attack. Robert Johnson had to fly back to England with his rudder shot up, controlling his P-47 via using the trim tabs.

The 63rd FS was equally active, but without the success. Their Yellow Flight went down to bounce Fw 190s that were preparing to attack the B-17s and Lt. Glenn Schlitz claimed one, but it was disallowed. Blue Flight, Capt. Lyle Adrianse and 2nd Lt. Frederick Windmayer, went after another and chased it until it dove through the B-17 formation, upon which they had to break away lest the Fortress gunners fire at them, too. Red Flight, led by Capt. Don Goodfleisch, went after an Fw 190 that was shooting at a B-17s whose crew was in the process of bailing out, and drove it away from the disabled bomber. Major Burke's White Flight attacked another, but came up empty handed.

Upon their return to England they found the weather to be a formidable foe, also. Most of East Angles was covered by a blanket of heavy fog, and the rest of the country by lighter patches of it. The fighters put down wherever they could. Lt. Jones, 62nd FS, landed at Boreham, which was still under construction. He hit a tractor that pulled out on the runway in front of him as he was landing. Stunned, he was rescued from his burning P-47 by troops from the Corps of Engineers, suffering second degree burns on his hands and face.

Group Headquarters, not being aware that Schlitz's claim was not going to be approved, considered him to be their fifth ace, while Robert S. Johnson, who also entered a claim this day, was their sixth. Johnson's claim was upheld, and he actually became their fifth ace, while Schlitz attained this status on November 12, 1943. To this point, however, four of the five P-47 aces in the 8th Air Force were from the 56th Fighter Group.

October 13: On a surprise turn-about, Italy declared war on Germany.

October 14: VIII FC FO 156. Five P-47 groups were supposed to provide long-range escort for the heavy bombers. But, because of the weather, only the 56th and 353rd Fighter Group's were able to accomplish the task. The 56th FG went out with fifty-three P-47s behind Major Schilling at 1204 to escort 295 B-17s to Schweinfurt.

Landfall-in was over Walcheren Island at 24,000 feet and RV was accomplished at 1306 near Sas van Ghent after one orbit, because the bombers were five minutes late. The B-17s were at 25,000 feet and Major Burke's 63rd Fighter Squadron provided top cover for the front two boxes, while the 61st FS went in on the north side and the 62nd FS took the right.

During the period of actual escort the bombers were unmolested by the Luftwaffe, but as the 56th FG broke escort at the limit of their range, near Dison, German fighters were seen lining up to attack. (They came under heavy fighter attack over the target, and the now escorting 353rd FG claimed 10-1-5. An initial report indicated that sixty B-17s were downed. True! The day became noted forever as "Black Thursday").

Approaching Aachen, groups of between four and twenty Nazi fighters were seen climbing at various altitudes. The 62nd and 63rd FS's proceeded towards home, while White and Blue Flights of the 61st FS, having a bit more fuel, went down to disturb the German's intentions. Lt.'s Frank McCauley and Norman Brooks each got an Me 110, and Major James Stewart, Hq. 56th FG, who was flying with the squadron, damaged another. Capt. Gerald Johnson nailed an Fw 190. Clouds and fog remained their nemesis on return. Seven 63rd FS Thunderbolts got back to Halesworth at 1437, while others had to divert to other bases. The 63rd had two P-47s written off in crash landings, one by Flight Officer Anthony Cavallo at Puddington, while Lt. Russell Westfall put his down on a farm near there.

October 18: VIII FC FO 162 sent the 56th Fighter Group out on penetration support for the heavies. All P-47s groups were up on this Field Order, with several on Rodeos, and this also marked the first operational mission for the 55th Fighter Group with their long expected P-38s finally being released for combat by the 8th Air Force after incurring months of delays brought on by problems in getting them ready.

Col. Zemke led the 61st Fighter Squadron off at 1351, and landfall-in was over Knocke. Ground control then informed Zemke that the bombers were ten minutes early, so Zemke cut off the intended dogleg on the flightplan and led the Group directly to Ans in an attempt to catch the bombers. Although weak radio contact was made with the B-17s, they could not be found, and the Group turned for home.

Near Maastricht, Zemke spotted an Me 210 and led his White Flight down on it, with Capt. Lamb bring his Red Flight along in trail. It was destroyed, the claim being shared by Zemke, Major Stewart, Capt. Lamb and Lt.'s Wood, Blake and Anderson. (Officially, the credit was divided between Major James Stewart and Lt. Melvin Wood). The Group RTB'd at 1604.

October 20: VIII FC FO 163. All seven P-47s groups up, along with thirty-nine P-38s of the 55th Fighter Group. Col. Zemke led the 56th FG from the front of the 63rd Fighter Squadron off Halesworth at 1250 to provide penetration support for the heavies.

In over Blankenburg at 1334 at 24,000 feet, RV was made this time over Chateau d'Ardenne with the Thunderbolts at 31,000 feet.

At the RV point vapor trails coming from the Lille area were seen, from as far away as twenty to thirty miles from their altitude. At 1400 Blue Flight of the 63rd FS spotted two Fw 190s and went after them while Yellow Flight saw ten more Fw 190s and bounced them. Capt. Goodfleisch damaging one. Then, South of Ans, Goodfleisch and Vogt each claimed an Fw 190. (Goodfleisch's claim was downgraded to a probable). Near the target, over Eindhoven, Col. Zemke took his White Flight into a batch of Fw 190s and got one. Flight Officer Archie Roby, Lt.'s Gordon Batdorf and George Goldstein each damaged one.

On the way out, White Flight of the 61st FS broke up a gaggle of eight Me 109s over Dison, but had no claims. Col. Zemke voiced his disappointment in the P-47s lank of range on this mission, as they were only carrying seventy-five gallon belly tanks. If they had more initial fuel through larger belly tanks to begin with, they could have stayed in the targeted area longer and shot down more German fighters, as well as being able to stay with the bombers longer. Other than Capt. Cook, 62nd FS, landing with a flat tire and "cracking up," and a few others having to seek out alternate airfields

On return from a Ramrod on October 20, 1943 Captain Walter Cook, 62nd FS, discovered that he had a flat tire when he landed. A new prop and an engine inspection made the P-47 airworthy once again. (USAF)

on the way home, the 62nd FS had an uneventful mission, much to their dismay.

October 22: VIII FC FO 165. Breaking tradition, all 8th Air Force fighter groups were up on Ramrods, providing escorts for 9th Air Force B-26s. (Now) Lt. Col. Schilling led with the 61st Fighter Squadron to escort seventy-two B-26s to Cambrai, and the Group was airborne at 1514. Approaching the French coast the mission was recalled because of bad weather over the continent, so the mission turned into a navigational training exercise that landed at 1636.

October 24: VIII FC FO 166 was a replay of the October 22 mission, with success. All fighter groups were up. This mission marked the largest American fighter force dispatched so far. Lt. Col. Schilling led the 62nd Fighter Squadron on this mission and they were off at 1128 to escort seventy-two B-26s to bomb the airdrome at St. Andre.

After making a large timing circle over the English Channel, landfall-in and RV was made over Fecamp at 1237 with the P-47s at 20,000 feet. Escort was made over the target, and bombing results looked good. On the way out many groups of German fighters were seen, but they concentrated on looking over the P-38s and except for a pair of Fw 190s that made a feint on Yellow Flight of the 63rd FS, the mission was uneventful. (This German interest in the P-38 portended the comments by many bomber crewmen that the best fighter escort they could have was the P-38, as the Luftwaffe found them far easier to shoot down than a heavy bomber, and they concentrated their attention on them instead of the bombers whenever they had the chance).

October 29: No mission, but a new commander. Colonel Robert B. Landry arrived at Halesworth to replace Colonel Zemke as both Station and Group Commanding Officer. Zemke was being sent home to the United States to present his views on how to win the war. Landry was truly the "Old Man," as he had attained the hoary age of thirty-four.

November 3: VIII FC FO 168 after a ten day curtailment of fighter missions because of fog and rain, the 8th Air Force fighters were once again able to fly. The was so much rain at Halesworth that the area was equated to the Pripet Marshes. A boring time for the pilots and miserable conditions for the ground crews to work in, but time enough to get their aircraft into tip-top shape. The 8th Air Force again launched a maximum effort fighter mission with all P-47 groups, as well as the P-38 equipped 55th Fighter Group and the 20th Fighter Squadron that was attempting to become operational. A total of 378 fighters were sent off on Ramrods.

No mission on Halloween 1943, but HV◆B was photographed over Norfolk on a training flight. Since there was three similarly coded "razorback" P-47s in the 61st FS, its identity is unknown. (USAF)

The 4th FG came over from Debden to use Halesworth as a forward staging base. It did not work out so well for them, as they lost one P-47 in a takeoff crash. Two more were lost with their pilots to Me 109s over Holland. They claimed one Me 109 destroyed, but were unable to make RV with the bombers they were to escort.

Lt. Col. Schilling led fifty-four Thunderbolts from Halesworth, the largest number the Group had ever put up for a mission. Airborne at 1230, they had seven aborts. Off Kijkduin, ground control informed them of bogies in the area, so they dropped their belly tanks early. The bogies turned out to be friendly fighters, and frustratingly their mission endurance was now shortened. At the RV point the 2nd Bomb Division B-24s that they were to provide withdrawal escort for could not be found. Thus they orbited the area and picked up the last box of returning B-17s over Baltrum Island at 1331. The Forts were under attack, with the attackers in turn being harassed by P-38s.

Lt. Robert Johnson, 61st FS Blue Flight leader went down to 15,000 feet and shot down an Me 109. He was followed by Capt. Bud Mahurin and Blue Flight of the 63rd FS who went after another Me 109 that was chasing a P-38, and Mahurin and Lt. Wayne O'Connor shot it down. Mahurin's Blue Flight then climbed back up and located the missing B-24s north of Norderney Island. Mahurin then led his Blue Flight against some Me 110s that were chasing a Liberator, and Mahurin claimed one, while Lt. Wisniewski damaged another. The mission landed at Halesworth at 1458.

November 5: VIII FC FO 170 had all fighter groups airborne on Ramrod missions. The 56th Fighter Group was tasked with providing penetration escort to the 5th Task Force, and Col. Zemke led the mission from the 63rd Fighter Squadron, which was airborne at 1222. Zemke, who was awaiting transportation home, had got wind of the Ramrod to Munster and showed up at Halesworth in time to bump Dave Schilling from the mission. (Landry was assigned an element lead position, in order to gain combat experience). Schilling was miffed, but RHIP!

Landfall-in was between Ijmuiden and Egmond at 27,000 feet at 1313. The belly tanks were dropped two minutes later, and RV was made at 1320. The B-24s were covered with the 63rd FS on the right side of the first box of Libs, the 61st FS on the left side, while the 62nd FS covered the rear box of bombers. South of the Rhine River an estimated thirty Fw 190s came in on the formation at 27,000 feet from the north.

The German fighters, seeing the Thunderbolts, apparently decided to hold off their attacks on the B-24s until after the P-47s has to break off at the limit of their endurance and go home, for they flew parallel to the formation without making any aggressive moves. This tardiness allowed the 61st and 63rd FS's to position themselves and attack the Fw 190s first.

Col. Zemke waded in on them from the rear and got one, followed by Lt. John Wilson. Flight Officer Robey and Capt. Adrianse each damaging one. The 61st FS followed suit, and Major Francis Gabreski claimed one destroyed and another as damaged. Lt. Eugen Barnum shot at the one that Gabreski had damaged, and received full credit for shooting it down. Upon being relieved over the Rhine by P-38s, the 56th FG turned for home.

Then, Lt. George Hall, 63rd FS Red Three, looked down and saw an Me 210 at 15,000 feet climbing to make an astern attack on the last box of B-24s. Hall dove on it and shot it down, receiving his first credit and also the distinction of destroying the 100th enemy aircraft by the 56th FG. (Hall would receive a silver cup as an award for this distinction on December 31). At the same time, a gaggle of Me 109s was observed preparing to attack the bombers, which were attacked by Blue Flight of the 63rd FS. Although no claims were made, the Me 109s were chased and dispersed and they were unable to make any attack on the bombers. The Group left the continent in pairs and groups of four in the vicinity of The Hague to land at Halesworth at 1435.

Hall had this to report on his first kill: "I spotted an Me 210 off my right wing and about five thousand feet below, heading for the rear of the last box of bombers. My position was up-sun to him, so I went down in a dive to the right. When I got to within approximately five to six thousand yards of him, the rear gunner must have seen me because the 210 started a turn to the left. I closed fast and realized I would have to lay off deflection. I opened up at approximately three hundred yards, at fifteen thousand feet, and immediately the canopy and parts of the fuselage around the pilot blew off. Both engines caught on fire at the same time. The Me 210 flipped to the left and then to the right, which made me pull to the right to avoid hitting him.

"A piece of the e/a caused battle damage to the leading edge of my right wing. I passed so close to the open cockpit, that I could see the pilot sprawled out in such a manner that I believed him dead. I saw the gunner frantically trying to get out, and a few seconds later saw a large object leave the plane. The plane went down in a spiral, with both engines burning."

The goal of attaining the 100 kill mark had been set, somewhat as a lark, for Sadie Hawkins Day, which happened to fall on November 6. Sadie Hawkins was a cartoon character created by an artist, Al Capp, for his Li'l Abner cartoon series. On "her" day, single women were free to select bachelors as their mate without all the normal romancing folderol. Li'l Abner was a favorite of the pilots and men of the 56th FG, and Capp had provided the basis for the artwork of his characters that adorned most of the 62nd FS P-47s, and some of the others. (His artwork would latter appear on Mustangs of the 18th FG in Korea, as his popularity spanned several wars). Thus the Group attained their goal by one day.

November 7: VIII FC FO 172. The P-38 groups did not participate on this Ramrod, as well as the 4th Fighter Group, as they were active on another Field Order of their own. For the 283 P-47s under FO 172, it was a pretty rough mission. The 355th FG lost five Thunderbolts, the 56th FG one. Only the 355th FG was able to score a single victory against the Luftwaffe. Lt. Col. Schilling led from the 62nd Fighter Squadron, to provide escort for sixty B-17s from three bomb groups to Wesel. Off Halesworth at 0955, the 56th FG entered Europe over Ijmuiden at 27,000 feet and climbed to 30,000 to make RV at Doetencheim and then proceeded on to the target. Escort continued to Turnhout, where the bombers met elements of the 2nd Task Force and the 56th FG was relieved. At 1114 the 63rd Fighter Squadron lost their pilot. Flight Officer Robert E. Sheehan announced: "Postgate (The squadron's radio callsign) White Two. My prop's flat, I can't hold it." Major Burke, replied: "Postgate Leader, 'How's that now?'" Sheehan came back: "I can't control it at all." One minute later, Sheehan continued, "I am going down. Its burning." He was last seen straggling behind the squadron over Doesburg at 1120 at 28,000 feet. Sheehan bailed out and became the 56th FG's first evader. He returned to England on January 25, 1944. The Group landed at 1225.

November 11: VIII FC FO 177 dispatched seven P-47 fighter groups and fifty-nine P-38s on Ramrods. The 56th Fighter Group was tasked with providing target and withdrawal support for B-17s bombing Munster. Major "Gabby" Gabreski, making his first mission as the Group leader, took off in front of the 61st Fighter Squadron at 1243 with a total of fifty-three P-47s.

Landfall-in was over Zandvoort at 1335 at 26,000 feet. The bombers were slightly late, thus one orbit was required over the RV point. The 61st FS positioned themselves to the left of the Fortresses, the 63rd FS took up the rear.

The 62nd FS, spotting some unidentified aircraft, dove through a cloud layer and engaged between twenty-five and thirty Fw 190s. Capt. Walter Cook, White Leader, shot down two, becoming the first 62nd Fighter Squadron pilot to destroy two enemy fighters on one mission. Blue Flight Leader, Capt. Eugene O'Neill, brought his flight on in and got four Fw 190s into a Lufberry circle with his flight. Shooting their way out, O'Neill got one, as well as Blue Three, Lt. George Goldstein, and Blue Four, Flight Officer Joe Icard. Another Fw 190 was seen attacking Ray Dauphin, and O'Neill

damaged him as he drove him off. Capt. Leroy Schreiber was also credited with a damaged.

As the B-17s came away from the target two Fw 190s and an Me 109 were seen flying parallel to the B-17s, as they turned in to make an attack, Major Burke, leading the 63rd FS, led his White Flight into them, and shot down the Me 109. The 63rd's Red Flight was providing top cover at 32,000 feet for White Flight's attack, and Red Flight entered some clouds while circling. Lt. Ludwig saw Lt. Wayne O'Connor just before they entered these clouds, but he was not seen to come out with the rest of the flight. He was killed in action, but the cause was never determined.

The only encounter the 61st FS had was when Lt. Melvin Wood was attacked by an Me 109 as the squadron swung over the bombers as they were turning away from the target. Wood's P-47 was damaged, but he got it home. The escort for the bombers continued to Nijmegan by the 61st and 63rd FS's, and to Dorsrecht by the 62nd FS on the way home. Lt. Malcom Van Meter, 62nd FS, ran out of fuel crossing the coast on the way out and had to bailout twenty miles west of The Hague. He was rescued. The remainder of the Group headed for Halesworth to land at 1542, but five of their pilots had to select other landing sites on the way, because of fuel shortages.

November 13: VIII FC FO 180 sent the 56th FG and six other P-47s groups on a Ramrod. Lt. Col. Schilling led the 56th Fighter Group from the 63rd Fighter Squadron, and the Group was airborne at 1116. Also flying with the 56th FG on this mission were Col. Robert Landry and Lucian Dade from Headquarters 56th FG.

Providing escort for a mix of B-17s and B-24s, the rendezvous was rather haphazard because the bombers were in a mixed stream. It took ten minutes for the three fighter squadrons to accomplish the RV, with the squadrons hanging on with the B-24s, but now and then overtaking the B-17s that were supposed to be on the left of the B-24s. With the exception of the 61st FS seeing four Fw 190s over the Zuider Zee, the mission was uneventful and pretty much an exercise in futility. Most of the Group RTB'd at 1342, but again several flights had to select alternate airfields because of fuel shortages on the way home. The seventy-five gallon belly tanks just didn't provide enough endurance, and supply couldn't keep up with the demand for the larger capacity 108 gallon tanks.

November 17: Now that the older P-47s had been retro-fitted with belly tank/bomb rack shackles, and the newer versions were coming onboard with them already installed, the squadrons practiced a new wrinkle with their Thunderbolts.

They would carry bombs, and formate with a B-24, and when the B-24 dropped its bombs, they would too. Several practice missions were carried out accordingly during the month of November when the squadrons were not committed to escort missions. The results, initially, were considered to be fairly good, although there were problems in determining the trajectory of the bomb drops in relationship between the B-24 and the P-47s, and in educating the bombardier with the flight characteristics of the P-47 and the reaction time between seeing the bomber dropping its bombs and the fighter pilot's being able to react similarly.

The last such training mission took place on November 17 with the 62nd Fighter Squadron and met with disaster. A flight of four Thunderbolts encountered a solid overcast at 22,000 feet and went into a long shallow dive to get out of the clouds. The fighters, without deicing equipment, immediately loaded up with ice that covered their canopies, wings and airframes. Two broke off at 16,000 feet and managed to recover on instruments, another broke out under the clouds at 500 feet and narrowly escaped crashing. Lt. Harry Coronios was never seen again, and was presumed to have crashed into the North Sea some fifteen miles east of Happisburgh, Norfolk.

The mentioned newer version of the Thunderbolt arriving were the P-47D-10RE and -D-11RA's that were improved from the earlier versions and now featured water injection and "paddle-bladed" Curtiss propellers. The added water injection gave a short term boost to 2300 hp, versus the non-injected 2000 hp. The wide-chord prop blades improved the aircraft's service altitude and its speed increased some ten mph. Between the two new features, the P-47s rate of climb was increased 600 feet per minute. The modifications came from kits supplied from the United States that were installed at RAF Wattisham, and the first of these "new" P-47s came to the 56th FG in mid-November 1943, although it would be April 1944 before the Group was fully equipped with these or the Republic factory built versions, the P-47D-16RE and P-47D-21RAs.

November 19: VIII FC FO 184 sent 288 P-47s from six groups on Ramrods for heavy bombers. Lt. Col. Schilling again led from the front of the 63rd Fighter Squadron and they were airborne at 1043. Over the English Channel the bombers called to say they would be late, so the Group orbited off The Hague until the B-17s caught up. Due to the weather over the target, the bombers could not bomb their primary, Gelsenkirchen, so they selected targets of opportunity. The 56th Fighter Group escorted for an uneventful hour, half of it over water, and broke escort at 1225, returning to Halesworth at 1305.

November 25: VIII FC FO 190. The 56th and 353rd Fighter Group's went out as bombers for the first time. Top cover escort was provided by the 356th FG.

Off Halesworth at 1204, and led by Lt. Col. Schilling with fifty-three P-47s, each carrying a single 500 pound General Purpose bomb on their belly tank shackles. They were to RV with the same B-24, "G' for George" that they had practiced with, only the B-24 had a new, inexperienced (with this type mission) bombardier, and its intervelometer failed. In addition, the B-24 was late at the RV point.

The mission started "downhill" at this point, as the Group had to orbit the RV point, and the squadrons started to get strung-out over the English Channel. Finally, when the Liberator arrived at 24,000 feet and was only about fifteen miles from the target, the airfield at St. Omer/Longuenesse, the squadrons had to attempt to take up their proper positions. Schilling positioned the 62nd FS to the right rear of the B-24, Major Gabreski's 61st FS to its left. Major Burke's 63rd FS's White and Red Flights tacked on to the rear of the 61st FS, while their Yellow and Blue Flights formated on the rear of the B-24. The bombardier failed to give a count down to the drop over the radio, and when he dropped, his bombs fell in a salvo one and a half seconds past the bomb release line. Some P-47 pilots dropped visually, and although a few were seen to hit the airfield, most fell in the woods a thousand yards beyond the MPI, Main Point of Impact. Three P-47s of the 61st FS were damaged by heavy, intense and accurate flak, but everyone got home okay at 1349.

November 26: VIII FC FO 191. Probably the most successful fighter mission of 1943 for any command. The 8th Fighter Command was credited with thirty-six destroyed, three probables, and nine damaged. The 56th Fighter Group claimed 23-2-7. All fighter groups were up on Ramrods, with the 56th FG tasked with providing withdrawal support for the 1st Task Force returning from Bremen.

The bomber missions, themselves, were the largest force of heavies dispatched so far in the war. A total of 405 B-17s and 103 B-24s went to Bremen. 120 B-17s went to Paris, but these had to return with their bombs as their target was obscured by clouds. 138 B-26s from the 9th Air Force were also out on tactical sorties. Fighter Command put up a total of 450 escorts.

Lt. Col. Schilling led from the 61st Fighter Squadron, and they were off at 1053. Landfall-in was accomplished north of Egmond at 1140 climbing to 30,000 feet, and the new 108 gallon belly tanks that everyone carried were dropped at 1145 over the Zuider Zee. The 62nd FS was the first to make RV with the returning B-17s, near Papenburg, and they were undergoing heavy attacks by Me 110s at the time.

The Messerschmitt's were making astern attacks, firing rockets and lobbing cannon fire at the bombers and then breaking away just beyond the range of the tail gunner's .50 caliber machine guns. The Me 110's were protected by their own top cover, Me 109s and Fw 190s, that prevented Allied intervention. Some were seen flying off to the side of the B-17s in formations identical to those flown by the B-17s. They were also painted similarly to the B-17s, light grey/white on their bottoms and olive drab on their tops. Just as the 56th FG got there, the escorting German fighters dove down to attack a group of P-38s, and the 62nd FS "Just sailed in."

The 62nd FS claimed fifteen German fighters, but had eleven P-47s damaged. Lt. Bryon Morrill had a fuel tank holed and started loosing fuel and headed for home with only one hundred gallons remaining. He was escorted by Lt. Wilbur Kelley, but Morrill bailed out while in the clouds over the Zuider Zee, and Kelley didn't get a chance to see whether his parachute opened, or not. Morrill became a POW. Lt. Anthony Carcione had to land at Framlingham. Lt. Eugene O'Neill had a piece of an Me 110 control cable wrapped around the tail of his P-47, so he became one of few fighter pilots to return from combat with a bonafide souvenir. Lt. Ralph Johnson's compass failed, so he and Lt. Fred Christensen and Flight Officer Irvin Valenta headed home, and almost made the mistake of landing at St. Omer. But they recognized their error when the Germans fired their flak guns at them. They then circled Dunkirk, orientated themselves, and flew home okay.

Major Horace Craig claimed one Me 110 and one Me 210 destroyed, but both claims were downgraded to probably destroyed. Capt. Walter Cook was awarded claims for two Me 210s. Capt. Ralph Johnson got two Me 210s. Lt. Stan Morrill got an Me 109 and another as a probable. Capt. Eugene O'Neill got an Fw 190 and shared another with Lt. Mark Boyle. Lt.'s Anthony Carcione and Fred Christensen each were awarded Me 110s. Flight Officer Irving Valenta claimed three Me 110s destroyed, and one damaged. Two were credited, and one was downgraded to a probable. Some, unidentified pilot from the 62nd FS, flying P-47 LM⊙F, also damaged a P-47 of the 4th FG! It should be noted that the Me 210s were considered more difficult to knock down that the Me 110s, the Me 210s had heavier armor protection and its gunner had heavier defensive firepower.

The 63rd FS, led by Major Burke, waded right in on the Me 110s also. Capt. Mahurin, Red Leader, shot down three in rapid succession, and also got a probable. 1st Lt. Harold Comstock got another Me 110, damaged one, and also damaged an Fw 190. Lt. John Truluck got an Fw 190, and damaged an Me 110. 2nd Lt. Raymond Petty damaged an Me 110, and 1st Lt. Jack Brown damaged an Fw 190. Bud Mahurin became the first 8th Air Force "Double Ace" on this mission.

The 61st FS got into the fray as the Luftwaffe fighters were scattering. Major Gabreski claimed two Me 110s, Major James Stewart, one Do 217. Lt. Col. Schilling claimed two Fw 190s destroyed and one Me 210 damaged. Flight Officer Frank Klibbe was credited with one Me 109.

Incident: Just prior to takeoff, a black cat was seen to enter the parachute loft, where the chutes and other survival equipment were kept. The cat sat, in turn, on the parachutes of Schilling, Craig, Cook and O'Neill. Contrary to the Post War movie "Fighter Squadron," the cat was welcome in the loft at its pleasure, as each of the pilots that it had paid special attention to was able to make multiple claims this day.

November 29: VIII FC FO 192. All Thunderbolt groups were off on Ramrods. For this mission the 56th Fighter Group was charged with providing penetration and target support for B-17s returning to Breman. Major Horace Craig led the mission from the lead position of his 62nd Fighter Squadron. Off at 1307, land fall-in and the exact point of RV with the bombers was not known for sure, because of a solid undercast, but they were on time and the RV was made on schedule.

Enroute to the target, Lt. Col. Schilling and Lt. Felix Williamson, 62nd FS, bounced two Fw 190s and between them knocked down one. At approximately the same time Capt. Leroy Schreiber and Lt. Harry Pruden saw the only twin-engine enemy aircraft during the mission, and between

Incident: "Sinbad" was Lt. Fred Christensen's pet cat. Prior to the mission on November 27, 1943 the cat climbed onto the parachutes in the loft of the 62nd FS, and despite all efforts would not come down off the chute's. The pilot of each parachute that Sinbad sat upon scored during the day's mission.

them shot it down, an Me 210. The flights from the 62nd FS rejoined the formation and had no more encounters during this mission.

However, Major Gabreski's 61st FS got into the Luftwaffe approaching the target. An estimated forty German fighters were seen preparing to make frontal assaults on the B-17s. Mostly these were Me 109s with a few Fw 190s thrown in for good measure. Gabreski claimed two Me 109s northeast of Breman. Lt. Joe Powers got another in this battle. Capt. Robert Lamb claimed one Fw 190 destroyed and one damaged (His claim was downgraded to a probable). Lt. Melvin Wood claimed one Fw 190 damaged, but was not credited.

At 1424 the 63rd FS had their first encounters near Leer. Capt. Mahurin leading White Flight (with LT.'s Charles Reed, Isadora Porowski and Frederick Windmayer), bounced three Me 109s and Mahurin got one. Then Red One and Two, Lt.'s Harold Comstock and John Wilson, who had attached themselves to White Flight, were attacked by a single Me 109. The Messerschmitt fired on Wilson, giving him painful wounds in the left knee and neck, as well as knocking out his left aileron. Comstock raked the offensive Me from nose to tail and sent it down spinning and smoking into the clouds below, and was credited with a probable. Comstock then escorted Wilson home for a successful crash landing.

After leaving the target, and just before breaking escort, the 63rd's Yellow Flight (Capt. Don Goodfleisch, Lt.'s Lucian Dade, Benard Smith and Russ Westfall), saw two Me 109s at 30,000 feet and started up after them, but then saw fifteen more down below them and trading altitude for airspeed and taking advantage of their height, changed their minds and started after the lower batch of German fighters. Yet, as they turned to the left in preparation for the attack, they saw eight more Me 109s coming down on them, as well as an additional fifteen more below them. Boxed in, they started a twisting climb to shoot their way out of there, with Smith damaging one enemy fighter.

Lt. Fred Windmayer, however, was in trouble. Capt. Schreiber and Lt. Pruden from the 62nd FS heard him calling, and they overheard him state that his engine was running rough and that he had but forty gallons of fuel left. Although his radio transmissions were sharp and clear, he could not be located. Schreiber gave him additional weather information, and assumed that he was climbing out. But Windmayer said that he was at four

hundred feet and was going to have to bail out. The assumption was that he drowned in the English Channel west of Ijmuiden.

It had been a rough mission, twenty-two B-17s had gone down, along with three B-24s. Although the fighter escorts claimed 36-3-9, the trade-off in manpower lost could hardly be compared. Each German fighter claimed had a crew of either one or two men. Each Allied bomber carried a ten man crew. The bomber crews, at the end of the day, had ten known dead, thirty-five wounded, and 215 men were missing in action.

Lt.'s Clamp, Vogt and Wilson would receive Purple Hearts for wounds received in action this day. On a more positive note, Capt. Walker Mahurin received the distinction of downing the fiftieth German aircraft by the squadron. The 63rd FS becoming the first American squadron in the European Theater of Operations to shoot down this number.

November 30: VIII FC FO 193 sent the seven P-47 groups on another Ramrod. The 56th Fighter Group was briefed to provide penetration, target and withdrawal support. 1st Air Division bombers were going to Solingen, and this would be the 56th FG's first trip to the Ruhr Valley industrial area. Led by Lt. Col. Schilling and the 63rd Fighter Squadron, they were airborne at 1029. The 61st FS, led by Lt. Col. Landry, was plagued by problems. They had a total of five aborts, and had to send three more P-47s back as escorts for those aborting. At the RV point things started to become confused. Four Combat Wings were seen to abort the mission and head back to England. The 56th FG picked up one Combat Wing of B-17s that was at 27,000 feet and took them to the target and out. No B-24s could be found. Lt. John Eaves, 62nd FS, was hit by flak, but he got back okay. Lt. William Grosvenor, 61st FS, reported that his engine was cutting out, and then quit entirely while at 30,000 feet. Grosvenor got it restarted by the time he reached 4,000 feet, so he decided to strafe a train on his way home. It exploded in front of him. Then he hit a steel tower and his P-47 came apart on him, but he was thrown clear of the wreck as it plowed into the ground in Belgium. After all this, he still managed to evade capture and returned to the squadron in September 1944.

Although some Nazi fighters were seen, they did not act to threaten the bombers, so they were in turn ignored. The 56th FG returned at 1318.

December 1943: Winter approaches. Many complaints that too much coal and coke is wasted in the heating stoves. All ashes are to be sifted with shovels and rakes and unburned fuel returned for further use. No one is allowed to fire-up their stoves before 1630, and to use them for more than two hours, regardless of the fuel in use. The contractor failed to deliver either the coal or coke contracted for, which meant many side trips to "borrow" (in various forms) fuel from other people.

December 1: VIII FC FO 194. All fighter groups on Ramrods. The 56th Fighter Group sent out fifty-two Thunderbolts under Major Gabreski, with his 61st Fighter Squadron in the lead. Off at 1035, Gabreski was advised while the Group was forming up over Halesworth that the bombers were running fifteen minutes late, so RPM's and rate of climb were reduced to loose time. Then Gabreski was advised that "The Big Friends" were not going to be as late as expected, so the schedule had to be revised once again.

The 56th FG provided escort for the lead box of 360 heavies headed for Solingen, and landfall-in was accomplished over Westhoofd at 1143. At 1212 Capt. Don Goodflesch, 63rd FS, led his Yellow Flight on a bounce of three Me 109s and a Ju 88 that were attacking the rear of the lead box. They made no claims, but lost Lt. Vance Ludwig. He was last seen by Lt. John Patton as they were both being attacked from the rear by two or three Fw 190s. Ludwig was seen to roll over on his back and go into a dive with an Fw 190 on his tail. He was killed in action.

Major Gabreski fired at two Me 110s, but made no claim pending assessment of his gun camera film, as his windscreen was so obscured by oil streaks that he couldn't tell for sure whether he was hitting the German fighters, or not. (No claims credited). Lt. Dick Mudge, 61st, did get an Me

After a Ramrod to Solingen on December 1, 1943 LM◯F of the 62nd FS was stood on its nose by its weary pilot on return. Again, actual damage was minimal. (USAF)

109, however. Gabreski and Mudge returned with their P-47s "all shot up." At the same time, Lt. Joseph Egan and Flight Officer Isadore Porowski broke up a flight of three Ju 88s that were attacking a straggling B-24, allowing the B-24 to escape the area.

Near Aachen, on the way out, Lt. Fred Christensen, 62nd FS, shot down an Me 109, while Lt. Justus Foster, 61st FS, got an Fw 190 near Beverloo that had been a part of a gaggle of five that came up upon their rear. Lt. Cleve M. Brown, 61st FS, was last seen at this time, and he became a POW.

The 62nd lost Lt. Harry Pruden. He had gone in to break up a flight of enemy aircraft that were positioning themselves to attack a straggling

bomber. After he forced them to shy away, he told his flight leader, Lt. Ray Dauphin, that he was "Now flying Number Four." This was the last that he was heard of, about fifteen miles west of Cologne. He too was killed in action.

Each squadron lost a pilot on this mission that claimed three enemy aircraft destroyed. And the return trip was equally hazardous. One P-47 landed at Wattleham with severe battle damage, another at Manston. Lt. Byron "Fats" Morrill, 62nd FS, had to belly-in, and another squadron P-47 was damaged in a landing accident on return. Four others had to put down at Manston because of fuel shortages.

On the December 11 Ramrod HV◯B, 42-74620 of the 61st FS suffered minor battle damage. (USAF)

December 4: VIII FC FO 195. Three Thunderbolt groups out on a dive bombing mission. The 56th Fighter Group Ramroding and 352nd FG on a Rodeo/sweep of the area, providing cover for the 353rd FG that did the actual bombing. Major Horace Craig and the 62nd Fighter Squadron led the Group off at 1415 and they made RV with the 353rd FG at 1436.

Landfall-in was over Haamstede at 1446 and the mission proceeded to Glize/Rigen where the 353rd FG bombed the airdrome. Two groups of enemy aircraft were seen on the way into the target, but they dove for cover after espying three groups of Thunderbolts and no encounters took place. Then Blue Flight of the 61st FS chased away three Me 109s just prior to the bomb release point, but no claims were made. The actual bombing appeared to be successful, with bombs seen to strike near the control tower and in the hanger area. The 352nd claimed two enemy aircraft destroyed. The 56th FG's portion of the escort mission returned at 1553.

December 5: VIII FC FO 196. All fighter groups in operation, including the first mission for the 354th FG from IX FC on loan to the 8th Air Force. The first Army Air Force P-51 mission in Europe. The 56th Fighter Group was to provide an escort to Paris for eighty B-17s, and Major Francis Gabreski led from the 61st Fighter Squadron.

Off at 1028, landfall-in was over Cayux at 26,000 feet at 1118. RV with the bombers was made over Grandvilliers with the Thunderbolts at 30,000 feet. Visibility was so bad that the bombers did not drop their "eggs." Ten minutes before landfall-out over Le Touquet, at 1204, Lt. George Goldstein's, 62nd FS, prop went haywire. He could not control it in either automatic or manual modes, and his P-47 started down. Capt. Leroy Schreiber escorted Goldstein down to 13,500 feet, where he bailed out over Poix. A good chute was seen, and Goldstein became a POW. No enemy aircraft had been seen at all, and the Ramrod landed at 1254.

December 11: VIII FC FO 198. All fighter units on Ramrods. Lt. Col. Schilling led fifty P-47s of the 56th Fighter Group off Halesworth at 1027. Landfall-in was over Tessel Island at 30,000. Four minutes later, the Luftwaffe hit the 56th FG from 36,000 and up-sun, forcing them to drop their belly tanks and thwarting their part of the escort mission.

Just south of Leeuwarden, with the 62nd Fighter Squadron on the right, twenty to thirty Me 109s bounced the 63rd FS, with half of the Me's staying high, the other half came down on the squadron and totally disrupted their formation, but did not do any actual damage.

Schilling ordered the 61st and 63rd FS's to proceed on course, and the 62nd FS to engage the interlopers. Then, Schilling decided that the 62nd FS had better get on with the mission at hand, too, and called for them to rejoin the Group. With the 62nd FS's formation totally disrupted and engaged in combat, only Major Craig's Blue Flight was able to disengage and continue with the mission profile and make RV with the bombers. The remainder of the 62nd FS then broke away from the German fighters, but being too low on fuel to continue with the mission, had to content themselves with patrolling Leeuwarden in an effort to protect straggling bombers. Only Lt. Stan Morrell was able to claim an Me 109 as destroyed out of this encounter.

At the bomber RV point more German fighters were encountered. Lt. Col. Landry's 63rd FS spotted six Me 109s coming in on them from the north. Landry got one of them, his only air-to-air kill, and the rest headed down out of the melee and did not bother anyone again. Shortly thereafter, two Me 210s and an Me 110 came in, attempting to get through to the bombers. Lt. Glen Schlitz got one Me 210. Underneath all this, at 15,000 feet, three Fw 190s attempted to draw down Blue and Yellow Flights of the 63rd FS. These were engaged by the flights, but no claims were made.

OPPOSITE: Paul Conger with his commemoration aircraft. Community War Bond drives often came up with enough money to "purchase" an individual aircraft, which then bore the communities name when it was assigned to a combat unit. This example was 42-7880, HV◓N. (via Davis)

On December 11, 1943 the 56th FG got into intense combat with the Luftwaffe while on a Ramrod. In the ensuing battle the Group claimed 17-0-5 German aircraft destroyed, but lost two pilots of their own through an aerial mishap. Three P-47s had battle damage, courtesy of the foe. 42-7871, Gabreski's second HV◓A, had 20mm damage to the supercharger, along with damage to the cockpit, enough to bruise the bottom of his right foot where it had rested against the demolished rudder pedal. (USAF)

The 61st FS would have had an absolute field day if it had not been for one extremely unfortunate incident that can only be recorded as one of the fortunes of war. Just as Major Gabreski started to lead his squadron down in what would have been considered as a classic tactical bounce of the German fighters, from above and out of the sun, a pair of his pilots collided. The wingmen in Yellow Flight, Lt. Lawrence Strand, Yellow Two, and Lt. Edward Kruer, Yellow Four, smashed together during the cross-over preparatory to the bounce. Their P-47s exploded at 30,000 and one empty parachute was seen. Both were killed.

In the combat that followed, Major Gabreski destroyed an Me 110. Lt. Paul Conger got two Me 109s. Capt. Robert Lamb got three Me 110s. Lt. Robill Roberts got an Me 110 and a Ju 88 and damaged another Ju 88. Lt. Sam Hamilton damaged an Me 110. Lt. Donovan Smith got two Me 110s and shared an Fw 190 with Flight Officer William Aggers, while also damaging another Me 110.

Smith: "We made an attack on three Me 110s flying at 27,000 feet, with two more Me 110s flying the same direction about 1,500 feet below. We started our attack at 34,000 feet and closed upon these first three rather close and plenty fast. I saw Capt. Lamb knock down the first one on the extreme left. He scored a great many hits on fuselage and wings, and one man bailed out. I was about eight hundred yards behind Capt. Lamb and drew a bead on the middle one. I fired around a 60-round burst and observed hits on the right wing root and cockpit. A second later his wing folded up and he spun down.

"I then started after Capt. Lamb's plane and was closing rather slowly, when I saw another Me 110 flying southwest over the target at about 19,000 feet. I told F/O Aggers to stick with me, and we dove down on him. I closed rather close and he started to pull up a little, then went into a violent dive. I led him about two rings and observed many hits on the underside of the fuselage. My aircraft was hit by pieces from this e/a. A second later, F/O Aggers and I saw him fall apart and one chute came out.

"When this combat was finished, I started a steep pull up at wide-open throttle only to be cut off by an Fw 190. He was red-nosed and had tan and green wings and fuselage. We maneuvered with him for at least three or four egg-shaped turns, and finally I got a good chance for a head-on attack. We both held our fire to a point-blank range and the e/a passed by me smoking from his engine. F/O Aggers fired at the same time, and when we turned around the enemy had bailed out and his ship was in a

HV◐P (bar), 42-75163, was stricken from the roles and used for spare parts after combat on December 11, 1943. Its pilot on the mission is unknown. (USAF)

steep spiral and smoking badly. I then pulled up to 27,000 feet to get into the shelter of some bombers since we were quite alone."

Lt. Joe Powers got an Me 109 and an Me 110 along with damaging another Me 110. Powers' combat demonstrates prowess not only in battle but the loyalty and necessity of a good wingman.

Powers: "At this time, my engine began to smoke and run rough, and my windshield became obscured with oil. I decided to go home. My wingman had stayed with me throughout all this maneuvering and due to the oil coming from a cracked cylinder, he had to lead me home. There is no more beautiful sight when you are trying to get home with a damaged airplane, than the sight of your wingman covering you. No praise is too high for Lieutenant Marangello, for his support and cooperation. Without his support, I would not have been able to press home my attacks, and I am sure that I could not have gotten home."

In all, the 56th FG claimed 17-0-5 for the loss of two through an accident. Three additional P-47s suffered battle damage, one of them having to be stricken-off as beyond repair. The Luftwaffe could claim none.

December 13: VIII FC FO 199. All P-47 groups up on escort missions, with the 56th Fighter Group ordered to provide withdrawal escort for B-17s returning from Breman. Major Craig led the 62nd Fighter Squadron and the Group.

Off at 1037, they crossed-in over Ijmuiden at 1119 between 25,000 and 28,000 feet. RV was made at Delmenhorst, with the B-17s at 28,000 feet, at 1210, relieving the 4th FG.

On the way out, Red Flight of the 63rd FS was jumped by four out of eight Fw 190s that were seen, but low on fuel, Red Flight could only evade them and could not make any pursuit. The remaining four Focke-Wulf 190s went after a box of B-17s withdrawing in the Tessel Island area. Again, fuel state prevented any encounters or assistance for the Flying Forts. The Group landed at 1321 to witness a couple exciting events.

Two 9th Air Force B-26s crashed at Halesworth. One could not get his nose wheel down, and had no brakes. He zipped down the runway and went through a fence. The other crashed two miles beyond the airfield's perimeter.

December 20: VIII FC FO 204. After a week of inactivity, due to inclement weather, VIII Fighter Command launched a maximum fighter effort. Eight P-47 groups went up, the mission being the first for the 358th Fighter Group, and the first with all three squadrons going up for the 359th FG.

Lt. Col. Landry led the 63rd Fighter Squadron and the Group off Halesworth at 1044. Landfall-in was over Egmond at 25,000 feet at 1126. RV was accomplished over Stadskanaal at 30,000 feet, with the P-47s keeping their belly tanks to this point. A group of P-51s was met head on just before reaching the target, Breman. Lt. Mark Boyle, 62nd FS, being fired upon by one of the overeager Mustang pilots.

Hot on the heels of the P-51s came fifteen Me 109s. Six of them "Blew right through Yellow Flight (of the 63rd FS) and attacked Red Flight." Lt.'s Harold Comstock and Charles Reed, Blue Three and Four, were attacked head on and tried to get at them, but the Me 109s turned in behind them. They were out turned and out climbed at 31,000 feet. Comstock got rid of the one chasing him by diving through a formation of B-24s. As Yellow Flight became engaged, they went into a Luftberry circle, and Lt. Charles Clamp fired at a long-nosed Fw 190D, seeing strikes on its left wingroot and top of its canopy and saw it fly away one wing low. It was credited as a probable. Major Horace Craig finally got a kill to make up for the one denied him in November, a Do 217. Capt. Eugene O'Neill got an Me 109.

Lt. Michael Quirk also got an Me 109, and then had to leave the area to escort Lt. Robert Taylor towards home. Taylor couldn't drop his belly tank and he couldn't get it to feed, either, along with having his engine act up. Approximately fifteen miles off Felixstone the Pratt & Whitney engine quit, apparently out of fuel, but then Taylor got it started again and decided to stick with his P-47. But then it quit again for good, and as he was by now too low to bailout, Taylor attempted to ditch his P-47. The belly tank snagged a wave and the P-47 flipped over in the water and Taylor was drowned.

Lt. Charles Reed, 63rd FS, had to belly land in a marsh near Dunwich on the way back, out of fuel. Flight Officer Walter Frederick landed with battle damage and first degree burns at 1336.

Capt. Joseph Bennett and Lt. Joe Powers from the 61st FS were also awarded kills. an Me 110 and an Me 109, respectively.

"Francis Ann II" belonged to an unidentified pilot of the 61st Fighter Squadron. (via Davis)

December 22: VIII FC FO 207 sent all 8th AF fighter groups out on Ramrods for all three Bomb Divisions. The 56th Fighter Group was ordered to provide target support for 350 B-17s of the 1st Bomb Division attacking Osnabruck. Col. Robert Landry led the Group, airborne Halesworth at 1232. They went in over Egmond at 1330 at 27,000 feet and took up escort position over the lead box of B-17s, but their speed soon put them over the rear box of B-24s going to Munster.

Coming into the Munster area, Capt. Walker Mahurin, leading the 63rd Fighter Squadron, saw fifteen Me 109s flying west at 20,000 feet and starting to turn in under the bombers. They did not appear to be a threat, so the squadron proceeded on. After leaving the target, some twenty more Me 109s were spotted, now circling to come in behind the bombers. One group of seven, and another of five were selected, and Mahurin took his squadron down to attack. Mahurin got two Me 109s and Lt. William Janson damaged another.

The 62nd FS's Lt. Felix Williamson got an Me 109, while Lt. Anthony Carcoine damaged an Fw 190. 1st Lt. Robert Johnson, 61st FS, got

his seventh kill, identified as either an Me 109G or an Me 209, as there was a lot of confusion at the time between whether the latest version of the Me 109 was a modification of the older design or an entirely new fighter. Johnson, with wingman Lt. Joseph Perry, having gone to the assistance of an aborting B-17 near Zwolle when Johnson picked this one off.

December 23: 65th Fighter Wing FO 81 and 66th Fw FO 37. The 56th Fighter Group was to provide fighter escort for the 353rd FG while they dive bombed Glize/Rijen airfield. Col. Landry led the mission, and after taking off at 0906, RV was accomplished over Oxfordness at 17,000 feet at 0935.

The 56th FG orbited the target while the 353rd Fighter Group "Thunderbombers" went to work, and although a partial undercast prevented an accurate assessment of the bombing, results were believed to be pretty good. They were back down by 1112 after a basically uneventful mission.

UN❂X was shared by Lt.'s George Compton and Charles Reed, 63rd FS. Reed belly landed it on December 21, 1943. (via Davis)

42-76363, LM❂F of the 62nd Fighter Squadron belonged to Billy Edens. (via Davis)

December 24: VIII FC FO 209 sent 459 P-47s on a sweep ahead of the bombers and also general target support for the bombers going to the Pas de Callis area. The 56th Fighter Group put up fifty-one P-47s, under Lt. Col. Schilling, who led with the 63rd Fighter Squadron. Takeoff from Halesworth was at 1249. The Group patrolled the Cambrai area between 17,500 and 22,000 feet uneventfully. Except for Lt. Adam Wisniewski, 63rd FS, having to belly land near Manston because he ran out of gas, the mission was uneventful. RTB'd at 1543.

December 30: VIII FC FO 210 sent all 8th AF Bomb Divisions and Fighter Groups out on bombing and Ramrod missions. The 56th Fighter Group, under Col. Landry, was off at 1135 on the longest P-47 mission attempted. (Except for Lt. Isadore Porowski, 63rd Fighter Squadron, who nosed over on takeoff. His P-47 inverted and came down on top of him, but he was unhurt. The 63rd FS had four other aborts, two prior to takeoff, and two after becoming airborne). The 56th FG was tasked with providing withdrawal escort to the B-17s returning from Ludwigshaven, and RV was accomplished southwest of Metz at 1246 with the bombers at 22,000 feet and the fighters at 25,000 feet.

Landry's 63rd FS took the second box, while the 62nd FS took the first and the 63rd FS took the third box of bombers under their escort. Although some Fw 190s were seen chasing P-38s, the mission was unopposed while under the care of the 56th FG. But the bombers were attacked after the 56th FG had to breakoff for home.

As the mission had pushed the range of the P-47 to its utmost, there were many problems with the lack of fuel on the way home. Lt. Fred Christensen, 62nd FS, crash landed short of the runway at Leiston out of fuel. Lt. John Patton, 63rd FS, ran out of gas taxiing-in at Halesworth. Several other P-47 fuel tanks held only ten to fifteen gallons of gas when they were "sticked."

December 31: VIII FC FO 211. Again all fighter and bomber groups were out on missions. The 56th Fighter Group was to provide withdrawal support for 1st Task Force heavies returning from Bordeaux, La Rochelle and St. Jean D'Angeley.

Col. Landry and fifty-two Thunderbolts were off Halesworth at 1225. On the way into Europe, Lt. William Marangello, 61st Fighter Squadron, was killed. His P-47 crashed off the Jersey Islands. The cause was believed to be an oxygen system failure.

Proceeding directly to the RV point, Molean, which was reached at 1343 at 30,000 feet, they were forced to descend to 18,000-20,000 feet to cover the B-17s that were down at 16,000 feet. The 61st FS took over the first box, Major Burke's 63rd FS the third box, and the 61st FS covered the middle one. Over St. Giles six Fw 190s came in under the 61st FS at 17,000 feet in an attempt to get at the B-17s from 7:00 O'clock. Yellow Flight went down to break up the attack and 1st Lt. Robert Johnson got a pair of them. His ninth and tenth kills, making him a "double ace."

The other squadrons saw other groups of German aircraft, but had no encounters. Landfall-out was over Peros-guirec at 1428. The 62nd FS had to land at Exeter for fuel on the way home, and then return to Halesworth after dark in bad weather. It was almost a disaster, as navigation got fouled up, and most had to call for Direction Finding, DF, steers to find "homeplate."

Towards the end of the month, the 56th Fighter Group had started a new transition school of their own for new pilots coming into the Group. This became necessary, for example, because the 62nd Fighter Squadron was now down to only twenty-three "old head" pilots, while the squadron had gained eleven rookies since September. The new pilots, while eager enough, were sadly lacking in many of the prerequisite skills that they would need to keep them alive in a combat environment. Training Command, demanding enough in its own right, was not teaching many of the exact requirements the new pilots needed.

Training in the sunny climes of the American Southwest hardly prepared them for English fog and icing conditions. The patchwork typography of England made pilotage navigational skills difficult, and the new pilots needed to be taught how to utilize the "buncher" and "splasher" radio beacons and DF. How to penetrate clouds and turbulence in formation without any deicing equipment on their aircraft. Physiological training on hypoxia and anoxia and the effects of Boyles Law on their diets at altitudes they never attained while flying in Training Command. Their earlier gunnery training was sorely lacking, if they had any at all, and everyone had to learn the new bombing techniques.

Another factor was the obligation of screening out those pilots who were found not to possess the necessary fighter pilot's attitude. Just because Training Command graduated an officer and designated him as having the skill of a fighter pilot, it did not necessarily make him one. If he was lacking in either ability or envisioned attitude, he had to be sent elsewhere, either for his own safety or for the safety of his wingman or squadron.

The new school, borrowing the name given to one in another fighter group, was "Clobber College." It was initially commanded by Capt. Walker Mahurin, and 1st Lt. Kenneth Mason, the 62nd FS Intelligence Officer was its Ground Training Officer. They were assisted by Lt.'s Egan, Quirk and Brainard, all from the 62nd FS. The curriculum ran for three weeks and included twenty-seven flying hours and sixty hours of ground schools.

January 4, 1944: VIII FC FO 212, Ramrods to Munster. All P-47 groups operational. This was the first mission by the 56th Fighter Group with all P-47s now equipped with the "paddle bladed" props. The new props had either Curtiss "long-wide" or A. O. Smith "short-wide" blades. Now all the pilots were equally impressed with the improved version, and not just the select few that had got the first ones received. As coupled with the water injection, their P-47s "gave fantastic rates of climb." They could outclimb a Spitfire IXb, a Messerschmitt or Focke-Wulf for the first time. Major Craig led the 62nd Fighter Squadron and thirty-six P-47s off Halesworth at 0908 to provide penetration, target and withdrawal support for 120 B-17s into Germany. In over Ijmuiden climbing to 27,000 feet, the belly tanks were dropped over the Zuider Zee eight minutes after landfall-in. RV was accomplished over Noordhorn at 1018 with the Group now at 30,000 feet.

Approaching Munster, approximately fifty "Jerries" were reported coming in on the "Big Friends" head-on, and then they broke away to turn in to come in on them from behind. Mahurin's 63rd FS also turned to intercept them, and bounced four Fw 190s near Hengelo, Mahurin and Lt. John Patton fired on them, but made no claims. The German fighters disappeared while the bombers were dropping their bombs, leaving the sky to the flak guns, but reappeared as the B-17s turned for home.

Major Gabreski's White Flight, 61st FS, broke up an attack of four Fw 190s that were desiring to attack a box of bombers from 11:00 O'clock, but again made no claims. Over Stadtlohn a straggling B-17 was bounced by five Fw 190s and were in turn bounced by Yellow Flight of the 62nd FS. Lt. Michael Quirk, Yellow Flight Leader, destroying one, for the first kill of the new year. Escort continued to the Dutch Islands, and then the Group RTB'd, landing at 1152.

January 5: VIII FC FO 213 sent 243 P-47s from the 56th Fighter Group and three other groups on a Ramrod to escort the 2nd Air Division to Elberfeld. The 56th FG was led by Lt. Col. Schilling. Major James Stewart, the new squadron commander of the 61st Fighter Squadron led his unit for the first time. In over Blankenburghe at 1110, RV was made west of Cologne at 1135 with the Thunderbolts at 30,000 feet.

Near Duren, two flights of four each Me 109s were seen at 20,000 feet preparing to attack the bombers. These were jumped by Lt. Stanley Morrill's flight, 62nd FS, and Morrill got one and scattered the rest. South of Bonn, White Flight of the 61st FS spotted three Fw 190s preparing for an astern attack on the bombers. Major Stewart got one of them.

Approaching the Liege-Ans area, a dozen plus Fw 190s came in on the bombers, and both the 61st and 62nd FS's went after these. Lt. Fred

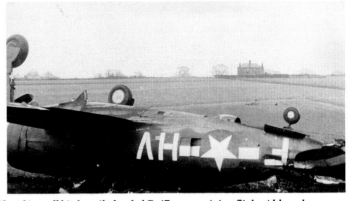

Left: On January 1, 1944 Lt. Evan McMinn hit a flak gun emplacement while taking off his heavily loaded P-47 on a training flight. Although damage appears reparable, HV✪F was scrapped-out. As an example of the wear and tear the fighters were getting at the time, 42-8458 had been hit by flak on November 25, and again on the 26th it was hit by flak, along with ingesting pieces of an Me 110 that Gabreski shot down. (He had three of his kills in this aircraft). (USAF) Right: The remains of 42-8458, HV✪F. The Jug's cockpit was built with an armored roll-over plate behind the pilot's seat, just in case something like this occurred. McMinn had only minor injuries. (via Davis)

Christensen, Red Flight, 62nd FS, destroying one that was attacking Lt. Caleb Reeder, with the Fw pilot bailing out. 1st Lt. Robert Johnson, White Three, 61st FS, chased down an Fw 190 whose own element leader was being chased by Gabreski and who was trying to knock down "Gabby." Johnson shot him off Gabby's tail. Due to unforecasted exceptionally high winds and the extra fuel consumed in combat, ten of the Group's P-47s had to seek out alternate landing sites in England on return, but everyone got down safely.

Rumors abounded that the Luftwaffe was now flying captured Air Force aircraft. Strange B-17s had been seen for months. On this mission a pair of P-47s were seen by pilots that were virtually positive that they identified as belonging to the enemy. Post War investigation showed that the Luftwaffe had somewhere around a half-dozen operational P-47s, about half of them being the early "Razorback" versions that were being flown at this time.

January 7: VIII FC FO 215. All Thunderbolt groups up to support all three 8th Air Force Bomb Divisions. The 56th Fighter Group was assigned to fly withdrawal support.

Airborne Halesworth at 1104 and led by Col. Landry, the Group provided top cover for the second box of B-17s of the 1st Task Force coming back from Ludwigshaven. RV was made at 27,000 feet over Mellier at 1214 and continued until 1253 over Guise-Villiers. After takeoff Capt. John Vogt's Yellow Flight, 63rd Fighter Squadron, had got separated from the rest of the squadron and wound up tacked on to the 352nd Fighter Group enroute to Paris. They got credit for flying the mission, but also caught hell from Mahurin for their navigation. Mahurin had more to say along the same line to 2nd Lt. Anthony Cavallo. Cavallo had been bounced by three Me 109s on the way home, and although he managed to shake them off, he got himself good and lost. He landed at Welsingham, Newcastle, some 250 miles north of Halesworth.

January 11: VIII FC FO 216. The 56th Fighter Group flew their first double-squadron/group mission. Each squadron was divided in half, with an "A" and a "B" squadron of twelve aircraft each. Thus the Group put up an "A" and "B" Group on this and similar succeeding missions, usually with thirty-six fighters in each. Normally these missions were tasked with different assignments, but came under the same Field Order and operated in the same general area as each other. Each had their own individual commanders, and operated on their own control times.

The 56th FG's "A" Group was off Halesworth at 0952, being led by Lt. Col. Schilling, to provide penetration support to the 1st Combat Wing to Oschersleben. The target was the final assembly plant for Fw 190s, so

the fighter pilots had a particular interest in the bombing results. RV was made just north of Nordham at 1054, with the B-17s between 16,000 and 20,000 feet and the fighters at 25-26,000 feet. This made the bombers difficult to cover, and the interest in the bombing academic.

As RV was being accomplished, in the general area of Lingen, somewhere between fifty and a hundred Me 109s with some Fw 190s thrown in, intercepted them and started attacking the first box of B-17s from all angles. Schilling's dozen P-47s from the 61st Fighter Squadron waded in on a dozen Fw 190s and two dozen Me 109s, with Schilling shooting down an Fw 190 and damaging an Me 109. Captains' James Carter and Joseph Bennett each claimed an Me 109, but Bennett's claim was downgraded. Carter also probably destroyed an Me 109 and damaged another. Lt. Justus Foster got the fourth, an Me 109, and damaged another.

Schilling called down Major Craig's 62nd FS for help. Lt. Stanley Morrill destroying an Me 109 that dove in. Lt. Michael Quirk also claimed an Me 109, but it was not credited. Thereafter, the 62nd FS went back up to provide top cover for the rest of "A" Group. The 63rd FS, White and Blue Flights, under Major Burke, went down next to bounce twenty Me 109s and Fw 190s. Burke, who hadn't had a claim in two months to the day, "Closed fast behind one of the 109s, opened fire and noticed hits all along the fuselage." The Me 109 then exploded and smoke from it filled Burke's cockpit. When the smoke cleared he spotted another and went after it, seeing strikes on its wings and fuselage. Burke got a probable on this one. Lt. Archie Robey, his wingman, hit another Me 109 which he set on fire and it was last seen tumbling into the clouds below. Lt. Glen Schlitz, leading Blue Flight, blew up two Me 109s in a row, and five minutes later got his third for the mission. Lt. Benard Smith, got separated from his White Flight while all this was going on, so he joined on Schlitz just as he was getting third kill, and while he was at it, he shot down an Fw 190 by blowing its wing off. On the way out Lt. Robey managed to damage another Me 109. Two more engagements took place on the way home, but they were ineffective for both sides. The 61st FS commented that this was the toughest dogfight they had ever been it, and their success was due to the outstanding protection given to them by Major Craig's 62nd FS. (It is noted, also, that the encounters over Europe this morning resulted in the first Medal of Honor awarded to a fighter pilot in the ETO. Colonel James H. Howard, 356th Fighter Squadron, 354th Fighter Group, single handedly took on a squadron of German fighters attacking a bomber formation, destroying three and disrupting their attacks).

"B" Group took off at 1041 under Major Gabreski's leadership to provide penetration support to the 3rd Air Task Force to Brunswick. Landfall-in over Ijmuiden at 24,000 feet. The bombers were all mixed up and strung-out from over the North Sea to east of the Zuider Zee. Because of deteriorating weather the bombers were recalled, so most of the bombers dropped their bombs on Lingen. Other than seeing two German fighters that were too far away to chase near Lingen, the mission was uneventful. Escort out was provided to north of Nordhorn at 1212, and landfall-out was again over Ijmuiden. They RTB'd at 1353.

On the administrative side: Colonel Robert Landry was relieved by Lt. Col. David Schilling as 56th Fighter Group Commanding Officer. Landry was transferred to Headquarters VIII Air Force Staff. Major Gabreski was promoted to Lt. Col. and relieved as commander of the 61st Fighter Squadron, being transferred to Headquarters 56th FG as Flight Executive Officer. Major James C. Stewart officially became the new 61st FS commanding officer.

January 14: VIII FC FO 217 sent both the "A" and "B" Groups of the 56th Fighter Group out on Ramrod and a Rodeo.

"B" Group, under Lt. Col. Landry, took off at 1342. This was a new type of mission for the Group, although other 8th Air Force fighter groups had been practicing them for a few weeks. Known at "Type 16" control, essentially, they were microwave early warning, MEW, radar monitored and vectored freelance missions. On this mission only two of the sixteen available radio frequencies were useable, and they had to be shared with the 4th Fighter Group. The RAF radar was primitive, had yet to be peaked, and the Army Air Force controllers inexperienced. The participating pilots were not the least bit impressed, particularly after being vectored around Paris against phantom radar targets. This feeling was moderated somewhat when they returned and discovered that the 4th FG had been vectored against real targets and scored eight kills for no losses.

Lt. Colonel David Schilling entering the cockpit of his P-47 prior to an escort mission. (USAF)

Lt. Prager Neyland got hit by 20mm fire on January 14, 1944 and "Pistol Packin' Momma" had a hole blown right through its radio compartment. Neyland was injured, but brought her home. (via Davis)

"A" Group was airborne from Halesworth at 1359 under Lt. Col. Schilling on the Ramrod, providing general support to B-17s and B-24s attacking "Crossbow" targets (V-1 weapon launching sites) in the Pas de Calais area. They went in over Dunkirk at 1442 at 21,000 and then descended to sweep Cambrai, St. Quenton and Valenciennes. Twelve miles east of Cambrai Lt. Preger Neyland, 61st Fighter Squadron, was chased by an unidentified fighter with no national markings, a long nose, and square wingtips. He was wounded by gunfire from it, whomever and whatever it was. Lt. Wilbur Kelley, 62nd FS, had a closer call. His P-47 was hit by flak, and if he had been three or four inches taller fragments would have got him instead of his headrest. Two more P-47s were flak damaged. The mission RTB'd at 1655.

January 19: Colonel Zemke returned from leave in the United States and reassumed command of the 56th Fighter Group. Lt. Col. Schilling again became the Group's Flying Executive Officer, and the position of Deputy Flight Executive Officer was created for Lt. Col. Gabreski.

For the aircraft enthusiast an item should be observed here. While under Landry's command the 56th Fighter Group had been offered an exchange of Mustangs for Thunderbolts, as the 8th Air Force wanted to re-equip all of its fighter groups with P-51s and the 9th Air Force wanted all the P-47s they could get. Col. Landry rejected the offer, and Col. Zemke was described as "livid" when he discovered that it had occurred during his absence and now the offer was a closed subject. Zemke would have made the switch to Mustangs for their longer range if for nothing else.

January 21: VIII FC FO 221. The largest concentration of Thunderbolts ever, 531 P-47s, went out in support of the three air divisions on a return engagement to Pas de Calais after a week of inactivity brought on by heavy fog. This would also be the largest force of bombers dispatched to date, a total of ten combat wings.

The 56th Fighter Group's "B" Group took off at 1250 behind Lt. Col. Landry and the "B" squadron of the 63rd Fighter Squadron. The Group went in over St. Inglevert at 1338 and swept to Poix, Noyon, Beaumont-sur-Oise, making landfall-out over Cayeux at 1525. While passing northeast of Compiegne, Landry took his White Flight down on a bounce against four Fw 190s out of a flight of sixteen. Landry fired, but his selected Fw broke hard and fast and no hits were seen. In the same area his Red Flight went after nine Me 109s, but they dove away. "B" Group landed at 1605, with one P-47 nosing over on landing. One additional P-47s crash landed at Manston.

"A" Group took off at 1307 led by Major Craig. They entered Europe over Dieppe at 1353 at 25,000 feet, flew to Aumale, and set up an orbit from there to Lonhueville, Gournay and Rouen between 18,000 and 20,000 feet. Near St. Seens four Fw 190s were seen attacking returning B-24s and were in turn jumped by Red Flight of Major Stewart's 61st FS. Capt. Leslie Smith damaged one, but his wingman, Lt. Allen E. Dimmick, on his first combat mission, was attacked from behind, hit in the wingroot and shot down. He was killed. Lt. Robert Johnson, in turn, brought his Blue Flight down and destroyed the Focke-Wulf for his twelfth kill. On return, eight P-47s had to land at Manston, and another at Lympne, with the remainder landing at Halesworth at 1615.

January 24: VIII FC FO 222. As the 8th Fighter Command now had the capability to send out between five and six hundred fighters as escorts for Bomber Command's missions, a new tactic was tried on this day's mission.

Instead of assigning P-47s to cover a specific unit as a close escort, P-47s were sent to geographical areas along the bombers course, to orbit there and cover each Combat Wing as it passed through their own area. Thus, the bombers passed from one fighter groups area of responsibility to another's along their entire track across Europe, and did not have to depend upon making a rendezvous with a fighter group for coverage, nor

find themselves without coverage when the Thunderbolts reached the point of their maximum combat range. When the bombers reached their Initial Point, IP, prior to bombing, further fighter coverage was provided from that point to the target, and out to within P-47 range once again by P-38s, and later by P-51s, when they became available.

On this particular mission, the 1st, 2nd and 3rd Bomb Divisions headed for Frankfurt with 840 B-17s and B-24s. Due to weather conditions, the bomber mission was recalled, but as it was not known whether all the bombers heard the recall message, or not, the fighters went out and stayed out, having to split their forces to cover all of the returning formations at once. Only two of the "Big Friends" were lost to enemy action.

The 56th Fighter Group's "B" Group was airborne from Halesworth at 0920 under Capt. O'Neill with thirty-nine "Jugs." In the Ans-Aachen area they picked up one box of bombers at 1030, and when they were recalled, "B" Group proceeded east to pick up another bomb group, and provided escort for them until 1119 over Brussels. Near Namur, the 61st Fighter Squadron's "B" squadron, under Capt. Robert A. Lamb, was climbing from 21,000 feet to 26,000 feet after six unidentified aircraft when they were jumped by four Fw 190s that were attempting a head-on attack on the bombers. They swung around to get on their tails, and found themselves being chased by a pair of Me 109s. The engagement was broken off without result, and the Me 109s did not press an attack, having deterred the P-47s from their own intentions.

"A" Group followed "B" by eight minutes, led by Major Gabreski, again with thirty-nine Thunderbolts. Major Burke led the 63rd FS "A" squadron, and when he had to abort, lead was passed to Capt. John Vogt. Although twenty-five German fighters were seen, an attempt to engage them ended when they dove into cloud cover and hid. The mission returned at 1217.

January 29: VIII FC FO 226. Weather finally permitted a return trip to Frankfurt. It was one of Fighter Command's better days. P-38s claimed 10-1-1, Mustangs claimed 5-1-4, for no losses. Thunderbolts claimed 34-4-9, with the 56th Fighter Group claiming 6-1-1 for the loss of one pilot. "A" Group, under Lt. Col. Schilling, with thirty-seven P-47s took off at 1020, making landfall-in over Knocke at 1107. RV was accomplished southwest of Koblenz at 1139 at 29,000 feet with the first box of the 1st Bomb Division.

Over Koblenz, Lt. Col. Schilling got an Me 109 at 25,000 feet. On the way out over Knocke, the 63rd FS's "A" squadron came under attack by a pair of Fw 190s. Lt. Kenneth Lewis was hit by one of them. He was last

Gabreski and Major Sylvester Burke on January 25, 1944. Gabreski had just got his 11th victory, made Lt. Colonel, and was celebrating his birthday. (USAF)

Up on a test hop with one of the new P-47s equipped with water-injection, Lt. Frank Klibbe, 61st FS, had to make a forced landing when the engine quit. HV◉T, 42-75604, was a write-off. The experience apparently inspired Klibbe to become one of the better known Engineering Officers in the Air Force, as he later worked with P-51H problems, F-80 transition, and F-84 aerial refueling. (USAF)

seen turning inland and going down, but he stated that he was okay. This was not the end result, however, as he was killed in action. Lt. Harold Comstock managed to damage one of the Fw 190s. "A" Group landed at 1334.

"B" Group was airborne at 1029 behind Lt. Col. Gabreski. They went in over Knocke at 1120, and came in behind "A" Group over Koblenz at 1152 to RV with the last three Combat Wings of the 1st Bomb division. At the RV point a dozen single and twin engine German fighters were met, and Lt. Anthony Cavallo, 63rd FS, went after four Me 210s. After exchanging his attacking position with Lt. Jack Brown, Cavallo got one. It rolled over and hung up in the air, as if suspended from a skyhook, apparently its pilot had been killed. Another came in on Cavallo's right, and he fired on it until he was out of ammunition, and he watched it spiral down. Brown saw the one he was shooting at roll over on its back and plummet into the clouds below. The latter two being credited as probably destroyed. 2nd Lt. Prager Neyland, 61st FS, back on missions after recovering from his wounds, also got a probable, an Me 110. Lt. Col. Gabreski got another, as well as Lt. Melvin Wood, Capt. Joseph Bennett destroyed one Me 110 and damaged another. (Neyland's probable and Bennett's damaged were assessed as a single total kill, and credit was split between them). The 62nd FS got skunked, and "B" Group landed at 1335.

Upon return, the first award presentation of the year had everyone in military formation out on the tarmac in Class A uniforms. Among the awards given out was the Silver Star to Lt. Col. Schilling.

January 30: VIII FC FO 227. The heavies went to Brunswick, and the fighters had another Field Day, Fighter Command claiming 45-15-31. Of this, the P-47s came out best, claiming 36-13-20. The 56th Fighter Group claimed sixteen for no losses.

Lt. Col. Schilling led "A" Group off first, airborne at 1131. The bombers, it appeared to the fighter pilots, were in a snafu situation as the three

air divisions were all interspersed and strung out in a sloppy moving block twenty miles wide and eighty miles long.

The first gaggle of German fighters, ten Me 109s, were encountered near Almelo, flying northwest to intercept the bombers. The 62nd Fighter Squadron went down on the bounce of them and Lt. Michael Quirk got one and damaged another. One Me 210, all by himself at 8,000 feet, was bounced by Lt. Anthony Carcione and destroyed. Lt. Stanley Morrill then jumped a Ju 88 that was trying to get at a straggling bomber, and claimed him as a probable. Morrill then turned his attention to an Me 210 and damaged it. (Oddly enough, the Official Credit List splits Carcione's claim with Morrill, awarding each .5 credit for the Ju 88 and ignoring the other claims). Lt. Eugene Barnum, 61st FS, claimed one Me 210 as a probable. The only damage to a friendly P-47 was incurred by Lt. Albert Knafelz, who had his windscreen shattered by either empty .50 caliber shell cases or by pieces of the Me 110 Carcione was firing at.

"B" Group, led by Lt. Col. Gabreski, was up at 1146, and the fifteen minute difference in departure time would make an even greater difference in scoring. In over Ijmuiden at 1235, RV with the bombers was near Drummer Lake, a location that the future would show to be the virtual hot bed of Luftwaffe activity. South of Quakenbruck, just prior to RV at 1255, Lt. Joseph Egan, 63rd FS, spotted four twin-engine enemy aircraft climbing up behind a box of B-24s. He dove down, fired from 400 yards, and saw the targeted Me 210 go down in a tight spiral. Lt's George Hall and Lloyd Langdon were escorting a box of B-24s on the way out when they spotted fifteen Me 109s below them and heading northeast. Hall went down and got one. Then, Langdon fired on another, who pilot either bailed out, or fell out of his Me 109. Langdon fired on another, damaging it, and then a third that just happened to pop up in front of him. He hit it in its belly tank and it blew up. A fourth Me 109 flew through the .50 calibers that Hall was shooting at another, and Hall damaged it, while destroying his intended target, too.

Capt. Mahurin got a Ju 88, and probably got another. Then he got into a Luftberry circle with a third, but ran out of ammunition. He was so caught up in the action that he had intentions of ramming it, but its prop wash kept throwing him away. It eventually rolled away and dove into the clouds. Mahurin's Ju 88 destroyed gave him a total score of 14.5 and placed him in the lead of 8th Air Force fighter pilots still flying combat missions.

Only Lt. Mark Mosley, from the 62nd FS had any luck for his squadron, as he damaged an Me 210 North of Hanskamp.

Lt. Col. Gabreski's 61st FS rounded out the day's scoring with "Gabby" getting an Me 109 and a Me210. Capt. James Carter got an Fw 190. Lt. Robert Johnson ran his score up to fourteen by getting an Me 109 and an Me 210. (In his book *Thunderbolt*, Johnson states that he got a kill and a probable this date, but he was officially awarded two claims for his day's

A view of the nose art on Frank Klibbe's first "Little Chief/Anderson Indians, HV◉V, 42-76179. (via Davis)

The second HV⊙V "Little Chief," HV⊙V belonging to Frank Klibbe. Note the larger war bonnet. (via Davis)

work). Lt.'s Joe Powers and Frank Klibbe got an Fw 190 and an Me 109, respectively. They returned, elated, at 1444.

The day's activities marked the 200th kill for the 56th Fighter Group. The event was dedicated to President Roosevelt, as it was his birthday.

January 31: VIII FC FO 229 was a short notice escort for B-24s to "Crossbow" targets near St. Poi-Siracourt with 114 P-47s of the 56th and 356th Fighter Groups.

"A" Group was off at 1249 behind Lt. Col. Gabreski. They went in at 20,000 feet and RV'd with two large and one small formation of B-24s. They escorted them to the target, northwest of Cambrai, over a solid cloud undercast, except for directly over the target. "B" Group took off at 1305 to provide area support for the same bombing mission. They went in over Calais at 20,000 feet at 1340, and Lt. Joseph Egan, 63rd Fighter Squadron, took his Red Flight down to look for enemy fighters. They found eight, but they all escaped. In the process, though, Lt. Isadore Porowski's Thunderbolt was hit by flak. He got back okay. All encountered problems on the return as the weather had deteriorated and the pilots had a hard time finding Halesworth's runways in snow, rain and fog.

February 3: VIII FC FO 233 sent all 8th Air Force fighter groups, and two borrowed from the 9th AF out to support the three air divisions. The 56th Fighter Group dispatched both their "A" and "B" Groups.

"A" Group, under Lt. Col. Gabreski, was off Halesworth at 0937 to give penetration support to the 1st Air Task Force enroute to Wilhelmshaven. Lanfall-in was over Egmond at 1027, and RV with the "Big Friends" was accomplished over the Zuider Zee with the middle box of the 3rd Bomb Division B-17s.

Although a pair of Me 109s were seen chasing a straggling B-17, they broke away when they saw the Thunderbolts and no encounters took place. Due to the length of the mission and the fuel consumed, four P-47s had to

put down at Orfordness, and Lt. James Fields, 62nd, ran out of fuel five miles short of Halesworth. He belly landed and pretty well wrote off his aircraft, but was unhurt.

"B" Group was off seven minutes behind "A" and also made landfall-in over Egmond, at 1032. The five minute time differential again made all the world's difference in encountering the "Jerries." Over Ruhlertwist, Major Craig, leading "B" Group (And who was also flying his last combat mission, as he was the first 56th FG pilot to complete his 200 combat-hour mission requirement.), saw ten Me 109s and fifteen Fw 190s at 30,000 feet in groups of vee's and trying to maneuver up-sun of the bombers before attacking.

Craig took the Group up a thousand feet above the Germans, and then sent the 63rd Fighter Squadron down on the pounce. White Leader, Bud Mahurin, fired on one Me 109 without noticeable effect, but another straightened out in front of him and he clobbered it. It was Mahurin's fifteenth kill, and it made him not only the top scoring fighter pilot but the first "triple ace" in the ETO. Lt. William Janson, White Three, was following Mahurin and fired on another 109. Janson saw pieces come off of it, and it started smoking, but he couldn't stick around to see what happened. Originally claimed as a "kill" it was credited as a probable. 1st Lt. Charles Reed, Red Three, got an Fw 190 which exploded in front of him.

The enemy fighters disappeared into the clouds and the 63rd FS set off to find the bombers they were supposed to escort, but without success. White and Red Flights turned for home, and Mahurin's supercharger failed and he had to start down to 10,000 feet. Escorted by Lt. Russell Westfall. Lt. Lloyd Langdon, Red Two, went with them, and soon was joined by Lt. Joseph Egan, Red One. As they dropped below the clouds they encountered eight Me 109s and a pair of Fw 190s. The Me's jumped Lt. Westfall, but were forced away by Lt.'s Langdon and Egan, with Egan claiming one Me 109. (Downgraded to a probable). All of this consumed too much fuel, and Lt. Langdon ran out of gas forty miles out to sea and had to bailout.

Egan circled him as long as he could, calling for assistance from RAF Air-Sea Rescue, and then headed for England. He had just enough fuel remaining, himself, to make the coast, and bellied in on the beach. Egan was unhurt, but Langdon was lost in the cold sea.

Blue Flight, after the fruitless search for the bombers also found themselves short on gas. Lt. "Bunny" Comstock bellied-in at Beccles, and Lt. Harold Matthews crash landed at Boxted. The remainder returned to Halesworth at 1311.

February 4: VIII FC FO 234 had all fighter groups out on missions covering bombers hitting Frankfurt. The 56th Fighter Group was to provide withdrawal support for the 1st Air Task Force.

"A" Group, behind Col. Zemke, went in at 1153 south of Blankenberge at 24,000 feet. They circled over Koblenz for twenty minutes, but none of the B-17s could be found, and as no German fighters were seen, they RTB'd, landing at 1353.

"B" Group crossed-in at 1212 over Knocke-Walcheren Island at 25,000 feet and proceeded to the RV point. After making three orbits and not seeing any bombers, Major Burke ordered them to turn for home. Finally, they caught up with three boxes of B-17s southwest of Antwerp, which they escorted out.

Near Charleroi the 62nd Fighter Squadron got into the only action by the Group this day. Their White Flight spotted some twenty-five Fw 190s and they dove on them, but the Fw's quickly escaped into cloud cover. Then, while climbing back up to altitude, four or five Fw 190s came back down on them. Lt. Valenta's P-47 being hit by a pair of 20mm cannon shells. Blue Flight then attacked six Fw 190s near Florennes. The Fw's went into Luftberry Circles, and then broke for the deck. Lt. Fred Christensen, Blue Three, attacked an Fw 190 that was firing on a P-47, and exploded it. He then made two more attacks without success. Capt. Michael Quirk got another Fw 190 that was flying with a wingman, but the wingman ran off when his flight leader was attacked. Lt. James Fields got another Fw 190. Quirk later came in behind a twin-engine enemy aircraft near St. Omer whose gunner bailed out when he saw Quirk's P-47. Quirk became so intent on watching the parachutist that he forgot about shooting at the aircraft, and it disappeared. Lt. Fields then was attacked near Lille by eight Me 109s and dove for the deck. He got so low in his attempt to escape that he found himself looking up at the trees flashing by his canopy. While his attention was thusly diverted, he flew right through a tree, which damaged his wings and prop. With a 20mm cannon shell in the left wing, Fields' had to belly land at Manston with no hydraulic systems. His P-47 was a write-off.

February 5: VIII FC FO 235. In an effort to curtail Luftwaffe interceptor operations, the heavies went to their airdromes in France to paste the German fighters while they were still on the ground. All fighter groups were up on various area support missions.

It should be noted here that the Air Force had previously done away with the Royal Air Force nomenclature for fighter missions. These missions would officially be no longer be referred to as Rodeo's, Ramrod's and Circus's but be identified as "free lance;" "area support," (Which included penetration, target and/or withdrawal support type missions.), "fighter sweeps," (Which included "Type 16" MEW radar vectored missions). Soon to become operationally effective, the fighter-bomber and dive bombing missions would often be referred to as "Thunderbolting" or "Thunder-bombing" in unofficial commentaries.

"A" Group crossed in over Dieppe at 1124 at 22,500 feet behind Col. Zemke to provide withdrawal support for the "Big Friends" returning from airfield attacks in France. RV was made east of Chartres and the bombers were escorted out. The mission was unopposed and uneventful for "A" Group.

"B" Group followed "A" by a half hour. They crossed in over St. Vallery at 26,000 feet. Near Rouen, the 63rd Fighter Squadron's Red Flight

encountered two Fw 190s that were following them and preparing to attack their White Flight. Capt. John Vogt called for Red Flight to break and he and Red Two, 2nd Lt. Evert Everett, made a left climbing turn to attempt to get at the Fw's. Lt. John A. Patton, whose own wingman, Flight Officer John Ross, had aborted, apparently did not hear Vogt's call to break and was shot down. Patton was last seen spinning into lower clouds. He was killed. Lt. John Bryant, 62nd FS, then chased another Fw 190, but it also escaped. The Group returned at 1357.

That afternoon at Halesworth 2nd Lt. Roger Phillips, 61st FS, was killed in a mid-air collision. He had been up on a training flight after just having been assigned to the squadron the previous week.

February 6: VIII FC FO 236 sent all P-47 groups up to support the three Bomb Divisions. Over five hundred "T-Bolts" were operational. The 56th Fighter Group sported their new colors for this effort. The previous white paint on the front of the P-47s cowlings was replaced by red for the 61st Fighter Squadron, yellow for the 62nd FS, and blue for the 63rd FS. This, actually, would last only a short time, until February 15, and then all of the cowlings would be painted red and the appropriate squadron colors were painted upon the aircraft's rudders.

"B" Group was up at 0916 behind Major Sylvester Burke and the 63rd Fighter Squadron. They crossed-in at 1008 at 25,000 under the control of "Tackline," their MEW controller, on a Type 16 mission. While over the continent, the 63rd Fighter Squadron saw some enemy aircraft, but the controller would not let them make the interception. Near Albert the 62nd FS saw a B-17 being shot down by Fw 190s (No parachutes observed.), at 10,000 feet and went down to help. Capt. Eugene O'Neill got one, and Lt. Joe Icard damaged another. Another B-17 was seen to be straggling out, so the 62nd FS formed up on him and provided an escort out, with one crew member seen to bailout of the Fort while it was under escort.

The 61st FS sighted six Me 109s climbing in pairs near Beauvais at 12,000 feet, intent upon attacking the bombers, and intercepted them. Capt. Robert Lamb and wingman Lt. Robert Rankin each got one of them at 7,000 feet.

Lamb: "I was flying Halsted White 1, we were on area cover patrol and were covering one box of B-17s. I saw three elements of two 109's approaching the big friends from the south and below. We dove down across the nose of the big friends as the lead Me-109 pulled up and fired at the bombers. I had two flights of three each. We closed on them and they turned south again, we closed into range. I dropped down behind the first two and pulled up even with the number two Hun. We were about 30 feet apart. I was then about 200 to 250 yards from the leader. I opened fire and immediately saw strikes on the wings and fuselage. A piece flew off the belly and another from the right wing. The 109 then started a roll to the right. Strikes were still appearing on the e/a. The pilot jettisoned his canopy and bailed out. As he left the e/a he must have jumped into the fire of my starboard guns because I saw him blow apart in mid-air."

As the squadron moved across Paris twenty more Me 109s were sighted at altitudes ranging between 5,000 and 20,000 feet. Two were destroyed by Lt.'s Samuel Hamilton and Joe Powers.

"A" Group did not takeoff until 1104, behind Lt. Col. Schilling. They crossed-in at 1149 at 26,500 over Dunkirk to provide withdrawal support for the returning bombers. RV was accomplished at Anverre at 1225. Other than seeing a P-38 go down in flames near Rouen, and three Me 109s that were not encountered, the mission was uneventful until they got back to England. "A" Group had to scatter themselves to other airfields to refuel before being able to return to Halesworth. Lt. Dick Thompson crashlanded at Manston on return, suffering a slight injury to his right eye. The Group was logged back at Halesworth at 1541.

February 8: VIII FC FO 238. The 1st and 3rd Bomb Divisions went to Frankfurt. The 56th Fighter Group was assigned to send "A" Group on penetration support, while "B" Group would provide withdrawal support under Type 16 control.

"A" Group was led-off at 0940 by Col. Zemke on his first mission after his return to the Group. They made RV with two boxes of B-17s of the 3rd Bomb Division at 1043 at 27,000 feet over a solid cloud layer that was 20,000 feet thick. Another P-47 group took over as lead escort, and all were relieved by other P-47 groups and a P-38 group. The other groups were seen encountering enemy aircraft, but "A" Group had an uneventful mission. Again, they had to land at advance bases in England to refuel before being able to get home. The P-47 simply did not have the range required.

"B" Group was up at 1130 with Major Burke leading. They had three aborts, and another withdrew as escort for them. They went in over Nieuport at 1212 and were vectored to St. Quenton where they met a pair of Me 109s. Major Burke took White Flight of the 63rd Fighter Squadron in for the attack as the Messerschmitt's made a 180 degree turn and started down. Burke damaged one. Flight Officer John Ross attacked the other, but made no claim. During his attack, he, in turn was jumped by two more Me 109s out of the sun. They hit Ross's wings, causing him to spin-out, but he recovered and got back to England okay.

Lt. Joe Icard, Red Four in the 62nd FS formation got an Me 109. Capt. Leroy Schreiber claimed a probable Me 109, which was changed to a claim for a damaged. Lt. Stanley Morrill also damaged an Me 109. This encounter took place over Cambrai-Valenciennes. Later, Major Stewart and Flight Lt. Michael Gladych from the 61st FS fired at a pair of Fw 190s, but made no claims. "B" Group also had to land at alternate airfields in England for fuel before returning to Halesworth.

February 9: Captain Leroy Schreiber became the Commanding Officer of the 62nd Fighter Squadron, vice Major "Pappy" Craig who was rotating home.

February 10: VIII FC FO 239. Eight P-47 groups, including one from the 9th Air Force, up on escort for 3rd Bomb Division B-17s to Brunswick. The 56th Fighter Group was delayed on takeoff because of a snowstorm that swept across Halesworth and they missed out on all the real action. The other P-47 groups claimed 37-0-15.

Airborne from Halesworth at 1238 behind Lt. Col. Schilling, the "A" and "B" groups were combined because of the delay. They dispatched fifty-five P-47s, but eight aborted, and the 61st Fighter Squadron was only able to get seven aircraft up for the mission.

In over Schouwen Island at 1324, they spotted some B-24s coming back from Glize-Rijen, but since these were not the bombers they were looking for, they turned north to intercept two boxes of returning B-17s. The Group split at this time, with half escorting these Forts across the North Sea, while the other half went looking for stragglers to escort home. They picked up three or four and escorted them back to England. Except for a single encounter that Schilling and Major Stewart had when they unsuccessfully attempted to bounce a couple German fighters, the mission was uneventful. They RTB'd at 1527.

February 11: VIII FC FO 240. A mission to Frankfurt was guaranteed to stir up the Luftwaffe. On this mission by the 1st Bomb Division, 486 P-47s from all groups went along as escort and claimed 14-0-14. In addition, the restriction against attacking ground targets had just been lifted by General James Doolittle, the new Commanding General of the 8th Air Force. And Col. Zemke got the first of 327 German aircraft destroyed on the ground by the 56th Fighter Group.

"B" Group was off first, at 0947 behind Major Burke and the 63rd Fighter Squadron. They entered Europe over Knocke at 1035. Major Stewart's 61st FS took the lead box, escorting to the front left, the 62nd FS, took the front, and the 63rd FS provided top cover. At 1110 the 62nd FS saw four Me 109s in the area of Hody-Spa. The Me's dove from 30,000

feet. Major Burke turned to intercept them and fired burst at two of them, but made no claim, pending assessment of his gun camera film. One claim was approved. (One of these being seen on fire and being chased by a pair of P-47s from the 61st FS).

About 1115 and north of Malmedy, the 61st FS spotted five Fw 190s at 29,000 feet starting down in a head-on attack on the B-17s. Their White Flight attacked and Major Stewart destroyed one. The 62nd FS got into it with four Me 109s south of Bierset, observing four Me 109s still carrying their belly tanks diving through the B-17 formation. Lt. Fred Christensen and Lt. Stanley Morrill each getting one. "A" Group returned at 1236.

"A" Group took off at 0954 with Col. Zemke leading. They crossed in at 1042 over Walcheren Island following the B-17s. Zemke sent the 63rd FS ahead to accomplish the official RV with the Forts, while taking the 61st and 62nd fighter squadrons after four Me 109s that he had seen near Liege.

The 63rd FS flew up the line of bombers to the lead box, and encountered four Me 109s east of Vogelstand. They dropped their belly tanks and went after them, but were without success. The 63rd FS escorted to the limit of their endurance and returned home on their own, crossing-out at Ostend at 1215.

The Me 109s that Zemke had seen were intercepted by White Flight of the 62nd FS over Ans. Lt. Joe Icard destroying one, while Capt. Leroy Schreiber damaged another. Zemke, realizing that they would never catch the B-17s, took the two squadrons down to strafe the airdrome at Juvincourt on the way home. He destroyed an Me 109 on the ground on his first pass, starting the trend of racking up ground kills for the 56th FG. Zemke probably destroyed another on his second pass, and damaged two more on successive strafing runs. Capt. Schreiber destroyed the second enemy aircraft on the ground, an Me 110. Lt. McClure, 62nd FS, damaged an Me 110, and Lt.'s Donald Funcheon and Richard Altschuler damaged another between them. They also shot up a couple of hangars.

RTB time was 1348, as most had to select alternate landing sites in England to refuel on their way home.

February 19: Major Sylvester Burke was transferred to Headquarters 2nd Bomb Division. He was replaced as squadron commander of the 63rd Fighter Squadron by Major Gerald Johnson.

February 20: VIII FC FO 245. After a little more than a week of non operational flying the 56th Fighter Group was prepared to commence their part in "Big Week." This would be a maximum effort by the 8th Air Force against industrial targets in Germany with the largest concentration of bombers and fighters to date. Anything and everything that was available for strategic bombing and escort would be participating. This would be the first time that the 8th Air Force would be able to send out over a thousand heavy bombers. Not only would all available fighters be up, but the Thunderbolts would be fitted with the new long-range 150 gallon belly tanks. For the first time they would be able to penetrate deep into Germany and still have enough fuel to loiter there and wait for the Luftwaffe to show up, or be able to range far and wide and go look for them, instead of having to take pot-luck in the event their paths crossed. On this first mission of "Big week" a total of 668 Thunderbolts were dispatched, and everyone of them was needed. Since the 8th Air Force had only been flying a limited number of missions in preparation for the assault, the Luftwaffe was able to also take an advantage of the respite to prepare for the ensuing bomber raids. Of the 964 bombers dispatched on the first day, twenty-one were lost. Bomber crewmen claimed 65-33-29 German aircraft. Air Force fighters claimed 61-7-37 for the loss of four, with two more written off with battle damage and four additional suffering repairable damage

"A" Group was to provide penetration support to the 1st Bomb Division going to Leipzig, Bernberg and Aschersleben. Major Burke led the Group off Halesworth at 1100. This would be his last mission for the duration, as he reached the 200 combat hour mark on the day's effort. RV with

"Penrod and Sam" was the last of the P-47s assigned to Robert Johnson. Coded LM✪Q, it was 42-25512, from the last of the "Razorback" series. Sgt. J. C. Penrod was Johnson's crew chief. (via Davis)

the last box of bombers occurred over the Zuider Zee. They flew up the bomber stream to assume the "point" on escort over Drummer Lake at 1214 at 24,000 feet. On the way out, with the 62nd and 63rd Fighter Squadron's remaining on escort, Lt. Col. Gabreski took the 61st FS down on a bounce of twenty Me 110s northeast of Minden that were flying below the bombers and were offset from the bomber stream by six miles. Gabby's boys had the proverbial "field day."

In combats that ranged from 17,000 down to 4,000 feet, Gabreski destroyed two Me 110s and damaged one. Lt. Robert Johnson shot down two and damaged two more. Lt. Don Smith shot down two and damaged one. Capt. James Carter and Lt. Samuel Hamilton each got one, with Hamilton damaging another. Lt. Justus Foster got a probable and a damaged. Three other Lt.'s damaged Me 110s: Don Funcheon, Richard Altschuler and Claude Mussey. As usual in three dimensional air combat, it was a matter of being in the right place at the right time, as neither the 62nd or 63rd FS's had encounters with enemy aircraft on this mission.

For Bob Johnson, the axiom also held true, as Bud Mahurin was on leave. Johnson's two kills this day were his fifteenth and sixteenth, not only making him the Group's second triple ace, but pulling ahead of Mahurin by .5. A feat in what the press was calling a scoring race.

"B" Group got up at 1123 behind Lt. Col. Schilling. They had seven aborts out of the thirty-eight P-47s dispatched, and had to send two more back as escorts for them. "B" Group was to provide penetration support to the 2nd Task Force to Halberstadt, Brunswick and Gotha, and they joined the B-24s over Drummer lake. Here it became a case of the 62nd FS getting all the action, while the 61st and 63rd FS's had few things to write home about.

Five Me 109s attacked the bombers head-on and Capt. Leroy Schreiber took his 62nd FS after them. Schreiber shot down three, and damaged a fourth Me 109. He then took his squadron down to lower altitudes to see what might be interesting. At Wuntsdorf airdrome Lt. Stan Morrill saw six twin-engine German fighters, believed to be Me 110s, all lined up on the runway preparing to takeoff after the bombers. He damaged all six of them sufficiently enough to prevent their interference with the 8th Air Force.

At Steinhuder Lake, Morrill spotted an Me 110 in the traffic pattern as it was returning from attacking the bombers, so he shot it down. Lt. Fred Christensen shot down a Ju 88 in the same area, and then he and Morrill then shared in the destruction of a Do-217. "B" Group landed at 1452.

It wasn't a bad day's work for the 56th FG, as they claimed fourteen enemy aircraft destroyed, two probably destroyed, and eighteen damaged.

One of the things that had tilted the odds in their favor was the addition of 150 gallon belly tanks that now gave an effective combat range of 350 miles. For Capt. Schreiber, it had been a damned good day. He had been sitting on 4.5 kills since November. Today he too joined the ranks of the aces. Only two 56th FG aircraft suffered minor battle damage.

February 21: VIII FC FO 246. Although the weather turned bad again, causing many of the bomber formations to bomb secondary targets, all three bomb divisions were active. All fighter groups were active as well, including two borrowed from the 9th Air Force. Primary targets had been Kiepholz, Brunswick and Bramsche.

"A" Group was led off by Col. Zemke at 1249. Seven of the thirty-nine Thunderbolts had to abort, and one more withdrew as an escort. They entered Europe somewhat scattered, with the 61st Fighter Squadron not joining-up until 1415 south of Osnabruck and the remainder of the group at Quackenbruck five minutes later. RV with two Combat Wings of the 3rd Bomb Division was initially accomplished at 1412 north of Munster at 27,000 feet by the 63rd FS.

The reason for the join-up delay being an encounter with a pair of Fw 190Ds, which were just coming into the German inventory in force. The "long nose" Focke-Wulf's were somewhat of a novelty item, as their capabilities remained an unknown and many of the fighter pilots wanted to see what they had in comparison to their own improved P-47s.

At the RV point, the bombers were undergoing attacks by Me 110s that were coming in on the rear of the withdrawing B-17s. Capt. John Vogt, Red One, 63rd FS, went after one, chasing it down to 15,000 feet. Vogt started firing at 600 yards, and continued firing until he had closed to 150 yards. He saw strikes all over its engines and fuselage, and watched it catch fire. His wingman, Capt. Richard Leary, damaged another. Leary was not a 56th FG pilot, but was on loan to the 63rd Fighter Squadron from the 368th Fighter Group.

"A" Group continued escort out to the Zuider Zee at 1448 and then set course for home, making landfall out over Egmond at 1501.

"B" Group was off at 1343 with Capt. Leroy Schreiber leading. Landfall-in was over Katwijk Ann Zee at 1420 at 22,000 feet. RV was made over Diepholz airdrome, in the Bramsche area, with the bombers that were attacking the airdrome, itself. The bombers were undergoing attacks by a determined Luftwaffe at the time. 1st Lt. Joseph Egan, Blue One, 63rd FS, saw four Me 109s and an Fw 190 fly head-on through the last box of B-17s and go after a straggler. The Fort's tail gunner got one, and Egan went after the third one in the formation and flamed it, watching it crash on the east bank of the Zuider Zee.

Capt. Glen Schlitz, White Leader, and leading the 63rd FS, climbed to 28,000 feet and spotted four Me 109s that over flew his flight to bounce another flight of P-47s ahead of them. Those P-47s broke, and the Me 109s followed them down, so Schlitz went after them, and shot down the third one in that formation, watching it splash into the Zuider Zee. For some reason, this claim was never officially approved.

Pilots of the 62nd FS had similar encounters. Capt. Leroy Schreiber saw an Me 109 going after another straggling B-17 near Osnabruck, and shot it down. Schreiber and wingman, Capt. Haesler, then damaged another Me 109. Near Soesterberg four Fw 190s and a pair of Me 109s were flying a parallel route to the bombers at 20,000 feet. These were attacked by Lt. Joe Icard and Lt. Charles Harrison, who each got one. Then, Lt. Roy Bluhm got another Me 109 near Zwolle.

The 61st FS did even better: Major Gerald Johnson claimed an Fw 190, which was not officially awarded. Capt. Michael Gladych claimed two Me 109s; Lt.'s Donald Funcheon, Claude Mussey, Frank Klibbe and Flight Officer Evan McMinn all were credited with destroying Me 109s. Although none of the 56th FG's P-47s had been damaged by enemy fire, several had been shot at by B-17 gunners during the mission. It was felt that the gunners were confused by the new colors on the noses of their P-47s and were mistaking them for Fw 190s.

February 22: VIII FC FO 247. All bomber and fighter groups on the offensive. Many had to also fight the elements as well as the Luftwaffe and flak.

"A" Group behind Lt. Col. Gabreski was off at 1116 with thirty-nine Thunderbolts. They went in over Zandvoort at 1215, and at 1225 they were advised that the 2nd Task Force that they were supposed to escort had been recalled because of the weather. They then sought out other bombers to cover, and RV'd with three boxes of B-17s of the 1st Bomb Division over Gutersloh. These Fort's were already under attack, and Lt. Joe Egan, Red One, 63rd Fighter Squadron, saw four Me 109s going after a straggling B-17s. Egan and 2nd Lt. Barney Casteel went after them. Egan hit the one he intended all over with .50 caliber fire and watched it tumble end for end three times before going down in flames. Egan would later damage an Fw 190.

Major Gerald Johnson, flying his first mission as Commanding Officer of the 63rd FS, then saw two Me 109s going in on the bombers. Johnson started after them, but they dove away, so Johnson started climbing back up and saw Fw 190s attacking the bombers. Intending to divert their attention, he fired at one from a far distance, but the German pilot either ignored the tracers or did not see them. Johnson closed in and fired again and it went down into the clouds below smoking and obviously out of control. It was claimed as destroyed, but credited as a probable.

The 62nd FS had a bit of confusion at the beginning of the mission. Their "B" squadron, when notified that their intended bombers to Schweinfurt had been recalled, joined up with "A" squadron (And "A" Group.), for the mission. At RV, with the bombers under attack, the 62nd's White and Red Flights went to the assistance of the bombers, while Blue Flight flew top cover for them. Capt. Schreiber and Lt.'s Fields' and Bryant shared in the destruction of an Me 109.

Then Lt.'s Quirk and Fields split a claim for an Fw 190. Then Quirk got another Fw 190, with Lt. Bryant credited with damaging it beforehand.

With the Luftwaffe beaten off for the moment, "A" Squadron sent down six P-47s to strafe Eindhoven airdrome. Lt. Anthony Carcione destroying an Me 109 on the ground, while Lt. Charles Ginn damaged a Do 217. Flak gunners in turn damaged two P-47s. "B" Squadron had rejoined the bombers at Gutersloh, and then broke escort at Paderborn. They then spotted twenty Me 109s and four Me 110s. Their White Flight made an attack on the Messerschmitts, and Lt. Ray Dauphin damaged an Me 110. In the process, two of their P-47s were hit by 20mm return fire.

West of Paderborn the 61st FS got into it with forty plus Fw 190s. "Gabby" got one, running his personal score up to fourteen. 1st Lt. Don Smith got another, his last for the war, but sufficient to make him an ace with 5.5 kills. Capt. Leslie Smith started his string to "Acedom" with his first two Fw 190s. Flight Officer Evan McMinn got another, and wasn't doing too bad for a pilot the Air Force had not made a full fledged officer, in fact, he would become an ace before he was commissioned. "A" Group returned, albeit scattered to four different airfields in England at 1407.

"B" Group had followed "A" by fifteen minutes, behind Major Stewart, and flew an identical path into Europe. "B's" 62nd and 63rd fighter squadrons picked up three boxes of 1st Bomb Division B-17s at Gutersloh at 1320, while the 61st FS escorted a box of B-24s to Doesburg, where they were recalled.

The 63rd FS's White Flight observed ten to fifteen Me 110s attacking their Forts at the RV point. Capt. John Vogt, White One, went after them, claiming one destroyed and one additional as a probable, and joining the ranks of aces in the process. Lt. George Hall, White Three, claimed two Me 110s, one of which was seen to crash. Capt. Richard Leary, White Two, damaged another. Capt. Lyle Adrianse, Blue One, also got an Me 110. Again, a red nosed, blue tailed 63rd FS P-47 was shot at by a returning B-17, this time just off the Dutch coast.

The 61st FS's Major James Stewart destroyed an Me 109, while Flight Officer Steve Gerick damaged an Me 110. Stewart's claim marked a true milestone, as the 61st FS became the first fighter squadron in the European Theater to score one hundred kills.

February 24: VIII FC FO 250. After a weather enforced day off, Fighter Command sent out over six hundred Thunderbolts, along with one hundred-fifty P-38s and P-51s to support the heavies going to Schweinfurt and Gotha. Although ten American fighters were lost, they claimed 60-11-27, with the P-47s claiming 31-0-13. The 56th Fighter Group claimed eight German fighters, for the loss of one pilot killed. Their first loss in just under three weeks. During this period they had cost the Luftwaffe at least sixty-four confirmed aircraft. This may not have been a record, but it was a far better average than anyone could have ever expected.

"A" Group took off at 1104 with thirty-eight P-47s, including mission leader, Col. Zemke. They crossed in north of Ijmuiden at 1151 and made RV east of Zwolle ten minutes later, providing escort for seven Combat Wing's of the 1st and 2nd Bomb Divisions. Between twenty and thirty single engine German fighters were seen to be attacking the bombers between Lingen and Herford, which were engaged by elements of "A" Group between Minden, Herford and Cassel at altitudes from 25,000 feet down to 500 feet.

Zemke led the attack on a pair of Fw 190s that he saw to the south and below the bombers, being accompanied by Lt. John Truluck's, 63rd Fighter Squadron, element. On the descent to intercept them, Truluck spotted two more below and behind the pair that Zemke was intent upon. Truluck cut in on them and opened fire at 400 yards, and hit one in its belly tank, which burst into flames. It canopy blew off, and its pilot did attempt to bailout, but without success.

Lt. Archie Robey, Zemke's wingman, got a probable on an Fw 190, but Zemke came up scoreless. As Zemke focused upon knocking down the lead Fw 190, the German pilot's own wingman swung in behind Zemke and cut loose on his P-47 with cannon shells, registering hits on the Thunderbolt's flaps and elevator. The German pilot, intent upon his quarry, had ignored Robey who was guarding Zemke, and paid for it the hard way. But Zemke came up scoreless. His reflector gunsight had failed, and the fixed "iron sight" was inaccurate.

Blue Flight of the 62nd FS was bounced by a "Long-nosed Fw 190," and then went after three of them that had attempted an interception on them. Lt. Stanley Morrill got one, its pilot bailing out (56th FG records state that it was a Fw 190). Several Fw 190s were then engaged by Capt. Michael Quirk and Lt. John Fields southwest of Paderborn, but without claims.

On the way out, Lt.'s Fred Christensen and Kelley strafed Quakenbruck airdrome. Christensen damaged an Fw 190 and an Me 110 on the ground, but during this attack, Lt. Wilbur Kelley disappeared. A victim of the intense airfield defensive antiaircraft fire. Kelley was the first of the approximately one third of the 56th FG's total number of pilot losses that were generated by this sort of action.

The 61st FS, led by Major Stewart, was equally active. Stewart shot down an Fw 190, and so did Lt.'s Gordon Blake and Joe Powers. Stewart's encounter report, while lengthy, is indicative of combat and worth relating:

Stewart: "I was leading Keyworth Squadron on penetration support to Schweinfurt. Our flight was made up of Stewart, Keen, Powers and Stauss. We made R/V with the rear box of Forts over Lingen about 1230. Shortly after R/V White Three called in a single Me 109 going through the bombers so I started an attack but the 109 had a too good a start and I had to let him go. So then continued on the track again until we reached the second box of bombers a few miles SE of Oonsbruck, where we made a pass at some Fw 190's. But we were cut out by some other P-47's so I let them go. Lt Powers said he was going down on two 190s on some P-47's tail so I started to follow to give him cover when another P-47 crossed in front of me and I lost Lt. Powers. I then went back to the bombers looking for some other aircraft of our Squadron to join and saw 2 A/C to the right and ahead of the bombers so I headed that way for about ten minutes before I identified them as P-47's. I started closing in toward them from their right side when I noticed them initiating an attack on three a/c way out in front of the bombers at about 15,000 ft. I and my wingman, Lt. Keen were at 20,000 ft. Upon being attacked two of the a/c turned left and dove almost immediately under me. I initiated an attack on the closest a/c diving to about 6 or 7,000 ft. gradually closing in on him as he started climbing and turning to the left. He leveled out about 10,000 ft. and I started firing at about 400 yards, missing him at first then closing in a little closer and really plastering him. His belly tank exploded and he caught on fire rolling over to the right and diving into the ground. I took a quick look to the left to see how my wing man was and noticed an Fw 190 about 600 yards from his tail just about ready to open fire. I called him to break hard and I winged over hard to the left and got behind the a/c. The a/c immediately broke off his attack and took mild evasive action. I was just about to get in good shooting position and range when the a/c moved over hard, did a half roll and hit the deck. I was low on gas so I started home climbing to 14,000 ft. and breaking off my attack. My wing man and Lt. Herman who made the initial attack on the a/c can confirm the hits on the a/c and Lt. Herman can confirm the fact that the a/c crashed to the ground and exploded. My wing man Lt. Keen saw my strikes and then took a short squirt at the a/c himself which nearly cost him his life."

"B" Group was off right behind "A" Group and made landfall-in over Ijmuiden at 1157. They made RV with the bombers west of Drummer Lake at 1232, where the bombers were being attacked. Major Gerald Johnson, leading the 63rd FS, spotted three Fw 190s climbing up to position themselves for an attack on the bombers and took his White Flight down upon them. One of the 190s made a one hundred-eighty degree turn to get away from the Thunderbolts, but it made easy meat for Johnson in the process, as he was able to fire on it from dead-astern. The Fw 190 went down in a mass of flames. Lt. Harold Comstock, leading Blue Flight, spotted an Fw 190 silhouetted against the snow, and damaged it.

As the formation proceeded on course, five Fw 190s attacked the second box of bombers northeast of Herford. Capt. Leroy Schreiber, leading the Group and the 62nd FS, went after an Fw 190 with his White Flight. Schreiber and Lt. Valenta damaged it, and Lt. Gordon finished it off by sawing its wing off with .50 calibers. On the outbound leg, Lt. Donald Funcheon, 61st FS, claimed two Fw 190s destroyed and one damaged, but was only awarded one claim Fw 190.

Funcheon: "I was flying White 3 to Capt. Lamb, White 1 . . . They were flying in a Vic, the leader and his wing man quite close and the third one out and a good ways from the leader. I took this third fellow and opened fire and about 300 yards, 10 degree deflection. I saw hits on the right side of the fuselage and right wing. At this time the first two broke left on the same level and my e/a kept flying straight then flicked over to the left on his back and went straight down from 5,000 feet. At this time Capt. Lamb, White 1, was firing at the No. 1 man. I tried to get shots at No. 2, but couldn't, all the time watching my e/a going straight down. I came very close to the No. 2 man in our flight and had to break away from this attack also loosing sight of the 3rd e/a. This all happened in a very short time, right after my wingman left. After that break I lost every one of the e/a and the three of us circled about 16,000 ft. looking for them with no results. We climbed up to 20,000 ft. flew with the bombers a short while and then Northgrove flight leader {Major Gerald Johnson} flying abreast of us spotted a Fw-190 on the deck. They went down and our flight gave them cover circling about 10,000 ft. All this time I couldn't find the target. Northgrove flight pulled up and we kept on circling going down. About 4,000 ft. over the town of Holzminden White 1 straightened and made a pass at this 190 with in-line engine. White 1 made a half turn with him and then broke and I got a shot at him but didn't see and strikes and broke off.This German pilot was very smart and he also had a good airplane. He rat-raced around there for awhile and White 1 yelled to break up which I did and circled about 3,000 ft. very mad and very determined. Capt. Lamb made a pass at him and broke off and the e/a leveled off and headed fest [sic], which he always did after anyone broke off their attack. He was drawing us in deeper and deeper. Well, after he leveled off right on the tree tops from Capt. Lamb's pass I got a long shot from astern at a great distance coming down from above. He didn't see me."

The fighters and bombers remained in constant contact with the determined Luftwaffe as far as the Zuider Zee where combat was finally broken off. The mission had been pure hell for the bomber crews.

February 25: VIII FC FO 251. Six hundred eighty-seven P-47s were up on escort for the three bomb divisions today. The largest force of Thunderbolts ever sent out. This was the last of the maximum effort "Big Week." Included were three fighter groups borrowed from the IX Fighter Command, along with nine groups of the VIII FC. It was not going to be too much longer that the rival 4th FG was going to be included in these totals, as they were presently undergoing transition into the P-51. For this mission, the 56th Fighter Group was to provide withdrawal escort and support for the Big Friends coming back from the notorious Regensburg and Stuttgart.

"A" Group, with Lt. Col. Gabreski leading, was off at 1332. They made landfall-in over Walcheren Island at 1414 at 20,000 feet, and RV'd east of Landau, over the Rhine River at 1500 with the second box of returning bombers. (P-38s were covering the lead box). "Mustangs and Spitfires were seen on withdrawal and P-47s were everywhere." Near Karlsruhe four Me 109s were seen attacking a straggling B-17, which in turn were attacked by the 61st Fighter Squadron. Capt. Robert Lamb, leading the squadron, shot down one, while Lt. Don Funcheon got another. Lt. Eugene Barnum damaged a third. For the 62nd and 63rd FS's, the mission was basically uneventful. All returned at 1659.

"B" Group, behind Major Gerald Johnson, was airborne Halesworth at 1334. They followed "A" over Walcheren Island by five minutes and made RV with the last box of returning bombers at Neukirchen at 1505, relieving six groups of P-47s and P-51s. Near Hamburg a pair of yellow nosed Fw 190s was seen on the deck, which were bounced by White Flight of the 62nd FS. Capt. Michael Quirk led them down, and Lt. Thaddeus Buszko shot at one, damaging it. Quirk then came in behind it and shot it down with its pilot bailing out. The "Jerry" pilot bailed out so close to Buszko that he had to avoid hitting him, but he had the opportunity to wave at him in his parachute, and the German pilot waved back! Other than Lt. Robert Cherry having to land at Chipping Onger on the return with minor flak damage, the remainder of the mission was without incident, landing at 1703.

February 28: VIII FC FO 253. An almost anti-climatic day after so many days of concentrated combat. The 56th Fighter Group dispatched a total of sixty-one P-47s from both "A" and "B" groups to cover operations of eighty-one B-24s of the 2nd Bomb Division on a mission to Ecalles Sur Buchy. Lt. Col. Schilling led "A" Group off at 1158, and Major Stewart led "B" Group off two minutes later. The two Groups provided escort in the Abbeville area, and out to mid-English Channel, and although many Spitfires, B-25s and B-26s were seen, there was no sign of the Luftwaffe. All were back to Halesworth by 1415.

February 29: VIII FC FO 255. The VIII FC sent up six P-47 groups, along with two more P-47 groups borrowed from the IX FC to provide support for the 3rd Bomb Division striking Brunswick. Only one pilot from the 56th Fighter Group managed to score.

"A" Group, behind Col. Zemke, was off Halesworth at 0915. For the first time in many missions, they had no aborts. Landfall-in was over Ijmuiden at 1000 and RV with four boxes of the penetrating bombers was made fifteen minutes later. Escort was broken west of Steinhuder Lake at 1105. Although their spare aircraft had seen four German aircraft before he turned for home, they saw him first and dove away. Thus, there were no encounters by "A" Group, and they returned at 1224.

"B" Group was led by Capt. Schreiber and was off ten minutes later. They also went in over Ijmuiden, at 1008, making landfall-in and RV at this time. Major Gerald Johnson, leading the 63rd Fighter Squadron, saw a twin-engine German fighter over the east side of the Zuider Zee, and dove down to investigate. Identifying it as a Ju 52, Johnson fired from 200 yards.

It burst into flames and crashed. At this point until out of range, very accurate flak followed Johnson's every move, which had to be quite an unsettling feeling. Escort was broken over at Minden at 1118. The 62nd FS then provided a shuttle service escorting out aborting bombers while the rest of the Group provided top cover for them. "B" Group landed at 1230.

In all, February 1944 had been one great month for the 56th Fighter Group. Although two of their pilots had been killed in combat, they initially claimed seventy-two German aircraft destroyed, nine probably destroyed, and forty-four damaged. In a three day period, they accounted for forty-four destroyed, February 20-22, for no losses. They were no longer mandated to stick with the bombers regardless of whether they were under attack or not, but freed to seek out the Luftwaffe where ever they could find them. The modified propellers and engines, along with the larger belly tanks, had made this job easier to do just that, and Zemke's Wolfpack was on the proverbial roll. It was also during February that the press termed the 56th Fighter Group as "The Wolfpack," or "Zemke's Wolfpack." A moniker that has since identified the Group in everyone's minds.

March 2: VIII FC FO 257. The 1st and 2nd Bomb Divisions went to Frankfurt. Providing escort, among others, were 445 P-47s from seven VIII Fighter Command groups and three from the IX FC. The 56th Fighter Group was on withdrawal support for the Big Friends.

"A" Group, with Lt. Col. Gabreski leading, was off at 1142 with thirty-six Thunderbolts. In over Walcheren Island at 1225 between 22,000 and 25,000 feet, RV was made over the Rhine River between Bonn and Koblenz at 1258. As only friendly fighters were seen, "A" Group went down to strafe an airdrome, where they damaged hangers, barracks and gun emplacements, but no enemy aircraft were reported damaged.

On the way home Lt. Edward N. Rougeau, 62nd FS, called Lt. Charles Ginn to ask for an escort, as he was having electrical problems that killed his generator and took away control of the propeller. Ginn made several turns in an attempt to find him, but could not. As it turned out, Rougeau had bailed out because his radio had then quit and he could not hear of forthcoming aid or find any assistance. He became a prisoner of war.

"B" Group took off at 1159 with Major Gerald Johnson at the helm. The twenty-four P-47s crossed in south of Schouwen Island at 1239 between 22,000 and 27,000 feet, making RV south of Bonn at 1308 with two Combat Wings of 2nd Bomb Division B-24s. One Me 109 was seen all by itself south of Liege just after RV, which was bounced and destroyed by Major Johnson. Johnson opened fire from 300 yards and saw strikes on its nose and canopy, where upon he closed to 100 yards to fire again, but the German pilot bailed out. Johnson came home with a piece of shattered plexiglas embedded in his right wing from the Messerschmitt's canopy.

March 3: VIII FC FO 259. The tactic of sending ten P-47 fighter groups out on bomber support seemed to be working well. On this date, eight were sent by VIII FC, and two from IX FC, for at total of 484 Thunderbolts as escorts for the three Bomb Divisions attacking Berlin in what was supposed to have been the first daylight raid against the German capital. However, the weather did not cooperate and the bomber force sought out their secondary target, Wilhelmshaven. There, the weather was still not very good, and only fifty-four "heavies" bombed out of the eleven Combat Wings of B-17s and three Combat Wings of B-24s.

Both "A" and "B" Groups were dispatched. Lt. Col. Schilling led "A" off Halesworth at 0957, and Major Stewart led "B" Group off one minute later. They went in over Tereschilling Island at 1041, and then flew up the coast to Blauort Island to accomplish the RV. Escort was continued until Juist Island, and then they turned for home. Although many "bogies" were called, they all turned out to be friendly fighters, and the Groups headed for home with "B" Group landing at 1253 and "A" Group at 1307.

March 4: VIII FC FO 260. The 1st and 3rd Bomb Divisions attempted to get to Berlin once again, and again the weather did not cooperate. Only one Combat Wing of the 3rd Bomb Division went to Berlin, while all the others sought out alternate targets. Whether the 13th Combat Wing missed hearing the recall, or chose to ignore it, remains an academic argument. Nevertheless, the issue made fame in both fiction and fact for the participating units.

"A" Group took off at 1028 to provide penetration support. Col. Zemke led them over Schouwen Island at 1056 and on to southeast of Cologne to make RV with the heavies at 1140. At 1200 all 1st Bomb division B-17s were recalled. As no German fighters were apparent, Zemke split his thirty-six P-47s to escort out several groups of the returning bombers as far as the coast before "A" Group's P-47s rejoined to land Halesworth at 1340.

"B" Group was off at 1358 behind Lt. Col. Schilling to provide area and withdrawal support for the heavies. At mid-Channel, the Group was turned due east to penetrate Europe. Two squadrons making landfall-in near Noordwal at 1430 and the 61st at The Hague at 1433. The 61st FS proceeded to Duisburg, where they encountered accurate and intense flak, and had two of their P-47s damaged. The 62nd and 63rd FS's encountered clouds to 24,000 feet that they climbed over, and then made three orbits over Rotterdam before setting course for home.

Just after breaking out on top of the clouds and twenty miles north of The Hague, Lt. Irvin Valenta, 62nd FS, encountered some sort of a problem, possibly an oxygen system failure. He was last seen at 23,000 feet descending at a thirty degree angle back into the clouds. Another fatal loss, as a pilot wearing an oxygen mask and passing out from a lack of oxygen had little chance of recovering even if he did reach a lower altitude, be-

March 4, 1944 was a busy day for the Wolfpack. The heavies were headed for Berlin, and the 56th FG split into their "A" and "B" Groups to cover the mission. Only one Combat Wing got to the "Big B," but there was enough excitement for the fighter pilots. Upon return from the mission, Captain Leslie Smith's P-47 struck another Thunderbolt in a mid-air collision and came close to giving Smith a headache. UN◉H (bar) was 42-74643 and was the personal aircraft of J. Carroll Wakefield. (USAF)

The Jug that Smith hit often was flown by Colonel Zemke, HV❂Z, 42-75121. It was repaired and damaged by enemy fire six weeks later. (USAF)

cause the mask would then prevent the denser air from getting to his lungs. Although many friendly fighters were seen, again there was no sign of the Luftwaffe, and the mission landed at 1628.

March 6: VIII FC FO 262. The weather had cleared and this was the big day that everyone had been waiting for. All three bomb divisions went to Berlin and its suburbs. Helping them along were eight VIII Fighter Command P-47 groups, along with three from the IX FC. A total of 615 Thunderbolts, and they acquitted themselves rather well, claiming 36-7-12, with the 56th Fighter Group claiming 10-2-4 for the loss of one pilot killed and one wounded.

"A" Group followed Col. Zemke off Halesworth at 1013. Three pilots had to abort the momentous mission, and one had to escort them home, leaving thirty-one to make the trip.

Landfall-in was between Ijmuiden and Egmond at 1100, where the bombers were seen, but the actual RV was not made until over Lingen twenty-five minutes later with the 1st Bomb Division. North of Drummer Lake the 61st Fighter Squadron spotted the Luftwaffe first, approximately one hundred single engine fighters that were coming in on the B-17s from 8:00 o'clock.

Zemke turned "A" Group around to meet them, and combat ranged between 25,000 and 5,000 feet. Zemke spotted an Fw 190 raking a B-17 with gun and cannon fire, and was able to shoot it down. He then got on an Me 109 and sent it spinning down on fire. This was followed by a joint effort that Zemke shared with Lt.'s Charles Reed, Donald Peters and Marvin Becker, 63rd FS. They spotted an Me 109 and bore down on it to see it catch fire for no ascertainable reason. They all watched it become almost totally consumed before it crashed. (All four pilots got .25 credit, and this

HV❂Y, 41-6385 was flown by Lt. Claude Mussey on the March 4 Ramrod. It was hit by flak in front of the wind shield and in the tail feathers. (USAF)

On March 6, 1944 the weather improved and all the heavies headed for Berlin. As expected, the Luftwaffe was up, and the flak guns were very active. LM◉P was hit in the tail by flak as it was flown by Lt. Dean Nordquist. (USAF)

ran Zemke's total score to 9.25 kills). Lt. George Hall, Red One, 63rd FS, spotted an Fw 190 attacking a B-17 that had pulled out of formation to let its crew bailout. Hall spotted five chutes blossom before downing the Focke-Wulf. Lt.'s Joe Icard and Jack Greene, 62nd FS's Red Flight, spotted a pair of Fw 190s while the 63rd FS was busy, and Icard destroyed one while Greene damaged the other.

Major Stewart, leading the 61st FS, became an ace and a half, destroying two Fw 190s and bringing his total score to 7.5. Lt. Robert Johnson got his seventeenth kill, another Fw 190, and damaged another. He was in an angry mood and would have gone after others if he had been given the chance, as he witnessed several instances were the "Jerry" pilots were firing at Allied airmen in their parachutes. The 61st FS lost Lt. Andrew Stauss in the confusion of combat, and he was later determined to have been killed.

"B" Group got airborne at 1032 with Major Gerald Johnson leading thirty-five P-47s. They had just one abort. They crossed-in over Egmond at 1117 and enroute to the RV point, near Lewestoft they passed over one box of B-24s. Approaching Bergen a second box of B-24s was seen to be orbiting, and these were joined by the first box that the Group had seen. After passing these groups of Liberators, "B" Group turned south to Emden to RV with their intended B-24s, accomplishing this at 1145 over Meppel.

Four Fw 190s were seen below them at this time and were attacked, destroying one and damaging another. Major Johnson got the damaged credit, but someone else from another unit slid in in front of him and shot it down before Johnson could get back into a shooting position. Bud Mahurin, Red One, 63rd FS, chased an Me 109 down into the clouds and then lost sight of it, but he did see an Fw 190 diving away, so he went after him. The Fw went into a cloud that was thin enough for Mahurin to keep him in sight, so Mahurin fired, and was close enough in the obscuration to see strikes on its fuselage. Mahurin claimed him as a probable. He then started to climb back up to rejoin his formation and found himself in a turning dogfight with an Fw 190 that was trying to shoot down a 78th Fighter Group P-47. After several turns the Fw 190 started a rapid climb which was followed by a "split-S," that was a mistake, as it placed Mahurin in perfect firing position. Bud fired, and the Fw 190 pilot bailed out.

Capt. Leroy Schreiber and Lt. Harold Gallagher, 62nd FS, attacked an Me 109 without success, but later Lt. Fred Christensen and Lt. John

Fields came upon an Fw 190 and an Me 109 that were picking upon a straggling B-17 north of Drummer Lake. Fields got in some good shots on the Fw 190s, damaging it, and then Christensen shot it down. One flight of the 61st FS went down to strafe Vechta airdrome on the way home. Capt. Michael Gladych destroying one Fw 190 there on the ground while Lt. Even McMinn damaged two Me 109s. McMinn also damaged several gun posts and barracks, but Capt. Paul Conger received painful wounds to his left shoulder and side from flak.

March 8: VIII FC FO 263. Back to "Big B," this time the VKF ball bearing works in the Erkner suburb was the target for the three bomb divisions. Again, eight VIII Fighter Command and two IX FC P-47 groups were on escort duties. Six hundred-thirteen P-47s and two hundred seventy-eight P-38s and P-51s to provide cover for five hundred thirty-nine effective bombers. An aerial armada that would challenge the Luftwaffe to the utmost, but they would rise over their snow covered country to the task with a vengeance. Again, however, the German fighters would come out second best, even though they extracted a heavy toll from those on this mission.

Thirty-two B-17s were lost, as well as five B-24s. The fighters did better, claiming 79-8-25 in the air and 8-4-7 on the ground, for the loss of eighteen. Of the claims/ losses, the 56th Fighter Group claimed twenty-eight German aircraft destroyed for the loss of three pilots killed and two becoming prisoners of war. One additional P-47 was lost when its pilot had to bailout over England.

Lt. Col. David Schilling led "A" Group off Halesworth at 1118 with thirty-seven P-47s dispatched. Five had to abort, and one additional returned with them as an escort. Providing penetration support to the 1st Task Force, "A" Group made landfall-in over Valkenberg at 1200 and made RV with the 3rd Bomb Division at 1240 at 24,000 feet over Drummer Lake.

Just after RV was accomplished, Major Gerald Johnson, leading the 63rd Fighter Squadron, saw ten Me 109s coming in on the bombers, and when they spotted the P-47s, they broke formation. Lt's Marvin Becker and Archie Robey each claiming the one they pursued. Then, Lt. John Truluck chased an Me 109 all the way to the deck. They went over airdromes, around trees and houses, with Truluck firing all the way. Truluck, pulled up to gain a more advantageous firing position, then dove down on

Capt. Paul Conger, 61st FS, was flying HV◯C (bar) on the Berlin mission. Hit by flak, Conger suffered painful wounds, but got his sick jug back to England, and both deserved their Purple Hearts. (USAF)

his prey once again as the Me 109 appeared ready to belly in. He fired and saw the Me 109 "smashland" in a field.

Lt. John Marcotte, Red Two, on Truluck's wing, was only on his fourth combat mission. He had followed Truluck down, and then as they were climbing back up, they spotted two P-47s engaged with two Me 109s. Truluck, out of ammunition, exchanged positions with Marcotte, and sent him down to help out the other two Thunderbolts. Marcotte fired on one Me 109, but overshot him, and then they got into a turning dogfight. At this time Truluck lost sight of him, but later he said that he was climbing back up through 11,000 feet with supercharger problems. Later Marcotte said that he couldn't stay with it and was going to bailout. He became a POW. Gerald Johnson got another Me 109 which he tore up its nose and canopy with gunfire. As he overran the target he saw its pilot slumped in his harness, obviously fatally wounded. Johnson then climbed back up to altitude to rejoin the bombers and found that they were still under attack. He fired on two Fw 190s without apparent results, then went after an Me 109 that had dove through the bomber formation. He chased that one down to 6,000 feet, where he ran out of ammunition. But he had inflicted enough damage on it that it was seen to crash.

Things were not going well for the bombers at this time, for between Drummer and Stienhuder Lakes over one hundred German fighters had come in on them. At least a dozen B-17s were seen going down by pilots of the 62nd FS in this region. Capt. Leroy Schreiber and Lt. Robert Cherry each claimed two Fw 190s, with Cherry damaging another. (Only one of Cherry's claims was upheld, the other being credited as a probable). Two pilots were lost, Lt's Joe Icard, who had just become an ace two days earlier, and Fred Roy. A pilot from the 63rd FS reported seeing a yellow nosed P-47 under attack by an Me 109, and the Thunderbolt exploded, but who the pilot was remained unknown. Both of these pilots were killed. On the way out Lt. Col. Schilling destroyed an Me 210 on the ground.

The 61st FS had no losses on this mission. In the air Capt. Bennett got one Fw 190 and two Me 109s. 2nd Lt. Klibbe got an Fw 190, as did Major Stewart, who also claimed an Me 110. Lt. Dick Mudge damaged an Fw 190. Both Klibbe and Bennett landed with minor battle damage to their P-47s.

"B" Group followed Lt. Col. Gabreski off two minutes behind "A" Group to provide penetration support for the 1st Bomb Division. They crossed in over Egmond at 1211 at 22,000 feet and took up coverage of the B-17s over Ankum. Again over Drummer Lake a hundred plus German fighters were seen, and the 61st FS was shadowed by nine single engine and three twin-engine fighters above them at 33,000 feet along their entire escort route.

The 62nd FS "was engaged by an aggressive and determined foe." Lt's Felix Williamson, Mark Mosley and James Field's each got an Fw 190, while Capt. Michael Quirk and Lt. Eaves shared a another. Lt.'s Fields

After flying the fatiguing mission to Berlin, accidents can happen, but fortunately the pilot, Lt. Adam Wisniewski, was unhurt. (USAF)

and Wendell McClure each damaged an Fw 190. Lt. Caleb Reeder was hit by flak east of Osnabruck and had to bailout to become a POW. "Tell the boy's to bite my butt," he said before bailing out. Lt. Anthony Carcione was last seen down on the deck, and he was later identified as killed in action.

The 63rd FS really had not seen any thing to attract their attention up to the time to turn for home, so Bud Mahurin took them down to low altitude to look for worthwhile targets on the way out. Approaching the Wesendorf airdrome, Mahurin spotted an enemy aircraft, so he went after him. Mahurin fired and forced the Fw 190 down into the trees, although he stated that his shooting was "rotten." Mahurin then pulled up over the airdrome to set course for home, but spotted an Me 110 that had just taken off and went down after him, but since he was too high, he ordered Lt. Bernard Smith to shoot, and Smith shot it down. Recrossing again over the airdrome at 600 feet they saw a Ju 88 takeoff, so Mahurin dove on it, setting its right engine on fire and causing it to crash into a wooded area. Again they recrossed the airdrome, this time at 6,000 feet, where a grey Fw 190 was seen. Mahurin fired, and fired again at it as it tried to evade him, but his windshield was smeared with oil from the Ju 88 and he couldn't really see it well enough to line up on it properly. The Fw 190 then started

to "beetle along the tree-tops," and climb over the trees. Mahurin fired on it again and set it smoking badly, and then he ran out of ammo. But, Lt. Harold Mathews, White Four, saw it roll over and crash.

The 61st FS again did rather well. Lt. Robert Johnson shot down two Me 109s that were about to shoot at Lt. Smith. These were identified as "new types." Lt. Gordon Blake got an Fw 190, as did Capt. Michael Gladych. Lt. Claude Mussey got an Me 109 and a probable on a Ju 88. Lt. Col. Gabreski damaged a pair of Fw 190s, and then they went strafing, where Gabreski destroyed an Fw 190, probably destroyed two more and damaged two additional. Capt. Gladych damaged three Fw 190s on the ground, and got his P-47 damaged badly enough that he had to bailout of it when he got back to England.

The afternoon's work set several new records. Capt. Mahurin became the leading ace in the ETO with an official score of 19.5. This placed him but .5 ahead of Lt. Robert Johnson. Also, the 56th Fighter Group was now the top scoring fighter Group in the ETO, having broken the 300 kill mark.

March 9: VIII FC FO 264. No respite for the 8th Air Force, or for the enemy. The 1st and 3rd Bomb Divisions went back to Berlin, while the 2nd Bomb Division struck targets at Hannover, Brunswick and Neinberg.

Capt. Mike Quirk blew a tire upon landing from a cross-country flight on March 7, 1944 and blew a tire. As usual, the P-47 would flip up upon its nose when such things occurred, and then settle back down. LM⬤K was 42-75242, a replacement for the previous "K" 42-7992. (USAF)

March 8, 1944 and back to the "Big B" with both the 56th FG's "A" and "B" Groups. The Wolfpack scored twenty-eight destroyed, for the loss of five to the enemy. (Three killed and two POWs). "Liberty Belle" of the 61st FS P-47, belonged to an unidentified pilot, and had flak damage to its wings. (USAF)

Twenty-three fighter groups were operational, and for the first mission in weeks, VIII Fighter Command had no claims for enemy aircraft destroyed. Only one P-38 was lost over Europe. Due to a solid overcast over the continent, the Luftwaffe was held on the ground, and most of the bombers were forced to hit secondary targets.

Both "A" and "B" Groups were off on penetration support and escort duties, with "A" led by Lt. Col. Schilling and "B" by Major Stewart. "A" was off Halesworth at 1016, and "B" at 1020. They both crossed-in over Ijmuiden and made RV west of Drummer Lake, "A" with the 1st Bomb Division at 1140, and "B" with the 3rd Bomb Division at 1155. The mission was entirely uneventful, and the Groups returned at 1345.

March 14: No missions, but "Brass Hat Day." Visiting Halesworth were Lt. General Carl "Tooey" Spaatz, commanding general of the US Strategic Air Forces in Europe; Lt. General James Doolittle, commanding general of the 8th Air Force, "Widewing;" Major General William Kepner, commanding general of VIII Fighter Command, "Ajax;" and Brig. General Jesse Auton, commanding general of the Group's parent 65th Fighter Wing. Among all the congratulations and inspections that took place, Colonel Zemke was awarded the Distinguished Service Cross by General Spaatz.

March 15: VIII FC FO 269. After almost a week of weather enforced inactivity, the 56th Fighter Group was back on operations. During the pre-

LM◉S, 42-76250. Of the five LM◉S's assigned to the 62nd FS, this was the only one that Dave Schilling did not claim as his own. Flown by Wendell McClure on the March 8 mission to Berlin, it was hit in the starboard aileron by flak. (USAF)

Above: Captain Joseph Bennett, 61st FS, got an Fw 190 and two ME 109s in aerial combat on March 8, 1944. The German pilots got a few hits on him, too, but he got back okay: Battle damage to his 42-75269, HV⚙O. (USAF) Left: An example of battle damage incurred to Bennett's HV⚙O on the March 8 mission. (USAF)

over Steinhuder Lake. As the primary targets were obscured by clouds, 185 B-17s and 143 B-24s bombed the city of Brunswick, itself. Although Gabreski's 62nd FS had no encounters with enemy aircraft, themselves, when German aircraft were seen near Drummer Lake, Gabreski ordered Stewart's 61st FS and Mahurin's 63rd FS down to attack them.

Mahurin took his White Flight down to 3,000 feet to assist in breaking up the German formation of thirty plus fighters. But they had no luck. Lt. John Truluck, leading Red Flight, with Lt.'s Marvin Becker, Archie Robey and Donald Peters, stayed higher, and took on forty plus mixed Me 109s and Fw 190s that had just made a firing pass on the bombers. They chased them down to the deck and got into a swirling dogfight, with Truluck shooting at an Fw 190, an Me 109, and another Fw 190, in turn, without apparent success. Then Truluck swung in behind another Fw 190 and hit him from wingtip to wingtip. Truluck then pulled up a bit, positioned himself to shoot again as the 190 was trying to make a forced landing. He fired from only ten feet above the ground. Truluck now had his seventh and last

ceding time, Bomber and Fighter Commands had flown limited numbers of missions, mostly into France and the Low Countries, but the 56th FG was not involved in these. But on this mission, they would provide penetration support to the 2nd and 3rd Bomb Divisions headed for the heavily defended target of Brunswick.

"A" Group, led by Lt. Col. Gabreski, took off at 0850 with the 62nd Fighter Squadron in the lead. They had to orbit over the Zuider Zee because the bombers were late and then moved on to finally accomplish RV

Left: Capt. Mike Gladych damaged three Fw 190s on the ground during the course of the March 8th missions, but return fire holed his fuel tanks and he ran out of gas over England on the way home and had to bailout. (USAF) Right: The terminal result of Gladych's 42-75140, HV⚙M, "Pengie II" after hitting the ground. (USAF)

Most flak damage to fighters was minor, if they got home. More severe damage usually meant that the pilot was lost. The fighter pilot did not have the benefit of additional engines and crew members to assist him with the ensuing problems that bomber pilots had. This 63rd FS P-47 was hit in the windscreen and right wing by flak on March 8, 1944, but the damage was so minor that the pilot was unidentified. It was the personal P-47 of Lt. Gordon Batdorf, Minneapolis, MN. (USAF)

kill of the war. Lt. Archie Robey, Red Three, chased an Fw 190 down from 4,000 feet, hitting him around the cockpit, and watching him go straight into the ground. He then continued on down to intercept the German's that Truluck was mixed up with, and shot down the other Fw 190. Lt. Donald Peters, Red Four, stayed with him, and nailed the Me 109. Lt. Samuel Stamps put in a claim for an Fw 190 destroyed, but it was not upheld.

The 61st FS had the greatest success, with Lt. Robert Johnson knocking down two Fw 190s for his twentieth and twenty-first kills, and then an Me 109 on the way home, bringing his total score up to twenty-two and making him the highest scoring pilot in the Theater. A grateful Air Force promoted him to Captain upon return.

Lt. Joe Powers got an Me 109 and an Fw 190, which made him a double ace. Lt. Robert Rankin also got at Fw 190 and an Me 109, and also claimed an Me 109 as damaged and another as probably destroyed. Powers damaged another Fw 190. Flight Officer Steven Gerick got an Me 109 and damaged another. Major James Stewart, leading the squadron, claimed an Me 109 as damaged and so did Flight Officer Evan McMinn. During these encounters the P-47 of Lt. John Kozey was hit by 20mm fire in the left wing with the blast of flame burning the National insignia off of the Thunderbolt's fuselage. With a large chunk of the wing missing and his engine failing, Kozey had little choice but to bailout near Quackenbruck and spend the rest of the war as a POW.

"B" Group followed Major Gerald Johnson off at 0852, this time with only twenty-four P-47s, instead of the usual thirty-six. Landfall-in was again over Ijmuiden, where they passed one group of B-24s, and then passed over a group of B-17s over the Zuider Zee. They made RV with their intended bombers at Quackenbruck at 1015, three Combat Wings of B-17s of the 3rd Bomb Division.

West of Drummer Lake the 62nd FS had been sent down to engage some forty Me 109s and Fw 190s that were seen milling around at 6,000 feet. Lt. Fred Christensen claimed two Fw 190s destroyed and damaged two more. Capt. Michael Quirk, Lt's John Bryant, James Fields, James Jones and Mark Moseley all entered claims for Fw 190s. Jones also damaged an Fw 190.

As the 62nd FS didn't appear to need any assistance during their encounters, the remainder of "B" Group pressed on. At Drummer Lake, itself, they made "S" turns and orbited awaiting the bombers, and when they came close enough, the Group proceeded on course ahead of them. Two gaggles of German fighters were then seen approaching from the northwest. Thirty-forty in one tight formation, and twenty-thirty in the other. "B" Group intercepted these just before they reached the lead box of bombers.

Major Johnson got an Me 109 that almost blinded him when it caught on fire. He then came in behind another and hit him in the canopy and wingroots. It caught on fire and went down smoking, and then its pilot bailed out. Lt. Joseph Egan, Red One, chased an Fw 190 down to the ground,

March 8, 1944 was a dual milestone. The Wolfpack got its 300th victory, and Bud Mahurin scored a Hat Trick. Congratulations are due, and expected! (USAF)

Inside of the windscreen on the early P-47s was a panel of armored glass to protect the pilot. Later versions had a flat windshield that was constructed of the same material. The Spitfire mirror idea was brought to the Wolfpack's attention by Lt. John Vogt and adopted by many pilots. (USAF)

1st Lt. Felix Williamson racked up thirteen air-to-air kills between November 1943 and February 1945. This photograph was taken at the end of his first tour when he had actually scored three, plus two .5 kills. (via Davis)

42-22772 became assigned to Lt. Anthony Cavello when it came to the Wolfpack's inventory on November 18, 1943 as a replacement aircraft. He named it "El Diablo" and "Eleanor III." (via Davis)

Another view of Cavello's "El Diablo," UN⊕G (bar). He had three kills with this Jug. (via Davis)

Major Leslie Smith's Jug was "Silver Lady," 42-26044, HV❖Z (bar). Smith had seven accredited kills. (via Davis)

and left him at 500 feet, still in an inverted position, where it had no chance of being recovered. Lt. Frank Klibbe and Capt. Leslie Smith scored for the 61st FS, with each getting an Fw 190. For Klibbe, this was his fifth kill, and he too joined the Group's ranks of aces.

March 16: VIII FC FO 270. Again, over six hundred Thunderbolts were up on bomber support missions. The 1st Bomb Division went to Augsburg, while the 3rd BD headed for Friedrichshafen. These targets in southern Germany would require an awful long time over enemy territory, and poor weather conditions did not help at all. Many of the bomb groups had to drop on secondary targets, and seven bombers had to put down in Switzerland with battle damage. The P-47 groups claimed 25-3-17, with the 56th Fighter Group claiming 11-1-5, for no losses.

"A" Group was off at 0911 behind Col. Zemke with thirty-six P-47s. Three aborted, and one additional returned as an escort for them. They made RV over Chalons at 1026 with the 1st Task Force, and just after RV

a gaggle of mixed Me 109s and Fw 190s was seen ahead of the B-17s. Col. Zemke attacked with White Flight from the 63rd Fighter Squadron and Lt. Anthony Cavallo, White Three, put in a claim for a damaged, but later withdrew it. Proceeding on course, another gaggle of thirty plus German fighters was seen coming in from the north. They made a 180 degree turn prior to starting an attack on the bombers, and over St. Dizler the 62nd FS pounced upon them. Lt. Arlington Canizares knocked down an Me 109 and shared another with Capt. Leroy Schreiber that they hit over Nancy in combat that ranged between 20,000 and 7,000 feet. Schreiber also got an Fw 190 over the St. Dizler airdrome. Lt. Felix Williamson got an Fw 190. Lt. Mark Boyle claimed an Fw 190 as a probable, and Lt. Charles Ginn damaged one on the ground at Burvinnes airdrome. Lt. Joe Powers, 61st FS, destroyed one Me 109 and damaged an Fw 190. Four of the P-47s that returned had minor battle damage, and the mission was back at 1235.

"B" Group followed Lt. Col. Gabreski off at 0919. They flew a similar course, making landfall-in north of Dunkirk at 0958 and RV north of

Even though the Luftwaffe was held on the ground, because of the weather, on March 9, German antiaircraft gunners were not hampered by clouds. Lt. Colonel Gabreski had his HV❖A 42-75510 hit in the wing by flak. (USAF)

Returning from an uneventful mission did not necessarily mean that everything was without event, as Lt. George Lovett, 63rd FS, found when he stood his P-47 on its nose on March 9, 1944. Lovett was killed on a local training flight six weeks later in this same P-47, UN❖T, 42-75137. (USAF)

Captain James Carter was another World War II Wolfpack pilot that would return to the Group in the Post War years. He had six accredited air-to-air kills. He is sitting in the cockpit of Major Leslie Smith's fighter. (via Davis)

March 14, 1944 and all the dignitaries descended on Halesworth to inspect the Wolfpack and bestow honors. Lt. Col. Gabreski is escorting Lt. General William Kepner, Commanding Officer, VIII Fighter Command, around the flightline on a tour of the base. (USAF)

Captain Robert Johnson, America's top ace at the time, discusses tactics with Lt. General Kepner, while Colonel Zemke makes sure that Johnson say's the right words. In the background is Lt. Harold "Bunny" Comstock. (USAF)

Major Gerald Johnson, Commanding Officer 63rd FS and Brig. General Jessie Auton, commander of the Wolfpack's parent 65th Fighter Wing. Both were from Kentucky. (USAF)

Captain Walker Mahurin, General's Doolittle and Auton, and Captain Joseph Bennett. Lt. General James Doolittle became the Commanding General of the 8th Air Force in January 1944. He died in the fall of 1993 as one of the World's true heros. (USAF)

General Doolittle, Colonel Zemke and Captain Robert Lamb. At the time, Lamb was Operations Officer of the 63rd FS, and would become their squadron commander on March 28, 1944 when "Jerry" Johnson became a POW. (USAF)

Capt. Robert Johnson and his scoreboard, effective March 15, 1944 when he got a "triple." he would add five more before completing his missions and an extension. (via Davis)

Major George Bostwick was the last wartime commander of the 63rd Fighter Squadron. He has eight accredited air kills, and seven more on the ground when this photo was taken, his final tally. (USAF)

Captain Donald Renwick (left), Lt. Norman Brooks and Captain Gabreski. Renwick had one air-to-air score, Brooks two, and Gabreski was running up his score. Note Gabby's RAF Mae West. (USAF)

Captain Gerald "Jerry" Johnson. His P-47 was "In The Mood," HV⊙D, 42-7877 when he was in the 61st Fighter Squadron. He became the Commanding Officer of the 63rd FS for six weeks before he was shot down on May 12, 1944 and became a POW. Post war Johnson commanded the 62nd FS before getting his own Group. (USAF)

Flight Officer Even McMinn's P-47 was also hit by flak (below left) on the March 15 mission. The fuselage, engine cowling and elevators all suffered flak damage, while the prop (below right) was nicked by a bullet. McMinn, in exchange, damaged an Me 109. (USAF)

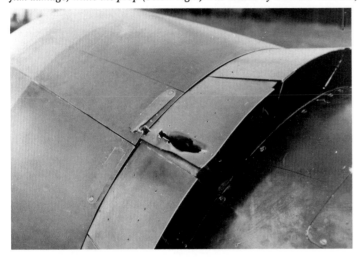

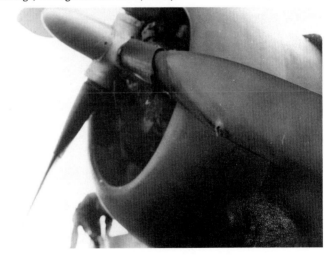

Vitry along the Marne Canal at 1032 with the 1st Task Force. Just east of St. Dizler "B" Group engaged thirty plus Fw 190s that were sitting up above the bombers at 30,000 feet. In individual combats that took them from the troposphere to the ground pilots from the 61st and 62nd FS claimed 7-1-0, with the 63rd FS not having any encounters at all while they provided top cover for the other squadrons.

From the 62nd FS, Lt. Fred Christensen claimed two while Lt.'s Stanley Morrill and Thaddeus Buszko each claimed one. Lt. James Jones claiming the probable. "Gabby" Gabreski destroyed two and Flight Officer Evan McMinn got another for the 61st FS. All of these downed German fighters were Fw 190s. None of the twenty-one participating P-47s on this mission were scratched, and they returned at 1240.

March 18: VIII FC FO 273. Five hundred-eleven B-17s and two hundred twenty-seven B-24s were effective on missions to Munich and Friedrichshafen by the 3rd and 2nd Bomb Divisions. Of the six hundred Thunderbolts dispatched, the 56th Fighter Group was tasked with providing withdrawal support for these Big Friends.

"A" Group was off Halesworth at 1348 behind Col. Zemke. They

entered the continent at 1324 climbing through 13,500 feet over Ostend. Over Rambervillers at 1516, RV with the returning bombers was made. Other than a pair of Fw 190s that were chasing a straggler, and were driven off, no other German fighters were seen. One P-47 received minor flak damage, and they returned at 1731.

"B" Group followed Lt. Col. Gabreski off at 1412 and they crossed into Europe over Ostend twenty minutes behind "A" Group. They made RV over Luneville at 1535. A single Fw 190 was seen east of Avesnes, which was downed by Lt. Joe Powers after Lt. Samuel Hamilton had expended all of his ammunition on it without effect. As this flight from the 61st FS was setting course for home, another Fw 190 was sighted, and Powers went after it, but by now he too was out of ammunition. In a feint, Powers pulled above and along side of it, and then started to dive on it. The Fw 190 pilot, tried to turn into his antagonist but he was too low and he struck a hilltop, shedding many pieces, including his prop. As the Fw 190 bounced back into the air, Lt. Dale Stream fired on it, and the German pilot made a hasty bailout. One might think that the claim would be shared, but Stream was given sole credit. Powers' didn't care, as he now had an even dozen credits, himself.

On a Ramrod to Brunswick on March 15, 1944 Lt. James Fields, 62nd FS, shot down an Fw 190. While this was taking place, he had both flaps holed by flak. The damage was repaired, and on March 27 Field's would be shot down in this aircraft to become a POW. (USAF)

UN✪V (bar) "Pat" was a P-47D-21RA assigned to the 63rd Fighter Squadron. Photographed over the North sea, its pilot is unidentified. (via Davis)

The March 15 mission, itself, was a Ramrod to Augsburg, and Lt. Arlington Canizares shot down an Me 109 and shared another with Captain Leroy Schreiber. Canizares' P-47 was hit by return fire in its right wing. (USAF)

Capt. Schreiber's P-47, LM✪T, 42-22537, was hit by flak on the mission. Schreiber also downed an Fw 190 during the course of events. (USAF)

Lt. Frank Newell was flying LM✪A, 42-75178, and he too was hit by flak on the Ramrod to Augsburg. All of the battle damaged aircraft were from "A" Group on this mission, while "B" Group was unscathed. (USAF)

LM&N, 42-74664 was flown by an unidentified pilot on the March 16 mission. It too had flak damage to its right wing. Repaired, it was assigned to the 5th Emergency Rescue Squadron as 5F✪U and was written-off as a result of a collision while landing on August 8. (USAF)

Bud Mahurin, with Lt. Fred Windmayer on the right, and two other pilots discuss the "plan" for a training mission on March 17, 1944.

Dave Schilling, Robert Landry and "Whisky" Wisniewski pose in front of Landry's "Lousiana Pirate," UN❂W, 42-75109. This Jug was also used by John Vogt. (via Davis)

March 20: VIII FC FO 275. The 1st and 3rd Bomb Division B-17s went to Frankfurt, the 2nd Bomb Division B-24s went to Braided, all with the intention of bombing Luftwaffe possessions. Weather conditions caused the recall of many of the bomber groups. VIII FC sent seven P-47 groups out (Along with other types, of course.), on escort services.

"B" Group was off first on this mission, at 0929. Major Gerald Johnson led. In over Le Treport at 18,000 feet, they RV'd with the 3rd Combat Wing of the 3rd Bomb Division at Amines. As the bombers entered the clouds near Charleville visual contact with them was lost, and never regained. The formation leader stated that he was going to lead the bombers down to a lower altitude, but radio contact kept getting weaker, and soon it was lost entirely. It was assumed that they aborted the mission. Between Charleville and Lenguyen a formation of between twenty-five and thirty Me 109s was seen at 18,000 feet heading north. These were jumped by Major Stewart's 61st FS, who fought them all the way down to fifty feet above the ground before loosing them in fog and clouds. But in the process, Stewart shot down two of them, and shared another with Lt. Dale Stream, while Stream got another by himself. (Official credit was not given to Stewart and Stream for the shared kill. These were the last accredited claims for both pilots, as Stewart soon finished his operational tour, with a total of 11.5 credits, and Stream was killed two days later).

"A" Group did not takeoff until 1209, to provide withdrawal support for the returning heavies. Lt. Col. Gabreski leading them into the sky at 1209. By this time a solid overcast was over Europe between 8,000 and 30,000 feet. They went in near Ostend and penetrated to near Brussels, but could not find any bombers to escort. The mission returned by flights and landed at 1401.

March 22: VIII FC FO 277. All three bomb divisions went to Berlin, covered by three P-47 groups from IX Fighter Command and seven from VIII FC. For the first time the 56th Fighter Group would also dispatch a "C" Group. It would prove to be a costly day for the 56th Fighter Group with little to show for it.

"A" Group followed Col. Zemke on a penetration support mission, becoming airborne at 1019 with thirty-six P-47s. Landfall-in was made over the Vlieland Islands at 1106. At Heligeland at 1146 they passed over elements of the 2nd Bomb Wing (B-24s) and accomplished RV with 1st Task Force B-17s southwest of Rendsberg at 1205. Escort was broken-off at Hagenow a half hour later. On the way out some low-level strafing was done, with Lt. John Fields, 62nd Fighter Squadron, destroying a locomotive near Meppen and Col. Zemke and Flight Officer Evan McMinn, 61st FS, destroying another loco and two box cars east of the Rhine River. "A" Group landed at 1412.

"B" Group was off at 1032, also on penetration support, led by Capt. Leroy Schreiber. About fifteen minutes after takeoff a flight from the 61st FS was climbing through a cloud deck that started at 5,500 feet. Something went wrong, and Lt.'s Donald Funcheon, Claude Mussey and Dale Stream all disappeared into the North Sea.

"B" Group continued into Europe, making landfall-in and RV over Heide at 1225 with the 3rd Bomb Division that "were considerably strung out." No German aircraft were seen during the escort, which was terminated at 1250. On the way out, "B" Group also went strafing. While strafing a train near Meppen, which was damaged by Lt.'s Dick Mudge and Herbert Holtmeyer, 61st FS. Two P-47s were hit by flak. Lt. Thaddeus Buszko, 62nd FS, receiving a cut on his forehead. Just prior to making landfall-out over Ijmuiden elements from the 61st FS decided to strafe a flak tower, which cost them another pilot. Lt. Melvin Wood had made a firing pass on the tower, pulled up, announced that he had been hit, ". . . and then fell off behind a hill. No chute seen." Wood did survive as a POW, however.

"C" Group went off on an area support mission at 1312 behind Lt. Col. Gabreski. The Group was composed of eight P-47s from the 61st and 63rd FS's. They crossed-in over Zandvoort at 1312 and made RV with returning bombers over Steinhudder Lake at 1354. Since there was no evidence of the Luftwaffe this day, they escorted a B-17 out as far as the coast and then broke escort and went strafing. Capt. James Carter, 61st FS, damaged a Ju 88 on the ground, along with a locomotive. Lt. Col. Gabreski damaged three, while Carter and Lt. Smith shared in shooting up a couple more.

March 23: VIII FC FO 278. The heavies went to Brunswick and Munster, along with a few other selected targets. All fighter groups were operational, including four from IX Fighter Command.

"B" Group took off from Halesworth at 0902 behind Lt. Col. Gabreski to provide penetration, target and withdrawal support. For this mission they only dispatched twenty-four P-47s. RV was made over Drummer Lake at 1020 with B-24s of the 2nd Bomb Division, which were escorted to their targets, and then out to Schouwen Island. At this point escort was broken with them, and "B" Group turned back inland to pick up returning B-17s, which were also escorted out as far as Schouwen Island. Uneventfully, they returned at 1230.

"A" Group was off ten minutes later behind Col. Zemke with thirty-five Thunderbolts with the same task ahead of them. RV was made at Osnabruck at 22,000 feet at 1038. The heavies were escorted for an hour, and out to the Dutch Islands before escort was broken. Only Bud Mahurin, leading the 63rd FS, had a shot at an enemy aircraft. Mahurin had seen a

Lt. Ray Kuhn and "Fireball." UN⬤K, 44-21225, it was shared by Kuhn and Russ Kyler. (via Davis)

Lt. Dale Stream's P-47 HV⬤P (bar) was damaged on the lower fuselage and landing gear doors during the Ramrod for the 3rd Bomb Division on March 20, 1944. During mission Stream shot down an Me 109, and shared another claim with Major Stewart, which was not credited. Dale Stream was killed two days later in 42-8461, HV⬤P. (USAF)

single Me 109 attacking a straggling B-17 and went to the Fort's assistance. Unfortunately he could not get there quick enough, and the B-17 went down. The Me 109 escaped into the haze. The mission landed at 1255.

March 24: VIII FC FO 279. Thunderbolt groups sent up 301 P-47s from four VIII FC and one from IX FC on escort for the 1st and 2nd Bomb Divisions. All other P-47 groups being grounded because of the weather over England.

"B" Group, behind Col. Zemke, was off at 0737 to provide penetration support. The prescribed route was flown as well as could be determined by their navigational techniques and equipment, but the weather was so bad that any accurate positioning could not be ascertained. They provided escort for the lead box of B-17s of the 1st Bomb Division enroute to the ball bearing factories at Schweinfurt. Then they proceeded as far with them as the Rhine River, they believed, and then turned for home. With Direction Finding assistance provided by "Darkey," they landed at 1053.

"A" Group had to abort the mission, as the weather had closed in over Halesworth before they could get off the ground.

March 27: VIII FC FO 282. All three Bomb Divisions went to targets in France to bomb Luftwaffe installations. Over seven hundred Thunderbolts from VIII and IX Fighter Command's were along on escort missions. P-47 pilots claimed 6-0-2, with the 56th Fighter Group claiming four destroyed. If the losses of March 22 were bad, today's losses would really sap the Group's morale, although they did not know at the time that three of the four downed pilots survived.

Lt. Col. David Schilling took "B" Group off at 1241 to provide target and withdrawal support to the 4th Air Task Force bombing Chartres and Tours. They crossed-in at St. Valery at 1329 at 15,000 feet, far below their usual penetration altitude. RV was made over the Loire River, near Saumer at 1354. Escort was provided until 1435, where they were southeast of Le Mans.

They then proceed to Chartres where the 63rd Fighter Squadron was to provide top cover for the 62nd FS that was going to go down and strafe. About fifteen miles southeast of Chartres Bud Mahurin spotted a Do 217 and went after it. Mahurin fired, and then left it to the rest of his flight to work over. Four parachutes were seen to come out of it before it crashed. (The credit was shared by Mahurin and Lt.'s Willard Johnson, Isadore Porowski and Samuel Lowman. This was Lowman's sole claim).

After Mahurin had pulled away from his second pass on the Dornier, he stated on the radio that he had been hit and would have to take it easy. A

Major Lucian Dade was an aggressive and determined leader. He was credited with three air-to-air kills. (via Davis)

2nd Lt Robert Cherry did not score in the morning conflict, but a Luftwaffe pilot could claim a "damaged" on him. Cherry's P-47 was hit in the fuselage, prop and left wing by 20mm fire.

few seconds later fire was seen trailing from his P-47s supercharger duct. Mahurin bailed out, at about eight hundred feet, which permitted only four swings in his parachute, before landing in an open field about a mile from where his P-47 crashed. He was seen to run into a wooded area, wave, and disappear into the trees. He evaded capture and returned to England. Later he was assigned to the Pacific theatre and would fly another combat tour there.

Schilling took the 62nd FS down to strafe the airdrome at Chateaudun, where he destroyed a Ju 52 on the ground. Lt. James Fields' was hit by flak while strafing and had to belly land his burning "Jug." As Fields' was seen to run away from the burning aircraft, Lt. Robert Cherry made a strafing run on it, to make sure that it was completely destroyed. Fields' was soon captured and spent the rest of the war as a POW. Lt. Wiley Merrill also got hit by flak, and was wounded on his left wrist. With his electrical and hydraulic systems out, he struggled back to England. Upon landing Merrill

ran off the end of the runway and his P-47 flipped over, but the built-in crash bar prevented further injury to him.

"A" Group did not take off until 1354 on a withdrawal support mission. Led By Lt. Col. Gabreski and the 61st FS, they crossed-in at Fecamp at 1454, and made RV with the returning 3rd Division B-17s at La Reche at 1530. Over the Loire River, northeast of Nantes, a pair of Me 109s were seen, so Gabreski went after them and destroyed them both. These were his seventeenth and eighteenth kills.

Escort was broken off at 1640 and the Group broke into flights and elements to seek targets of opportunity on the way home. Major Gerald Johnson, 63rd FS, led his White Flight down to strafe some trucks. The flight, composed of Johnson, and Lt.'s Everet Everett and Archie Robey had just completed a pass on a line of trucks and were heading for home when someone called out a position on some more trucks entering the town of Conde. They overflew the town at a thousand feet in an attempt to find

Captain Ray Dauphin was a part of "B" Group that took off at noon to provide withdrawal support for the March 20 Ramrod, but since the weather had curtailed the bombers efforts, the mission was, basically, uneventful. The German AA guns didn't not know this and fired anyway. Dauphin's LM✪D, 42-75160. (USAF)

UN◉A, "Huckle De Buck" with D-Day "Invasion Stripes." Initially, the black and white bands circled both the fuselage and the wings. Later on, they were removed from the wings upper surfaces and the top of the fuselage. (via Davis)

the trucks and came under anti-aircraft fire. Robey was hit by .303 and 20mm fire, and caught up with Johnson to tell him of his plight just as Johnson announced that he to had been hit and was going to have to make a crash landing.

Johnson set his P-47 down in a field between Isigny and Carenten and was seen to get out of the cockpit and then set his parachute on fire inside of the cockpit. Robey called the Group's Command Post, Yardstick, and informed them that Johnson was down and asked if he could, or should, make an attempt to land in the field and try to pick Johnson up.

On March 22 the 56th FG launched all three of their made up "A," "B" and "C" Groups. After their parts of the Ramrods were over, the groups went train busting. Capt. James Carter, 61st FS, destroyed a locomotive, but got hit by both flak and a 20mm shell in the process. The open door below the canopy is the baggage compartment. (USAF)

On the train-busting portion of the mission, Lt. Herbert Holtmeier, 61st FS, was flying Mike Quirk's (62nd FS) LM❂K 42-75242, and got a wing holed by flak.

Robey dropped his landing gear in the attempt, but could not get his flaps down because his hydraulic system had been hit by flak, so he had to give up on the idea. Everett then made an attempt to get into the field, but he clipped a tree with his wing and also had to abandon the idea. Then Robey discovered that his landing gear would only retract to the half way point, so under escort by Everett, they headed for home over Aromanches, where they were both hit by small arms fire. About five miles off the coast, Everett said he was going to have to turn back and attempt to ditch his Thunderbolt. Robey told him to bailout instead. Robey then called Air Search and Rescue and alerted them. They had a launch in the area, but they failed to find the downed pilot. Everett was drowned. Johnson became a POW.

Robey struggled to the RAF base at Ford to attempt an emergency landing. His prop was in fixed pitch and he had no flaps. He did manage to get his landing gear down again, but he had no brakes. Then he got cut out of the traffic pattern by a pair of Mustangs and had to make a second attempt to try to get his sick Jug down again. As he landed, his engine froze up, and he skidded off the runway, but he was not injured.

March 28: VIII FC FO 283. The heavies went back to hit the Luftwaffe bases in France once again. The 56th Fighter Group only flew one mission this day, a Type 16 control mission to provide area support for the three Bomb Divisions on their return.

Airborne at 1435 with Lt. Col. Schilling leading forty-nine Thunderbolts, they made landfall-in over Cayeux at 1511 at 18,000 feet. Then they were vectored by the controller to Amines, Paris, Evereux and finally to Beauvais where RV with the Big Friends of the 2nd Task Force that had attacked Dijon and Reims was accomplished. The bombers were shepherded home by the 62nd and 63rd Fighter Squadrons's, while the 61st FS made one more sweep towards Paris before returning. No German aircraft were seen at all, and the mission landed at 1720.

March 29: VIII FC FO 284. The 1st Bomb Division went to Brunswick and were provided escort by five P-47 Groups.

Preceding the main 56th Fighter Group units, Col. Zemke, Capt. Michael Gladych and Lt. Archie Robey went in ten minutes ahead of them on a freelance mission. Zemke chased a diving Me 109, but blacked out during the dogfighting. Lt. Robey chased it some more, but neither made a claim on it. They then went strafing and Robey destroyed a locomotive while Gladych and Zemke each damaged one, along with shooting up some railroad installations and a oil dump.

As the fighters were being prepared for the day's missions a tragedy occurred near Halesworth at 1045 when a pair of B-24s from the 93rd Bomb Group collided as they were forming up to proceed on their own mission into Europe. At approximately 1120 a 2000 pound bomb in one of the burning hulks exploded while attempts were underway to recover the bodies of the fallen airmen. Many of the men from the 56th Fighter Group were participating in these efforts, and Lt. Stanley Morrill and Cpl. Benny Cala from the 62nd FS were killed in the explosion. Another seventeen GI's were killed and thirty-eight injured, along with four civilians. The 2010th Engineers were decimated, while the 15th Station Complement Squadron and the 33rd Service Group, all of which were supporting units for the 56th FG, had heavy casualties.

"A" Group, behind Lt. Col. Gabreski was off at 1252 with forty P-47s. They crossed-in over Ijmuiden at 1333 to provide withdrawal escort for the returning heavies. RV was made at 1410 northwest of Neinberg. At this time six to eight Me 109s came in on them from the southeast at their altitude, 23,000 feet. Lt. Robert Rankin, 61st Fighter Squadron destroying one of them. North of Drummer Lake nine plus more Me 109s came in on them at 26,000 feet out of the sun, but no claims were made during the ensuing encounter that took them all the way down to the deck. After this, they too went strafing, and Lt. Edward Sisson, 61st FS, damaged a train.

"B" Group took off ten minutes behind "A" Group with twenty-four P-47s behind Lt. Col. Schilling. RV was made over Sulingen at 1425 with four Combat Wings of returning Flying Fortress's. The Forts were being chased by a dozen Me 109s that were attacking them from the east. "B" Group interceded and Lt. Col. Schilling shot down one and damaged another, which made him the Group's newest "double ace" with ten and a half accredited kills. "B" Group landed at 1619.

April 1: VIII FC FO 286. The 2nd and 3rd Bomb Divisions went to Ludwigshaven and other targets in southern Germany, or at least they tried to. Heavy weather encountered over France caused the recall of many of the bombers, while the same weather created navigational problems for the remainder. Several bomb groups got off course by as many as a hundred miles, and one group bombed Switzerland by mistake. An error that cost the US taxpayers a million dollars in the form of an apology.

"A" Group followed Col. Zemke off at 0818 with thirty-two P-47s. Takeoff times were getting earlier each day as the days were getting longer. In over Knocke at 0858, they were supposed to escort B-17s, but the 3rd Division was recalled, so they went to Namur and picked up some B-24s, which were escorted as far as Marches. A couple of German fighters were seen in the air, but not encountered.

On the way home the 61st Fighter Squadron dropped down to inspect a suspected dummy airdrome northeast of Lille, and seven fake Ju 88s were spotted in a field. Then they flew to near Valenciennes, where they saw a dozen mixed single and twin-engine fighters parked. Flak was too heavy to mess with them, as the P-47 flown by Lt. Thomas Owens was hit on the first look-see. Owen's pulled up to 1,000 feet with flames pouring out of his supercharger duct, rolled over and dove straight in. He was killed.

"B" Group was led by Capt. Robert Lamb, the new squadron commander of the 63rd Fighter Squadron. Lamb led them off at 0827 and they made landfall-in over Ostend at 0905. RV was accomplished just south of Ostend with four Combat Wings of B-24s and they were escorted for a half hour, with escort being terminated southwest of Trier. No enemy aircraft were encountered and they returned home at 1120.

April 5: VIII FC FO 288. The 8th Air Force decided to hit the Luftwaffe hard on the ground this day. Only three 2nd Bomb Division B-24 groups and one P-47 fighter group went after strategic targets, while all the other fighter groups went to Luftwaffe airdromes in Germany on a mission known as Jackpot I. The new long-range Mustang really showed its stuff, as they accounted for 96-4-120 German aircraft destroyed, almost all on the ground. P-47 pilots claimed but 2-0-2.

Major Schreiber led "A" Group off at 1331, while Lt. Col. Schilling led "B" Group off at 1338. A total of forty-eight P-47s. The mission plan called for a strafing sweep on Eschwege, Husum and Schleswig airdromes, but the encountered weather made navigation so difficult that they had to give up on attacking those targets. "A" Group swept in over The Hague, where Schreiber's P-47 was hit by flak, but they kept going on to southeast of Arnheim, south to Ans, where they saw a pair of Me 210s, but the Germans ducked into clouds and evaded. They then crossed out over Schouwen Islands.

"B" Group went in over Terschilling Island, where Lt. Samuel Lowman's Thunderbolt was hit by flak, but he was not injured. They "stooged around" for awhile, and RTB'd at 1547.

The only real event of the mission was that it was the last one for Capt. Harold "Bunny" Comstock. He had reached the magic 200 combat hour mark and was eligible for rotation home. Comstock had three kills, one probable, and four damaged. Although not an ace (At this point.), Comstock was pretty well known, for back in December 1943 he and the deceased Capt. Roger Dyar had reached compressibility in their P-47s over Long Island. They had registered 725 mph on their air speed indicators, and the unknowing believed that they had broken the sound barrier. A big to-do was made of it at the time.

April 8: VIII FC FO 291. The three Bomb Divisions went to targets in Germany and the fighter groups were out on escort missions, and then sought targets of opportunity on the ground.

"A" Group followed Col. Zemke off at 1224 to provide target and withdrawal support for the heavies, and then a Rodeo. RV was made over Drummer Lake and the 3rd Bomb Division B-17s were followed to Hesepe, where the bombing looked good to the fighter pilots. Zemke sent his Red Flight, 63rd Fighter Squadron, down to strafe, so (Now) Capt. John Truluck, Lt.'s Sam Dale and Isadore Porowski went down and damaged a pair of locomotives. They were about to strafe Hesepe airdrome, but got beat out by the 62nd FS so they went home. Major Leroy Schreiber, 62nd FS, and Lt. Arlington Canizares shared an Me 410 and an Me 109. Capt. James Jones got a Ju 88, all on the ground. The 61st FS strafed at Salzbergen, where Major Stewart blew up either an ammo dump or gas storage dump. It exploded so violently that he couldn't tell which it had been, but the explosion was powerful enough to damage his aircraft. Lt. Edward Sisson shot up a hanger while they were there.

"B" Group was led by Lt. Col. Gabreski and they were off Halesworth at 1251. They crossed-in over Egmond at 1334 and made RV with 1st Bomb Division B-17s at Oldenburg, their target, at 1413. Escort was broken at 1510 over Egmond. They turned around there and picked up a straggling B-17 that they then escorted across the North Sea, and RTB'd at 1555.

April 9: VIII FC FO 292. Bomber Command sent the heavies out in force, over 540 B-17s and B-24s, but only four hundred were effective. Once again, weather was a major factor that reduced the numbers over the targets.

"A" Group followed Lt. Col. Schilling at 0908 to provide penetration support for B-24s of the 2nd Bomb Division, 1st Task Force, heading for Tutow. RV was made thirty miles northwest of Husum, and they crossed-in over Husum. They provided escort to northeast of Eckernfurde.

Enroute, two groups of twenty each Luftwaffe fighters came in on them in the vicinity of Kappeln, and engagements with the 61st and 62nd Fighter Squadrons took place while the 63rd FS flew cover. Lt. Col. Schilling destroyed two Fw 190s and damaged a third. Capt. Charles Harrison damaged an Me 109, while Lt. Wendell McClure damaged an Fw 190, all flying with the 62nd FS. Capt. Robert Johnson, 61st FS, got an Fw 190, while Lt. Samuel Hamilton, Johnson's wingman got an Fw 190 and damaged another over the Baltic Sea.

Schilling's Combat Report: "My wingman (Lt. Wendell A. McClure) and I had become separated from the Group when we sighted a gaggle of between 30 and 35 Fw-190s flying a tight formation and circling to the right at 21,000 feet about twenty miles northeast of Schleswig.

UN⬧E (bar) was assigned to Joe Egan. Details on its belly landing are unknown. (via Davis)

"The Greek," 42-7866, LM⬧G, was lost on September 5, 1944 over England, due to a faulty prop control. (via Davis)

Thaddeus Buszko normally flew a Thunderbolt named "Flack Sack," but he flew LM⦿E (bar), 42-75125, on March 22, 1944 and brought "Hakkey" back with battle damage to its windscreen. (USAF)

"We immediately swung around to the rear of the formation and sneaked in range from the underneath and the outside. I opened fire from about three hundred yards with about a ten-degree deflection from above and immediately saw strikes all over the aircraft. I continued firing until I had closed to 150 yards when I pulled up violently to avoid a collision with particles from the aircraft, which had exploded. Several pieces struck my aircraft, knocking two holes in the leading edge of my right wing and one in the blister of the canopy. Immediately following this, several of the rear-end Charlies saw my wingman and I flick-rolled to the deck. I picked another target at about a 30 degree deflection at about 300 yards and opened fire. He saw me, turned right, rolled and went down. I saw several strikes and followed him to 15,000 feet, where I broke off and climbed back up. I then saw my wingman diving on the tail of a Fw-190 as I rejoined the rear end of the formation. By this time they had me spotted and split into two formations, half of them getting behind me.

"I flicked, hit the switch, and went down. At about 12,000 feet I overboosted my engine due to excessive rpm and blew a cylinder head, causing a lot of oil and smoke to come out of the left side of my engine.

"I had no sooner hit the deck, with everything cut back trying to stop the smoke, when I saw two Fw-190s ahead, turning to the left. I was still indicating over 400 (mph) and lined him up from about 380 yards with a ten-degree deflection. I noticed a large concentration of strikes on the wing roots, cockpit and canopy. As I passed over him, he pulled up steeply to the left, winged over, and went straight in and exploded, leaving a large column of smoke.

"I continued on course out and happened across a lake several miles southeast of Schleswig, saw a Arado 196 on floats ahead and fired at it from about 900 yards. I undershot but raised my sights and hit it squarely with a heavy concentration of strikes all over it. It began to smoke just as I passed over it.

Another flat tire caused the damage to 42-75283, LM⦿J (bar). It was flown on a training flight by a Lt. Pfliger, VIII Service Command, on March 26, 1944. (USAF)

"After I crossed the lake, I saw a JU-234 [sic] ahead and slightly to the right preparing to land at Schleswig airdrome. I was over-eager and fired too soon, and only got about five to seven hits before I ran out of ammunition. I then proceeded out on course and saw a Fw 190 firing at me from about 500 yards. I figured that excessive pressure would set the accessory section on fire but took the chance. As I did so, smoke and oil again poured out of the cowling, and the Fw 190 pulled up to my right and turned back. I waited until he was out of sight and then cut back to 1800 (rpm) and 29 inches (of mercury). The fire stopped and I figured I might make it. Shortly after I had crossed out, I saw Heligoland out ahead and to my right and turned left, but due to the haze almost flew over a large convoy led by three destroyers. I turned right and figured that I could get between them. They must have been asleep because I was past the two of them before they opened up, and then they shot everything from both places.

"After getting out of range, I called the boys and told them of my predicament, speed, course, and time I passed (the enemy coast going) out. The trip home was uneventful."

After escort was broken, the squadrons sought targets on the ground. Red Flight of the 63rd FS damaged a locomotive and a trawler, along with a high speed launch. They RTB'd at 1357.

"B" Group was off at 0923 with twenty-four P-47s following Lt. Col. Gabreski. They made RV with a box of B-17s off Nordstond Island, and ten minutes after RV they spotted a dozen Me 109s in the distance, about 8,000 feet above them. Since their originally intended B-17s had aborted the mission, and the B-17s they were presently were with were already protected by another group of P-47s, Gabreski took "B" Group after the Messerschmitts. They climbed to 30,000 feet, but the Me 109s remained four thousand feet above them and would not come down, and the heavy Jugs could not climb up to them, so they had to forget the idea.

They turned back to parallel the bombers course, and soon spotted two gaggles of mixed Me 109s and Fw 190s. One was a group of eight to twelve, and the other composed of twenty. The 62nd Fighter Squadron went after these, and Capt. Leroy Schreiber got an Me 109 and probably another. Capt. Joe Powers got an Fw 190. The 61st FS then joined in and Capt. Tadeusz Andersz got an Me 109, and so did Capt. Leslie Smith.

Smith: "I was going too fast to stay behind (the Me 109) long and as I went by I saw the canopy fly off. I came so close to the plane I could look into the open cockpit and see the pilot." Smith circled on it twice more and saw the German pilot bailout before the aircraft crashed and exploded.

After breaking escort they went to strafe, making a run over what they believed was Luneburg airdrome. Major Scheriber probably destroyed an Me 109 and damaged two more. On a lake east of Schleswig five seaplanes and a flying boat were seen. "Gabby" Gabreski damaged an He 115 and shared in the destruction of a large four-engine flying boat that was similar in appearance to the China Clipper.

"Gabby" had this to say: "We encountered a tremendous amount of light small arms fire from the banks of the lake, which we caught head on. I never saw so many tracers in all my life. For a minute after the attack all I could visualize were red tracers meeting me head-on. The light stuff scared the hell out of me, but I venture to say that those eight fifties scared the living daylights out of about twenty-five gunners as I sprayed the length of the bank."

Sharing in the destruction of the flying boat was Lt. Harold Matthews, 63rd FS. Lt. Warren Kerr got an Arado 196, while Lt. Walter Frederick got an He 115 and damaged another.

On the way home one of those more unfortunate things of war occurred. Lt. Anthony Canizares, 62nd FS, ran out of fuel while crossing the English Channel. He bailed out, but struck the tail of his P-47 in the process. Air-Sea Rescue picked him up, but he died soon thereafter as a result of his injuries and exposure.

April 10: VIII FC FO 293. Bomber Command selected targets in France and the Low Countries for the day's targets for the three Bomb Divisions.

"A" Group was off at 0818 behind Col. Zemke to give target and withdrawal support for the 1st Air Task Force attacking Brussels and targets inside of France. They went in over Knocke, flew over Mons, Brussels, and Glize-Rijen, crossing out over the Schouwen Islands, and provided escort half way back across the North Sea before heading for home.

"B" Group took off Halesworth at 0829 to give penetration and target support to the 3rd Air Task Force attacking Charleroi. They met the first box of bombers at Ostend and circled there until the second box showed up in the vicinity of Armentieres. It was a mess, as the bombers broke into ten or fifteen smaller groups and the fighter pilots could not determine which ones they were supposed to escort. They had to content themselves with criss-crossing over Charleroi. The bombers confusion continued, as they missed their first run on the target and had to circle and come back again for another run.

Red Flight stuck with one box that went to Aostmalle, fifteen miles northeast of Antwerp, where they bombed, but two other groups that were escorted by White Flight, apparently did not bomb at all. "B" Group RTB'd at 1131.

April 11: VIII FC FO 295. Nine P-47 groups were up, including two from IX Fighter Command, to provide escort services to the three Bomb Divisions. The 56th Fighter Group, for the first time flew two missions with both their "A" and "B" Groups participating on each. Not only a tribute to the participating pilots, but to the ground crews that were able to get so many of their Thunderbolts off on the four missions. It had just been a year since their first few orientation flights across the channel, and they had gained a lot of experience and ability in the meantime.

"B" Group was up at 0846, led by Capt. Charles Clamp and the 63rd Fighter Squadron to provide penetration support for the 1st Air Division. RV was made at Zwolle and escort broken off at Drummer Lake. They crossed out over Ijmuiden and it was considered an uneventful mission.

"A" Group took off at 0907 to give penetration and withdrawal support to the 3rd Air Division. They made RV over Egmond and flew a similar route and also had an uneventful mission, landing at 1156.

"B" Group's second mission was off at 1252 and was led by Lt. Col. Schilling. They provided withdrawal escort for the heavies coming back from targets in the Baltic area. RV was made north of Eckernforde at 1413 and the Big Friends were escorted without opposition until 1450. Then they went strafing at Schleswig where Lt. Mark Boyle, 62nd Fighter Squadron, destroyed an He 115 on a lake. Three additional unidentified types, single-engine, were damaged on the ground by Boyle, Lt.'s Roy Bluhm and Wendell McClure. Dave Schilling, Lt.'s Dean Noordquest, John Eaves, McClure and Jack Greene then went to Heligoland where they sank one minesweeper and damaged three more.

"A" Group was off at 1322 behind Col. Zemke. They crossed-in over Hiede at 1510 and made RV with the bombers over Keil Bay at 1515. Escort was broken ten minutes later, and they too went down to strafe. Zemke and his wingman, Lt. Harold Matthews, 63rd FS, strafed and derailed a train north of Husum, then went after a passenger train, whose passengers bailed out of its doors and windows when they realized they were under attack. Lt.'s J. C. Wakefield and Robert Campbell shot up a marshalling yard and a radar station. Lt.'s Felix Williamson and Thaddeus Buszko destroyed and damaged another train, respectively. They RTB'd at 1720.

April 12: VIII FC FO 296. The Big Friends attempted to go to targets in France and Germany, but heavy weather conditions forced their missions to be aborted. The 56th Fighter Group went in under the weather on Rodeo sweeps.

"A" Group got off at 1306 behind Lt. Col. Gabreski, with twenty-three Thunderbolts. They made landfall-in over The Hague at 1348 and swept over Hanover, Munster, Steinhuder and Drummer Lakes, all quite uneventfully at 16,000 feet. Since the heavies were not about, the Luftwaffe, apparently, did not want to play. Although some barges, tug boats and locomotives were strafed, nothing profound occurred and they returned at 1629.

"B" Group took off at 1313 with Col. Zemke in the lead. They intended to strafe Varel, Ardorf and Hafe airdromes, but because of intense flak, these were given a pass. Along the Kusten Canal many barges were sighted and strafed, destroying and damaging quite a few. Zemke also shot up three barracks. Landfall-out was over Treschilling Island at 1556 and they landed at 1645.

April 13: VIII FC FO 298. Nine Thunderbolt groups were up, along with the other fighter types, on support missions for the three Bomb Divisions. This date marked the first anniversary for actual combat operations for the 56th and 78th Fighter Groups. Both groups would fair better today than they had on their first missions.

"A" Group was led off Halesworth at 1352 by Lt. Col. Schilling. They crossed-in over Walcheren Island at 1451 and made RV with the returning heavies from the 2nd Task Force east of Mannheim at 1553. Withdrawal support was provided until 1645 west of Koblenz.

Just after RV was accomplished five Me 109s were seen heading for the bombers. They were intercepted by Red Flight of the 62nd Fighter Squadron, Lt. Joe Powers and Mark Boyle, as well as White Flight of the 61st FS, led by Schilling. Powers damaged one Me 109, and Boyle then shot it down. Schilling claimed another as damaged, but later gun camera assessment credited him with his fourteenth kill.

This was the last combat mission for Capt. John Vogt, 63rd FS, who had been on detached service with the 65th Fighter Wing since February. He had become an ace on Feb. 22, 1944, and would take his experience to the 365th Fighter Group, where he became the squadron commander of the 360th FS. He would score three more kills while leading that squadron.

"B" Group was led by (Now) Major Lamb with eight P-47s from each squadron, also on a withdrawal support mission. Off at 1410, they crossed-in over Walcheren Island at 1451 and made RV in the area of Speyer at 1555. While escorting, a straggling B-17 was approached by three Fw 190s from below and behind, so White Flight dove on them to give the Fort a chance at survival. Capt. Robert Johnson, 61st FS, shot down two of them, his twenty-fourth and twenty-fifth kills. One German pilot bailed out, the other crashed. "B" Group RTB'd at 1751.

On the administrative side, Lt. Col. Gabreski was transferred from Headquarters 56th FG to take over the command of the 61st Fighter Squadron. Gabreski would continue in his position as Flying Executive Officer as well. Major James Stewart, having completed his combat tour, was transferred to Headquarters VIII Fighter Command.

April 15: VIII FC FO 299. Seven P-47 groups went into Europe to conduct strafing sweeps against high priority Luftwaffe airdromes, on the "Jackpot II" mission. These missions were rather aptly named, as one could either hit the jackpot and score pretty well, or miss out and take some heavy losses, or as the 56th Fighter Group discovered, do both. These pre D-Day missions only portended the heavy losses that the fighters (and later fighter-bomber) missions would incur on the low-level "air-to-mud" strikes. "B" Group took off at 1218 with twenty-four Thunderbolts behind Lt. Col. Gabreski. Two P-47s aborted, and one returned with them as an escort. Landfall-in was over the Meldorf area at 1345 at 20,000 feet. They swept Stade Neumunster, Keil, Schleswig, Albertdorf and made landfall-out in elements and flights over St. Peter and Wesselbures a hour later.

While passing over Swade they observed fifty to sixty German aircraft on the ground that were being worked over by another squadron. Then they saw a group of Fw 190s approaching, with seven flying in line-abreast formation and three more struggling to catch up. The 62nd Fighter Squadron dove down to 7,000 feet to pounce on them. Lt. Fred Christensen claimed one of them, along with an Me 109 that appeared from somewhere and should have stayed there instead of getting mixed up with the battle

between the Fw 190s and P-47s. Lt. William Chataway damaged a pair of Fw 190s, with one of them later being awarded as a kill: his only one. Lt. Jack Greene probably destroyed one and damaged another. Lt.'s Wiley Merrill and Harold Gallagher each damaged one.

Capt. Charles Harrison was seen to be hit by fire from an Fw 190 and his P-47 went down on fire. Although a parachute was seen at 1,500 feet, there was no way of knowing who was in it, and apparently it was not Harrison, as he was reported to have been killed.

The 61st and 62nd FS's then went to Neumunsterand strafed the airdrome with moderate success. The 63rd FS remained as top cover during the entire mission, and for Capt. Charles Clamp and his pilots, the mission was uneventful.

"A" Group got off at 1225 behind Col. Zemke with twenty-four P-47s and had no aborts. They crossed-in west of Heide at 1347 and arrived over Rendsburg at 1355 at 18,000 feet. Over Flensburg airdrome a regular traffic pattern was set up as they orbited, strafed, etc. Lt.'s Samuel Stamps and Willard Johnson, 63rd FS, shared an Fw 190 that had just taken off from the nearby Husum airdrome for the only air-to-air claim.

Air-to-ground work was more fruitful, as Col. Zemke destroyed three He 111's and damaged three more. Lt.'s Stamps' and Johnson each destroyed an He 111 on the ground. Lt.'s Samuel Lowman, 63rd FS, and Edward Sission, 61st FS, got one each, while Sisson damaged two more unidentified type twin-engine aircraft. Flight Officer Evan McMinn got an Me 210 and damaged another, along with damaging an He 111. Lt. Charles Reed, 63rd FS, damaged two He 111s, and Lt. Herbert Holtmeyer, 61st FS, damaged a Ju 88. Capt. Leslie Smith destroyed one He 111 and damaged another.

Portions of "A" Group were also working over Eggebeck and Handewitt airdromes. Over Eggebeck, Capt. Dick Mudge, 61st FS, encountered problems and had to bailout to become a POW.

Major Leroy Schreiber, Commanding Officer of the 62nd Fighter Squadron, had just destroyed an unidentified type twin-engine aircraft and pulled up to make another pass when his P-47 was hit by flak over Flensburg. He was seen to climb to seven hundred feet, apparently intending to bailout, but his P-47 nosed over and dived into the ground before he could get out of it, and had no chance to survive.

Although many other ground targets were worked over and well and truly clobbered, it was without the same initial enthusiasm. Schreiber had been a good squadron commander and leader in the air, with ten accredited air-to-air kills, and he had also unselfishly shared four more air-to-air claims with other pilots. Major Lucian Dade was transferred from 56th FG Headquarters Squadron as his replacement.

April 17: Today, and for the next two days the 56th Fighter Group ground echelon was quite busy with a move from Halesworth to Boxted, AAF Station 150. Boxted, three miles north of Colchester, had originally started out as an 8th Air Force bomber base, but had been loaned to the 9th Air Force as a P-51 base between October 1943 and April 1944, being the home of the 354th Fighter Group. The new location, some fifty miles southwest of Halesworth, was now half the distance to London, good for recreational purposes, and just a little closer to Europe, particularly the Low Countries and France, in preparation for the upcoming invasion. Halesworth now became a B-24 base for the 489th Bomb Group. (Most of it is now a turkey farm).

April 18: VIII FC FO 304 sent fighter support out for the three Bomb divisions. The six dispatched P-47s groups claimed 2-0-1, for the loss of one Thunderbolt. The 56th Fighter Group had no claims or losses.

Lt. Col. Schilling led "A" Group off Halesworth at 1404 on their last mission from their old air base. Landfall-in was north of Ijmuiden, and RV with returning elements of the 3rd Bomb Division was made southwest of Hamburg. Escort continued until 1710 in the middle of the North Sea, where they broke escort and flew to Boxted, landing there at 1737.

"B" Group was led by Major Lamb and the 63rd Fighter Squadron. They were off at 1450 and crossed-in over Den Holder at 1537, making RV south of Scharhorn Island at 1619 with B-24s of the 2nd Bomb Division that were ahead of schedule. Escort continued until 1650 near Ameland Island and the Thunderbolts headed for their new home, landing at 1757.

April 19: VIII FC FO's 305 and 306. Two separate Field Orders were cut this date effecting 56th Fighter Group operations, both calling for the Group to provide withdrawal support for heavy bomber operations.

"A" Group took off Boxted on their first mission from their new base at 0957 under Field Order 305. Col. Zemke leading twenty-four P-47s. Landfall-in was over Walcheren Island at 1035, and RV made southeast of Bonn at 1110 at 19,000 feet. Escort was broken over Dunkirk at 1225. The mission was uneventful.

"B" Group was off at 1004 behind Major Lamb under Field Order 306. They went in over Knocke at 1050 and made RV at Ans at 1115. Escort was broken over Ostend as they made landfall-out. Pilots had reported a marked decrease in flak over the coastal areas during the previous two weeks, and they encountered none at all on this mission that landed at 1200.

April 20: VIII FC FO 307. Only five Thunderbolts groups were sent up as a part of the fighter escorts for the three Bomb Divisions going to "Noball" targets in France.

"B" Group was first off, at 1722, behind Capt. Leslie Smith, with twenty-four Thunderbolts to provide area support for the heavies. Landfall-in was over Cayeux at 1813 and they orbited in the Amines-Poix area for a period between 12,000 and 16,000 feet. Although intense flak was observed up to 20,000 feet, none of their P-47s were damaged and no enemy aircraft were seen. They RTB'd at 2048.

"A" Group got off at 1727 on the latest takeoff and landing mission to date. Major Lamb led, with twenty-four P-47s. They made a sweep down to Paris, and made ten plus orbits in the area until 2005. North of Paris Capt. Felix Williamson and Lt. Wendel McClure destroyed a Ju 88 that was "stooging 8,000 feet." It exploded. Immediately thereafter, Lt. Dayton Sheridan damaged an Me 410. All were from the 62nd Fighter Squadron. They landed at 2057.

April 22: VIII FC FO 309. The fighter groups were all up on various missions in support of Bomber Command. Some dive bombed, while others conducted sweeps or escort missions. The 56th Fighter Group was assigned withdrawal escort for the Big Friends.

Since the missions were not scheduled until late in the day, several pilots went up on maintenance, training or proficiency flights. These could

be as hazardous as combat missions under the right, or wrong, circumstances. Two pilots were killed. Lt. George Bracken, 61st FS, and 1st Lt. Archie Robey, 63rd FS. Robey, who had joined the squadron as a Flight Officer, was an experienced pilot with four kills. He went down twenty miles off Orfordness into the cold North Sea. The circumstances involving Bracken's loss are unknown.

"A" Group followed Lt. Col. Gabreski off Boxted at 1823 with twenty-three Thunderbolts. Landfall-in was over Walcheren Island at 1858 at 16,000 feet. RV was accomplished over Koblenz at 1935 with four Combat Wings of B-17s from the 1st Bomb Division returning from Hamm and Bonn. Other than witnessing a P-47 from an unknown group being shotdown by flak West of Bruges, the mission was uneventful.

"B" Group was off at 1844 with Col. Zemke leading twenty-four P-47s. They also went in over Walcheren Island, at 1923, and made RV near Koblenz, at 2000. They provided escort for three Combat Wings of B-24s from the 2nd Bomb Division. The B-24 gunners were jumpy, and fired on the 56th FG as they approached, but then settled down and escort was continued uneventfully. RTB time was 2146.

April 24: VIII FC FO 312. Six VIII Fighter Command P-47s groups were up, along with four from IX FC in support of the three Bomb Divisions. A total of 490 Thunderbolts, who claimed 2-1-0 in the air, and 36-0-16 on the ground. The 56th Fighter Group got 14-0-15 of these ground kills.

"A" Group was led by Lt. Col. Gabreski. Off at 1047 on a penetration support mission for the 1st Task Force, they made RV with the B-17s twenty miles west of Chalons at 1202. They escorted to southwest of Strasbourg and then headed for home. While escorting, a dozen Me 109s attacked the 2nd Combat Wing from 27,000 feet over Nancy, but were too far away for "A" Group to intercede. Near Luneville, four more Me 109s attacked the bombers, making a diving pass through their formation and continuing down to the deck, but again they were too distant for the Group to encounter. On the way home, "Gabby" and his wingman strafed Frieburg airdrome, where eight He 111s had been observed. Gabreski damaged one.

"B" Group got most of the action. Off at 1055 behind Major Stewart to provide penetration support to the 2nd Task Force of the 3rd Bomb Division. The Group made landfall-in over Calais at 1139 and RV at 1215 west of St. Dizier. The three squadrons broke escort at five minute intervals, with the 61st Fighter Squadron "heading for the barn," while the 62nd and 63rd FS's went "astrafing."

Capt. John Truluck, who was leading the seven P-47s furnished by the 63rd FS on this mission, took them down to the deck with the intent to strafe a railway shed. But then he saw the airdrome at Thalheim that was packed with German aircraft. The operation was tricky, as Truluck led his two flights through a narrow rocky gorge below mountain peaks to hit the

41-6261 UN◉B, had been the personal P-47 of Lt. Gordon Batdorf. It was stood on its nose during a taxi accident on April 21, 1944, another training day. (USAF)

This P-47 was reported as having crashed on April 22, 1944, but the only reported loss by the 63rd FS this day was Lt. Archie Robey, who went down in the North Sea, thus identification of what occurred here is unknown. (USAF)

Lt. Victor Bast, 61st FS, and his ground crew. Bast came to the squadron as a 2nd Lt. and became their Post War Assistant Operations Officer as a Captain. (USAF)

field unexpectedly. Parked there were some twenty Me 109s, fifteen Fw 190s, eight Ju 52s, ten Do 217s, along with several Me 110s and 210s and other unidentified twin-engine types. Trueluck got two Do 217s and an Me 109. 1st Lt. Donald Peters got an Me 109 and a 210, along with damaging another Me 109. 2nd Lt. Warren Kerr got two Me 109s and a 110. 1st Lt. Adam Wisniewski got an Me 210, a unidentified twin-engine type, and damaged an Me 210 and a Ju 87. 2nd Lt. John Aranyos got at Do 217 and damaged another, along with damaging an Me 210. 2nd Lt. Donald Marshall destroyed a Ju 52 and an Me 210. Flight Officer Sam Dale destroyed an Fw 190 and an Me 109. 2nd Lt. Harry Warner got a Ju 87. A pretty good deal for them all, as they were unopposed and had the opportunity to make four unopposed passes over the airdrome, and everybody got at least one. After deciding not to press their luck any longer at Thalheim, those that had ammunition remaining made one firing pass at Eutingen, where forty more German aircraft were parked. The 63rd FS made no claims there, but Major Stewart came in with a flight from the 62nd FS, and Stewart believed that he damaged two Me 109s, and an unidentified biplane. The afternoon's effort was enough for the participating pilots to receive a Letter of Commendation from Brig. General Auton.

April 25: VIII FC FO 313. Another support mission for the three Bomb Wings, with most of them going to targets in France.

Col. Zemke led "A" Group off at 0810 with twenty-four P-47s. In north of Ostend at 0842, they made RV with the heavies northeast of Luneville at 0924 to provide target and withdrawal support. Escort was broken over Romilly at 1045. The 62nd and 63rd Fighter Squadrons headed for home, while the 61st FS decided to go down to see what the bombers might have missed at their target, Metz. Zemke discovered forty to fifty aircraft parked there, some hidden under camouflage netting, others hidden in bushes, and additional dispersed in nearby fields. In strafing, they claimed 3-0-7, but left ten to twenty more claims open pending assessment of gun camera films. Zemke claimed two Ju 88s destroyed, and held his claims pending on the remainder. Flight Officer Steve Gerrick destroyed one Me 109 and damaged two Fw 190s. Capt. Michael Gladych damaged an Fw 190, a Ju 87 and an unidentified twin-engine type. Lt. Richard Heineman damaged a Ju 52 and an Me 109. Other members of the squadron shot up structures on the airdrome. (Zemke's two claims were upheld, and no others that were pending were awarded).

"B" Group was up at 0908 behind Major Lamb to provide withdrawal support to the 1st Task Force. Lt. Campbell, out of Red Flight, 63rd FS, was the only abort. In over Hardelot at 0942, RV was made at Bar de Duc at 1020. The bombers were escorted to the coast, and then one squadron

went back to pick up another bomb group to escort out. They witnessed a rather stupid incident where another P-47 squadron made a simulated attack on a returning group of B-17s while they were still over enemy territory, and narrowly escaped being fired upon. Otherwise, their mission was uneventful.

April 26: VIII FC FO 315. Bomber Command sent their three divisions to targets in Germany. Thirteen Fighter Groups were up on escort missions, and the Luftwaffe ignored them.

"A" Group was led off at 0742 by Col. Zemke, and "B" Group tookoff immediately behind them, led by Lt. Col. Gabreski. A total of forty-eight P-47s dispatched, with no aborts from either group. The heavies were to attack Paderborn and Gutersloh, but did not bomb, apparently because of the solid undercast and as the B-24s did not have a path finding radar aircraft along with them on this mission. An uneventful "milk run" mission that returned at 1115.

April 27: VIII FC FO 316. All three Bomb Divisions were active, but P-47 operations were limited to five fighter groups.

The 56th Fighter Group sent out their "A" and "B" Groups on a Type 16 Control mission to the Pas de Calais area. "B" Group, led by Capt. Leslie Smith, 62nd Fighter Squadron, was off at 0837, while "A" Group, led by Capt. Don Goodflesch, 63rd FS, got off at 0843. Both Groups orbited over the Low Countries twenty-thirty times before crossing-out over Dunkirk at 1130 and landing at noon.

That evening a second mission was flown by both "A" and "B" Groups, this time a Ramrod and target support type. Lt. Col. Gabreski led "A" Group off at 1704 with twenty-four P-47s, while Major Lamb led "B" Group off at 1711 with twenty-four more. Escort was uneventfully provided for 2nd Bomb Division B-24s to Noball targets that the bombers had difficulty hitting because of a low heavy haze. They returned at 2015.

April 28: VIII FC FO 318 sent the heavies and fighters out on scattered small scale missions. A three mission day for the 56th Fighter Group.

"A" Group, led by Col. Zemke, got off at 0841 on a Type 16 Control mission. The morning weather was bad over the continent, so pilots were never quite sure of their positions and had to rely upon radar vectoring for navigation. In over approximately Dieppe at 0922, they were vectored to Chartres, to orbit between there and Orleans, and then out near Pas de Calais at 1108. Several groups of friendlies were seen, but the only sign of the Luftwaffe was twenty plus fighters spotted through a hole in the clouds on the ground at Orleans/Bricy airdrome. RTB was at 1148.

"B" Group was led off at 0951 by Lt. Col. Gabreski. Again on a Type 16 Control mission, they went in over Caen at 1034, flew to Le Mans, thence along the Huisme River, northeast bound, to Chartres and Vire before out over Pas de Calais at 1230. RTBing at 1323.

65th FW FO 97. The Wolfpack's first attempt at fighter-bombing.

Col. Zemke led "A" Group out on a "Thunderbombing" mission at 1552 with eight P-47s from each squadron. Each "Thunderbomber" carried twelve 20 pound M41 fragmentation bombs. Landfall-in was over Le Treport at 1634 at 12,500 feet. As the primary target of Orleans/Bricy airdrome was obscured by clouds, they flew to an unidentified airdrome northeast of Paris and near Soissons. Commencing the dive bombing run between 11,000 and 13,000 feet, the bombs were dropped between 7,000 and 10,000 feet at an angle of around forty-five degrees. Although the results were not known for sure, it was believed that the mission was ineffective.

Three 63rd Fighter Squadron P-47s had their three-bomb clusters hang up in their bomb arming wires on their racks and their pilots had to jettison them into the North Sea. Two others could not jettison their loads at all and had to return with their bombs to make nervous landings. As bombs were a new type ordnance for the armorers to deal with, errors in hanging the bombs to begin with could be expected, but the pilots could not be blamed for being unhappy with the situation.

April 29: VIII FC FO 320. Back to the "Big B" with all three Bomb Divisions and all fighter groups up, including four on loan from IX Fighter Command. It was another expensive day, as sixty-three of the Big Friends went down over Europe.

Lt. Col. Gabreski led "A" Group off at 0807 on a sweep ahead of the bombers. Again weather conditions made accurate navigation impossible. They went in to the area of Bad Ostenhausen and then headed for home without seeing any evidence of the Luftwaffe. RTB time was 1100.

"B: Group got off at 0812 behind Major Stewart on a Ramrod ahead of the bombers. Landfall-in was around Bergen at 0900 at 20,000 feet, and course was set northeast to about thirty miles west of Oldenberg, and then to Breman and Emden. Between Oldenburg and Bremen the flak was of heavy caliber, and intense. Two P-47s were damaged, and Lt. Samuel Hamilton, 61st Fighter Squadron, was slightly wounded. Landfall-out was near Ijmuiden at 1020, and RTB accomplished at 1126.

The second mission was to provide withdrawal escort for the Big Friends on their return from Berlin.

"A" Group was off at 1204 behind Lt. Col. Gabreski with twenty-four P-47s. RV was made at Munster with four Combat Wings of B-17s from the 1st Bomb Division. The high altitude sky was full of friendly aircraft, but there was no sign of the Luftwaffe up there, although they were called down below the clouds twice to help straggling bombers that were under attack at lower altitudes. These distressed aircraft could not be found, nor could the Germans be ferreted out.

"B" Group was led off by Major Stewart at 1216. They were to have met B-24s of the 2nd Bomb Division over Drummer Lake, but the Liberators were late, so fuel constraints dictated that they escort others home. They picked up four Combat Wings of B-17s and a few B-24s and escorted them out to midway across the North Sea. One group of P-47s then went back to look for stragglers and brought out a pair. Major Stewart's 61st FS still had their long range belly tanks on their P-47s, so they were able to proceed a bit further east to look for the bombers. At Steinhudder Lake they found five Me 109s at 15,000 feet that were coming in on the tail of some bombers. Stewart managed to damage one. RTB time was 1531.

April 30: VIII FC FO 321. The 1st and 2nd Air Task Force's went to targets in France. The 56th Fighter Group gave withdrawal support to them. Although other P-47 groups claimed 9-1-5, the 56th FG was scoreless.

"A" Group tookoff at 1102 with Major Robert Lamb, 63rd Fighter Squadron, leading twenty-four P-47s. In over Le Treport at 1142, RV was made over Orleans at 1212 with four Combat Wings of B-17s of the 1st and 3rd Bomb Divisions. Escort was broken and landfall-out made over Trauville at 1300. Moderate accurate flak was encountered over Chateaudun, and one 61st FS P-47 was damaged, otherwise it was an uneventful mission that RTB'd at 1405.

"B" Group was off at 1110 with Capt. Leslie Smith, 61st FS, in the lead. They flew a similar route to that of "A" Group, and made RV with two Combat Wings of 1st and 3rd Bomb Division B-17s over Chateaudun at 1215. They were escorted to a point twenty-five miles off Beachy Head, at 1325, and the P-47s RTB'd Boxted at 1407.

During the course of the day at Boxted, Lt. George Lovett, 63rd FS, was killed on a training flight.

April 1944 had been an exceptional month for the 56th Fighter Group in all respects. The disruption of moving from Halesworth to Boxted and settling into unfamiliar quarters was taken in stride, without curtailing any combat missions. Credit for this has to go almost entirely to the ground troops, for it was they who had to pack and unpack their tools and equipment and sort out their required aircraft parts and make sure that they were accessible when the fighters were there to be worked upon. Paperwork can be shuffled and taken care of at leisure, but aircraft maintenance during combat operations is far more demanding and important.

During April, the Group's pilots destroyed fifty-five "Jerries," seventeen in the air and thirty-eight on the ground. Two more were probably destroyed, one in the air, and one on the ground. Some fifty additional were damaged, fifteen in the air and thirty-five on the ground.

The two "Field Day's" for the month occurred on the 15th and 24th, just as the ground crews were preparing for the move, and just as they were getting settled in afterwards. Pilot's, of course, deserve all the credit they can get for their role in this, but at this April point, midway through World War II as far as the 56th Fighter Group's role was concerned, one must reflect upon the fact that it was the ground crews that made it all possible. This was their forth move in a little more than a year. A lot of packing and unpacking and work; lack of sleep and late and cold rations were the norm for these men.

During the course of the month an officer that was not a pilot became an "ace." Major Wilbur R. Watson was the 56th Fighter Group's Air Inspector and he had begun collecting the thirteenth kills from the top scoring fighter pilots. Capt. Robert Johnson was the first to donate a claim for a downed German aircraft to Watson, in sort of a half-joke, half serious show of respect for the "desk weenie." Watson's score mounted when Lt. Col. Schilling donated his thirteenth, followed by Lt. Col. Gabreski and Capt Joe Powers. When Zemke shot up four on the ground on April 15, he gave credit for one of them to Watson, which made him an ace, on paper, anyhow. While of little value in the grand scheme of things, this sort of gesture contributed to the esprit de corps within the Group and bolstered morale of all.

May 1: VIII FC FO 323. Six P-47 groups up on escort for the three Bomb Divisions.

"A" Group was led by Major Lamb and they were off at 1601. Landfall-in was over Schouwen Island at 1633, whereupon they swept the Venle-Liege area before going back to pick up B-24s near Eindhoven, which were then escorted to Brussels to bomb a marshalling yard. Escort was provided out as far as Knocke, at 1825. RTB'd at 1903.

"B" Group followed Major Dade off at 1851 with the standard twenty-four ship Thunderbolt formation. They crossed-in over Dunkirk at 1925 and were fired upon by the lead B-17 of a returning mission. White Flight had two P-47s hit by .50 caliber fire, damaging those flown by Lt.'s Anthony Cavallo and Samuel Lowman, 63rd Fighter Squadron, who thusly had to return to Boxted. One nosed-up on landing, but neither pilot was injured during the incidents. The remainder of "B" Group arrived over Charleroi at 1927 to start a sweep over the Low Countries that was uneventful. They RTB'd at 2126.

May 4: VIII FC FO 326. Four of the P-47 groups went out in support of the 1st and 2nd Bomb Divisions.

"A" Group went out on escort of the bombers, but the bombers were recalled, so they made a sweep on their own. Col. Zemke led them off at 0827, and landfall-in was over Katwijk at 0915. They swept over Osnabruck, Nordhausen, Halberstadt, Eiselehen, Brunswick, Hanover, Salzwedel, and south of Bremen. Landfall-out was over Knocke and Egmond between 1205 and 1230, as the Group had split while on their sweep.

In the vicinity of Brunswick and Hanover many vapor trails were seen, an indication that the Luftwaffe had been up in anticipation of bomber raids. At Nordhausen, about twenty Me 109s and Fw 190s were caught returning to their airdromes and were attacked by the 62nd Fighter Squadron, as they and the 61st FS had already gone down to do some strafing in the area. Lt.'s Robert Cherry and Eugene Bennett got an Fw 190 in the traffic pattern and shot it down. It crashed into the center of Nordhausen. Cherry then saw an Me 210 and shot it down. Its pilot making a belly landing and two of its crew members were seen to run away from the burning wreckage.

1st Lt. Felix Williamson, Red One, spotted a whole slew of aircraft parked on the ground and prepared to strafe them, but had his attention diverted by two gaggles of eight Fw 190s and an Me 109, followed by eight more Fw 190s coming in to land. He prepared to attack them, only to discover that he had run himself out of ammunition while shooting up and destroying four locomotives. While ten additional trains were either destroyed or damaged by pilots of the two squadrons, these German fighters escaped unscathed.

The 63rd FS had remained as top cover during all of this, and for them the mission had been "uneventful." Upon return, two "A" Group P-47s were force-landed out of fuel, one at Felixstone, and the other just off the base. Two additional had been damaged, one by flak and the other by pieces of a locomotive.

"B" Group also went out on a escort mission that became a sweep, taking off at 0852 behind Capt. Leslie Smith. They went in over Ijmuiden at 0935. RV with B-17s of five Combat Wings of the 1st Bomb Division was made near Kampen at 0955, but the bombers turned back over Lingen at 1015, so escort was broken off at this point. "B" Group then headed for Drummer Lake where Lt.'s Joe Powers and Roy Bluhm were bounced by eight Me 109s that came down on them from 32,000 feet. Powers shot down one and damaged another. Bluhm damaged another. The unusual thing about these Me 109s is that they all were fitted with large scoops under their noses, apparently "tropicalized" versions that had either been intended for, or were withdrawn from the North African Theater. The 61st and 62nd FS then proceeded to shoot up some more rolling stock, while the eight P-47s of the 63rd FS remained as top cover and had another uneventful mission.

May 6: VIII FC FO 328. The 56th Fighter Group went out by itself to provide area support for the 1st and 2nd Bomb Divisions. Targets were Noball in the Pas De Calais area, and the 1st BD returned without dropping their bombs, as the targets were obscured by cirrus clouds. The 2nd BD bombed via Pathfinder PFF aircraft.

Major Dade led "A" Group and Capt. Smith "B" Group, with "B" getting off at 0655 and "A" at 0714, their earliest morning takeoffs of the war so far. Going in under Type 16 Control, they swept the Low Country's uneventfully at altitudes above the cloud decks and only one flight of German aircraft was seen, which evaded interception by diving into the clouds. RTB time was 1020.

May 7: VIII FC FO 330. The 1st and 3rd Bomb Divisions went to Berlin on the 1st mission for the day. The 2nd BD went to Munster on the afternoon's mission.

Major Lamb led "A" Group off at 0816 on support and area sweeps ahead of the bombers. Due to a solid cloud cover, they made landfall-in over Ijmuiden, and got, maybe, to Ulizen, before heading out over Ijmuiden again. Navigation being imprecise because of the clouds. The bombers were never seen, and there was no sign of the Luftwaffe. They returned to Boxted at 1220.

"B" Group was led by Lt. Col. Gabreski, and they were off at 1741 to provide penetration, target and withdrawal support. Landfall-in and RV was made over Schouwen Island. They escorted to the target and as far out as Nieuport, but again there was no sign of the Luftwaffe. RTB time was 2030.

Also on May 7 Detachment "B," 65th Fighter Wing, was formed at Boxted to provide air-sea rescue services. Under the command of Capt. Robert Gerhart, this was the only such 8th Air Force unit. The unit started with 105 enlisted men, but increased to 150 by January 1945 when they were detached from the 56th Fighter Group and relocated to Halesworth. By this time they were redesignated as the 5th Air Rescue squadron.

Initially equipped with hand-me-down P-47Ds, of which a third came from the 56th Fighter Group after they had been declared as "war-weary," the squadron pilots came from two sources. Roughly half were assigned on ninety day details from one of the three 8th AF Fighter Wings, while the remainder were assigned from a casual pool of fighter pilots that had been deemed unsuitable for combat missions for one reason or another.

Regardless of their source, these pilots were a courageous breed. They were expected to scramble in search of downed aircrew regardless of the weather and spend hazardous hours searching for life jackets and dinghies amid dark waves of the sea. In a year and a half they had responded to nearly five hundred distress calls and contributed to the rescue of over a thousand airmen.

May 8: VIII FC FO 331. The long-haul to Berlin was again scheduled for the 1st and 3rd Bomb divisions. The 2nd BD went to Brunswick. Five hundred B-17s would drop almost a thousand tons of bombs on the center of Berlin, while eight hundred tons would fall on Brunswick.

"A" Group was led by Lt. Col. Gabreski and they got off at 0734 to provide a fighter sweep ahead of the bombers. They crossed-in at Neerdwijk at 0826 and arrived in their assigned area to sweep at 0924. Over flying Brunswick, Drummer Lake and Celle, they crossed-out at Haarlem by flights and elements at 1050.

The excitement began as they approached Celle when a dozen Me 109s were seen to be attacking the lead box of B-17s. As "A" Group moved into to break up the attack, they were intercepted by another gaggle of Me 109s and Fw 190s. Capt. Robert Johnson got one of each, which ran his score to the final total of twenty-seven. This effectively ended his career as a fighter pilot, as this feat tied and then broke Capt. Eddie Rickenbacher's World War I score and Johnson was ordered off further combat missions and returned to the United States. Johnson would then go on "Warbond" tours, making speeches to exhort the public and production workers. Liking this work, he later joined Republic Aviation and became vice-president of public relations.

Lt. Harold Hartney damaged an Fw 190 and Lt. Herman King an Me 109 for the 62nd FS's contribution. Gabreski, leading from the 61st FS, got an Me 109. Lt. Frank Klibbe, 61st FS, got an Me 109 and an Fw 190 and Lt. Joseph Perry, also from the 61st FS, got an Fw 190.

Lt. Gordon Lewis, 62nd FS, is officially credited with shooting down an Fw 190 during the course of this mission, although it is not mentioned in either the 62nd FS or 56th FG records. What is mentioned, however, is that Lewis was shot down by a blue-nosed P-51 coded PE-P (352nd FG, 328th FS). Lewis had to bail out over Oschersleben and became a POW. The same Mustang continued firing on White Flight and hit Lt. Robert Cherry's P-47 in the prop. Cherry returned to Boxted okay. Lt. Thad Buszko, 62nd FS, also got back okay, also, after being wounded in his right arm by flak. His P-47 caught on fire, but he dove down and blew the fire out, and then got it back to be salvaged.

"B" Group followed Major Dade off at 0753. They made landfall-in over Ijmuiden at 0847 at 22,000 feet and accomplished RV with the B-24s north of Amsterdam at 0855. The bomber formation was reported as poor, which made escorting them quite difficult. Two squadrons broke escort at Steinhuder Lake, while the 62nd FS broke off at Bremen to attack seven Me 109s. The only score was a damaged Me 109 by Lt. Herman King. They returned at 1142.

May 9: VIII FC FO 333. All fighter groups were up in support of the three bomb divisions. The 56th Fighter Group flew Ramrod missions to Laen-Athies and Laon-Couvron in support of the 3rd Bomb Division.

Major James Stewart led "B" Group off Boxted at 0804, while Col. Zemke led "A" Group off one minute behind them. They went in over Cayeux, and made RV north of Beauvais, escorting the bombers on penetration, target and withdrawal. Escort was terminated at mid-channel on the way home at 1030. No German fighters were seen and Zemke went on record to state that one fighter group providing an escort for this type of short-range mission would be sufficient. The area over the target on this short ranged mission had been just too congested by friendly fighters for safeties sake.

May 11: VIII FC FO 335. Only B-17s represented the strategic force this date, going to targets in northwestern Europe. The 56th Fighter Group was to provide penetration support for those heavies going to Chartres area.

Flying as a single Group on this mission, Lt. Col. Gabreski led forty-eight P-47s off at 1257. They went in over Cayeux at 1335 climbing from 10,000 to 14,000 feet. RV was made in the area of Chartres. Just before RV was joined, Capt. John Eaves, leading the 62nd FS, was warned by the radar controller of enemy aircraft in the area and saw six Fw 190s starting to attack the lead box of B-17s. He led his squadron after them, but they were too far away to engage and were soon lost in the haze. Another milk run mission.

May 12: VIII FC FO 337. No milk run, this one. P-47s claimed 26-0-8, with the 56th Fighter Group claiming eighteen destroyed. They lost three fighter pilots, but fortunately all survived as POW's.

Ever since the 8th Air Force obtained the P-47, the P-51 and P-38 in Europe they had been working on revising their tactics to utilize these fighters more effectively. It was all a learning experience, as the original tactics had been based upon those used by the RAF, and some they had seen the Luftwaffe using, and tried to adapt these for their own use.

Flights had originally been composed of three aircraft flying in Vee's, or in RAF parlance, "Vic's." These fighters had been positioned in various relationships to each other in several manners, to be able to maneuver to cover each other or swing into an attack by one flight and have the succeeding flights able to either come in behind and above them for top cover, or to also continue the attack through larger squadron or group formations. Line-abreast formations, which the Luftwaffe continued to use, were also attempted, but they often resembled a crack-the-whip effort, with those closest to the action being able to attack effectively, while those on the far end were often so far away as to be not only ineffective but vulnerable to attack, themselves.

The most effective formation that was devised was the "finger-four," which resembled the position of extended finger tips. The Flight Leader was farthest out in front, while his wingman was off to his short side and positioned slightly above and to his rear. The Element Leader took up the long side, with his own wingman above and behind him. The flight could be positioned either as a right or left hand, which depended upon its position in the larger squadron formation, which was composed, usually, of four such elements arranged in either a diamond formation or also spread as a larger finger-four formation. A fighter group then went into combat composed of three squadrons of sixteen aircraft each, arranged in a "Vic" with the high squadron leading, the second squadron five hundred feet below them and off to one side. The third squadron was on the opposite side of the lead squadron, and five hundred feet below the middle squadron. Arranged thusly, the middle and low squadron could criss-cross below and behind the lead squadron during turns without a threat of collision. It was also effective, when tightened up, for cloud penetration, as the leaders could keep sight of the other flights and formations. Operating in the clear, the elements, flights and squadrons could spread out, but still be in a position to effectively cover each other for defensive purposes's or to make an attack. The element/flight leader's were "the shooters," while the wingmen provided protection for them. This formation, developed in 1943 became the standard for decades and through two more wars, before the advent and improvements in airborne radar created a need for a newer tactical formation.

One of the tactics attempted to increase the effectiveness of the fighters was the "Zemke Fan," a method of spreading out the fighters over Europe to increase their chances to find and attack the Luftwaffe. The first mission trying this tactic was the fighter sweep conducted by "A" Group this morning. Col. Zemke led twenty-four P-47s off Boxted at 0946, but they had three aborts, which would have an effect upon the mission. They flew to Koblenz where they spread into the fan, to cover an area of one hundred-eighty degrees from that point. One flight flew to south of Glissen, another to east of Glissen. Another to Marburg, and a fourth to Berghausen. The fifth flight headed to Baden-Baden, and the sixth to Mannheim.

Zemke's flight, after having Lt. John McDonnell, 63rd FS, White Four, abort, was composed of Zemke, Lt. Col. Preston Piper and Lt. Willard Johnson. South of Glissen they were jumped by seven Me 109s that had both a height and speed advantage over them, diving down on them from 29,000 feet. Piper and Johnson were both shot down in flames at 20,000 feet, but both were able to bailout and became POW's. Piper, on his seventh mission, had been a B-17 pilot that General Curtis LeMay personally asked Zemke to put in fighters, hence his higher rank, but lack of a command position.

Zemke dove away, and then ran into four more Me 109s near Wiesbaden. He managed to evade these, only to find himself in a position to attack four more Me 109s over the Rhine River south of Koblenz. After watching these being joined by others until he found thirty plus assembling, Zemke started calling for help. This formation, now mixed Fw 190s and Me 109s was climbing, and Zemke climbed with them, hoping to either get into position to get a shot, or to get some help. Finally, as they reached the contrail level, Lt's Robert "Shorty" Rankin and Cleon Thomton, 61st FS, spotted the contrails and came to Zemke's assistance. Zemke then picked an Me 109 that was too loose with his wingmen and raked it from end to end. It did two quick rolls and fell off into a spin, catching fire, and its pilot bailed out.

A pair of Me 109s had come in on Zemke's tail during this conflict and Rankin selected one, firing until it started smoking and its landing gear fell out of its wheel wells. He then concentrated upon its wingman, firing with identical results.

Rankin had to fight his way to Zemke's assistance to begin with. After hearing the call for help, he and Thomton had headed in Zemke's direction, only to encounter another batch of Me 109s. Rankin went after the last two, and fired at one that dove away, so he chased him down to see him fail to pull out of his dive and crash into a village. Climbing back up, Rankin saw another Me 109 that was descending, so he went after him and put many rounds into its fuselage. Its pilot bailed out, but his parachute was not seen to open.

Zemke, Rankin and Thomton then witnessed one of the stranger incidents of the war. While they were positioning themselves on a flight of Me 109s at 15,000 feet, three of the German pilots bailed out. None of the P-47 pilots had fired a shot, and none took any credit for the incident.

Zemke, low on fuel, headed for home, but Rankin continued to mix it up with the Luftwaffe, knocking down one more Me 109 and becoming the second fighter pilot in the Theater to destroy five German aircraft in the air during one combat mission. For 2nd Lt. Cleon Thomton, the mission was one that every future fighter pilot dreamed of and set his goals toward. Thomton found himself head-on with an Me 109 and fired. The Me 109 lost glycol coolant, started smoking, and its pilot bailed out. He had gotten his first kill on his first combat mission.

The fan had the fighters spread all over, so the exact sequence of events is not positive: The flight heading for east of Glissen encountered a dozen Me 109s northeast of Koblenz. Lt. Carroll Wakefield, 63rd FS, got three of them.

The 61st FS, going to northeast of Marburg spotted forty plus in an orbit, marshalling to attack the bombers. They waded in on them from 25,000 feet and destroyed four. Capt. Paul Conger got two Fw 190s and damaged another. Lt. Arthur Maul got an Me 109. Flight Officer Steven Gerick got an Fw 190 and damaged two Me 109s (One of which was later shot down by Rankin, and Rankin is also credited with two additional Me 109s damaged). Lt. Praeger Neyland was credited with a probably destroyed Me 109.

"B" Group took off at 0951 behind Lt. Col. Gabreski. Landfall-in was over Walcheren Island, and they proceeded to Worms-Frankfurt-Bad Mergentheim areas, with the squadrons splitting into elements, and the Group fanning out. Capt. Felix Williamson's 62nd FS encountered eight Me 109s near Frankfurt, and they fought them down to the deck at Bad Mergentheim. In the process, Capt. Joe Powers and Flight Officer Joseph Vitale shared an Me 109. It is believed that the downed German pilot was Major Gunther Rall, who had previously shot down Lt. Col. Piper and Lt. Johnson, and taken a pot-shot at Col. Zemke. Rall, at the time was the

Luftwaffe's third top scoring fighter pilot. He survived his bailout, with injuries, but soon returned to operations and finished the war with a total of 275 Allied aircraft destroyed.

Lt. Herman King got an Me 109. Lt. Jack Greene shot down an Me 109, but in turn was shotdown himself. His P-47 was seen on fire over Frankfurt, and he was seen to bailout at 16,000 feet to become a POW.

The 63rd FS had their encounters east of Koblenz with seven to ten Fw 190s. Lt. Anthony Cavello getting two of them, with one crashing into the center of Koblenz, itself.

Whether the Zemke Fan was a good idea or not was never conclusively proven. The 56th Fighter Group had claimed 19-1-6 in the air for three losses. If they had all been together in the area where the combats had taken place, their scores in all probability would have been higher. Likewise, the two portions of "A" Group that went to Mannheim and Baden-Baden that morning had not seen a single German fighter. Again, it was all a matter of being in the right place at the right time.

May 13: VIII FC FO 338. A mission to Tutow and Politz by the 2nd Bomb Division. The 56th Fighter Group's "A" Group covered their penetration, while "B" Group covered the withdrawal.

Major Lucien Dade led "A" Group off at 1145. They went in over Heide, where they made RV with the Liberators. Escort was provided to Neumunster, where the 63rd Fighter Squadron spotted a single Fw 190 that they chased away. Dade's 62nd FS then located forty Fw 190s and they went after them, with Dade destroying one. Lt. Harold Hartney was killed, however. His Thunderbolt was seen to be hit by enemy antiaircraft fire and his P-47 exploded on impact with the ground.

"B" Group was off at 1353, led by Major Robert Lamb. They RV'd with the returning bombers at Aabenraa, just north of the boarder between Germany and Denmark. First they encountered a group of bogies that turned out to be P-51s, then a group of German aircraft that was already engaged by friendly fighters, so they let them go. Then, a group of Fw 190s came in on the rear of the returning bombers, and the 61st FS dove in on them. 1st Lt. Robert Keen knocking down three of them with the first two German pilots being seen to bailout and the third one dying when his aircraft exploded. 2nd Lt. James Jure got another Fw 190.

In all, the 56th Fighter Group claimed five kills for the day's efforts, with all of them being the first ones credited to the mentioned pilots.

May 17: Lt. James E. Elliott, 62nd FS, was killed in a mid-air collision with a B-26 while he was up on a training flight.

May 19: VIII FC FO 342. After almost a week where few fighter missions were flown because of the weather over Europe, the three bomber divisions went to Keil, Berlin and Brunswick. Only four P-47 groups assisted them, but they accounted for 26-0-16 German aircraft in the air and two more on the ground. The 56th Fighter Group chalked up five of these.

A single group was dispatched by the 56th FG for this day's effort. Forty-eight P-47s being led off Boxted at 1112 by Col. Zemke on penetration support. They went in south of Ijmuiden and made RV with the rear boxes of the Big Friends near Zwolle, continuing over their formation to take up station with the lead boxes. Near Meppel, thirty plus enemy aircraft came in on the rear boxes, and the 62nd Fighter Squadron turned back to intercept them, but was unable to close on them enough to make contact, so they reversed their course and continued escorting.

Blue Flight of the 63rd FS was then bounced between Drummer and Stienhudder Lake's by three Me 109s, with the P-47 of Lt. Barney Casteel being damaged. This same flight was again bounced on the way out and Blue Leader, 1st Lt. Benard Smith and Blue Three, Casteel, had a good fight on their hands for a moment as the black Me 109s came down on them, and then jumped back up to 36,000 feet to avoid the P-47s firepower. Lt. Anthony Cavallo, in the 63rd's Red Flight, went down on a bounce between Drummer and Stienhudder Lake's only for Cavallo's engine to go kaput. He managed to keep it running long enough to make it

midway across the North Sea, where he had to bailout. He was rescued by the ASR troops.

Some fifty German fighters were in the area intent upon harassing the returning Big Friends and managed to make one pass on the heavies before being intercepted by the 56th FG. Major Leslie Smith, leading White Flight of the 61st FS sent one Fw 190 down smoking and forced another's pilot to bailout, along with damaging a third. The two claims put Smith into the ranks of aces, giving him a total of six for the time being. Capt. John Eaves, 62nd FS, also got two Fw 190s, which gave him a total score of 3.5. 2nd Lt. Richard Heineman, 61st FS, claimed his first, an Fw 190.

This mission had been the first for the new bubble equipped P-47D-25 "Superbolt." Those fortunate enough to have one were impressed with the visibility from the cockpit. No more of the "birdcage" canopy bracing to contend with, and visibility to the rear was outstanding. Yet, due to the cut-down rear fuselage, the lack of area/mass did make the fighter a tad less stable. Later retro-fitting of a dorsal fin would cure this problem. But in the meantime, the pilots would have to be content with being able to see better and put up with the "snakeeness."

May 20: VIII FC FO 343A. The three bomb divisions were scheduled to hit targets in France and Belgium. The weather was worse than lousy. The 3rd Bomb Division gave up on going, and most of the 2nd Bomb Division was recalled. Several incidents and accidents occurred within the bomber forces because of the weather, including both ground and air collisions.

The 56th Fighter Group was led off by Lt. Col. Gabreski at 0843 to provide penetration, area target and withdrawal support. RV was ten miles northwest of Furnes at 0940 with the B-17s and landfall-in was over Furnes. Escort continued to the targeted airdromes in the Paris area, and out to over The Hague at 1115. No enemy fighters were encountered, and because of the cloud cover, bombing results were not seen. RTB time was 1220.

May 21: VIII FC FO 345. The 1st and 2nd Bomb Divisions went to targets in France. Most of the fighter groups went out on the new "Chattanooga" missions. Chattanooga operated the same as Jackpot, only the targets were rail and other transportation targets instead of German airfields. Generally, each effected fighter group was assigned a specific area to fly these missions in. That way they would have a better knowledge of the geographical area and could plan their tactics in the most effective manner.

The 56th Fighter Group's "B" Group tookoff at 1302 behind Lt. Col. Gabreski on a Type 16 Control mission with twenty-four P-47s. They made landfall at Le Treport at 1347 at 18,000 feet. Flew to Amines, then to Lille, Namur and Antwerp, and crossed out in the vicinity of Dunkirk. An uneventful patrol providing area cover for those fighters looking for targets down on the deck.

"A" Group was off at 1318 behind Capt. Donald Goodfleisch and the 63rd Fighter Squadron. They made RV with the first box of bombers ten miles west of Sangette at 1345 and crossed-in five minutes later. Escort was provided to the Noball target and out to the coast where they picked up a second box of bombers, took them to their Noball target and out to Nieuport at 1505. The mission was uneventful, and as usual, the pilots had little clue of what a Noball target was to begin with. It would be another month before the V-1 Buzz Bombs would be launched against England and their presence and identification became generally known to the aircrews that had been bombing obscured targets in wooded areas for the past few months without any idea of the meaning of the target. What they did know, however, was that whatever they were, they were pretty well defended by flak guns.

May 22: VIII FC FO 346. The first of two major fighter missions this day was an escort for the Big Friends. Two P-47 Groups went out, the 56th and the 356th. The 56th Fighter Group claimed 12-1-2 in the air, the 356th was scoreless. Still, it was an expensive mission for the 56th FG, as two pilots were killed and three more P-47s were destroyed.

Col. Zemke led the 56th off at 1027 with forty-eight P-47s. Landfall-in was over Katwig at 1142 at 16,000 feet. Over Drummer Lake the Group spread into the Zemke Fan, with the 61st Fighter Squadron going to the Breman area, the 63rd FS to Hanover and the 62nd FS to Paderborn-Einbeck and Brunswick.

Over Hepenhefen airdrome, east of Breman, a dozen P-47s of the 61st FS went down to 15,000 feet when they saw fifteen German fighters taking off line-abreast formation. Then more were seen getting off in pairs, so Lt. Col. Gabreski called in the remaining four Thunderbolts from his squadron and they all went down to 3,000 feet to encounter the Luftwaffe.

"Gabby" took his White Flight after the first eight Fw 190s, and he set the first one that he had selected on fire, and then went after another that he clobbered until its pilot bailed out. As he then started a climbing turn he saw one P-47 smoking and another going down in flames. There was no way of knowing who was who, as he had left his Red and Blue Flights to take on the remaining Focke-Wulfs. Although three parachutes were seen, it was not known to whom they belonged. Lt.'s Richard Heineman and Cletus Nale were both killed during the combat.

The 61st FS reformed over the airdrome and then saw twenty-five more Fw 190s below them at 5,000 feet. Diving down on them, the German flak open up on them all, and continued firing until one of the Focke-Wulf's fired a green flare to warn them to stop. The 61st FS continued to engage these Fw 190s with Gabreski getting another. Also scoring were Capt. James Carter getting two and Capt. Withhold Lanowski, a Polish exchange pilot, getting one. Flight Officer Evan McMinn got two, which made him an ace, and he damaged another. Not too bad for a pilot the Air Force hadn't made a full fledged officer.

2nd Lt. Heineman was seen to knock down one Fw 190 before he went down, but Post War assessment credited him with two this day. Lt's Praeger Neyland, James Clark and Reginald Herin were each credited with one Fw 190, and Clark damaged another. On the way home, near Hamburg, Gabreski damaged another. In all, not exactly a "Turkey Shoot," but not a bad day's work, either.

But it wasn't over yet: McMinn had taken 20mm hits in his wing and it was burning. He almost bailed out, but decided to stick with it as long as he could. It continued to smoke until he reached the Zuider Zee, and just in the nick of time the smoking stopped, as McMinn didn't want to attempt to fly a burning fighter across the Channel. He did get it across the Channel and managed to put it down in a field near Leisten. It again caught on fire and it was written off in the ensuing blaze, but he was back safe.

The other two squadrons had to content themselves with strafing. A total of six locomotives were destroyed and seven more damaged. Eighteen barges were damaged, along with all sorts of other items. On the way home Lt. Billy Edens, 62nd FS, had a narrow escape. Out of fuel, he had to ditch in the cold waters of the North Sea. After a lonely hour in his dingy he was picked up by a RAF rescue launch.

VIII FC FO 347 sent the 56th Fighter Group out on a glide bombing mission. Col. Zemke led twenty-four P-47s off at 1647, with one aborting. They carried forty-six 500 General Purpose bombs to the target of a railroad bridge at Hasselt, Holland. Two P-47s went in on the deck to bomb, three dropped from 1,500 feet in a glide. Eight bombed from between 6,000 and 10,000 in (almost) vertical dives, and eight more dropped at a forty-five degree angle from 8,000 to 12,000 feet. All in an attempt to ascertain exactly what was the optimum tactic to use in this role. The results were inconclusive, as the bombing results were determined to be only fair regardless of the technique utilized.

The 63rd Fighter Squadron's sixteen bombs had been dropped from 6,000 feet, and all landed three hundred yards west of the target, with only one being seen to explode. Again a frustrating mission for the involved pilots.

This was the last combat mission for Major Robert Lamb, who led the 63rd FS. Lamb, one of the original members of the 61st Fighter Squadron, had been on his second extension of his 200 hour tour when Major Gerald Johnson was shot down, and was selected to be his replacement. In order to take and hold the position, Lamb had to first obtain a fifty combat hour extension, and then one for twenty-five hours more. Thus, when he finished his stint, he had a total of 275 combat hours and had scored seven German fighters shot down, one probably shot down, and two damaged.

Capt. Donald Goodfleisch replaced Major Lamb as the squadron commander of the 63rd FS on May 27, 1944. Goodflesich, one of the original members of the squadron, had returned to the squadron on March 20 after a short assignment to Hq. 56th FG, and had been serving as their Operations Officer since that date.

May 23: VIII FC FO 348. The three Bomb Divisions went out to strike airfields and rail targets in France. Escort was provided by fourteen fighter groups, and none made any claims.

Lt. Col. Gabreski led the 56th Fighter Group off at 0711 to provide penetration support for the heavies. RV was made with six combat wings of B-17s near Dieppe 0750, just prior to landfall-in. They provided escort until east of St. Dizler at 0900, and crossed out over Calais at 0945 to land Boxted at 1020. A solid undercast made navigation difficult and the Luftwaffe did not show up.

May 24: VIII FC FO 349. A two-mission day. For the first mission the 56th Fighter Group went out along with three other P-47 groups to provide escort for the 2nd and 3rd Bomb Divisions.

Col. Zemke led forty-eight P-47s off at 0842 to provide penetration support, but five had to abort, and one came back as an escort for them. The made RV north of Heligoland at 1012 at 25,000 feet, and from then on the continent was obscured by clouds. Landfall-in was estimated over St. Peter at 1025. Escort was broken a half hour later in the vicinity of Hamburg. At this point the 62nd and 63rd Fighter Squadrons went below the overcast to strafe, destroying one locomotive and damaging six more. A good deal of rolling stock was also heavily damaged. RTB time was 1306.

The evening mission was led by Major Dade under Field Order 99, (65th Fighter Wing). Dade led twenty-eight P-47s off at 1650 on a train busting mission. With the 62nd FS providing top cover, the 61st and 63rd FS's dropped thirty-two 500 pound General Purpose bombs on rail and bridge targets. They claimed five locomotives destroyed, including one entire train, which in itself was an exceptional and rare feat. Two additional trains were damaged, along with twenty plus freight cars and a couple barges that were tied up near a railroad bridge.

May 25: VIII FC FO 350. The three bomb divisions were again given penetration and target support by the P-47s who then went out on their own to seek worthwhile ground targets.

They got off at 0708, as the days were getting longer in mid-Spring, which permitted ever earlier takeoffs. Lt. Col. Gabreski led forty-eight P-47s across Cayeux at 0750 to make RV northeast of Meaux at 0828. One squadron broke escort at Luneville to go strafing, while the other two continued to over Luxembourg before going down to do the same. Twelve locomotives were claimed as destroyed, along with other rolling stock. There was no sign of the Luftwaffe, and no damaged was incurred to the Thunderbolts.

May 27: VIII FC FO 351 called for two Ramrod type missions. The first was to Ludwigshafen, and the second to Noball targets around Pas de Calais. Col. Zemke led the first group of forty-eight P-47s off at 1005 to cross-in over Cayeux at 1050. RV was made in the area of Poix at 1100, and escort was broken off over Chaumont a hour later. A total of five Fw 190s were seen, but they were too far away to encounter. A couple of trains were shot up on the way out, and RTB time was 1420.

Major Lyle Adrianse led the second mission, a short one with just seven P-47s. They got off at 1222 and made landfall-in east of St. Valery at 1315 at 17,000 feet. RV with the first group of A-20 Havoc light bombers was west of Dungeness at 1255, and the second group off Fecamp at 1330. Escort was broken with the second box almost immediately, and the P-47s made six orbits in the area looking for action, but found none, and returned at 1540.

Col. Zemke led twenty-four Thunderbolts off at 1817 under 65th Fighter Wing Field Order 102 to dive bomb a convoy of barges between Willenstadt and Meerije. Armed with 500 pound GP bombs with instantaneous fuzes, they dove from between 10,000 and 13,000 feet to between 5,000 and 7,000 feet to bomb from a seventy-five degree angle. It seem to be a good combination of tactics, as at least two barges were destroyed and the convoy was scattered.

May 28: VIII FC FO 352. The three Bomb Divisions went out to hit thirty separate targets, their most widespread missions so far.

Forty-eight Thunderbolts were led off Boxted by Lt. Col. Gabreski at 1054 on a sweep in advance of the bombers and to provide general area support. They arrived over Drummer Lake at 1217 and divided into squadrons to sweep Breman, Hanover, Steinhudder Lake, Celle, Ulzen, Quackenbruck, Paderbern, Nordhausen and Brunswick. Other than seeing one vapor trail over Nordhausen at 30,000 feet, there was no sign of the Luftwaffe.

Yellow Flight of the 63rd Fighter Squadron strafed some barges on a river north of Lingen, otherwise the mission was uneventful. (Again, it was a matter of being in the right place at the right time, as the P-51 groups claimed 25-1-5, and the bombers called the German fighter opposition "heavy.").

May 29: VIII FC FO 343. Again the P-47 groups were up on escort for the three bomb divisions. Again, the P-47 groups were not where the action was. P-51s claimed 38-1-4 in the air and 18-0-15 on the ground.

Col. Zemke led forty-four P-47s off at 0954, with one flight from the 63rd Fighter Squadron not making the mission. RV was made at Neumunster, ten minutes late, with the last three Combat Wings of the 3rd Air Division that were all strung out. Escort continued to Parchim, and then the Thunderbolts went down to strafe, but there was little to be found. Near Gifhorn, a radar station and several trains were destroyed or damaged, but it really wasn't what the pilots were looking for.

May 30: VIII FC FO 354. Another two mission day. The first was to provide penetration support for the heavies.

Lt. Col. Gabreski led them off at 0857 and they began to catch up with the Big Friends over the Zuider Zee at 1000. The reached the front of the bomber formation over Drummer Lake and took up escort at that point. West of Neinburg Capt. Donald Goodfleisch's 63rd Fighter Squadron broke off to go strafing. They damaged a pair of steam locomotives and a pair of diesel engines, and some rolling stock near Kopenbrugge. The 61st FS hit the airdrome at Hepenhefer, hitting three hangers and a large storage dump. Once again they missed seeing the Luftwaffe. The lucky Mustang groups claimed 48-3-2 in the air and 7-0-3 on the ground.

VIII FC FO 381, 65th Fighter Wing FO 102 sent one hundred P-47s out "Thunderbombing." The 56th Fighter Group, for the first time went out with a "Droopsnoot" glass-nosed P-38 to pin-point the target.

Col. Zemke led eight P-47s from each squadron off at 1558. Sixteen carried two 1,000 pound GP bombs with minimum delay fuzes, while the other eight served as escorts for them. Landfall-in was over Cayeux and they headed for the railroad bridges at Canly-Le-Jouuque, where they encountered heavy flak that caused them to scatter. Zemke, flying the P-38, with Lt. "Easy" Ezzel from the 20th Bomb Group as bombardier, decided that the flak was just too heavy in the area to try and reform the group to strike at the target again, so he led them to another span on the same railway line five miles down the road near Chantilly. Bombing results were deemed satisfactory, but the mission, as such, unworkable. The P-47s were just too heavy with the under-wing bomb loads. Takeoffs were hazardous, the rate of climb poor, and formation flying dangerous and difficult. Zemke recommended 500 pound bombs as far more practical.

May 31: VIII FC FO 355. Over a thousand B-17s and B-24s were sent against marshalling yards and aircraft industries in Germany, along with rail targets in France and Belgium. Due to weather conditions, only a third of the force was effective.

Col. Zemke led the 56th Fighter Group off on their first mission of the day at 0904 to provide penetration support for the heavies. They made RV with five Combat Wings of B-17s from the 3rd Bomb Division over the Zuider Zee. Escort was provided to south of Gutersloh, and then the 62nd Fighter Squadron went down to strafe the airdrome at Gutersloh, itself, where thirty aircraft were seen parked. Two hangers were damaged, but the pilots lost count of the aircraft they damaged and no claims were awarded. The 63rd FS had better luck hitting trains, destroying two locomotives, damaging another, and shooting up rolling stock.

VIII FC FO 356 called for a fighter-bomber strike against German airfields by the 56th and 353rd Fighter Groups. Eighty-one Thunderbombers were dispatched against Gutersloh, carrying 500 and 1000 pound bombs. It was hoped that the German's would not expect them back.

Col. Zemke was again in the lead, and the 56th Fighter Group's forty-five P-47s got off at 1656. They crossed-in over Ijmuiden at 1804 and reached Gutersloh at 1850 to dive bomb the airdrome for an half hour. Dropping 500 pound GP bombs by squadrons, the results were determined to be excellent.

While orbiting over the airdrome at 21,000 feet the 62nd Fighter Squadron engaged thirty Fw 190s that came in from the southwest between 21,000 and 24,000 feet. Half of this number soon peeled off to attack the 62nd FS that was climbing back up after bombing. But Col. Zemke, leading the 61st FS, took the squadron down to intercept the German attack and he shot down two, probably got another, and damaged one. Lt. Wendell McClure got one. Capt. Charles Tucker got another and also damaged one, which wasn't too bad for an ex-bomber pilot on his first mission as a fighter pilot.

While this was going on, the 63rd FS had just completed their bombing and was in the process of reforming and climbing through 15,000 feet. Thirty more Fw 190s came in on them in a tight formation. As the German's had all the speed and height advantage, along with the P-47s being low on fuel, Capt. Don Goodflesch had to take his squadron off into the haze to avoid combat. Nevertheless, Lt. Donald Peters got an Fw 190.

June 2: VIII FC FO 358. The first missions of Operation Cover, a faker-feint to make the Germans think that the future invasion would take place in the area of Pas de Calais. All bomber and fighter groups were up to hit targets in France. Cloud cover hampered bomber operations to a degree.

The 56th Fighter Group went out on an area support mission at 1049, being led by Lt. Russell Westfall and the 63rd Fighter Squadron. All of the "Wheels" were occupied elsewhere, and the three squadrons were all led by Lieutenants.

Landfall-in was over Dunkirk and the group proceeded to St. Omer-Lille-Cambrai-Amiens to make seven or eight orbits in that general area. The heavies hit Boulenge, which were observed by a Major Franklin and Capt. Jack Brown from "Ajax." (Brown had been one of the original members of the 63rd FS and completed his operational tour on March 22, 1944 as the squadron's Assistant Operations Officer. He would later be assigned to Peterson Field, Colorado). The mission was uneventful with the exception of two P-47s being hit and slightly damaged by flak, and they landed at 1355.

June 3: VIII FC FO 363. The Big Friends continued to devote their attention to the Pas de Calais area. Over five hundred B-17s and B-24s pounded the coastal defenses, although many were ineffective because of cloud cover. Lt. Col. Gabreski led forty-eight Jugs off at 0942 on a Type 16 Control mission. Landfall-in was over Cayeux at 1023, and they arrived over Montdidier at 1032 to commence being radar vectored to Paris, Brussels and Lille. There was a notable lack of flak during the course of the uneventful mission that RTB'd at 1315.

June 4: VIII FC FO 365. The heavies went to France, with B-17s concentrating on rail targets while the B-24s went after airfields.

The 56th Fighter Group launched its first mission of the day at 1119 with Major Dade leading forty-eight Thunderbolts on an area patrol. They crossed-in over Gravelines at 1208 and flew to Lille, circled three times then flew a racetrack between Arres and St. Omer three times before heading for home to land at 1425.

FO 368: The evening mission got off at 1810 behind Lt. Col. Gabreski to provide general penetration, target and withdrawal support for Big Friends hitting Noball targets at Pas de Calais with the Group specifically escorting the heavies attacking an airdrome at Bourges. The bombers "did good," and escort was broken by squadron to RTB at 2145.

June 5: VIII FC FO 369. Once again the heavies went back to the coast of Europe, this time to both Cherbourg and Pas de Calais.

Col. Zemke led the Group of forty-eight P-47s off at 0813 on another Type 16 Control mission. Lt. James Jure, 61st Fighter Squadron, crashed just after takeoff and he was slightly injured.

Landfall-in was at St. Valery at 0902 climbing to 18,000 feet. They penetrated to north of Evereux, and then set up an orbit Rouen-Bernay-Le Havre-Treport. Cloud cover, with tops to 34,000 feet created many problems in keeping the Group together, and even some of the squadrons had to split up to get around and through "the clag." Again, there was an obvious lack of the presence of the Luftwaffe and flak was nil.

June 6: VIII FC FO 371. "D-Day" and everything one might expect to go along with it. For everyone it was a maximum effort. For the pilots it was pure excitement in participating in the long-awaited invasion. For the long suffering ground crews it was excitement and work, and more work to the point of exhaustion. Their work continued from the return of the P-47s from the previous day's sorties and did not let up.

Post mission maintenance had to be taken care of, and there filtered down "the word" that everything had better be in extra tip-top shape for tomorrow. Then the gates were locked, everyone was restricted to Boxted and the outside telephone lines were disconnected. In the evening, orders were given to paint the fuselages and wings of the P-47s with black and white "Invasion Stripes." When Col. Zemke called the Group's key officers to Base Operations at eight O'clock that evening, there was no doubt at the big show was on for June 6. Most of the ground crews were now faced with a thirty-six to forty-eight hour endurance test to maintain their aircraft, being able to only catch a cat nap while the aircraft were gone. They lived on coffee and adrenalin: and accomplished an outstanding job. Sleep, even in the little time for it, did not have a chance to take place. At 0045 a British Bren Gun carrier exploded on the Colchester Road, just off base. By the time the excitement from that incident was over the continuous drone of bomber engines was overhead and the sky was full of red, white and green navigation lights as the bombers jockeyed for position in their formations that were assembling.

Lt. Col. Gabreski led the first mission with thirty-two P-47s of the 61st and 63rd Fighter Squadrons, taking off at 0336. A "Fullhouse" mission to provide an area patrol over the English Channel in the vicinity of Dunkirk. The intent was to provide a high cover on the north side of the landings from 17,000 feet against any interlopers coming down from that direction. Intelligence was expecting that the Luftwaffe would be moving torpedo bombers from Norway to attack the invasion shipping.

Since there was heavy cloud cover between 11,000 and 12,000 feet, the fighter pilots could not see a thing going on beneath them. Encountering strong winds, the Group was blown inland to near Abbeville, and the radar controller had to vector them back to their orbit point. The German's were aware that something big was going on at this early hour, as the radio frequencies were being jammed. One transmission kept repeating "Death, Death, Death" over and over. Another stated, "Come on in-plenty of room-the food's fine." On the way home, 2nd Lt. Robert Magle, 63rd FS, could not resist a "look-see" and went down to 7,000 feet, where he got shot at by "everything including rockets and the kitchen sink." They returned at 0801.

The 62nd Fighter Squadron put up sixteen P-47s for the second mission, becoming airborne at 0608 behind Major Lucian Dade. Eight Thunderbolts went in under the cloud cover between 1,000 and 4,000 feet, while the other eight flew between 1,000 and 5,000 feet. On another "Fullhouse" mission, they flew to Amines to patrol uneventfully. RTB time was 0956.

Lt. Russell Westfall, 63rd Fighter Squadron, led the third mission with sixteen P-47s, all from the 63rd FS. They were airborne from Boxted at 0945 on a "Stud" mission, to divebomb rail targets. They crossed-in over Dieppe and flew directly to Les Andelye to bomb a dam, marshalling yards and railroad tracks. Carrying 250 pound General Purpose bombs, the results were not gratifying. None of the bombs were seen to explode. The dam was missed entirely, a rail bridge had already been knocked down. Although some bombs were seen to hit railroad tracks, no rail cars were destroyed. They crossed back out over Dieppe to land at 1206.

Mission Four was another "Stud" dive bombing run, flown by sixteen Thunderbolts of the 61st FS. Capt. James Carter led them off at 1048 to make landfall-in at Le Treport at 1128. One train was attacked by four P-47s, all of which missed. Another flight bombed three strings of forty each railway cars with moderate success. RTB time was 1316.

The 62nd Fighter Squadron went back out at 1057 to fly the Fifth mission with fifteen P-47s. A "Stud" led by Capt. Fred "Chris" Christensen. The Germans were awake now and moving around a bit. The bombing was far more successful, as twenty plus trains were hit and damaged. Three locomotives were destroyed and all sorts of rolling stock shot up. Staff cars, busses and trucks also deserved attention, and were destroyed or damaged. Lt. William McElhare drew the first blood in the air, destroying an Fw 190 five miles east of Rambouillet.

Capt. Donald Goodfleisch took the 63rd Fighter Squadron out for mission Six, their third for the day. Another "Stud" with sixteen Thunderbolts that got off at 1428. They made landfall-in over Dieppe at 1612 and went to bomb a single-track double-width railroad bridge. Again, fourteen 250 pound bombs were dropped, and not a single one was seen to explode. "Colgate," their radar controller, then vectored them after four Fw 190s near Dieppe, but they could not be caught.

Mission Seven got them back into the big time again. Under Field Order 372, they went out on a "Royal Flush" mission, Type 16 Control. Col. Zemke led thirty-one "Jugs" of the 61st and 62nd FS's, but seven "tired" P-47s had to return early. Off at 1845, they went to Rouen to orbit. The 61st FS then broke-away to circle an airdrome south of Elbey, but nothing was happening there, so they went to Evereux and dive bombed and strafed the Fanville airdrome, damaging several parked aircraft. Proceeding to look for targets, they spotted a convoy that was already under attack by the 352nd Fighter group, which at the same time was engaged with fifteen Fw 190s.

Zemke took the 61st FS in to help out, destroying an Fw 190, himself, and confirming three more that 352nd FG pilots shot down. Zemke's claim was entered, and credited, even though he had not fired a shot, as the Focke-Wulf spun-in while trying to escape being fired upon. Also scoring was Flight Lt. Michael Gladych, who knocked down his fifth German fighter while flying with the 56th FG and became an ace by our Air Force standards. (He previously was credited with destroying five while flying with his Polish Air Force, and three while with the Royal Air Force, including one that he had deliberately rammed). The 61st FS worked over the convoy for an half hour, but claims for damages were far outweighed by the loss of Flight Officer Evan McMinn who was killed during the strafing of an armed convoy.

The 62nd FS had little success. The only targets they found were trucks in a convoy that was being worked over by P-51s. Capt. Christensen, leading the squadron, claimed a couple of trucks destroyed, but no enemy aircraft were encountered. The day closed with the return of this mission at 2018.

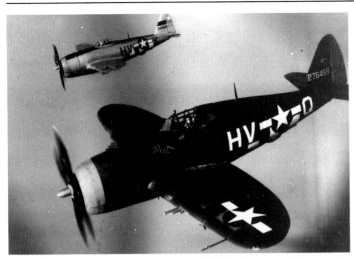

"Pat" and wingman over a haze layer. HV⊙K had previously belonged to Major Stewart, CO of the 61st FS. Stewart left the Wolfpack in April 1944, and was not flying this aircraft at the time, as attributed elsewhere, as it now bears post D-Day markings. HV⊙K belonged to Lt. Robert Baughman. (USAF)

June 7: VIII FC FO's 373 & 375. Over five hundred Thunderbolts were active during the day's activities in support of the invasion. Whereas the Luftwaffe had been hard to find on D-Day, they made up for it today. 29-1-12 were destroyed, probably destroyed, or damaged in the air and 25-0-12 hit on the ground by 8th Air Force fighter pilots. The 56th Fighter Group claimed twelve destroyed, but it cost them five P-47s and three pilots were killed.

Major Lucian Dade led the first mission off in the pre-dawn, at 0450. Composed of sixteen Thunderbolts from the 62nd Fighter squadron, they went out on a dive-bombing strike to the Bernay area carrying ninety clusters of M40 fragmentation bombs. Landfall-in was south of St. Valery at 14,000 feet, where the mission had to split into flights and elements to penetrate the clouds. The Thunderbombers selected random targets, which turned out to be less than fruitful, and far too expensive. Ten P-47s dropped sixty clusters of frags, with only Blue Three and Four specifically claiming three trucks. Two had to return still carrying their three clusters each. Three Thunderbombers were lost before they had a chance to even drop their ordnance. Lt. Eugene Bennent, Red Three, was hit by flak near Orbec while going in to attack an armored column of a hundred plus vehicles. He had to bailout at 1,500 feet and was last seen running into a wooded area. He managed to evade capture. Lt. Alfred Evans, Yellow Three, was hit by flak at Bucky, near Argeuil, and bellied-in his P-47. He was not seen to escape from the cockpit and it was discovered later that he was killed. Lt. Donald Furlong was seen to dive in from 1,500 feet over Argeuil after being hit by flak, and he too was killed.

Then, seven Fw 190s jumped the squadron, and Lt. Thad Buszko got his P-47 shot-up. He got it back to Boxted, but it was so damaged that it was written-off. Three other pilot's, all named "Bill" were lucky or unlucky, depending on how you looked at it. Lt.'s William Chataway, William Davenport, and William McElhare all had to divert to land at the Manston emergency landing field with battle damaged aircraft.

Lt. Col. Gabreski led the Second mission, which was made up of sixteen P-47s of the 61st Fighter Squadron. They got airborne at 0656 to go skip-bombing, with each P-47 carrying two 500 pound GP bombs. Gabreski's White Flight attacked a train, but missed with their bombs, so the train was destroyed by .50 caliber fire. Red Flight attacked a bridge, and at least one bomb was seen to cause some damage. Blue Flight hit a railroad siding composed of four tracks near Forges. They damaged 10-15 boxcars and tore up some trackage. Yellow Flight's Lt. Joseph Perry hit a marshalling yard successfully, while the other three P-47s in the flight

bombed a railway station and destroyed it and damaged the tracks. RTB time 0838.

Lt. Russell Westfall led the 63rd Fighter Squadron on the Group's third mission. The "Stud" got off at 0935 with sixteen Thunderbombers of the 63rd FS composing the strike to Gournay where they bombed the marshalling yard inside of the town. Lt. Roach Stewart's comments, while atypical of the cryptic combat reports, are worth recounting as to what was encountered:

"Our flight arrived in the target area, marshalling yards in the city of Gournay, France. White One and Two went down and dropped their bombs while Lt. (Harry F.) Warner, White Three and I, White Four, circled. Then Blue Flight descended to strafe the yards. After Blue Flight completed their strafing, Lt. Warner called in that he and I were coming in at a ninety degree angle to bomb. We went down, leveled off at approximately 50 feet; cut our speed to 250 m.p.h., flying a close formation. We released our bombs at 35 feet, aiming at a mass of cars assembled in the yards and passing over them at 20/25 feet. Just before passing over these cars, I saw Lt. Warner's bombs strike in the midst of them. At the same time a terrific explosion occurred, which completely demolished the latter half of Lt. Warner's plane. The remaining front half was engulfed in flames as it immediately crashed into the ground." Warner had no chance to survive.

Lt. Joseph Curtis, Red Three, was just pulling out of his dive after bomb release at five hundred feet when he spotted an Fw 190. Curtis chased after it, and the Focke-Wulf pilot mistakenly reversed his turn, which closed the range. Curtis hit it with a full burst of .50 caliber fire, and it dove into some trees, cartwheeled into the ground and exploded.

The mission's Yellow Flight proceeded to Beauvais, where they encountered a pair of Me 109s, which turned-tail upon sighting the Jugs. The Flight then bombed a marshalling yard, destroying two locomotives and damaging a third. They also strafed an airdrome near Beauvais, damaging some flak positions.

Mission Four came under FO 375, which was another "Stud" against an airdrome at Dreux. This mission was led by Lt. Col. Gabreski and was composed of sixteen Thunderbombers, all from the 61st Fighter Squadron. Airborne at 1043, they arrived over Dreux at 1205 at 12,000 feet. The target was obscured by cloud cover, so the mission proceeded to a marshalling yard two miles east of Chateaudun. They dropped twenty-four 500 pound GP bombs there, while another flight bombed a second marshalling yard four miles south of Chateaudun.

Free of their ordnance, they returned to Dreux, where they encountered a flight of Fw 190s on the deck heading southeast that were covered by another group of mixed Fw 190s and Me 190s between 3,000 and 4,000 feet. In the following battle "Gabby" knocked down an Me 109 and an Fw 190. Flight Officer Steven Gerrick got two Me 109s. Capt. (Flight Lt., actually), Michael Gladych got an Me 109. 2nd Lt. Joel Popplewell got his first and only kill on his sixth mission, an Me 109.

Popplewell: "Our Flight bounced the rear box and I singled out a Hun to my right. I fired and saw many hits on the fuselage and wing roots of the enemy aircraft. Smoke started pouring from the German plane. I fired again and the Nazi plane exploded in flames."

Two P-47s were slightly damaged, one by cannon fire and the other by flak.

Mission Five was made up by sixteen P-47s, all from the 62nd Fighter Squadron. Capt. Fred Christensen led them off at 1152 on yet another dive bombing mission, this time to Poix and Fourges. This time they carried 250 pound GP bombs, and all but four were dropped effectively upon marshalling yards. The four bombs that were not effective and to be jettisoned were by White Two and Red Two, Capt. Charles Tucker and Lt. William McElhare, when they were bounced by two Me 109s near Beauvais. They evaded being shot down by climbing into the clouds, but Tucker's P-47 was so shot-up that it had to be salvaged upon his return.

Yellow One and Two, Lt.'s Wendell McClure and George Bostwick, were bounced by three Fw 190s near the Grand Villers airdrome while at

4,000 feet. They too climbed into the clouds to escape, and when Bostwick exited the clouds he found himself on the tail of an Me 109, which he destroyed. Unfortunately, McClure did not fare so well, and he was not seen again. Shot down, he did manage to evade capture, however.

1st Lt. Mark Moseley and 2nd Lt. Jack Pierce shared a Ju 88 that they caught at low altitude just after it took off from Lisieux airdrome. The mission returned at 1545.

Capt. Donald Goodfleisch took the 63rd Fighter Squadron out for Mission Six at 1255. Again with sixteen Thunderbombers on a dive bombing strike. They crossed-in over Le Treport at 14,000 feet at 1338 and found targets of opportunity at Beauvais through a hole in the clouds. Three separate marshalling yards were bombed with 250 pound GP's, but only six bombs were seen to explode. Nevertheless, a train and twenty railroad cars were claimed as damaged. RTB time was 1611.

Col. Zemke led Mission Seven. Fourteen P-47s were dispatched, with one aborting. Armed with 500 pound GPs, they hit the marshalling yards at Gournai between 1755 and 1805, and again the results were frustrating. Only six bombs out of the twenty-eight were seen to explode, although they all were fitted with instantaneous fuzes.

Southeast of Nantes a group of fifteen Fw 190s and Me 109s were encountered. Col. Zemke shot down two Fw 190s and damaged a third. This feat making Zemke a "triple ace" with an official total score of 15.25 kills. These would also be Zemke's last air-to-air kills as "Leader of the Pack," although he would be credited with three more in the fall as Commanding Officer of the 479th Fighter Group.

Lt. Robert Rankin, 61st FS, got an Me 109. Capt. Zbigniew Janicki, one of the Polish exchange pilots assigned to the 61st FS, probably destroyed an Fw 190 and damaged another. But in return, Janicki's P-47 was heavily damaged by a German pilot and when he got back to Boxted he could not get his wheels down. He was not injured in the following belly landing, but his P-47 was a write-off.

The last mission for the day, Mission Eight, was the third mission flown by the 63rd Fighter Squadron during the day. Lt. Russell Westfall again led sixteen Thunderbombers out, with their getting off at 1800. Landfall-in was north of Dieppe at 1834 at 9,000 feet where they started looking for targets of opportunity.

White and Blue Flights went to drop their bombs on railroad tracks near Chateaudun, where they destroyed the tracks and sixteen out of the forty parked rail cars. Yellow Flight hit tracks eight miles west of Chartres and severed them. 2nd Lt. Eugene Timony then went to make a strafing pass on ten parked rail cars. One of them exploded, followed by the rest. Apparently they were loaded with ammunition, as the sound of the explosion could be heard at 8,000 feet over the noise of the P-47s engines, and the concussion was felt by pilots at 10,000 feet.

At landfall-in Red Flight had gotten themselves separated from the rest of the squadron while dodging clouds. Soon thereafter they spotted a pair of Fw 190s and dropped their bombs to give chase. After a ten minute pursuit one evaded, but the other was eventually caught by Red Two, 2nd Lt. Sam Dale. Dale fired at it until he was out of ammunition, and then 2nd Lt. Marvin Becker dove on it as the Fw 190 passed under him with its canopy open. Becker fired on it until its pilot had enough and bailed out. Each received a half credit. The flight then proceeded to Tillieres, where they spotted a convoy of forty trucks. The convoy conveniently stopped when its drivers saw the P-47s, and made easy meat of themselves for the pilots. Unfortunately, they had all gone "Winchester" (Out of ammunition.), and could only claim one truck as destroyed.

June 8: VIII FC FO 377. The 56th Fighter Group got a partial break from the dive bombing role on this day's mission requirements. A Ramrod for other groups that were doing the actual dive bombing was the first mission, while their second mission was back to dive bombing again.

Major Dade led the mission, which was composed of the 62nd Fighter Squadron and was partially curtailed by the weather. With a solid overcast, the fighter bombers had to proceed to alternate targets and Dade's group broke escort over Dreux. Seeking targets of opportunity, they flew over Illiers airdrome, where many German aircraft were seen taking off. Catching the Luftwaffe unprepared, Lt. Mark Moseley, destroyed two Fw 190s. Lt. Billy Edens, doing what a good wingman should, shot two Me 109s off Moseley's tail while Mark was getting his two and then got an Fw 190 without actually seeing any strikes. Perhaps it stalled-out while avoiding Edens' fire? Lt. George Van Noy got an Fw 190 on his first combat mission, which also marked the date of his mother's birthday. Not a bad gift, but also a jinx, as the rest of his tour would be scoreless. 2nd Lt. George Butler got an Me 109, the first of a string of three.

Lt. Col. Gabreski led the second mission to dive bomb near Pitres and Gondecourt. Red Flight hit a convoy proceeding north out of Pitres with eight 500 pound GPs. Several trucks were also destroyed by the strafing of Lt. Sisson. The unusual thing about this particular stretch of road was that it had featured camouflaged revetments for hiding trucks.

June 10: VIII FC FO 380-381. After a day's forced respite because of the weather, the fighter-bombers and their escorts were back on missions. It would be a tough day for the 500 Thunderbolts dispatched, for although they claimed 8-0-2 in aerial combat, fifteen were lost to various factors. The 56th Fighter Group flew three missions, and made no claims for enemy aircraft, for the loss of one aircraft.

Col. Zemke led the first mission off at 0728. It was composed of thirty-six P-47s, which composed "A" Group for this mission. Landfall-in was St. Valery, and from there they sought targets of opportunity in the area of Argentan. Bombing results were poor, while strafing was gratifying. RTB'd at 1105.

"B" Group was led off on the same mission by Capt. James Carter, 61st Fighter Squadron, at 0730 with sixteen Thunderbombers. Two flights bombed a seven arch bridge at Sables, considerably damaging it. Two more flights hit a electric powerplant at Morannes, and then all aircraft went strafing with good results against truck convoys. Two P-47s from the 63rd FS were shot at by a tank, and another from the 61st FS was damaged by cannon fire from an over eager P-38 pilot.

Lt. Col. Gabreski led fifty Thunderbolts off on the next mission, to go skip-bombing, at 1345. St. Valery was becoming an old friend as they passed over it again on the way in at 1455. Targets of opportunity were once again sought, and so many were hit that they cannot be recounted.

Over Chambois, Flight Officer Joseph Vitale, 62nd FS, was hit by flak and had to bailout. He managed to evade capture and returned via the underground on Sept. 4. On return, a Lt. Clark had to crashland in England, but the Group historian did not identify which Clark from which squadron. He was uninjured.

The Third Mission was another dual mission with both "A" and "B" Groups participating under Field Order 381. Col. Zemke led the forty-eight P-47s off at 2000 and they crossed over St. Valery at 2047 to split into the two groups of twenty-four aircraft each at that point. Again seeking targets of opportunity, "A" Group went to the marshalling yard at Echauffer, which was bombed with poor results. "B" Group went to the yards at Verneuil and Aube-sur-Risle, which were hit with greater success. The mission closed out the day at 2255, their latest return so far and a rare Group night landing.

June 11: VIII FC FO 382. Not a whole lot of rest for the pilots, and even less for the ground crews. An "O'Dark-thirty" briefing and Lt. Col. Gabreski led the first mission off at 0546 on a combination escort, area support and dive bombing strike.

The mission was composed of fifty-three P-47s from the 61st and 62nd Fighter Squadrons, and had one abort. Back over St. Valery once again, at 0640, the 61st Fighter Squadron went off to escort the Heavies for an half hour on the Big Friend's way to Munich. After escort, the 61st FS dive bombed east of Mayenne with good results. The 62nd FS, carrying 500 pound GP's, bombed Liffre, with poor results, but then strafed in the area with and did better. The mission returned at 1015.

The second mission got off an hour and a half later, at 1144, with Lt. Col. Gabreski again in the lead. The 61st and 62nd FS's put up a dozen P-47s each for this dive bombing strike, while the 63rd FS sent out ten. Across St. Valery again, they went to a marshalling yard at Pre-en-Pail that was well clobbered. Other sections went to a marshalling yard at Lisieux, which was hit with excellent results. Over a hundred flat cars loaded with half-tracks were put out of commission there.

June 12: VIII FC FO 383. Three P-47 groups on Ramrod and Stud missions to the areas around Tours/Paris.

Col. Zemke led the first mission off at 0728, an escort and dive bombing strike with fifty-three aircraft. The route over St. Valery might as well be paved with concrete, it was so well traveled, and it was crossed over again at 0818. Capt. Don Goodfleisch took his 63rd Fighter Squadron off from the rest of the Group to escort a B-24 mission for a hour, and then they went to the marshalling yards at Chaillous to drop their 250 pound GP bombs with fair results.

The 61st and 62nd FS's went to Sees to hit a marshalling yard, which was struck with good results, and then went strafing. Just after bombing, Lt. Billy Edens, 62nd FS, was jumped by seven Me 109s that he had to evade in a hurry, but he got away okay. The mission returned at 1131.

Lt. Col. Gabreski led forty-four Thunderbolts off at 1233 for the 56th Fighter Group's second mission. In over St. Valery at 1320 they proceeded towards Paris under the direction of "Colgate," (Headquarters 65th Fighter Wing at Debden).

Passing over Evereux, the 61st Fighter Squadron's fourteen Jugs encountered a dozen Me 109s that were climbing through 3,500 feet in line-abreast formation. Combat was joined with them, and then another dozen Me 109s joined in. They were aggressive and fought with sound tactics, but definitely came out second best in the melee that ranged between 4,000 feet and the deck. Flight Officer Steven Gerrick claimed four Me 109s destroyed, and was officially awarded two, given two as probables, and he damaged two more. Lt. Oscar Belk got one. Lt. Col. Gabreski shot down two, which made him an ace five times over, plus one, and placed him just one behind Robert Johnson for the ETO's highest scorer. Lt.'s Warren Patterson, Charles Dudley and Arthur Maul each damaged an Me 109. 2nd Lt. Earl Hertel, 61st FS, claimed another distinction of sorts. Low on fuel, Hertel put his P-47 down on an emergency airstrip on the Normandy beach-head, becoming the first 56th pilot to legitimately land on the continent. Hertel called out, "Having trouble. Am going to try and hit new allied landing strip on coast." Covered by 1st Lt. Praeger Neyland on the way to the airstrip, Hertel overshot his approach and "plowed up the nearby turf before his plane slid to a stop." He was uninjured and spent the night on a ship in the harbor before returning to England the next day.

The 62nd and 63rd FS's, flying as escort and high cover, swept Paris and environs without encounters. RTB time was 1635.

June 13: VIII FC FO 387. The 8th and 9th Air Forces went after tactical and strategic targets in France. The 56th Fighter Group went bombing again, this time carrying 1000 pound GP's. Fifty-two Jugs went out, and five had to come back early, being escorted by two more after dropping their bombs in the English Channel.

Enroute to Europe one of the aborting pilots, Flight Lt. (AAF Captain) Zbigniew Janicki, Polish Air Force, assigned to the 61st Fighter squadron was lost. Apparently he encountered some sort of mechanical problems, and he informed Col. Zemke that he was turning back. Subsequently he was overheard asking the radar controller for a vector to rejoin the Group, but he could not understand them and was then told to return to Boxted. Later he was heard to say that he was going to have to land and to "give regards to friends." He was later reported as killed in action.

In over St. Valery at 1942 after a 1830 takeoff, a solid overcast at 3,000 feet was encountered enroute to Le Port Boulet, so the Group searched for targets of opportunity. A couple of bridges were attacked, but with little success. An overshooting or undershooting bomb kicked up a lot of dirt,

but did little actual damage. Most frustrating to the pilot who had to lug them to the target. A few marshalling yards were also hit, with greater success. RTB'd at 2231.

June 14: VIII FC FO 388. The 1st and 3rd Bomb Division B-17s struck targets in France. The 56th Fighter Group flew area support during this exercise.

Off at 0641, Lt. Col. Gabreski took forty-four P-47s in over Le Treport at 0732. Capt. Don Goodfleisch's 63rd Fighter Squadron took up high cover escort duties for the Flying Forts at 27,000 feet while the other two squadrons flew to Senlis area to orbit, looking for action. North of Paris, near Reims, the 63rd FS encountered ten Me 109s. Lt. Walter Frederick, Yellow One, went after them with his flight and Frederick damaged three before the rest fled into the clouds. For the rest of the Group the mission was uneventful and they returned at 1021.

The second mission was led off by Col. Zemke at 1929 with the 61st and 62nd squadrons carrying 250 and 500 pound GP bombs, while the 63rd FS flew as top cover for the mission. In over Cayeux at 2021, they went looking for a Panzer convoy reported in the area of Amiens, but it could not be located. The 62nd FS then flew to Beauvais where they dropped thirty-two 500 five-hundred pounders on a mile long stretch of railway tracks. A hundred box cars were believed destroyed. The 61st FS dropped their "eggs" on Poix airdrome without being able to access the damage. RTB'd at 2237 with one P-47 suffering minor flak damage.

June 15: VIII FC FO 390. Two hundred P-47s out on escort for the three Bomb Divisions hitting targets in France and Western Germany. In fact, all 8th Air Force Fighter Groups were up but one.

Lt. Col. Gabreski led forty-eight Thunderbolts off at 0615 on a welcome respite of bomber escort. They crossed-in over St. Valery at 0702, escorting the B-24s to Paris and Orleans. After escort was broken west of Bernay, the Group went under Type 16 radar control on fruitless searches until fuel considerations dictated that it was time to head for home.

Col. Zemke led a strafing sweep that afternoon that took off at 1413. Crossing-in over Dieppe they proceeded to Grosley and Bernay to strafe a train and a convoy, inflicting satisfactory damage. RTB'd at 1845.

June 16: VIII FC FO 393. The 1st and 2nd Bomb Divisions hit airfields and Noball targets. The "Wolfpack" went up on area support.

Forty-eight Thunderbolts were off at 1410 behind Col. Zemke, with two aborting. In over Le Treport at 1500 among heavy clouds, they swept to Dreux where they found some action. Six Me 109s were circling over the airdrome at 3,000 feet and they bounced the Group, but without results. The 56th FG then proceeded to a wooded area near Laigle where a convoy was strafed. On the way out four Me 109s were encountered, and (Now) 2nd Lt. Steven Gerrick, 61st Fighter Squadron, made the ranks of the aces by shooting one down for his fifth kill. Enroute home Lt. Timothy Sullivan, 61st FS, went down due to unknown difficulties near the Normandy beach-head. He was killed.

June 17: VIII FC FO 394. The 1st and 2nd Bomb Divisions went back to airfields in France.

Lt. Col. Gabreski led the 56th Fighter Group off on their first mission of the day at 1146 on a Ramrod covering the heavies. In south of Dieppe at 1228, they made RV with the returning heavies west of Chartres and escorted them out to east of Argentan. There was no sign of the Luftwaffe. RTB'd at 1548.

Field Order 395: Another Ramrod, again led by "Gabby" Gabreski. Off with forty-eight Thunderbolts at 1852 to provide penetration, target and withdrawal support, RV and landfall-in was accomplished over Cabourg at 1953. The heavies hit Angers airdrome with "good to fair" results. Escort was broken at Quillebouf and the Jugs crossed out over St. Valery to land Boxted at 2248.

56TH FIGHTER GROUP AIRCRAFT PROFILES

1. P-47B Thunderbolt, s.n. 41-5999, A/C #24 of the 61st FS.
First type in service at Selfridge Field late 1942.

2. P-47C-5-RE Thunderbolt, s.n. 41-6322 of the 61st FS.
Operational training in Wales, U.K., march, 1943. A/C #201 has a yellow bordered fuselage insignia of the European theatre, circa 1943, and it fitted with a standard 50 gallon drop tank. The A/C was later designated HV-W "LITTLE BUTCH" and assigned to major Loren McCollum.

3. P-47-343-RE Thunderbolt, s.n. 41-6343 of the 62nd FS.
LM-W "LITTLE COOKIE" was assigned to Capt. Walter Cook who scored the first kill for the Group in the A/C on 12 June 1943. The A/C is displayed as of July when bars and red border were added to both fuselage and wing insignia.

4. P-47D-5-RE Thunderbolt, s.n. 42-8458 of the 61st FS.
HV-F displays five reversed white swastikas under the cockpit, three of which were recorded by Capt. Francis "Gabby" Gabreski on missions flown in November and December of 1943. The A/C bears fuselage and wing insignia with standardized blue borders of that era, and is fitted with a pressed paper 75 gallon drop tank. The A/C was written off after Lt. McMinn's takeoff accident on New Year's Day 1944.

5. P-47D-10-RE Thunderbolt, s.n. 42-75121 of the 61st FS.
HV-Z is very likely the A/C flown by Group Leader Hub Zemke during April and May, 1944, when he attained double-ace status while initiating his "Fan-formation" tactics against the Luftwaffe. The colonel was probably flying HV-Z when he was nearly shot down over Koblenz by Luftwaffe super-ace Günther Rall (275 victories) on May 12.

6. P-47D-22-RE Thunderbolt, s.n. 42-26024 of the 61st FS.
HV-O is one of the first bare-metal models equipped with the broad-bladed Hamilton propeller which increased the Thunderbolt's rate of climb. It carries a U.K. built 125 gallon drop tank. This A/C was often flown by Flight Officer Steve Gerick who scored two confirmed victories plus five damaged in the March-June missions of 1944. The ten plain black victory crosses and full span D-Day invasion markings shown here indicate late June.

7. P-47D-20-RE Thunderbolt, s.n. 42-76363 of the 62nd FS.
LM-F displays the typical 62nd Squadron camouflage treatment to obscure both the bare aluminum and D-Day stripes of the post-invasion era. Ten white swastikas on the black foil beneath the canopy verify seven aerial kills and apparently three ground kills for Lt. Billy Edens who flew this Thunderbolt throughout June and July of 1944.

8. P-47D-28-RE Thunderbolt, s.n. 42-28796 of the 63rd FS.
UN-V is a standard bubble-canopy "Super-bolt" (so named by Zemke) from the late 1944 era and displays abbreviated D-Day markings solely on the lower fuselage. It carries a pair of 1000 lb. HE bombs, one on each wing rack. The 63rd briefly used a dark blue rudder designator color in this era which later gave way to a much lighter shade. The pilot of this A/C is unknown.

9. P-47M-1-RE Thunderbolt, s.n. 44-21213 of the 62nd FS.
LM-I was one of the late model high-speed Thunderbolts assigned to Capt. Felix Williamson as of March, 1945. The A/C displays another variation of the 62nd Squadron camouflage treatment and lacks the fin strake later installed to the spine of the rear fuselage.

10. P-47M-1-RE Thunderbolt, s.n. 44-21118 of the 63rd FS.
UN-S was assigned to Lt. Arthur Schupe. The A/C displays the bold two-tone camouflage and bare-metal squadron letter codes used by the unit. The M-model often carried two 150 gallon drop tanks to fuel the voracious 2800 H.P. engine. The over-sized upper wing insignia is typical of the April-May 1945 era for all three squadrons as is the fin strake on the spine of the rear fuselage.

11. P-51H Mustang, s.n. 44-64308 of the HQ Squadron/56th FG.
Capt. Donovan Smith flew this A/C at Selfridge AFB as a member of the base aerobatic team which flew demonstrations at numerous air shows throughout 1946-1947. The score board displays five aerial victories plus the four damaged victims scored by Smith in his tour with the 61st FS in late 1943 and early 1944.

12. F-80A Shooting Star, s.n. 44-85275 of the 61st FS.
A/C #1 of Squadron CO LtCol Richie at Selfridge AFB in late 1947. The A/C designator "PN" would soon be changed to "FN" and would be one of the planes to make the first all-jet trans-Atlantic crossing in the summer of 1948.

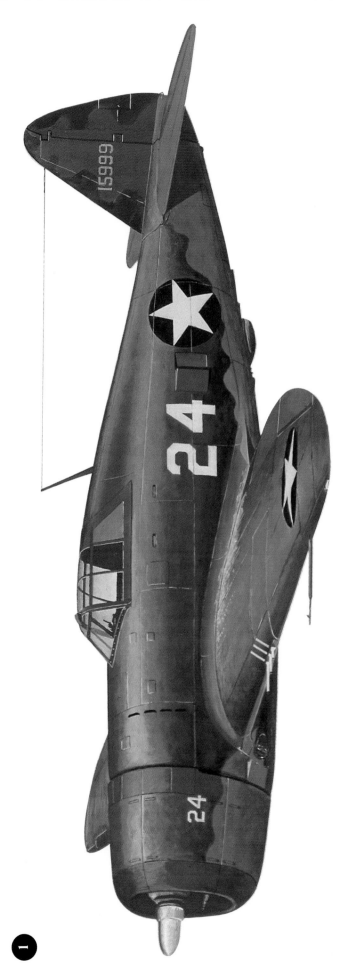

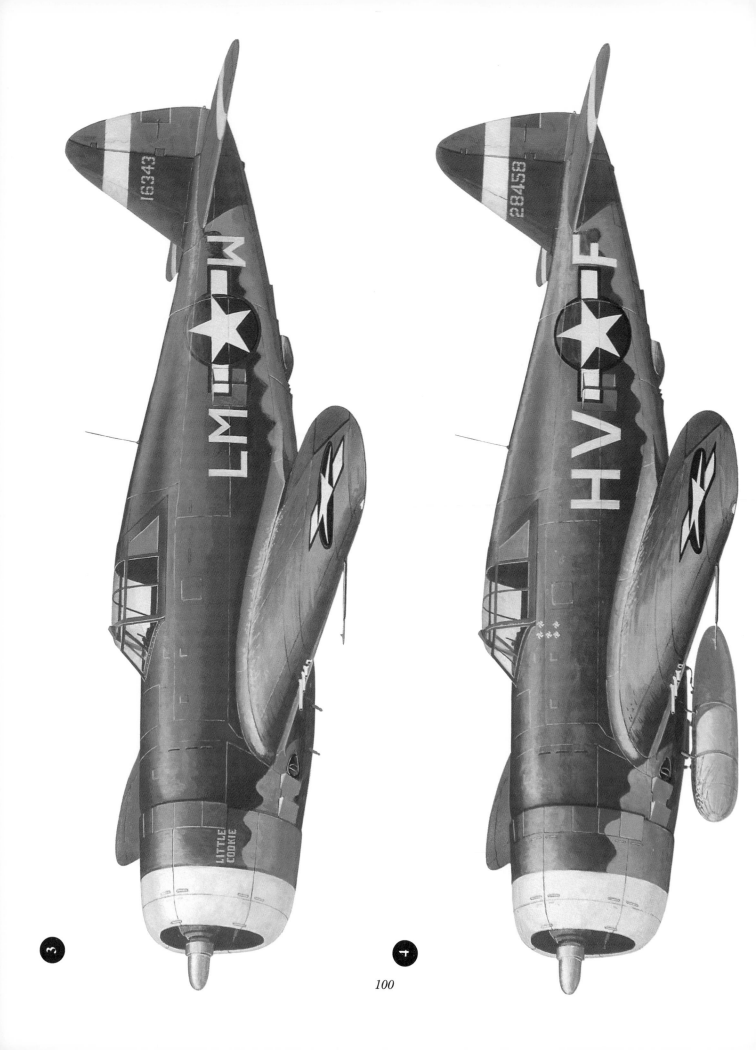

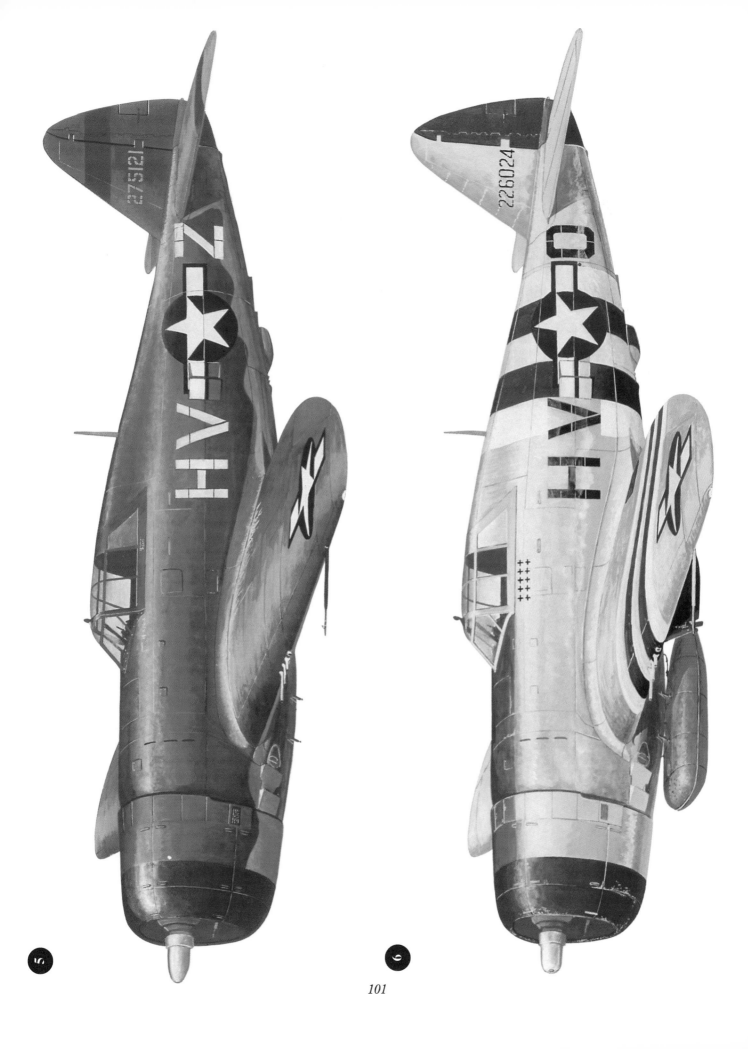

9

10

103

Hub Zemke leads the future Wolfpack over Long Island, New York during the fall of 1942. Note that his P-47 bears the colors of all three 56th Fighter Group squadrons, while the remainder are from the 61st Fighter Squadron. (Davis)

Another view of Zemke and the 61st Fighter Squadron in a line-astern formation over Long Island. Impressive in appearance, this type of formation was tactically dangerous. (Davis)

The P-47 was a massive fighter for its era. The pilot had to chin himself in order to check the carburetor intake and oil coolers for birdnests and other debris before each takeoff. (Davis)

Somber faced pilots "get the gen" at a briefing prior to a mission. (AFM)

Lt. Gerald "Gerry" Johnson's "In the Mood," HV✪D, 42-7877, aka., "Spirit of Jackson County Michigan."
Note the red surround to the national insignia that was applied for a short period during the summer of 1943.
(Davis)

Time, speed, distance, rendezvous points, while "Stormy" awaits his turn to give the weather briefing. (AFM)

"...And this is where...", debriefing was as important as the intitial mission briefing. At what altitude did the contrails form? How concentrated and what caliber was the Flak? Fighters? It all had a bearing on succeeding missions. (AFM)

44-21112 was Captain George Bostwick's "Ugly Duckling." He finished up his string of thirteen kills in this P-47M. (Davis)

Bostwick and his "ship." the 63rd Fighter Squadron experimented with all sorts of outlandish camouflage schemes after they received the P-47M. All proved of little value at that stage of the war. (Davis)

It wasn't all serious. Maybe they are selecting future "nose art" for a P-47. Such displays of pin-ups are no longer considered good for the country. (AFM)

An impressive scoreboard – Gabreski and his tally. He was the highest scoring American pilot in the ETO, and remains an inspiration for fighter pilots to this day. (Davis)

Bud Mahurin and the "Spirit of Atlantic City," another War Bond presentation aircraft. Mahurin was shot down in this aircraft on March 27, 1944 to become an evader. (Davis)

"Teddy" belonged to Major Michael Jackson. Jackson had eight air-to-air kills and 5.5 destroyed on the ground. (Davis)

42-75033, HV⭐L, leads the tactically loose "finger four" formation towards home. The white cowl and empanage bands helped in recognition between friend and foe. (Davis)

June 18: VIII FC FO 398. The first major attacks on Germany since D-Day. All three Bomb Divisions participating.

Col. Zemke led the first mission off at 0659 to provide target and withdrawal support for the heavies. In north of Kijkduin, they made RV north of Breman and escorted out to east of Egmond. One observation of note: The pilots observed that if the fighter groups flew a half-mile off to the side of the bombers, the flak would usually come up into the open area between them. Apparently the German flak guns were radar controlled and were unable to differentiate the exact distance between the formations, so they split the distance and fired ineffectively into the open area.

Col. Zemke also led the second mission. Off at 1632 they went dive bombing with 100 pound GP bombs. In west of Cherbourg, they bombed fuel dump in a forest outside of Branguilly, six miles southeast of Pontivy. Several forest fires were started and although the foliage obscured actual targets, the results were believed to be good. They RTB'd Boxted at 2030.

June 19: VIII FC FO 399. B-17s of the 1st and 3rd Bomb Divisions went to Bordeaux, France. The weather stunk, with clouds to 30,000 feet. The 56th Fighter Group was recalled immediately after takeoff because of the weather.

June 20: VIII FC FO 402. The heavies went to targets in Germany and Poland. Over 1,600 of the 1,965 Big Friends dispatched flew effective missions.

Up at 0706, the 56th Fighter Group's first mission was to provide target and withdrawal support. They crossed-in over Ijmuiden and flew to Hamburg where RV was made. Escort was provided to out over Nordholz and Terschilling Island. It was uneventful.

The second mission got off at 1912 to provide high cover for the returning heavies. RV was made just short of the target of Lens where two airdromes were bombed. "Bombing looked good." Again there was no sign of the Luftwaffe, and they returned at 2207.

June 21: VIII FC FO 407. The 1st and 2nd Bomb Divisions went to targets around Berlin. The 3rd Bomb Division hit Ruhland, and then continued on to land at Poltava, Russia under Operation Frantic, the first Shuttle Mission. Mustangs of the 4th Fighter Group went along as an escort for them. "A" and "B" Groups went out together on a Ramrod at 0716. "A," led by Major Lucian Dade, 62nd Fighter Squadron, escorted the 1st Task Force of the 3rd Air Division to Magdeburg. RV was made thirty miles northwest of Nordholz and continued to Stendal, and they then joined with "B" Group to strafe. They returned via The Hague to land at 1253.

"B" was led by Lt. Col. Gabreski and they flew a similar route. RV was made north of Borkum Islands and escort continued to east of Madgeburg. Upon breaking escort they went down to strafe. About ten miles northeast of Paderborn a number of trains were sighted and one locomotive was destroyed and four more damaged, along with a number of rolling stock.

1st Lt. Harold Matthews, 63rd FS, Red Three of "A" Group, joined with 2nd Lt. Sam Dale, White Four of "B" Group to strafe one of these trains. White One and Two, (Now Captain) Russ Westfall and 1st Lt. Thomas Guerrero, from "B" Group were going down right after them to strafe another train. After making their pass, Westfall and Guerrero were hitting 350 mph, indicated air speed, and pulling on their control sticks for all they were worth because of a heavily wooded area that was right in front of them when they saw Matthews skim, strike and disappear into the trees, after which a column of smoke was seen billowing into the sky. Dale had been so busy trying to avoid the trees, himself, that he had not seen a thing. Matthews was killed.

June 22: VIII FC FO 431. The three Bomb Divisions went to bomb airfields and industrial targets in France. All Fighter Groups participated except for the 4th that was in Russia.

Col. Zemke led the first mission off at 0941 on a Type 16 Control and dive bombing strike. They flew to Beauvais, Compiegne and Montdidier airdrome's to dive bomb, with the 63rd Fighter Squadron providing top cover for the other two squadrons attacks. Then reversing positions, the mission proceeded to Rosierres-en-Santerre airdrome and Becquicourt where the 63rd FS bombed with some success.

The mission had been basically uneventful with little flak and no sign of the Luftwaffe. But upon return the ever present threat of a mid-air collision in England's crowded sky manifested itself once again. Captain Charles E. Tucker, 62nd FS, was killed in a mid-air collision over Boxted while in the traffic pattern. Of six former bomber pilots that had joined the 56th FG in May 1944 to become fighter pilots on their second combat tour, Tucker was the second to perish in a mid-air collision over England. Two more of this group would die while flying combat missions.

A second mission got off at 1718 to dive bomb barges on a canal between Compiegne and Noyon, in the general area of Dunkirk. The 63rd FS hit this area with poor results. The 62nd FS dive bombed Estrees St. Denis with better results, but again the pilots witnessed another tragedy of war. A B-17 was spotted going down over Abbeville and two parachutes appeared from it, but one of them was hit by ack-ack and blown to oblivion.

June 23: VIII FC FO ? The Big Friends went to hit airfields and rail targets in France, along with Noball targets.

Col. Zemke led "A" Group off on an area support and strafing mission at 1819. In over Dunkirk, RV was made north of Laon with the returning heavies, and they were escorted out to Walcheren Island. The bomber formation was reported as poor and strung out, which gave the fighter pilots a bit more work to do. "B" Group followed "A" over Dunkirk by seven minutes and made their RV with the bombers northeast of Siossons, escorting them out to Schouwen Island. Since it was getting late in the day, the idea of strafing was given up and the Group's returned at 2145.

June 24: VIII FC FO ? The 1st and 3rd Bomb Division B-17s went to Breman, while 2nd BD B-24s hit Noball targets, bridges and airfields in France.

The 56th Fighter Group got up at 0931 on a fighter sweep and area patrol. In over Calais, they swept to south of Paris, north to St. Omer, southwest to Evereux and then out west of Dunkirk. A solid overcast kept to Luftwaffe grounded. RTB'd at 1254.

The second mission got off at 1731, another Rodeo. In over Dunkirk, they flew to Amines, where they orbited three times before proceeding on course to east of Dieppe, St. Quentin and Cambrai. Some strafing accounted for a narrow gauge locomotive and some boxcars, along with some vehicles. RTB'd at 2109.

June 25: VIII FC FO 417. All of Bomber Command's efforts were directed to France with over nine hundred heavies hitting airfields, bridges, and for the first time, the electrical grid's transformers and power plants. All 8th Air Force fighters but the 4th Fighter Group were over France on escort and tactical area support missions.

Lt. Col. Gabreski led the first mission off at 0608 to provide escort service. Just before RV was made a dozen Fw 190s attempted an attack on the bombers and dove through their formation. The 56th Fighter Group attempted an interception of them, but the German fighters were lost in the haze. RV was accomplished near Argentan at 0719 and continued until broken off by two squadrons at 0820 and the third at 0930. The Group then went to strafe, destroying six locomotives and a fair share of rolling stock. As the Group was reforming seven Me 109s attempted an attack on one flight from the 61st Fighter Squadron, but it was ineffectual, and contact with them was again lost in the haze.

Col. Zemke led the second mission, off at 1040 with thirty-two Jugs. Eight each from the 61st and 62nd FS's and sixteen from the 63rd Fighter Squadron. There were four aborts, and three more returned with them as escorts. Landfall-in was over Dieppe at 20,000 feet and RV was made over Evereux at 1155 with five Combat Wings of B-17s that were escorted from Conches to the Seine River. After breaking escort, the Group went on a Type-16 Control mission over Chartres, Chateaudun, Dreux and out southwest of Bernay. A little strafing accounted for only two trucks, and they returned at 1440.

June 27: VIII FC FO 420. The haze thickened into a solid cloud cover, and although all three Bomb Divisions were active, they only dispatched two hundred-fifty heavies against Noball targets and Creil and Chantilly. All had to seek out targets of opportunity as their main objectives were obscured by clouds.

Lt. Col. Gabreski led the 56th Fighter Group off at 1827 to go dive bombing at Connantre airdrome. Each Thunderbomber carried twelve 20 pound fragmentation bombs. Major (He had finally been promoted the day before.) Donald Goodfleisch's 63rd Fighter Squadron provided top cover while the other two squadrons bombed, and then took their turn.

While the squadrons were exchanging positions, Gabreski's 61st FS was bounced by Me 109s, so Capt. Fred Christensen's 62nd FS provided them with a top cover while Gabreski damaged one and then exploded another. Flight Lieutenant Withold Lanowski got the next one as Gabreski flew as his wingman. Lt.'s Warren Patterson, Steven Gerrick and James Jure also claimed Me 109s destroyed, but Gerrick's claim was downgraded to a probable. Jure also was credited with a claim for a damaged.

This evenings claims ran the 61st Fighter Squadron's total score to 230 enemy aircraft destroyed in the air. It also brought "Gabby's" total score to twenty-seven confirmed kills, tying Robert Johnson's record. "I caught him at 3,000 feet, pulled up behind him at fired, but observed no hits. I closed in again and fired. This time a big explosion occurred in the fuselage and flames bulged out of the tail of his plane. The whole tail appeared to melt, and he went down in flames." Gabreski stated in his after mission report.

After this little incident was cleaned up, the 62nd FS went down to bomb, and as they were finishing twenty/twenty-five more Me 109s came in on them at 7,000 feet, just below the cloud bases. The German pilots were aggressive and believed experienced. Nevertheless, Christensen shot one down, as did Lt. Robert Cherry. The squadron then reformed and headed for home, but on the way out, over Cambrai, four additional Me 109s bounced the squadron, concentrating on White Four without success. 1st Lt. William McElhare, one of the ex bomber pilots, shot down one and damaged two more. The mission RTB'd at 2222.

June 28: VIII FC FO 421. While the Big Friends went to Paris and Saarbrucken with almost a thousand heavies, the fighters were up on escort and fighter-bomber missions.

The 56th Fighter Group sent out both their "A" and "B" Groups at 0444. Col. Zemke led the mission, and his P-47 did not carry bombs, while the other forty-five carried two 250 pound GP's each. They arrived over La Perthe airdrome at 0620 between 17,000 and 20,000 feet and rolled-in to commence their dive bombing runs around 12,000 feet, dropping the bombs between 4,000 and 8,000 feet in fifty to eighty-five degree dives. Results were noted as poor. Although many Me 109s were observed on the airdrome preparing to takeoff, none were claimed as damaged. They RTB'd at 0825.

June 29: VIII FC FO 422. Over one thousand Big Friends made their first major raid on Leipzig, Germany to strike at synthetic oil plants, strategic industries and aircraft construction facilities.

Lt. Col. Gabreski led the first mission off Boxted at 0729 to provide penetration support to the heavies. Due to the distances involved, two radio-relay P-47s were dispatched to forward communications between the Group Headquarters and the forty fighters.

In over Ijmuiden at 0823, RV was made north of Lingen at 0840 with ten boxes of 2nd and 3rd Bomb Division B-24s and B-17s heading to the airdrome at Vectha, (Which was) "plastered with good results." Escort was terminated over Hanover/Naumberg at 0915 and the Wolfpack indulged in ground strafing on the way home. There was no sign of the Luftwaffe.

Major Don Goodfleisch led the second mission off at 1047 with twenty-three P-47s to provide withdrawal support for any stragglers coming back from the same mission. In over Ijmuiden at 1150 they proceeded to Lingen under Type 16 Control, and were vectored around Zwolle, and then out over Egmond. None of the 8th Air Force heavies were assisted, but over the North Sea a downed Royal Air Force Walrus was sighted with six men in a dinghy. The area was capped until an Air-Sea Rescue launch arrived on the scene. RTB time was 1536.

June 30: VIII FC FO 424. The heavies flew but three hundred effective sorties against airdromes in Belgium and France. 8th Air Force fighters were all out on tactical missions.

The 56th Fighter Group flew one dive bombing mission that got off Boxted at 1834. Armed with 250 pound GP's, they crossed in at Cayeux and proceeded to a marshalling yard at Cheny. The bombing results were reported to be the best the Group ever had. A round house was destroyed, along with at least fourteen boxcars that were believed to contain ammunition, as when they exploded they tore up more railroad track than the Thunderbombers ordnance.

In some air-to-air action, Lt. Marvin Becker, 63rd Fighter Squadron, chased down a Ju88 that was all silver in color with no national markings. He closed on it to 300/400 yards, and the Ju88s rear gunner started firing on him. Becker continued to hold down the trigger and sprayed the German bomber with .50 calibers until he overran the slower aircraft. It crashed into a field.

The 63rd FS strafed on the way home, hitting a parked train that was loaded with twenty plus trucks and ten tanks. Four other locomotives were destroyed. Passing over Albert Meaulte airdrome they encountered a heavy barrage of flak and Lt. David Kling's P-47 was hit in the cockpit and fuselage. Kling was wounded in the eye by a shard of plexiglas and with his hydraulics shot out, "Had rather a bad time landing at the base."

In all, one might have expected June 1944 to be a more spectacular scoring month than it was with D-Day and all. The weather over the continent was one factor in keeping the air-to-air scores down, as the Luftwaffe was not as active as one would have thought they would have been.

Again, too, it was all in being in the right place at the right time. The rival 4th Fighter Group, having flown the shuttle mission to Russia was out of action for several days, and they only scored twenty-one kills in comparison to the 56th FG's thirty-seven. The selection of missions flown by the 56th FG was another factor, as their dive bombing missions against rail and road traffic did not place them in a position of being able to rack up an expected high air-to-ground score against aircraft. It did seem strange, though, that the airdromes they did hit were so devoid of German aircraft. Still, the daily average amounted to nearly two German aircraft destroyed, probably destroyed or damaged for each day's efforts.

July 1944: The 56th Fighter Group's "Clobber College" was shut down. The training of new pilots was now conducted by direction of the squadron commanders and operations officers. The new pilots were given lectures on the various aspects of combat flying by the more experienced individual squadron pilots. In addition, Link Trainer instruction was emphasized to better prepare the pilots for instrument flying. Skeet shooting was utilized to sharpen the eye. Lots of formation work and practice missions were flown prior to releasing a fledgling pilot for combat, and standards for graduation to this point remained high. One thing that was added, to the enjoyment of the ground crews, was an air-to-ground target range on the edge of Boxted. This gave the ground-bound ones something to watch that they could at least relate to, and of course compare and critique their pilots.

July 1: VIII FC FO 424. The heavies went to hit Noball targets, while the "Little Friends" went out as fighter-bombers against rail and road targets in northern France. Almost all were recalled before reaching either the coast or their objectives because the weather was deteriorating. The 56th Fighter Group was scheduled to hit the airdrome at Auxerre, but "Colgate," recalled them before crossing in. The Group historian apparently also got fogged-in, as he confused the mission with the previous day's.

July 4: VIII FC FO 427. Weather limited bomber operations and almost curtailed all fighter missions for several days. Independence Day was still murky, bothering the heavies, but all but one fighter group was operational. For the 56th Fighter Group, it was a celebration in style!

The first mission was basically uneventful. Lt. Col. Gabreski led it off at 0551 with forty-eight P-47s on a penetration, target and withdrawal support mission. Landfall-in and RV was made over Cabourg an hour later, and escort provided until on the way out over St. Valery at 0755. A broken to solid undercast prevented the fighter pilots from observing bombing results, and except for escorting four stragglers that they went back in to pick up there was little to do. The mission landed at 0916.

Col. Zemke led the second group of forty-eight P-47s off at 1538 under Field Order 429. Weather immediately was a factor in that the group had a difficult time forming up and setting course because of clouds over Boxted. Thus they were a half hour late getting started. Approaching the coast at St. Valery at 1705 a solid line of clouds came from the south and ranged out of sight to the north and northeast.

Instead of aborting the mission to Nevers, France right then, Zemke turned the Group southeast, and then south and then southwest to the limit of their range in hopes of finding a hole in the thunderstorms and finding targets of opportunity. Just at the fuel limit, "Bingo," a hole occurred and Zemke took White and Red Flights from the 63rd Fighter Squadron down to bomb a marshalling yard, which were hit with excellent results, all sixteen 250 pound GP's exploding within the yard's confines.

The radar controller then directed the Group to La Harve Lyre, twenty miles southwest of Everux, where the 63rd FS's Blue and Yellow Flights bombed successfully. Right after this bombing took place the Luftwaffe showed up.

Over Everux airdrome twenty plus "bandits" were reported. Major Lucian Dade's 62nd FS spotted thirty-five Me 109s and ordered his squadron to jettison their bombs, but his own failed to drop.

Eight of the Messerschmitts were at 5,000 feet, and the rest at 300 feet, so they dove on the lower ones. In spite of being encumbered by the bombs, Dade destroyed two and damaged two more. 1st Lt. George Bostwick destroyed three and damaged another. Captain's Mark Moseley and Michael Jackson each got one. Lt. Wiley Merrill got two and probably destroyed another. Lt.'s Baird Knox, William McElhare, Dayton Sheridan and Albert Knafelz each were credited with one destroyed. Knafelz, Knox and McElhare were also each credited with a damaged. Lt.'s Darrell McMahan and Frank Newell split an Me 109 between them. Major Gorden Baker was credited with a damaged, also. Moseley became an ace on this mission, with a total of 5.5 kills to date.

Only Capt. James Carter was in the right place to score for the 61st Fighter Squadron. In one of the historical oddities, Lt. Edward Sisson is also officially credited with a kill on this date with the 61st FS. Yet, although he was flying this mission, there is no evidence of a claim being entered by him for downing an enemy aircraft nor mention in either his squadron or 56th Fighter Group records of an encounter. Col. Zemke, who was leading the 63rd FS got a damaged, but it was his Yellow Flight that got all the action. An Me 109 came in on Flight Officer Robert Magel, who then chased it until its pilot bailed out. Lt.'s Walter Frederick and Joseph Curtis joined a dogfight that was already in progress. Curtis got on the tail of an Me 109 and just as he was ready to shoot the German pilot bailed out, and Curtis had to make a quick turn to avoid the German pilot's tumbling body. Below the "Bingo" fuel state, Curtis headed for home, but then spotted another Me 109 at 4,000 feet. He fired three quick short bursts and the Messerschmitt went into a spin. Frederick then fired at it and its pilot bailed out, so they split the credit on that one.

Frederick then spotted an Fw 190 near Louivers, and since he had more fuel, he went after it. He closed to 100 yards and fired, right on the deck, but he overshot it and missed. He then chased it to Evereux, but it wouldn't go down. "We both hit trees on the deck, and once I saw his prop dig up dirt from a field. As my tracers appeared, I knew my ammo was low, but I kept on firing, the last of my ammo going into his right wing. I damaged this 190 severely, but he still wouldn't go down."

2nd Lt. Sam Dale, 63rd FS, was lost just as the fighting was ending. His flight leader, 1st Lt. Walter Frederick, had this to report: "I was leading Red Flight of my squadron with Lt. Dale as my element leader. My whole flight had several engagements with the enemy near Evereux and over Conches airdrome. When it was almost time to leave and head out for home, I called my flight to break off so we could set course for base. I could see a P-47 climbing up on my left and thought it was Red Three, Lt. Dale, with enemy aircraft after him. I broke right into the Fw 190s at 3,000 feet, and I saw Lt. Dale breaking right at 2,000 feet in the light flak over Conches airdrome. I also saw the enemy aircraft breaking right and firing, but at the time I was not sure they were firing at Lt. Dale. I called Dale to ask him if he was coming out O. K. and thought I heard him say 'Red 3 and Red 4 okay,' but Lt. (Walter) Flagg (Red Four) says he gave the only call which was 'Red Four, Roger!' This was the last I saw of Lt. Dale." Dale was killed, but it was never known for sure whether it was the flak or the Fw 190s that brought him down.

Two 62nd FS Thunderbolts still carried bombs after this engagement, being flown by Major Dade and Major Gorden Baker, and they went down to bomb and strafe Conches airdrome, while four P-47s from the 61st FS attacked a railroad bridge. During the course of this action, 1st Lt. Dayton Sheridan, 62nd FS, was slightly wounded. A total of four P-47s suffered battle damage, with three getting back to Boxted, and one putting down at Manston.

The returning pilots were elated with their successes. A total of seventeen German aircraft were knocked down, and ten more damaged, for the loss of one. The 56th Fighter Group now had a total of 508 German aircraft to their credit, being the first fighter group in the ETO to surpass the five hundred kill mark. All of these claims had been entered since June 12, 1943 when Capt. Walter Cook had knocked down the first German Fw 190, some thirteen months previously.

July 5: VIII FC FO 431. The 8th Air Force went into the skies over France to bomb marshalling yards and Noball targets, and over Holland and Belgium to bomb Luftwaffe airdromes. The 56th Fighter Group went out to provide withdrawal escort for the B-17s returning from Italy as a part of June's Operation Frantic shuttle mission.

Forty-eight P-47s got off at 1327 behind Lt. Col. Gabreski. There were three aborts, with one more turning back as an escort for them. In over Cayeaux at 17,000 feet at 1411, the Group flew to Chateauroux to RV with the Flying Forts. As the B-17s were running a half hour late, Gabreski sent the 63rd Fighter Squadron, under Capt. Lyle Adrianse, their Operations Officer, down to search for targets of opportunity while the other two squadrons went into an orbit to await the heavies.

Lt. Donald Peters and his Yellow Flight got a truck that was loaded with sheet metal, while Ardianse's White Flight strafed thirty railroad cars. They then proceeded towards Evereux to rejoin the rest of the Group, and met fifteen to twenty Me 109s over the rally point. Lt. Walter Flagg got one and probabled another, while Flight Officer Robert Magel fired at another, being credited with a damaged.

The remainder of the Group made RV with the bombers at 1525 and escorted them to twenty miles west of Dreux and then turned back to sweep St. Andre and Everux's airdromes. They encountered the same batch of Nazi fighters that the 63rd FS was engaged with and in a running dogfight claimed 10-1-3 additional German aircraft.

Capt. Fred Christensen, leading the 62nd FS, found himself bounced by three Me 109s and his P-47 was hit in the wing by 20mm cannon fire. Regardless, Christensen went after them in a chase that lasted for ten min-

The ground crews never get enough recognition. Two of the people that made Gabreski a success. S/Sgt. Ralph Safford and Corporal Felix Schacki. USAF via Davis

utes, and nailed one of them. Lt.'s George Butler, Robert Cherry, Billy Edens and Jack Pierce all were credited with Fw 190s that came in on the scene. Lt. Herman King and Michael Jackson each damaged an Fw 190.

As Gabreski led the 61st FS down on the attack from 14,000 feet against the Me 109s at 6,000 feet the squadron was bounced from above by Fw 190s. Lt. Timothy Sullivan was shot down on this, his sixteenth mission, and was killed. But they made up for his loss. Representing the Polish Air Force, Major Gladych and Flight Lt. Lanowski each destroying an Me 109. 1st Lt. Robert Keen shot down three Me 109s to become an ace, plus one. "Gabby" got one Me 109, his last air-to-air kill during World War II and giving him a total score of twenty-eight.

Gabreski: "Two tried to lure me down, while the third stayed up to jump me. But I realized what they were trying to do, so I banked sharply and went after the top man. He saw me coming and we cut a dozen patterns all over the sky, each of us attempting to get the other . . ." "I banked out of the turn and gave him a 90-degree deflection shot, more or less to scare him, but the dope flew right off to come in again. I had to make about three turns and then he started to dive. At about 1,000 feet he straightened out. I overtook him fast and caught him in a steep turn and let him have it. His ship made a half-roll to the left and lit up like a huge ball of fire."

This score also placed Major Gabreski in a tie with Major Richard Bong, 5th Air Force, as the two leading scoring fighter pilots in the Air Force at the time. In the course of history, Bong would become America's top scoring fighter pilot of all time, while Gabreski remains America's top scoring living ace. (Bong was killed in a P-80 accident in August 1945.)

July 6: VIII FC FO 432. The 8th Air Force sent out over thirteen hundred heavies against Noball targets by the 1st and 3rd Bomb Divisions, while the 2nd Bomb Division also hit Noball targets, Keil and bridges south of Paris. The 56th Fighter Group went out on two missions. The first bombing and strafing, and the second as a screen/sweep to keep the Luftwaffe away from the bombers attacking Noball targets.

Col. Zemke led the first mission off Boxted at 0502 with forty-eight Thunderbolts. They crossed in over Dieppe, and south of Bernay they got bounced by forty plus Me 109s and Fw 190s. Jettisoning their bombs, the 63rd Fighter Squadron took the first attack from the Messerschmitts in a line-abreast formation. As the Me 109s dove on them, one exploded, due, they believed, because he was pulling too much manifold pressure. These German pilots were eager and aggressive, as all of them were trailing heavy black smoke, indicating that they were running their Daimler-Benz engines all-out. (Yellow Flight of the 63rd FS, Lt.'s Joseph Curtis, John Ross and Richard Warboys, along with Flight Officer Robert Magel all claimed the exploded Me 109 as a kill, since it intended to attack them. It was disallowed).

Lt. Samuel Lowman, Red Three, 63rd FS, was in a right break as the Me 109s came in on them. Lt. James Kyle, Red Four, and Lowman's wingman, was turning also when he heard an explosion off to his left. He looked at Lowman's P-47 just as it was hit in the inner-cooler doors. Lowman "seemed to pull straight up and hang there . . ." He was killed.

Curtis got into a turning dogfight with a pair of Me 109s that were protected by six more above them. As he was turning he realized that he had forgotten to drop his belly tank when he salvoed his bombs, so he dumped it and was able to tighten his turn on the one he was chasing. The fuel tank flew back and smacked the Me 109 that was chasing him at the moment. It tore off the Messerschmitt's left wing and it was last seen spinning in. Curtis and the Me 109 he was after made twenty turns, but neither could bring their guns to bear on the other, and when the German pilot realized that his top cover had left him, he reversed his turn and escaped. Curtis put in a claim for a damaged on the one hit by his fuel tank, but was awarded a kill.

Red One and Two, Lt.'s Barney Casteel and Thomas Guerrero, were bounced by two Fw 190s east of Chartres that were at 10:00 O'Clock to them. They turned into the diving German fighters, with Casteel taking the one on the left and Guerrero the other. Guerrero fired a long burst at his target as it pulled back up into a steep climb, aborting his own attack. The Focke-Wulf rolled over on its back and its pilot bailed out. Casteel's selected target was hit in the fuselage and its belly tank exploded, and then it crashed into the ground.

The 62nd FS was at 14,000 feet when bounced out of the sun by the estimated forty Me 109s and four Fw 190s at 18,000 feet. 1st Lt. George Bostwick got one Me 109, while Capt. Mark Moseley got another. This was Moseley's last kill of the war, giving him a total of 6.5. And Bostwick joined the roster of aces. During this battle, Col. Zemke had his left wing holed by Me 109 cannon fire and lost the use of his left aileron. He was escorted home by Bostwick.

Major Dade led the second mission off at 0836 to provide withdrawal support for the Big Friends coming back from Keil. Only sixteen P-47s were sent off, and they made RV with the heavies over Drummer Lake at 1012, sweeping over the main force to join with the tail end of the formation over Steinhudder Lake. The heavies were in good stead, already being covered by P-38s and P-51s, and the escort out to Egmond was uneventful. They RTB'd at 1220.

July 7: VIII FC FO 436. A major mission into Germany was conducted by the 8th Air Force for the first time in several weeks. Over a thousand heavies participated, and thirty-seven were lost.

Lt. Col. Gabreski led the Group off at 0706 to provide penetration support for the Big Friends. As they crossed-in near Ijmuiden they started seeing the bombers, and then passed over the main formation to make RV over Drummer Lake at 0843. Escort continued to east of Brandenberg, where the 63rd FS turned for home.

Passing over Gardelegen airdrome Capt. Fred Christensen, leading the dozen Thunderbolts of the 62nd FS, spotted thirty-five enemy aircraft parked there. Christensen led his squadron to the east to position them for an attack upon the ground targets, but when they reversed their turn back over the airdrome they came upon a dozen Ju 52s in the traffic pattern. It was a mission to write home about, as Christensen set a new ETO record by destroying six in the air on one mission. This feat also ran his total score to 21.5 air-to-air kills. 2nd Lt. Billy Edens knocked down three, which made him an ace, plus two. These would be the final airborne kills for these two pilots. Capt. Michael Jackson got one, which added to his string towards "Acedom." Oddly enough, only Lt. Steven Gerick, 61st FS, was able to destroy an aircraft on the ground.

Christensen had this to say about his part of the attack: "I fired at the tail-end one and saw several strikes about the wing. I flew past him and the Hun blew up. I stayed in the pattern formed by the Jerries, fired at a second Jerry aircraft, and hit a motor and one wing. It blew up in flames, and I had to pull up to avoid striking debris . . ." "Singling out a third plane, I concentrated fire on one wing. This one took evasive action and, in so doing, smashed into the ground. I headed after a fourth and my engine stopped momentarily. I thought I was a goner but I switched on the main gas tank and my engine started clicking again . . ." "The fourth plane dived into the ground after I had fired several shots into one of its engines. I was making a slow turn when I ran into a fifth Ju 52. I peppered its wings and it exploded in the air . . ." "I saw another one near the ground, flying low. I fired at it and got strikes one wing and engine. I think it was attempting to land when I attacked. The plane exploded and looked like a blazing torch skimming across the field."

The second mission got off to provide withdrawal support to the returning bombers with only eight P-47s of the 62nd FS. Led by Major Dade, They met the returns over Drummer Lake and escorted them out to Emden. Intense and accurate flak hit a straggling B-24 they were escorting over Emden, and it was later seen to ditch.

July 8: VIII FC FO 437. The B-17s and B-24s concentrated on tactical and Noball targets in France. Over a thousand went out, but less than five hundred were effective, as weather conditions caused a massive recall of most of the heavies.

Col. Zemke led the first mission off at 0518 on a Type 16 Control sweep ahead of the Big Friends. Crossing-in over Dieppe at 0617, they flew to Rouen and started a radar vectored patrol for awhile. Zemke then took the Group down to strafe fifteen parked aircraft on an airdrome at St. Andre/Le Favril, but only one was claimed as damaged by Lt. Merton Gillies, 61st FS. RTB time was 0908.

Col. Zemke also led the second mission. Airborne at 1130 under 65th Fighter Wing Field Order 106, the forty-seven Thunderbolts returned to St. Andre/Le Favril, but the only thing they found was a truck, which Lt. Robert Cherry, 62nd FS, destroyed. The weather turned sour, so they returned early after but a 3:25 hour mission, landing at 1454.

July 11: VIII FC FO 441. Although the heavies and some fighter groups flew July 9 on limited missions, they all took the 10th off, as the weather continued to hamper operations. On July 11, over a thousand heavies headed to Munich and other targets in southern Germany. Close to eight hundred fighters were sent out in support of them, but the Luftwaffe did not show up to interfere with either of the forces.

Lt. Col. Gabreski led the first mission, penetration escort, off at 0932. RV and landfall-in was estimated to be over Walcheren Island, as cloud cover obscured landmarks. Escort continued to Stuttgart, and then they reversed course and flew back over the eastbound bombers on their way out looking for any aborts that might need an escort home. RTB'd at 1332 after an uneventful mission.

Major Donald "Goodie" Goodfleisch led the second mission of the day off at 1400 with twenty-four P-47s to provide withdrawal support. RV with the returning heavies of the 2nd and 3rd Bomb Divisions was made thirty miles northwest of Charleville, and they orbited there until the last of the stragglers had cleared that point and then followed the last of them out to RTB at 1700. This mission marked the 300 combat hour mark for Goodfleisch, and he was ordered home on leave. He was replaced by Joe Egan, effective July 17, as Egan had returned to operations after leave in the States.

July 12: VIII FC FO 446. The weather remained bad. The B-24s that were supposed to hit Noball targets in the Pas de Calais area all had to return with their bombs because they couldn't find their targets. The B-17s and B-24s headed for Munich attempted to bomb visually, but had to bomb by

PFF with undetermined results. Once again the Luftwaffe was absent. Col. Zemke led the 56th Fighter Group off at 1036 to provide penetration support for the 1st Bomb Division B-17s headed for Munich. RV was made over Walcheren Island at 1118, and escort provided to Kaiserslautern at 1235. They flew the reciprocal course home, passing over the bomber formations, and landed uneventfully at 1436.

July 13: VIII FC FO 444. Back to Munich again for the heavies, with all having to bomb by radar because of the cloud cover. Over a thousand Big Friends flew this mission, with only a 1% loss. Exceptional!

Major Lucian Dade took forty-eight P-47s off to escort home ten Combat Wings of the 1st and 3rd Bomb Divisions at 0918.

RV was made over Strasbourg at 1058 and continued uneventfully to Mons at 1212. As the Group was terminating their portion of the mission a mid-air collision occurred that took the life of Lt. James Palmer, 62nd Fighter Squadron. Palmer's P-47 was hit by a P-38 of the 55th Fighter Group and both pilots were killed. RTB time was 1313.

July 14: VIII FC FO 446. A rather limited but unusual mission by Bomber Command. Operation Cadillac, which supplied arms and supplies to the French Maquis resistance fighters, was flown by 359 B-17s.

Lt. Col. Gabreski led the 56th Fighter Group with forty-eight Thunderbolts off at 0552. They escorted three Combat Wings of 1st Bomb Division B-17s from Calbourg to Bourges, and then the 62nd and 63rd FS's dive bombed La Chappelle airdrome while the 61st FS provided their top cover. Nothing truly worthwhile was seen and damage could not be accessed. RTB'd at 1013.

As of this day, the 65th Fighter Wing had forty-four aces that were flying combat missions. Of these, nineteen belonged to the 56th Fighter Group, and nine of them belonged to the 61st Fighter Squadron.

July 15: VIII FC FO 449. Bomber Command took the day off while Fighter Command went after ground targets around Paris.

Col. Zemke led forty-eight P-47s off at 1727 and they arrived over the targeted Blois at 1850 to find the area blanked out by clouds. They then went after targets of opportunity at La Chapelle airdrome and Vendome marshalling yard.

As 2nd Lt. Robert Jenkins, 63rd FS, White Two, was at 8,000 feet and preparing to roll-in on a dive bombing run at La Chapppelle his P-47 was seen to be emitting white smoke from his supercharger duct. His wingman assumed that it was because Jenkins had retarded his throttle before starting his dive. Then, after completing his dive bombing run and pulling up to 2,000 feet, heavy grey smoke was seen coming from the duct, with occasional flames.

Lt. Marvin Becker, White Three, called to ask him what his problem was, and Jenkins replied: "I don't know. My carburetor air temperature is 150." (Degrees). Someone else told him to check the position of his intercooler doors, and them Major Goodfleisch told Jenkins to head for home and find someone to give him an escort. Becker told Jenkins that he would go with him, but Jenkins next transmission was: "I am at 1,500 feet and will have to bail out." A few seconds later Becker saw the P-47 go into a steep dive and trailing flames it crashed into the woods just west of Blois. Possibly, Jenkins' control cables had burned through before he had a chance to bailout. He was killed.

July 16: VIII FC FO 450. Over a thousand B-17s and B-24s headed for Munich, Stuttgart, Augsburg and Saarbrucken. A wall of clouds up to 30,000 feet got in their way, and most sought secondary targets. Again the Luftwaffe was notable in their absence, as the bomber crews claimed but 2-3-2 and none of the over seven hundred fighters dispatched made a claim.

Col. Zemke led the Group off at 0725 on penetration support. The made RV over Charleroi at 0839 with twelve Combat Wings of the 2nd Air Division and provided escort for them for a hour before going down to strafe. Claimed were 3-0-4 locomotives and 1-0-42 railway cars. Also strafed was a military encampment at Saarbrucken that held sixty barracks and a troop train that was being loaded. Eight to ten of the barracks were hit, as well as the train engine and seven cars. Grisley work, but necessary "for the war effort." No claim for casualties inflicted against the enemy troops was made.

July 19: VIII FC FO 456. After an improvement in the weather finally occurred, the heavies sought out the German industrial targets in Western and south-western Germany. Over twelve hundred were sent out, and over a thousand bombed effectively. Only one group of B-17s encountered the Luftwaffe. Everyone was wondering where they were except for three P-51 groups that claimed twelve.

Lt. Col. Schilling was back on missions after returning from leave in the States. He led the penetration support mission off at 0638. They had seven aborts out of the forty-eight P-47s dispatched, an unusually high number, particularly after a three day stand-down where the ground crews had all the time they needed to fine tune the Jugs.

RV with four Combat Wings of B-17s from the 1st Bomb Division was made twenty miles north of Antwerp at 0740 and they were escorted to southwest of Stuttgart at 0850. At this time Schilling took them down to strafe, between Saarbrucken-Metz and Nancy-Chalons.

Near Grindorff the 63rd Fighter Squadron got four locomotives and damaged fifteen boxcars, but lost their new squadron commander. There was no flak on their first pass, but as they started a repeat one the flak guns opened up from three concrete block houses. Capt. Joseph Egan's Thunderbolt was seen to be hit by a burst of flak on the right side of the fuselage and cockpit. It did a slow roll and crashed into a field. Egan, an ace, was flying just his second mission on his second tour after returning from furlough in the United States when he was killed.

Capt. Fred Christensen led the second mission off at 0945 with thirteen P-47s to assist in providing withdrawal support for the returning heavies. They flew in as far as Mannheim, Germany, but failed to find any Big Friends that needed their assistance, so they returned after an uneventful flight at 1347.

Major Gordon Baker was transferred from the 62nd Fighter Squadron to assume command of the 61st FS, as Lt. Col. Gabreski had finished his combat tour.

July 20: VIII FC FO 457. Again the 8th Air Force had over a thousand of their heavy bombers effective against oil and industrial targets in Germany. An incident occurred within the 56th Fighter Group occurred that showed just what can happen when a fighter pilot pushes his luck beyond the edge but still retains the favor of Lady Luck, herself.

Lt. Col. Schilling led the Group off Boxted at 0906 to provide penetration, target and withdrawal support for three Combat Wings of the 3rd Bomb Division. In at Schouwen Island with the heavies already under escort, they took them to bomb targets on both sides of the Rhine River at Merseburg and Halle and then escorted them out until 1140. At this time the squadrons split to seek strafing targets. The 63rd Fighter Squadron, under Schilling, hit Bruck and Eusenkirchen, getting three locomotives and seventeen boxcars.

The 61st FS hit the airdrome at Bassenbeim where at least a dozen He 111s were parked. Eight were destroyed and three damaged, all by individual pilots. Gabreski, who had completed his tour and had his bags packed for his return to the United States on furlough and to get married just had to get in one last mission. He also got too low on his last pass down the runway and slashed the turf with his prop, bending it and placing himself *hors de combat*. With his engine kaput, he rose, skimmed over some trees and bellied into a field. Uninjured he climbed from the cockpit and ran off into some woods while his shocked squadron mates prepared to strafe his abandoned Thunderbolt. Normal procedure, to prevent its re-use by the enemy.

Gabreski spent the rest of the war as a POW with several of his acquaintances, including Gerald Johnson, and would be joined before too long by Col. Zemke.

Capt. Fred Christensen led another small mission out that afternoon to provide withdrawal support for the returning heavies. Again there was no sign of the Luftwaffe and the mission was uneventful.

July 21: VIII FC FO 458. The Big Friends went on an all-out attack against the German aircraft industry and airfields in Germany, along with the infamous ball-bearing works.

For the first time in a long time the 56th Fighter Group sent out both their "A" and "B" Groups. Major Dade led "A" Group off at 0725 with thirty-one P-47s from the 61st and 62nd Fighter Squadrons to provide escort for B-24s of the 2nd Bomb Division headed for Munich. RV was made at Antwerp and escorted completed near Hamburg at 0919. Dade's White Flight did a little strafing on the way home, with Dade destroying a train. The remainder of the 62nd FS escorted a struggling B-17 that made it as far as forty miles from Clacton before it dove into the sea. They orbited the area until air-sea rescue got there to recover four bodies, two of which had their parachutes on.

July 22: Capt. Howard "Bunny" Comstock assumed command of the 63rd Fighter Squadron. Major Donald Goodfleisch having completed his tour and permitted combat flying hour extensions.

Capt. Fred Christensen led "B" Group off at 0738 with twenty Jugs to provide support for 2nd Bomb Division B-24s. RV was made at Walcheren Island at 0830 and escort provided to near Saarbrucken at 0940. Except for a few strafing claims of minor vehicles, the mission was uneventful and returned at 1122.

July 24: VIII FC FO 461. Bomber Command was active in supporting the US 1st Army in the St. Lo Offensive. All three Bomb Divisions participated with over fifteen hundred Flying Forts and Liberators, but only a quarter of them were considered as effective, as most were either recalled or otherwise returned with their bombs because ground visibility made safe bombing impossible.

The 56th Fighter Group tookoff at 1155 on an area support mission with forty-eight Thunderbolts and Lt. Col. Schilling at the helm. They arrived over Bernay at 1255 and remained in the general area for a half hour as moral support for the heavies. At 1320 they flew to Paris for a ten minute patrol before heading out for home over Compeigne. Only Lt. Col. Dave Schilling and wingman Lt. Arthur Bux went down to strafe. At Villaroche airdrome they shared in the destruction of one Me 210 and the damage of another on the ground, along with shooting-up the control tower and a couple flak positions.

July 25: VIII FC FO 462. The heavies again went out to support the 1st Army at St. Lo. This time almost seventeen hundred B-17s and B-24s were dispatched, and fifteen hundred bombed effectively. A couple Bomb Groups bombed short of their intended targets, killing over a hundred US Army troops and wounding 380.

The 56th Fighter Group sent out two missions. Col. Zemke led the first one, off at 0945 with forty-eight Jugs on an area patrol. They patrolled the Puntanges area for a half hour, and then the 63rd FS went off to sweep Bernay-Evereux-Dreux. The mission returned at 1339 after uneventful patrols, with the exception of the 63rd FS destroying a truck and a staff car with six passengers.

VIII FC FO 463. Lt. Col. Schilling led the second mission with thirty-five P-47s and Col. Zemke in a "Droop-Snoot" P-38 off at 1820. Each Thunderbomber carried a 150 gallon belly tank filled with oil, and the targets were a forested area near Bois de Mont, the airdrome at Montdidier and a fuel dump at Fournival.

Capt. Don Smith, Operations Officer of the 61st Fighter Squadron, and leading the squadron this day, was advised that they were under impending attack. They jettisoned their tanks "All over the French countryside." The attack did not materialize, so they contented themselves with strafing runs. Schilling's 62nd FS struck Bois de Mont and Fournival and strafed for forty minutes. Their action "provoked no enemy action." The 63rd FS also hit Bois de Mont, starting two large fires and five smaller ones where a railroad and a hard-surfaced road intersected. The sole actual claim for all this effort was one truck.

Zemke's P-38 experience was a little different. While on a bomb run at 12,000 feet over Montdidier the P-38 was hit in the right engine just at the bomb release point. The entire prop on the right side and a part of the Allison engine was blown away. The Lightning went out of control momentarily, but Zemke recovered and headed for home, sweating out an oil leak in the left engine. After touchdown at Boxted, the brakes failed and the P-38 went out into a field before coming to a stop. An exciting experience for bombardier Lt. Arthur Scroggins who had been confined in the glass nose of the Droopsnoot.

July 26: VIII FC FO 465. Bomber Command was not active this day, and only four P-47s groups from Fighter Command were sent out as Thunderbombers. The targets were again Bois de Mont, Fournival and Givet.

Col. Zemke led the mission off at 1707. This time each of the P-47s of the 62nd and 63rd Fighter Squadrons carried two 108 gallon fuel tanks, each filled with a mixture of fifty percent each of gas and oil. Sixteen P-47s of the 61st FS were without underwing ordnance, being assigned to fly top cover for the others. Although all but four tanks fell in the targeted area, they were basically ineffective. Many of the bomb shackles were found to be bent upon their return, believed to be caused by diving at too high of an airspeed with these tanks, as their aerodynamic characteristics were different than bombs. Zemke believed it would take 500 pound GPs to neutralize the area. On the way home some strafing was done, with five trucks being destroyed and a couple locomotives damaged.

July 27: VIII FC FO 468. A limited force of B-17s and B-24s were to bomb Belgium's coastline, but weather hampered the mission and only half of the 146 heavies dispatched were effective.

Lt. Col. Schilling led forty-eight P-47s off at 1737. The 62nd Fighter Squadron flew as top cover for the other two squadrons that were armed with two 250 pound GP's each. They flew to Paris, and they on to the marshalling yard at Abancourt, which were bombed with good results. While diving on the target, the 63rd FS's Blue Two, Capt. George Hall, prop went out of pitch. Someone told him to drop his landing gear and flaps, as this would help him keep the aircraft under control. Under escort by his wingman, Lt. Edward Albright, who was trying to steer him around all the known flak positions, Hall's P-47 was hit twice more by bursts of flak. They barely made it across the Channel to put down in forced landings south of Dungenees. The rest of the Group landed at 2055.

July 28: VIII FC FO 469. The 2nd Bomb Division went to targets in France, while the 1st and 3rd Bomb Divisions headed for targets in Belgium and Germany. The 56th Fighter Group provided area support for the 2nd Bomb Division.

Col. Zemke led forty-eight P-47s off at 0657. They arrived over Cayeux at 0740 between solid layers of clouds. Flying under radar control, (After a rather strange directive had ordered the removal of all of the IFF transponders from the P-47s.), they orbited Abbeville, then proceeded to north of Amines and St. Omer. No enemy aircraft were encountered and it was considered a "milk run." RTB'd at 0957.

July 29: VIII FC FO 470. The heavies went back to Germany to attack strategic oil targets with twelve hundred B-17s and B-24s.

The 56th Fighter Group was airborne Boxted at 0933 with forty-seven Thunderbolts behind Lt. Col. Schilling. RV was made with ten Combat Wings of B-17s of the 1st Bomb Division returning from Merseburg southeast of Minden at 1100 and escort was broken off an hour later. Again there was no sign of the Luftwaffe by the 56th FG, although the P-38s that had preceded them on the escort-in scored 21-2-3 on this mission.

July 31: VIII FC FO 472. Most of the three Bomb Divisions went to targets in Germany, while a portion of the 3rd BD struck airfields in France.

Col. Zemke led the Group off at 1117 to provide escort for four Combat Wings of the 3rd Bomb Division. RV was made over Schouwen Island and the Group split into "A" and "B" Groups, with "A" taking one pair of Combat Wings and "B" the other pair. "A" escorted the heavies to Laon, while "B" took theirs to Creil. In both cases the cloud layers prevented assessment of the bomb damage, but after escort was accomplished the fighters dove through the clouds to strafe targets of opportunity, destroying five trucks and damaging a pair of locomotives along with a number of freight cars.

August 1: VIII FC FO 473. The 1st and 2nd Bomb Divisions attacked tactical targets in France. The 3rd Bomb Division B-17s air-dropped supplies to French Resistance fighters as a part of Operation Buick, while their B-24s hit Noball targets.

The 56th Fighter Group got off at 1257 on an area support/ Rodeo and Type 16 Control mission. Lt. Col. Schilling led. They arrived over Chartres at 1350, where the 1st Bomb Division was attacking, and then the Group split into squadrons and elements. France was swept in all directions, but no German aircraft were encountered, yet intense flak discouraged any attempt at attacking ground targets. RTB'd at 1652.

August 2: VIII FC FO 474. The heavies went to France to hit tactical targets under escort by Mustangs. Other P-51s, along with P-38s and P-47s went to France as fighter-bombers.

Major Dade and the 62nd Fighter Squadron led the rest of the Group off at 1749. They crossed-in over Schouwen Island at 1849 and then split into the three squadrons, all Thunderbombers carrying two 250 pound GP's. The 61st FS, behind Major Gordon Baker struck the marshalling yards at Bohlen, getting eighteen out of thirty-two good hits. The 62nd FS hit marshalling yards at Enghinen with poor results. The 63rd FS was led by 1st Lt. Robert Campbell, their Assistant Operations Officer. They hit the marshalling yards at Vaux Andigny, getting only four direct hits on the yards and one on the railroad station. Again there remained no sign of the Luftwaffe, although all squadrons "stooged" around for a period after bombing looking for them.

August 3: VIII FC FO 476. Bomber Command attacked strategic and tactical targets along the boarder between France and Germany, along with tactical targets around Paris.

The 56th Fighter Group again went dive bombing. Col. Zemke led them off at 1306 with thirty-two Thunderbombers carrying one 250 pound GP each and fifteen P-47s as escort. The 62nd Fighter Squadron hit the marshalling yards at Saarebourg with only fair results coming from the bombing. However, strafing accounted for twelve locomotives destroyed and ten damaged. The 61st FS, Led by Capt. Smith, flew as top cover for the other two squadrons, and with no Luftwaffe to be seen, went down to strafe. They accounted for two locomotives destroyed and sixty boxcars damaged.

Ten miles southwest of Saarebourg, on the railroad line to Luneville, Zemke spotted a cement factory and sent three flights of his 63rd FS down to bomb it. And then Zemke spotted a slow moving train. On his second strafing pass at the train an Fw 190 came in behind him, and White Two, 2nd Lt. Richard Anderson, cut in behind it and started to fire. The Fw 190 broke left and Anderson kept after him, firing again. The Fw 190 straightened out, and Anderson fired once again and the German pilot had enough and bailed out. A classic example of a good wingman doing exactly what he was supposed to do.

Capt. Roy Fling, leading Yellow Flight, 63rd FS, saw what he believed to be the loss of 1st Lt. Roach Stewart, Blue Three. "The plane was flying over an area which was heavily defended by light (caliber) flak and there was a heavy concentration at the time. The plane continued in a straight course, taking no evasive action whatsoever, and then started a gentle turn, loosing altitude slowly. Flames appeared around the cockpit and it rolled over to the left, crashing in a wooded area just east of Luneville and burst into flames immediately." When Fling had first spotted the P-47 it was already trailing smoke, so possibly Stewart had already bailed out, as he survived the war.

August 4: VIII FC FO 478. The Big Friends went back to Germany enforce with almost twelve hundred of the heavies flying effective missions. A smaller force also went to Noball targets and the super-secret Peenemunde site, but none were aware of the value of that target at the time – it was the V-1 and V-2 weapons development location.

The 56th Fighter Group flew three missions this day. The first was led by Lt. Col. Schilling and "A" Group with thirty-two P-47s as a Ramrod in support for the 3rd Bomb Division B-17s to Hamburg and Breman. Off at 1107 they made RV over Bremerhaven at 1300 with the last Combat wings enroute to their target. Escort was provided over the target and continued to east of Breman at 1340. At the time escort was broken, the P-47s still had a little extra fuel, so they went into an orbit looking for action. They were not disappointed, as three Me 109s were soon encountered. Schilling went after them with the 61st Fighter Squadron, and although he missed, Lt. Arthur Maul, got one. Ground strafing on the way home chalked-up two locomotives destroyed and twenty-five boxcars damaged.

"B" Group got off at 1158, forty-five minutes later, and was led by Major Dade. Each squadron put up eight P-47s. RV with the heavies was made west of the Tessel Island at 1240. At landfall-in Dade took the 62nd FS to escort two Combat Wings of B-24s to Husam airdrome, their target, and then uneventfully swept the area. The other two squadrons took five Combat wings to Keil and broke escort at 1530. Major Baker's 61st FS spotted two four-engine flying boats on Selenter Lake, near Keil, and Baker destroyed one. The other was destroyed by Lt.'s William Barnes, Earl Hertel, Stuart Getz, James Jure and Carl Westman.

Col. Zemke led the evening mission off at 1812 with thirty-three P-47s armed with one 250 pound fragmentation bomb each. They arrived over Plantlunne airdrome at 1935 and worked it over for fifty minutes. 6-0-5 He 111s were hit, with Lt. Billy Edens destroying one with a direct bomb hit and two more by strafing. He also damaged two more. Col. Zemke destroyed one, and shared in the destruction of another with Lt. John Ferguson of the 62nd FS. Lt. Steven Murray, 62nd FS, destroyed another. Capt. Michael Quirk damaged one. All of the aircraft on the airdrome were believed destroyed, as what the 56th FG didn't get, the 353rd Fighter Group did.

August 5: VIII FC FO 483. The 8th Air Force Bomber Command sent most of its forces to attack strategic targets in Germany.

Lt. Col. Schilling led the 56th Fighter Group off at 1041 with fifty-one Thunderbolts. Initially they were on a Ramrod to provide escort for five Combat wings of 1st Bomb Division B-17s enroute to Neinberg. RV was made at Neinberg, and five minutes later they were warned of bandits between Hanover and Drummer Lake. They broke escort to go look for them, but they could not be found, so Blue and Yellow Flights of the 61st Fighter Squadron and the 63rd FS went on a strafing sweep while the 62nd FS continued escort for the returning Big Friends as far as Egmond. Four locomotives were claimed destroyed, along with other rolling stock and vehicles by those who had gone strafing.

This was the last fighter mission for 1st Lt John Aranyos, who had joined the 63rd FS in January. It had taken him eight months to get in three hundred combat hours in his fighter's cockpit. This was significant, as in April 1944 it had been decided to extend the normal combat tour for a fighter pilot from 200 to 300 hours. Aranyos milestone of eight months provided an indicator to others of just how long it would take to complete a normal combat tour. Those that wanted to could extend their tours in 100 hour increments after a furlough home. Some, like Schilling, sought extension after extension and "pencil whipped" their logged hours so that not too many were logged at a time and fought the entire war. Aranyos opted for an Air Training Command position at Yuma Field, Arizona.

August 6: VIII FC FO 487. Bomber Command went back to Germany with over eleven hundred heavies. The 357th Fighter Group and some 3rd Bomb Division B-17s made the second shuttle mission to Russia.

Major Dade led "A" Group off at 0933 to provide escort for Hamburg bound B-24s. RV was made five miles west of Tonning, and escort was provided to within sight of Hamburg before escort was broken to go strafing. The 63rd Fighter Squadron had their Gold Flight along with hopped up Superbolts to provide top cover for the others that strafed. Again, four locomotives were destroyed, along with miscellaneous other vehicles.

"B" Group was led off by Capt. Don Smith at 1051 with twenty-four P-47s on a Type 16 Control Rodeo. They arrived over Rouen at 1200, flew to Paris, orbited Melun, Le Mans and then back to Rouen at 1315. The 63rd FS was led by 1st Lt. Armand LaFlam on his last mission. His White Flight got two staff cars, one of which was a highly polished black; "In which rode three former Officers of the Wehrmacht. They have had it."

August 7: VIII FC FO 490. Bomber Command again turned their attention on France, going after bridges and fuel dumps. Again there remained little evidence of the Luftwaffe, but Mother Nature interfered once again and only half of the dispatched bombers were effective because of heavy cloud cover.

The 56th Fighter Group flew two missions. The first, off at 1043 behind Col. Zemke, sent out thirty-five Thunderbombers with the 61st and 63rd Fighter Squadron's carrying two 250 pound GP's each, while the 62nd FS provided top cover. They attacked the marshalling yard at Albert, France with good results, but with one loss.

Flight Officer Robert Magel, 63rd FS, Blue Three, was followed down by his wingman, 2nd Lt. Chester Frye, on the bombing run. They bombed at 4,000 feet, and Frye last saw Magel at 6,000 feet orbiting in the haze while looking for a slot to get back into his squadron's formation. There was no flak at the time, nor any sign of German fighters. What knocked him down was unknown, but Magel survived the war as a POW. The next day his twin brother, David, took his place in the 63rd Fighter Squadron.

Col. Zemke also led the second mission. Off at 1739 with forty-eight P-47s, they went back to Albert to finish the job. This time each carried one 500 pound GP and one 500 pound incendiary bomb. Over a mile of railway was destroyed, along with thirty-five boxcars and two locomotives damaged. Two locomotives were destroyed.

Again the mission came with a cost. Upon pulling out of their dive bombing run Lt. Arthur Maul had a mid-air collision with Lt. Warren Patterson. Maul had damage to his left wing and was heard to say, "Yellow Three, bailing out." Maul's P-47 was seen to hit the ground and explode at 2010 near Poix. There was no sign of a parachute, and Maul was later identified among those killed. Patterson got back with the rest of the Group at 2010, missing a horizontal stabilizer.

August 8: VIII FC FO 494. All the B-24 groups hit Noball targets, while all the Flying Fortresses concentrated on attacking tactical targets around Caen, France in support of the ground forces.

Each 56th Fighter Group squadron put up sixteen P-47s to attack the marshalling yard at St. Just and to provide area support for the heavies. The 63rd Fighter Squadron flew as top cover for the other two squadrons. The mission was off Boxted at 1126 behind Lt. Col. Schilling, with four aborts and one returning with them as an escort. The 62nd FS hit St. Just, damaging forty boxcars. The 61st FS hit a railway tunnel entrance east of Poix that had fifteen to twenty boxcars waiting to enter the tunnel. Between bombing and strafing thirteen boxcars were destroyed and fifty-seven damaged. RTB'd at 1450

August 9: VIII FC FO 497. Bomber Command sent their heavies to southeastern Germany to attack strategic targets, but again weather interfered and only two-thirds of the force were effective. Most of the fighter groups supported the heavies, while the 56th Fighter Group did both escort and Thunderbombing.

Col. Zemke led the first mission off at 0936 with forty-eight Jugs, and again there were five aborts. RV with B-24s of the 2nd Bomb Division returning from an attack on Strasbourg was over Trier at 1120 and withdrawal escort was terminated south of Liege at 1215. Again there was no encounter with the Luftwaffe by the 56th FG. (Although the 20th and 364th FG's had their best day so far). After breaking escort the Group strafed a marshalling yard at Pondrome, destroying seven locomotives and damaging seventeen. Ninety-four freight cars were destroyed or damaged.

Lt.'s George Van Noy and Darrell McMahan, 62nd FS, had a rather rare incident, as they shot down an abandoned B-24 of the 458th Bomb Group over Malmedy. (They looked it over good first, to be sure that there was no one on board. It had its right wheel hanging down, and its machine guns were also hanging loose in their turrets or mounts. There was no sign of anyone on board).

Major Dade led the second mission off at 1725 with thirty-five P-47s to dive bomb and strafe Chevillon, Revigny and St. Dizler. The 61st Fighter Squadron provided top cover while the other two squadrons worked over the area for five minutes short of an hour quite successfully. RTB'd at 2125.

August 10: VIII FC FO 498. Only Liberators were active from Bomber Command this date. They attacked bridges and fuel dumps southeast of Paris.

Lt. Col. Schilling led them off at 0929. Forty-eight P-47s on a Thunderbombing mission to Menzines, Brussels and Antwerp areas. The 61st Fighter Squadron actually struck a marshalling yard north of Givit, while the 62nd hit Muizon, as their primary target at Fismes was full of Red Cross cars. The 63rd FS hit a marshalling yard at Mamur as a target of opportunity for the same reason. Twenty-three locomotives were damaged all together, while twenty-two freight cars were destroyed or damaged. Many casualties were inflicted on over a hundred Germans that were attempting to abandon the trains that were under attack. Grisley business that was not relished by the pilots in any way shape or form.

Major Dade led the second mission off at 1631 under Field Order 501. The target was Foret de Montange, but it was so heavily defended by flak that the Group sought other targets. The 63rd Fighter Squadron flew as top cover, while the 61st FS attacked a marshalling yard at Jonchery, where they strafed and bombed a train. The 62nd FS hit a marshalling yard at Muizon, destroying sixteen boxcars. The mission RTB'd at 2031.

August 11: VIII FC FO 502. Almost a thousand heavies went out to attack tactical targets on the Brest peninsula.

Col. Zemke led his last mission at the helm of the 56th Fighter Group this morning. Off at 1112 on a Type-16 Control sweep, they arrived over Orleans at 1225, and then flew to Chartres, Blois, Etampes and Dreux. The weather was "severe clear," and Zemke believed that it was actually too good for the Luftwaffe to be up and about. After an uneventful sweep they were back at 1527.

August 12: VIII FC FO 506. A busy day for both Fighter and Bomber Commands against tactical targets in France. 650 heavies went out, along with over thirteen hundred fighters. The 56th Fighter Group flew four missions, and finally got some air-to-air action.

The first mission got off at 0446 with Lt. Col. Schilling leading on his first mission as the 56th Fighter Group's Commanding Officer. A pitch-black takeoff after a pilot's briefing at 0330. They hit the marshalling yard at Charleville with each P-47 carring two 250 pound GPs. Results were good, as both the 62nd and 63rd Fighter Squadrons's claimed five locomotives each.

Major Dade led the second mission. Off at 0712 with twenty-three Thunderbolts armed with five hundred pound GPs. The marshalling yards at Courcelles and Charleroi were hit by the 61st and 62nd FSs, while the 63rd FS flew top cover. Then all went strafing with moderate success.

The third mission got off at 1041 with Major Gordon Baker leading twenty-three P-47s armed with two 500 GPs each. They hit the marshalling yard at Fourmies, claiming fifty box cars destroyed and thirty-four damaged. Twenty-one trucks were also destroyed.

The fourth mission had all the excitement. Led by Lt. Col. Schilling, they got off at 1310 with another batch of twenty-three Thunderbolts armed with 500 pounders. One bomb fell off while the P-47s was still in the traffic pattern at Boxted. The mission went to the marshalling yard at Maubeuge, which contained 150 plus boxcars, and the comment was that each future mission should contain a "T. S. Slip for the yardmaster." The 63rd FS, alone, accounted for fourteen locomotives and thirty-five boxcars, along with damaging eighteen more.

Capt. Ray Fling, Red One, 63rd FS, spotted an Me 109 that bore no markings on it whatsoever. Fling "blindsided" the unsuspecting pilot from 300 yards and exploded it all over a pasture. Capt. (Now Squadron Leader) Michael Gladych, 61st FS got a Ju 88 in the air near Gambral.

On the loss side, the 61st FS lost Lt. William Barnes. He had radioed that his cylinder and oil temperatures were hot, and that his engine was running rough. His P-47s was seen to be trailing blue and white smoke at two thousand feet, and he could not maintain altitude. Barnes bellied-in at 1520 hours and was last seen running away from his fighter. He evaded capture.

August 13: VIII FC FO 511. Bomber Command continued to pound targets in France, while the Fighter Command concentrated on tactical targets near the front lines. The 56th Fighter Group once again split into their "A" and "B" Groups, with each group flying two missions -"From dawn until fuel ran down."

Major Gordon Baker led the first mission off at 0435 with twenty-two Thunderbombers armed with forty-four 250 pound GP's. Six pilots jettisoned their bombs at landfall-in to chase V-1 "Buzz Bombs," but without success. Various rail targets were hit by the remainder, claiming three locomotives destroyed and fifty-one boxcars damaged.

"B" Group got off at 0645 on their first effort with twenty-three Thunderbombers led by Capt. Harold Comstock. They went to a marshalling yard at Auxouville, and then attacked a bridge near Estoute. Both were successful and no flak was encountered.

Major Dade led "A" Group off on their second effort at 1422, again with twenty-three P-47s armed with two 500 pound GPs. Few worthwhile targets were found, and resultant attacks, for some reason, were poor.

Major Baker took "B" Group out at 1550. Again few targets of value could be found, so the pilots had a free for all shooting and bombing whatever suited their fancy. RTB'd at 1905.

August 14: VIII FC FO 513. The Liberators hit airdromes and rail targets in France, while the B-17s went to Germany. All fighter groups were active, which was unusual, as for the last month at least one per day had been on a stand-down

As of this date, no longer would people on the ground in France be vulnerable to strafing, as a moratorium had been placed on air-to-ground strafing in France. Too many Allied forces were about and it was too difficult to tell them from the Axis from the air. However, any and all personnel on the ground in Germany remained a fair target, as it was known that civilians were abusing downed airmen. Often far worse than the Nazi troops, themselves.

The 56th Fighter Group sent out their "A" Group at 0449 with Lt. Col. Schilling leading eight Thunderbolts from each squadron. Each P-47s

carried two 250 pound GP's to hit transportation targets. The 63rd Fighter Squadron hit the marshalling yard at Mariembourg and severed the tracks. The 62nd FS struck the canal at Cambrai, attacking the locks and barges there. The 61st FS hit the marshalling yard at Hirson. It was a successful mission, and none of the Jugs was even scratched by flak for a change.

"B" Group got off at 0905 with Major Baker leading another batch of P-47s. Eight from each squadron on a Ramrod to escort B-24s to south of Paris. RV was made just west of Charleville, and the Libs were taken under tow. South of Paris, Baker thought that they had RV'd with the wrong formation, so they broke escort and went back to almost Soissons looking for other B-24s, but none were seen. Thus, they turned around and rejoined the original B-24 formation south of Compiegne. These were escorted to northeast of Compiegne, where escort was broken off again and the Group went strafing. Capt. Roy Fling's Red Flight, 63rd FS, had the only success, destroying a locomotive and a motorcycle (Along with its rider).

August 15: VIII FC FO 517. The RAF and 8th Air Force Bomber Command went after airdromes in Germany and the low countries. Most of Fighter Command was accordingly involved with escorting the heavies.

Lt. Col. Schilling led the first mission off at 0952 to provide escort for RAF Lancasters attacking St. Trond, Le Culot, Tircemont and Brussels airdromes. After their services were no longer needed, escort was broken and again they went down to strafe. Capt. Michael Quirk, leading the 62nd Fighter Squadron, took them down to attack a marshalling yard where they destroyed three locomotives and damaged seventy boxcars.

Schilling led the 63rd FS down to strafe St. Trond airdrome while the 61st FS provided top cover for both squadrons. Capt. Robert Campbell, Assistant Operations Officer of the 63rd FS, who had just been promoted the week before, was lost at St. Trond.

Leading Blue Flight, Campbell was hit in the left wing by flak as he made his first strafing run across the airdrome. He damaged an Me 109 on this pass, and then started a second run on another 109 that was parked under some trees. There was an installation of heavy flak guns on the southwest corner of the airdrome, and they apparently hit him as he was concentrating on the Me 109. His P-47 crashed in the middle of the field and exploded.

Lt. Col. Schilling led the second mission off at 1527 to dive bomb the marshalling yards at Braine le Compe. Ten of the Thunderbombers carried 260 pound fragmentation bombs, fourteen carried 500 pound GP's. Two carried 250 pound GP's and something new for the Group, six rockets each. This was the first mission flown by the Group where some of their aircraft had "bazooka" type rocket tubes attached to their wings. The target was a locomotive repair shop, and forty locomotives were destroyed or damaged. The remainder of the damage could not be immediately accessed because of the smoke and dust they had stirred up during their attacks.

August 16: VIII FC FO 518. Over a thousand heavies went to synthetic oil refineries and aircraft factories in Germany.

Major Dade Led forty-eight P-47s off at 0739 on a "Zemke Fan" with the intention of intercepting the German fighters that would be taking off to pick on the heavies that would be bombing in the area. They arrived over Drummer Lake ahead of the Big Friends, but the only Luftwaffe aircraft that were encountered were three Ju 88s that White and Red Flights of the 61st Fighter squadron found in the traffic pattern at Arboim.

The three German aircraft landed before they could be attacked in the air, so Capt.'s Smith and Lanowski, along with Lt.'s George Levkulich, William Bour and Merton Gillies shot them up on the ground. The rest of the Group provided escort-out to a battle damaged B-17 and B-24 and landed at 1205.

August 17: VIII FC FO 519. Weather over the continent deterred heavy bomber operations, so all the fighter groups but two sought transportation targets in France and Belgium.

The Wolfpack flew two missions. "A" Group, led by Lt. Col. Schilling, got off Boxted at 0941. The targets were a railroad repair yard at Soignies and a marshalling yard at Braine le Comte. (South of Brussels). Twenty-eight 500 pound GP's and twelve 250 pound GPs were dropped on Braine le Comte where there were thirty plus railroad cars and locomotives. At least five locos were destroyed, but by the time the 61st Fighter Squadron bombed the target was so obscured by smoke and dust that a final tabulation of claims was impossible. In all, the mission claimed 10-0-10 locos, 4-0-21 box cars, and 15-0-2 trucks, and RTB'd at 1248.

Again several aircraft carried rocket launching tubes, as the 56th Fighter Group was the first 8th Air Force fighter group to be so equipped, but the results of the rocket attacks were inconclusive as far as accuracy was concerned, and the pilots were not happy with the corresponding drag and instability the tubes created.

"B" Group was led off at 0944 with Capt. "Bunny" Comstock leading twenty-four Jugs. The main target was a radio station near Wildenberg, where its eight transmitting towers were knocked down and the roof was blown off the transmitter site. Addition air-to-ground work accounted for 4-0-9 locos and 3-0-50 boxcars. RTB time was 1240 with one P-47 receiving minor flak damage.

August 18: VIII FC FO 523. With an improvement in the weather, Bomber Command sent out over 750 B-17s and B-24s to attack Luftwaffe installations and tactical targets. The 56th Fighter Group dispatched two separate missions in support of the heavies.

Major Baker led the first one off at 1221 with thirty-five P-47s to go Thunderbolting between Rouen and Poix, in France. Although only one locomotive was destroyed, thirty-one boxcars were obliterated. RTB at 1533

The second mission, a Ramrod to Rouen, got off at 1708 with thirty-five Thunderbolts, led by Major Dade. The 61st Fighter Squadron, Led by Capt. Smith provided top cover for the 62nd and 63rd FS's that attacked targets of opportunity. A railroad bridge was destroyed in one attack, while a road bridge was missed in another attack, but the road itself was well potholed.

August 23: VIII FC FO 526. The 56th Fighter Group had flown thirty-one missions in eighteen consecutive days, and then got a four day respite from missions because of the weather. Weather in Europe also kept the heavies on the ground this day, but four P-47 groups, including the 56th, got off to strike rail targets in France. The big new was that Paris was now entirely in Allied hands.

Lt. Col. Schilling led thirty-five P-47s off to hit targets at Ham, Abbeville and Amiens areas at 1441. Capt. George Hall, the newly appointed Operations Officer of the 63rd FS led that squadron to provide top cover for the other two squadrons.

Arriving over the Ham area at 1545, they worked over the general area for 1:15 minutes. The mission accounted for 2-0-19 locomotives and 11-0-55 boxcars, along with 10-0-35 empty oil tankers.

August 24: VIII FC FO 527. Over thirteen hundred heavies went to Germany to attack German oil and aircraft industries.

Capt. Michael Quirk led the escort mission off at 0911 with forty-eight P-47s flown by pilots happy to be back on a Ramrod. RV was made at Brunswick with B-24s of the 2nd Bomb Division headed for Hannover at 1120. Although informed of "bandits" near Madgenburg, none could be found, and escort was broken northeast of Mappel. The 62nd Fighter Squadron did some strafing on their way home, but the mission was considered uneventful.

August 25: VIII FC FO 529. Again over thirteen hundred heavies went out to attack German oil and aircraft industries. The Wolfpack flew two Ramrods in support of Bomber Command.

Lt. Col. Schilling led the first mission off at 0845 with forty-eight Thunderbolts. Assigned area patrol and general support, they went in over

Egmond and flew to Lubeck to orbit for a period, and then proceeded to Neumunster to RV with B-17s that they escorted out over the North Sea in batches covered by the three individual squadrons. Other than having two P-47s suffer minor flak damage, the mission was uneventful.

The second mission got of at 1613 with thirty-six P-47s led by Major Baker. RV was accomplished over Trouville with two Combat Wings of B-17s of the 1st Bomb Division at 1720. Although some bogies were announced, they turned out to be friendly fighters, and there was no sign of the Luftwaffe at all. Escort was broken at Ostend-Dunkirk, and Capt. Quirk's 62nd FS indulged in a little strafing, damaging one locomotive and eight cars and having one of their P-47s suffer minor flak damage.

August 26: VIII FC FO 532. Almost a thousand B-17s and B-24s went out to strike targets in France and Germany. The emphasis was on hitting POL targets (petroleum, oil, lubricants).

Capt. Comstock led the 56th Fighter Group with thirty-six Jugs to provide area support and escort. RV was made just to the west of Zwolle at 1220 with two Combat Wings of 1st Bomb Division B-17s, which were escorted uneventfully as far as Haamstede at 1310. They then went Thunderbolting, destroying five locomotives and three boxcars. 1st Lt. Walter Flagg, who had set an all-time 63rd FS record for flying the most combat hours in June (105:15), was slightly wounded by flak while attacking ground targets. He would receive the Purple Heart.

August 27: VIII FC FO 536. Over twelve hundred B-17s and B-24s were sent out to bomb Berlin and targets in northern and central Germany. However, heavy cloud cover caused the recall of most of the force, and less than two hundred bombed effectively. While the P-51 and P-38 fighter groups were up on escort missions, the P-47 groups concentrated on tactical fighter-bomber missions.

Capt. Quirk led the 56th Fighter Group up at 1055 with thirty-nine Thunderbombers carrying 500 pound GP's. They arrived over the Kaiserlauten area at 1240 and set to work striking the marshalling yard at Landsthul where 15-09 locomotives were hit, as well as 10-0-21 freight cars. The attacks came with a price. (Absolutely no pun intended). Lt. Thomas J. Price, 62nd Fighter Squadron, got too low while making a strafing run and struck the ground, his P-47 becoming a ball of fire and he was killed.

Captain Donovan Smith led a second mission back to the same area that afternoon with thirty-six Thunderbombers. Results were again very good with eighty-five freight cars damaged and ten destroyed. Thirty-six passenger cars were damaged and two locomotives destroyed. The pilots were pretty happy with the quick-release Lockheed Interstate electric bomb shackles that reduced the number of bomb hang-ups and also dropped when they were supposed to, which improved their ability to hit their intended targets.

August 28: VIII FC FO 538. Bomber Command stood down this day, but over eight hundred fighters went out to attack rail targets in Germany, France and the Low Countries. Many of the 56th Fighter Group's P-47s now featured the new K-14A gyro computing gunsight that the pilots were told would almost guarantee them a score if they encountered the Luftwaffe. After almost four weeks of not encountering any air-to-air action, they would find out today if the sight worked as advertised.

Lt. Col. Schilling led forty Thunderbolts off Boxted at 0700 for the 63rd Fighter Squadron to strike the marshalling yards at Winneiller and Diekirchen while the 62nd FS was to hit similar yards at Waldwisse and Courcilles. Twenty-four P-47s carried 500 pound GP's and the 61st Fighter Squadron flew as top cover.

On the way to the targets four He 111s were spotted flying down "on the deck" near Saarbrucken. Lt. Edward Albright, 63rd FS, Red Three, got one while Capt. Joseph Curtis and Lt. Walter Groce, Blue One and Two, shared another with Capt. Landowski, 61st FS. (Groce officially got 1/2 credit, but Curtis and Landowski were not credited at all). The smaller marshalling yards were then hit with fair to good results, and they the Group moved over to bomb Courcelles with excellent results. A single He 111 was spotted on the ground at Waldwisse, which was destroyed by Major Gordon Baker, 61st FS. As the Group commenced to reform to go home, Capt. Michael Jackson, 62nd FS, spotted a Ju 88 in the vicinity of Jarny, which he destroyed. Lt. Col. Schilling got an He 111 overhead Saarburg. One more He 111 was knocked down by Capt. Paul Conger and then he and Lt. James Jure, 61st FS, shared another.

Jure: "I was flying Whippet White 4 at about 7,000 ft. in the vicinity of Saarbrucken on a course of 100 (degrees) when I sighted a He 111 going in the opposite direction at an altitude of around 500 ft. I dove to the attack and the e/a started to turn. I gave one radius lead and opened fire at about 500 yards. My lead was not enough so on the second burst I gave a 1 1/2 lead and observed hits on tail as I closed to within 30 yards of the e/a. I hit him many times on the wing and forward part of the fuselage. The rear gunner on the e/a fired on me continuously until the e/a exploded.

"I learned later that Whippet Red Leader fired on the e/a and also got good hits on the wing which came off the e/a before it exploded. The e/a was definitely destroyed.

"I claim one He 111 destroyed (shared) with Whippet Red Leader, Capt. Paul A. Conger."

The action continued on the way home. As the 63rd FS passed near Sharleville, a Ju 88 and several single-engine aircraft were spotted parked on the grass at an unidentified airdrome. Their Red flight went in to strafe them, and encountered four Me 109s that were returning to land. Lt. Walter Flagg shot down one of the Messerschmitts, while Lt. Thomas Queen destroyed the Ju 88. Another, previously unseen, Ju 88 was damaged on the ground by Lt. Baird Knox, 62nd FS.

Major Lucian Dade led the evening mission off Boxted at 1658 with twenty-four Thunderbolts. Their mission was to provide tactical air support to ground forces from Charleroi to Brussels. The 62nd FS P-47s flew as top cover, while the other two squadrons sought targets of opportunity. First hit was the marshalling yard at Mone, and the second was another yard at Braine le Conte. A lot of rolling stock was damaged, but only ten boxcars were actually claimed as destroyed. RTB time was 2019.

August 29: VIII FC FO 540. Adverse weather over the continent curtailed strategic operations, so only one P-38 group and the four remaining 8th Air Force P-47 groups were active against tactical targets in France and Belgium.

Major Dade got little rest, as he led this mission off at 0659. Thirty-five P-47s went Thunderbolting to the Rethel area, but six had to abort, and three more returned as escorts for them. All sorts of miscellaneous ground targets were hit, including an inconclusive attack on a railroad tunnel. Ninety-five trucks were destroyed and forty-five horse drawn wagons.

August 31: Boxted was on the receiving end of German V-1 bombs. Although many pilots had seen them launched, the others now got too good a look at them. Seven passed over or near their base, and one exploded within two miles of their billets.

September 1: VIII FC FO 543. The 56th Fighter Group did not fly the last two days of August, and the other strategic and tactical units saw little action because of the weather over Europe. On September 1, the weather continued to effect strategic operations and most of the dispatched bombers were either recalled or unable to reach their primary targets. The P-38 and P-51 groups went out as escorts for the heavies, while the P-47 groups concentrated on tactical ground targets behind the German front lines.

Major Dade led the mission off at 0745 with thirty-six P-47s to once again go dive bombing and strafing. They bombed northwest of Eindhoven with excellent results, and then strafed near Tilburg and Breda with good results.

Lt. Col. Schilling led the second mission, at 1545 with thirty-three P-47s on another Thunderbombing strike to Holland. The excitement oc-

curred when a train that was being strafed by the 62nd and 63rd Fighter Squadrons blew up infront of them. The 62nd FS had three P-47s suffer repairable damage, but one more, although its pilot got it home, was damaged beyond repair. The 63rd FS also had three damaged in the same explosion. The train was suspected of carrying V-1s, due to the size of the explosion. In all, 220 boxcars were claimed destroyed by the Thunderbombers.

At Boxted, 2nd Lt. John Allen was killed on a training flight. It was his first day flying with the 62nd Fighter Squadron.

September 2: VIII FC FO 109. The weather was so bad over Europe that only the 56th Fighter Group out of the entire 8th Air Force flew a mission. Lt. Col. Schilling led them off at 1144 and they flew "on the deck" to Knocke-Ostend, and then strafed targets of opportunity on the way south to Courtai. Of the thirty-six P-47s sent out, an even dozen were damaged by various types of ground fire during this mission.

Lt. Jack Pierce, 62nd Fighter Squadron, had his P-47 damaged by an explosion of the target he had selected. It took him fifteen minutes just to get the sick Jug back up to five thousand feet, and the best speed he could get was a meager 150 mph. This made him a sitting target for the flak gunners who had him constantly silhouetted against the low clouds. Squadron mate Lt. Darrell McMahan escorted Pierce home, and each time he came under antiaircraft fire, McMahan either was able to silence the guns or divert their attention. McMahan was put in for a Distinguished Service Cross for his courageous work.

Two additional P-47s were damaged by striking ground objects: One hit a tree, another a telephone pole, but both pilots were able to get them home, although both were written off as a result of the incurred damage. The other nine P-47s all suffered varying degrees of flak damage.

September 5: VIII FC FO 550. VIII Bomber Command sent 882 B-17s and B-24s to southeastern Germany to hit aircraft and synthetic oil plants, of which 812 aircraft bombed effectively. The 56th Fighter Group went out in advance of them on a strafing sweep to attempt to catch the Luftwaffe on the ground before they could takeoff to intercept the bombers.

Major Dade led the thirty-six Thunderbolts off at 0938 on what would be one of the most interesting and eventful missions in weeks. Arriving in the vicinity of Koblenz at 1110 between ten and fifteen thousand feet, the first targets were sighted on the airdrome at Mershausen Airdrome.

With Capt. Comstock's 63rd Fighter Squadron providing top cover, the 62nd and 61st FS's went down to strafe the German aircraft with gusto. Pilots from the 61st FS awarded claims for ground kills were: Lt's Cleon Thomton and William Clark sharing an Me 110, and Clark getting an Me 110 and an Me 410 by himself; Major Lucian Dade, two Me 210s and an He 111; Lt. James Jure an He 111; Capt. Benjamin Cathers a Ju 88. Pilots from the 62nd FS awarded claims were: Lt. Herschel Womack one Me 110; Capt. Herman King one Me 110; Capt. William Wilkerson one He 111; Lt. Steven Murray two Ju 88s; Lt. Fred McIntosh one Me 110 and one unidentified type twin-engine aircraft. Each squadron also had one claim denied.

Capt. Quirk's 62nd FS then moved their attention to the airdrome at Limburg, where thirty to forty planes were seen parked. Capt. Michael Jackson destroyed two Ju 88s and an Me 109; Lt. Steve Murray and Jackson shared an Me 210, and Murry got two Storch's. Not seeing any need to provide top cover for the others, Comstock led the 63rd FS down to strafe the Autobahn ten miles northeast of Koblenz. During this effort they found themselves bounced by ten plus Me 109s, and in a dogfight that took them up from the deck to as high as 9,000 feet, they shot down seven and damaged one. 2nd Lt. Richard Anderson, who had only been in the squadron six weeks and got his first kill a month ago protecting Col. Zemke, got two; 2nd Lt. Robert Daniel got one; 2nd Lt. Cameron Hart started his string to "Acedom" with one; 1st Lt. James Kyle got his only kill of the war; 1st Lt. Richard Warboys also got his only kill of the war, and he would finish his tour five days later without getting another chance at scoring.

The raid on the airdrome at Gelnhausen on September 5, 1944 resulted in the destruction of seventy-eight German aircraft, and nineteen damaged. A new ETO record. UN✪D overflies the burning airdrome. (USAF, via Davis)

Having dispatched the German fighters without any damage, the 63rd FS returned to strafing, claiming one car, six trucks and a locomotive. As they overflew Eupen, the squadron turned northeast to avoid flak from Bonn, except Lt. Chester Frye, Red Four, who turned south instead. "He appeared," according to wingman, Lt. Hart, "to be out of the flak area and in no apparent trouble. He never rejoined the formation." Frye spent the rest of the war in Stalag Luft I as a POW.

The 61st FS was now concentrating on a train near Siegberg when 1st Lt. William Heaton was killed. Heaton had made one pass on the train, consisting of a locomotive and three boxcars, and was making another run at it when flak from a nearby airdrome smashed a round directly into his canopy. His P-47 was seen to hit the ground and explode.

Two other 61st FS pilots, Lt.'s William Clark and James Jure had their P-47s shot up by flak, but both managed to get them across the lines to friendly territory before having to settle for belly landings in France, and they both returned to the squadron a few days later.

The 62nd FS had shifted to Grozenlinden and Wetzlar airdromes where they racked up more ground kills. Capt. Herman King got one Me 110, one He 111, one Ju 88, and shared another Ju 88 with Lt. Steve Murray. Lt. Fred McIntosh destroyed one Me 210 and damaged two more. Lt. Herschel Womack destroyed an Me 210 and damaged another.

After being shadowed half way home by an Me 262, the mission returned at 1341.

VIII FC FO 110. Lt. Col. David Schilling led the late afternoon mission off at 1609 with twenty-nine Thunderbolts to Gelnhausen Airdrome. Major Gordon Baker led the 61st FS with eight of this number to provide top cover for the others on this eventful strafing sweep.

At Gelnhausen, some fifty aircraft were parked, mostly single-engine. Schilling, and his wingman, 2nd Lt. Charles Rotzler, 63rd FS, made the first diving strafing pass to ascertain if there were any flak guns, and to silence them if there were. They knocked out some on the east side of the field, and then proceeded to each damage a pair of Fw 190s before calling down the rest of the Group. On their second pass, Rotzler destroyed an Fw 190, and 1st Lt. Edward Albright got a Ju 52. On the third and fourth passes, Schilling got an Fw 190 and Rotzler got another one. 2nd Lt. Robert Daniels also got an Fw 190. During pass number six, Schilling spotted a hanger with two aircraft inside, so he fired and set the hanger on fire, which consumed two more. Rotzler continued to run his total up: on his fifth run he got an Fw 190, and on his sixth he spotted a hanger with aircraft and flak guns inside, which he also set on fire with incendiary ammunition.

Also scoring for the 63rd FS were: 1st Lt. Richard Warboys, one Me 109; 1st Lt. Eugene Timony two Bucker 131s and an Fw 190; 2nd Lt. Thomas Queen one Fw 190; 2nd Lt. Everett Henderson one Fw 190; Lt. Albright also added an Fw 190 to his score on a later pass.

The 62nd FS ran up the score even higher, claiming twenty-nine destroyed out of the total of forty-seven. In addition, a total of sixteen were damaged, of which seven of them were not claimed by the squadron, as they were also known to have been hit by pilots from the 63rd FS. 62nd FS pilots making claims were: Capt. Michael Quirk, four Fw 190s; Lt. Eugene Beeson, one Fw 190 and one unidentified type; Capt. Robert Keen, six Fw 190s; Lt. Roy Patterson, two Fw 190s; Lt. George Butler, two Me 109s and one Fw 190; Lt. Darrell McMahan, four Fw 190s; Lt. Jack Pierce, two Fw 190s; Lt. Robert Winters, one Fw 190; Lt. Fred McIntosh, two Fw 190s.

The 61st FS, not wanting to miss out on all the action, also came down for a little strafing. 1st Lt. William Hartshorn damaged an unknown type; Lt. Thomas Queen damaged an Fw 190; and Capt. Paul Conger and 2nd Lt. Fred Barrett shared in damaging three more Fw 190s. In all, Dave Schilling estimated that only two aircraft might have remained undamaged when the Wolfpack finished working over the field.

On the way back to Boxted, Lt. Col. Schilling spotted a lone Fw 190 flying down on the deck near Koblenz. Being out of ammunition, himself, he sent Lt. Eugene Timony, 63rd FS, Blue Two, after it. Timony closed to 400 yards and started firing at it from its seven o'clock position. As the distance reduced to 100 yards, Timony started seeing strikes on it, and as he overshot it, he was able to watch its pilot open the canopy and slide over its left wing as he bailed out.

Near Fulds, a lone German Fw 44 trainer was seen flying on the deck. It was dispatched by 1st Lt. George Butler, 62nd FS, for his third and last air-to-air kill.

All of this action, however, did bring on the not unexpected aircraft losses. 1st Lt. Earl Hertel, 61st FS, was seen to be hit by antiaircraft fire coming from a revetment near the bank of a canal on the outskirts of Antwerp. Hertel bailed out at 900 feet just west of Hulet. He landed safely and commenced to try and walk out of Holland, only to meet a girl who told him that the Maquis was at his crashed aircraft, so he returned to it. The Maquis took him to the Military Police of a Polish tank corps at St. Nicholas who saw to it that Hertel got back safely. He returned to Boxted on September 22.

2nd Lt. Claude Chinn, 63rd FS, lost his oil pressure on the way back and was last heard from at 2,000 south of Frankfurt. Chinn had to make a forced landing south of Troyes, near Lantages, in no man's land between the battle lines. He put his Thunderbolt down in an open field, set fire to it, and then made his way back to meet friendly troops who saw to it that he got headed back to his squadron okay.

1st Lt. James Clark, 61st FS, had to put down on an Allied airstrip in France for fuel and was considered a NYR (Not Yet Returned), for a period. 1st Lt. William Hartshorne, also from the 61st FS, was in the process of being placed on the NYR roster when he was the last to return to Boxted. His arrival was so much later than the others that he had been given up upon, and he had to be aided to a safe landing by the use of searchlights.

September 6: VIII FC FO 555. Once again bad weather over Germany kept the heavies out of action. Only the P-38s and P-47s were active on interdiction type missions.

Off Boxted at 1200 with thirty-five P-47s, the Wolfpack was led by Major Dade. They arrived in the secondary target area, roads between Maastricht and Aachen, at 1345, after discovering that the primary area, Frankfurt, was obscured by low clouds. Among the many vehicles destroyed or damaged were two Panther tanks, the first claims of this type. RTB was at 1605.

September 8: VIII FC FO 557. With an improvement in the weather, a thousand B-17s and B-24s went to industrial targets in the areas of Mainz and Ludwigshafen. 350 Mustangs were off on escort missions for them, while the other P-38, P-47 and P-51 groups went out on interdiction missions.

Major Baker led the Wolfpack off at 1307 to the Bonn area to bomb and strafe. 1st Lt. George Bostwick led the 62nd Fighter Squadron to provide top cover for the other two squadrons. Near St. Vity two flights of the Thunderbombers had to jettison their bombs after spotting bogies, but they turned out to be P-38s. After the remainder hit transportation targets near Rouen, the 56th Fighter Group proceeded to Euskirchen to attack the airdrome there where fifteen plus He 111s and Fw 190s were seen. Baker, leading from the 61st FS, got an He 111.

The remainder of the squadron then proceeded to silence the antiaircraft guns, and then the 62nd FS came down to workover the parked aircraft. Bostwick destroyed two Fw 190s and damaged three more; Lt. Jack Carwell got an Me 109; Lt. Louis Brown destroyed an unidentified twin-engine type and damaged an Fw 190; Lt. Billy Edens destroyed another unidentified type twin; Lt. Jack Pierce damaged an Me 109.

The 63rd FS was equally busy, with Lt. Gene Timony destroying a Ju 88; Lt. James Lister damaging three more Ju 88s; Lt. Russell Frederickson damaged an Me 110 and Lt. Walter Groce damaged an Me 109; Lt. Edward Albright damaged an unknown twin-engine type. It wasn't a bad afternoon's work. Although four P-47s suffered battle damage, all got home to Boxted okay.

September 9: VIII FC FO 560. Most of the Bomber Command force went to targets in western Germany. Two P-51 groups and all of the P-47 groups flew tactical missions, while the remaining fighter groups covered the heavies.

Major Dade led thirty-five Thunderbombers off Boxted at 1630 to attack German held Dutch islands. In over Schouwen Island, they patrolled to Rotterdam-Gilze Rijen-Antwerp, looking for worthwhile targets without much success. Those targets selected for bombing were hit with poor results, and the marshalling yard at Axel was missed by everyone.

Strafing was more successful, destroying thirty-one horse drawn vehicles and twenty-eight railway cars, among many other targets.

For such a short-ranged type mission, and after some of the heavier obstacles faced by the Group on missions deep into Europe, this one should have been of the "milk run" category, but it was not the case.

The 63rd Fighter Squadron suffered three losses. 2nd Lt. Everett Henderson, a new pilot flying Major Dade's wing as White Two, was killed as he strafed a truck near Noordewg and got too low and flew into the ground. Capt. Roy Fling, leading Red Flight, spotted a convoy near Hulst. He told his element leader, Lt. Cameron Hart, Red Three, to lead-off on the strafing run, which Hart did, but afterwards Hart found himself all alone. Hart called Fling on the radio, and everything was reported as being okay, so Hart continued to strafe the convoy, and when he was out of ammunition he called Fling again and said he was heading for home. Fling acknowledged this, but was never seen or heard from again. 2nd Lt. David Magel, Red Two, also disappeared, but he turned up okay after being forced down in friendly territory.

September 10: VIII FC FO 561. Bomber Command sent 1145 B-17s and B-24s to targets in and around Stuttgart. For a change, the Wolfpack got to participate in an escort mission.

The mission with thirty-five P-47s got off to a bad start, as five Thunderbolts had to turn back with various problems. Led by Capt. Michael Quirk, Commanding Officer of the 62nd Fighter Squadron, they had gotten airborne at 0901 and then made RV with B-24s of the 2nd Bomb Division near Eberbach at 1100. Escort was broken a half hour later at Wurzburg.

Passing over Wertheim, they spotted many German aircraft on the ground, but they were already being worked over by P-51s, so they continued on to Seligenstadt airdrome where some thirty German aircraft were seen parked.

Quirk led his squadron down to strafe, and they encountered "intense light accurate" antiaircraft fire from three sides of the airdrome. Quirk destroyed an He 111, but then was hit by flak and had to bailout. His parachute opened and he was seen to land in a tree to become a POW. 1st Lt. Billy Edens was also hit by flak, and was escorted to near Trier by 1st Lt. Townsend Parsons before Edens had to bailout to become another resident of a Stalag. The loss of these two pilots was particularly heavy, as Edens had been a member of the 62nd FS for quite awhile and was an ace with seven kills, while Quirk was a double ace and the last of the original squadron members to have come to England in 1943.

The Thunderbolt was tough, tough enough to bring Capt. Ray Fling back after flying through some trees on a strafing mission. Yet, fate and the enemy still had their way and Fling was killed on September 9, 1944. (via Davis)

The Polish contingent assigned to the Wolfpack. The majority of these pilots escaped from Poland when it was overrun, then fought with the French and the RAF before being attached to the USAAF. Left to Right, Mike Gladych, Flight Lt. Sawicz, Gabreski (Whose ethnicity brought them together.), Flight Lt.'s Zbigniew Janicki (KIA with the 61st FS.), Andersz and Lanowski. (via Davis)

Nevertheless, the mission continued and Lt. Jack Pierce destroyed an He 111 and Lt. George Van Noy damaged a Ju 88 while Lt. George Butler damaged a single-engine type.

For the 63rd FS the mission was uneventful, but the 61st FS lost their Operations Officer, Capt. Donavan Smith for a short period when he became a NYR. He had to land in France for fuel, and did not get back to Boxted until the next day.

Upon their return, Major Leslie Smith, who had led the 61st Fighter Squadron on this mission, was transferred to the 62nd FS as their new squadron commander to replace the missing Captain Quirk.

September 11: VIII FC FO 563. The 8th Air Force Bomber Command made an intensive attack against synthetic oil production with over eleven hundred heavy bombers. For the first time in four months the Luftwaffe attempted to thwart the bombers with a similar effort, putting up over an estimated five hundred fighters. This resulted in the loss of forty heavies (Along with those lost to flak.), and the highest bomber and fighter claims for German aircraft knocked down to date.

The Wolfpack got off at 1017 to provide target and withdrawal support on a Ramrod mission, making RV at Oschersleben at 1219 with the 3rd Air Task Force of the 2nd Bomb Division going to the heavily defended Magdeburg. Escort was provided uneventfully, being broken between Egmond and Quakenbruck, except by a couple of P-47s that escorted-out a crippled B-24. It was a frustrating mission for Major Baker, as

no German fighters were seen by the Group while the 55th Fighter Group flying nearby got twenty-eight in the air.

September 12: VIII FC FO 565. A similar mission by Bomber Command against the German oil industry, this time with eight hundred effective heavies. Some of the targets were the same as the previous day, but the Luftwaffe was not back up with the same defensive strength.

Lt. Col. Schilling led the Jugs off at 0824. Forty were sent out, but eight were early return aborts, and one more returned as an escort. The depleted Group met the 2nd Air Task Force of the 3rd Bomb Division southwest of Luneburg at 1025 while flying at 27,000 feet. Penetration and target support was provided to Madgeburg, where the bombing looked good until the target became obscured by smoke.

Over Brandenberg, twenty plus Me 109s were sighted slightly above the 56th FG and were thusly engaged by "Whippet Red Flight."

The 61st Fighter Squadron flight, down to three P-47s, got 2-0-1 Me 109's with Lt.'s James Clark and James Jure each getting a kill and Lt. Stuart Getz getting credit for the damaged.

South of Brandenburg, the 62nd FS was bounced by six more Me 109s, one of which was destroyed by an interloping P-51, and another by Lt. Darrell McMahon. Near Havelberg fifty more German fighters were seen, but they were too far away to encounter and the P-47s, by this time were starting to hurt for fuel.

As the Group turned for home, it became obvious that due to the length of the mission and the time spent at high power settings in combat, that many of them were not going to be able to make it back to Boxted. Both Lt.'s Clark and Jure had to belly land in Belgium out of fuel. Although they put down within a half mile of each other it took them two hours to get back together on the ground. The enthusiastic crowds that came out to meet them were that thick! Lt. Warren Patterson, also from the 61st FS, had a similar experience. After making a forced landing in Belgium, Patterson left his P-47 under guard by a force of the Free French, and then British troops: While waiting for transportation he had to shake the hands of a hundred Belgians.

2nd Lt. Fred Barrett, 61st FS, made a forced landing at the Merville airdrome, west of Lille. As two of the three runways were flagged to indicate they had been mined, and the third runway was blown-up, Barrett put his Jug down on the grass, borrowed gas from a RAF Typhoon squadron that had just moved in, and flew on home that night. Lt. Dean Nordquist, 62nd FS, had to land at Brussels because of flak damage. An eventful day.

September 13: VIII FC FO ? Back to oil and industrial targets by Bomber Command, this time in southern Germany. Over a thousand heavies went out, but less than eight hundred bombed effectively.

Major Baker led the Ramrod to Merseburg off at 0855. Escort was provided to the 3rd Air Task Force. RV was accomplished over the target and escort provided out to west of Dusseldorf. No sign of the Luftwaffe and an uneventful mission that RTB'd at 1402.

September 16: VIII FC FO 573. Bad weather kept the heavies on the ground, while only 327 P-47s and P-51s went out as fighter-bombers.

Capt. Harold Comstock led the thirty-six Thunderbombers off at 1535, and they arrived the Ahlhorn airdrome area at 1710. This was a new target that had not been touched before and had some intriguing facets. There was a lake painted on the ground on the east tip of the airdrome, and the woods on the southeast showed indications of heavy traffic going into them. While the 61st Fighter Squadron flew top cover, the other two squadrons bombed with each P-47 carrying 260 lb. fragmentation bombs. Bombing results were considered poor but several buildings on the north side of the field were set on fire and destroyed.

Lt. Francis Nolan destroyed three He 111Ks with his bombs and damaged another. Strafing accounted for even better results with Capt. Comstock torching an He 111 parked in a revetment; Capt. Don Smith, 61st FS, destroyed another, and Capt. Robert Keen, 62nd FS, got a Ju 88. An interesting target of suspect purposes was a train that was destroyed. Composed of ten flat cars that each held two cylinders, the containers "gave off a yellowish-white smoke when hit."

September 17: VIII FC FO 576. The major emphasis was on supporting the airborne invasion of Holland. Only B-17s from Bomber Command were participants, primarily to silence flak batteries. From Fighter Command, all groups were active, either to escort the B-17s or to provide tactical support to the airborne invasion that turned into a terrible debacle. Known as Operation "Market-Garden," "Market" was the paradrop of the First Allied Airborne Army at Nijmegen, while "Garden" was the British counterpart dropped at Arnhem that would be intended to linkup the two forces and permit the bypass of the Siegfried Line and the crossing of the Rhine River in Holland. Overextended and under supplied with both men and arms in the face of a determined German resistance, the British force was wiped out after a week of heavy fighting with heavy losses.

Lt. Col. Schilling led the mission off Boxted to hit the marshalling yard at Amersfoort where there was a concentration of 170 plus boxcars and eight plus locomotives. The mission, while successful in damaging or destroying German rolling stock, proved costly.

1st Lt. Edward Albright, who had just become the commander of the 63rd Fighter Squadron's "B Flight" the week before, was leading Red Flight and they dove intrail on the marshalling yard. During the dive, Albright's

On September 17 1st Lt. Carl Westman, 61st FS, was wounded while strafing. He managed to get back to England to bailout when his P-47 caught on fire. The remains of his P-47. Westman received the Purple Heart. (USAF)

belly tank was hit by flak and exploded. Then it either came off or he jettisoned it before pulling up into a cloud formation. His wingman, 2nd Lt. Frank Ogden, followed him up, but when Ogden broke out on top of the clouds, there was no sign of Albright. Radio contact between the two was made, and Albright said that he was heading south and still trying to get on top, but then he stated that he was going to have to bailout, as he had lost his oil pressure. This was the last that he was heard from, and he was later reported as killed in action.

1st Lt. Darrell McMahan, 62nd FS, was personally hit by flak which shattered his knee and broke his arm. McMahan fought his pain and injuries back to England where he had to make a forced landing at Boxted without being able to use either his brakes or flaps. 1st Lt. Carl Westman, 61st FS, was also injured on this mission. After being hit by flak, Westman flew his damaged Jug back to England, but it caught on fire before he could land. When he opened the canopy to bailout, the flames were sucked into the cockpit and set his clothes on fire and burned his exposed skin. Purple Hearts were awarded to these pilots.

September 18: VIII FC FO 578. The last Operation Frantic shuttle mission to Russia was launched with 110 B-17s and 150 P-51s. The primary objective for them was to attempt to supply trapped Poles during the Warsaw rising. An unsupported exercise (by the other Allied powers) in futility.

All other Fighter Command groups were active in supporting Operation "Market-Garden," either escorting the B-24s making parachute drops with relief supplies or on tactical missions.

For the Wolfpack this would be the most costly mission in their history. Assigned the role of flak busting: ". . . an operation dreaded by all fighter pilots because it involves flying over areas suspected of enemy flak, waiting until the guns fire to determine their locations by the flashes, and then destroying them." Literally flying into the enemy's gun barrels.

The initial assessment of losses was shocking. Sixteen pilots were missing, and of the twenty-three aircraft that returned, twelve had major battle damage. Of the sixteen pilots, eight either bailed out or belly landed in Allied territory. Three were wounded and had to be sent back to the United States. One was killed when he bellied-in, one was known to become a POW, and three were MIA.

Major Harold Comstock, who had been promoted the day before, but wasn't aware of it yet, and thusly is still listed as a Captain on the mission roster, wasn't supposed to lead this mission, but he got saddled with it, anyhow. Comstock led thirty-nine P-47s off Boxted at 1437, with only one having to abort.

Major Harold Comstock leading elements of his 63rd FS. Comstock's personal aircraft was UN✪V. UN✪R (bar) belonged to Major Burke. (USAF)

They arrived over the area of Turnhout, Holland at 1550 right "on the deck" as low clouds forced them down closer to the ground than desired. Clouds ranged from 500 to 1000 feet in patches, with higher cloud bases around 3500 feet, but surrounded with heavy haze. Because of the weather conditions and intense flak around Turnhout, the Group was split into two forces and things started downhill at this time. First off, the B-24s they were supposed to escort could not be located, and were not found until later by Comstock's 63rd Fighter Squadron on the way out.

The Group had been restricted by higher headquarters not to fire upon ground targets until actually fired upon first, because of a perceived belief that there were so many Allied troops in the area that the fighter pilots might strafe the wrong troops. True in conception. In reality it worked in reverse, as one 56th Fighter Group pilot was known to be shot down by an Allied tank concentration near Eindhoven. The remainder of the ground fire came up so thick and heavy it was impossible to tell whether it came from Allied or Axis forces.

Donavon Smith's "Ole Cock III," HV✪S. 42-28382. The original "Ole Cock" was a P-47C, and the 2nd was a "razorback" D. (USAF)

A barrel-chested Thunderbolt returns from a mission. LM✪A was P-47D-28RE, 44-19960. (via Davis)

UN✪A (bar) 44-19786 was lost on September 17, 1944 over Zoelen, Holland. Its pilot, Lt. Edward Albright, was killed. (via Davis)

Comstock's 63rd FS was so badly shot up and scattered that individual pilots had to look for targets of opportunity. While claiming three flak positions, one staff car and three trucks, they had to contend with: "The German flak guns tracked them, and then shot at them from the side as they went by at such low altitudes. Thus they were shot down before they could peel off, descend even lower and attack." 1st Lt. David Kling, flying as the squadron's spare, was shotup and crash landed west of Turnhout and was seen to escape from his wrecked aircraft. He returned to England before the month was out. Newly promoted 1st Lt. Charles Rotzler, flying Comstock's wing, bellied-in in friendly territory with flak damage and returned to the squadron a few days later.

Captain Gordon Stevens, one of the ex-bombardiers, was killed. Leading Blue Flight, Stevens was one of the pilots shot at from the side at Turnhout. Separated from his flight, he circled to come back and silenced the anti-aircraft guns and then reported that he was setting course for home, and was never heard from again. His wingman, 2nd Lt. Robert Kelley, was not seen after they became separated and he became a POW. 1st Lt. Thomas Guerrero, leading Red Flight, was last seen five miles west of Tilbourg when he stated that his engine was acting up and that setting a course southwest for friendly territory. He made it to behind the lines for a crash landing, but suffered head injuries and amnesia as a result. Flying as Red Four, 2nd Lt. Elwood Raymond, had his P-47 hit in the tail by flak and lost the use of his rudder. Making it back to Boxted, Raymond thought that it would be unsafe to attempt to land and elected to bailout over Bradwell Bay. For some reason Raymond did not get clear of his aircraft and was found in the wreckage of it in the flats of the bay.

The 61st Fighter Squadron did not suffer as heavy losses. 1st Lt. William Hartshorn was seen to bail out after suffering flak damage northwest of Schjudel. It was presumed that he landed in friendly territory, but he became a POW instead. Capt. Paul Conger had to land at airdrome A-25, Douai, after his aircraft was riddled with friendly .30 caliber fire. He returned to Boxted two days later. 2nd Lt. William Bartle was hit by flak at Tilberg. He headed south and bailed out in friendly territory and also was back by the 20th.

Capt. Herman King led the 62nd Fighter Squadron, and they suffered the heaviest losses. Of the twelve Thunderbolts they sent out, only five returned. Fortunately, four of the missing pilots did manage to get back within two days. 2nd Lt. Trevor Edwards had only been with the squadron a month when he was killed. He had told Capt. King that he was going to belly in, but the circumstances of what actually occurred went unseen. 1st Lt. William McElhare announced that "he'd had it," but he survived as a POW. Capt. William Wilkerson reported that he saw Lt. James Hodges P-47 down in friendly territory near Kornelimunster in damaged condition. Hodges suffered a broken leg in the crash landing and was hospitalized in a US Army hospital, and was later removed from flying status and returned to the United States. Wilkerson became one of the NYR's and was a real

surprise when he turned up on the 20th okay. His P-47 had been seen spinning down in flames twenty-five miles east of Aachen. Lt.'s Philip Fleming, George Van Noy and Herschel Womack all went down in unidentified circumstances, but all also returned to Boxted by the 20th.

September 19: VIII FC FO 579. The 1st and 3rd Bomb Division B-17s went to Germany, while the 2nd Bomb Division B-24s had the day off. In spite of the losses and battle damaged aircraft suffered by the Wolfpack the previous mission, they went up on an escort mission for the 1st Bomb Division.

Lt. Col. Schilling led thirty-two P-47s off at 1136. RV with the 2nd Air Task Force attacking Hamm was made at St. Trond at 1220, and escort was provided to the target and out to Maastricht and Aachen. RTB at 1552.

September 20: VIII FC FO 580. Bad weather got in the way of strategic missions, so they were canceled. The only heavy bomber operations were "Truckin," where forty B-24s flew fuel to France for the use of 9th Air Force operations. All 8th Air Force fighter groups but one were out on cloud forced very low-level missions.

Major Baker led thirty-six Thunderbombers on a Ramrod to the Arnhem area at 1531. With the cloud bases at 2,000 feet, dive bombing proved difficult, and actual damage inflicted impossible to determine. All but two of the 62nd Fighter Squadron P-47 pilots had to jettison their bombs in the English Channel on the way back because they could not position themselves properly for bombing.

All those targets that were bombed were then strafed, but claims amounted to only two flak gun positions destroyed. As usual, the flak was heavy and Lt. Robert Walker, 61st Fighter Squadron, had to crash land at Manston with battle damage on the way back with his P-47 a write off.

The "Scarsdale Scout" apparently was bellied in after an aborted takeoff, as the belly tanks are still attached. (USAF)

September 21: VIII FC FO 582. 8th Air Force Bomber Command struck targets in Germany, being escorted by P-38s and P-51s. Other Fighter Command P-51 groups and the P-47 groups were active over Holland.

The 56th Fighter Group drew a different type of mission, to provide area support for Royal Air Force Stirlings operating around Arnheim. Arriving over Arnheim at 1404 at 18,000 feet, Lt. Col. Schilling led the Group to Nijmegen, then north to Deventer, reversed course their course and headed them south to Lochem in a gradual descent.

As they approached Lochem, fifteen plus Fw 190s and at least a pair of Me 109s was seen flying on the deck and heading towards Germany. Schilling and the 63rd Fighter Squadron led the attack from 3,500 feet in a textbook bounce.

"The E/A were surprised by the attack but fought to survive, dragging the engagement NE towards Osnabruck." 1st Lt. Cammeron Hart was leading Red Flight with 2nd Lt. Harold Spicer on his wing while 1st Lt. Richard Anderson brought down the rest of Red Flight. As Lt. Col. Schilling was getting the first of the three Fw 190s he shot down this afternoon, Red Flight also engaged the Fw's with Hart going after the one he selected and Anderson doing likewise. Successfully in both cases. Lt. Harold Spicer had also selected an Fw 190 and was last seen chasing it northeast near Denekamp, but he was never heard from again and was later declared killed in action.

1st Lt. James Kyle was leading Blue Flight with 2nd Lt. Frank Ogden as his wingman and 2nd Lt. Walter Groce as his element leader, who had 2nd Lt. Oscar Cagle as his own wingman. As they dove through the 1,000 foot level, Ogden looked back and saw Groce and Cagle behind them where they should be, but this was the last observation of Lt. Cagle, and he too was killed in action. Lt. Groce was credited with one Fw 190 and Lt. Kyle with a damaged. 2nd Lt. Walter Pitts, out of Schilling's White Flight also destroyed two Focke-Wulf's.

The 62nd Fighter Squadron was led by Capt. Michael Jackson and they scored five Fw 190s for no losses. Jackson was credited with one, which brought his score to four. Additional claims were credited to 2nd Lt.'s Lewis Brown, Donald Henley, Roy Patterson and Robert Winters. These would be the only earned claims for Brown and Patterson, while Henley and Winters would add to their's later.

Squadron Leader Michael Gladych led the 61st Fighter Squadron, and Gladych became a double ace by AAF standards, scoring his ninth and tenth (and final) kills. 2nd Lt. Russ Kyler got his first kill, and 1st Lt. Stuart Getz and 2nd Lt. William Osborne shared another.

September 22: VIII FC FO 584. A marginal improvement in the weather permitted sending over six hundred heavies to Kassel with escort provided by P-51s. The P-38 groups were not active, while two P-47 groups went to the Arnheim area.

Lt. Col. Schilling led the Wolfpack off at 1406 on the Rodeo to Arnheim, arriving in the area at 1510. They patrolled the area a hour and a half and then set course for home. Except for observing contrails from a couple of German jets, the patrol was uneventful and they landed at 1811.

September 26: VIII FC FO 589. Bomber Command sent over a thousand effective B-17s and B-24s to Germany with an escort provided by Mustangs. Other P-51s, as well as P-38s and P-47s were busy over Holland supporting the 1st Allied Airborne Army.

After a couple days off, Lt. Col. Schilling led the 56th Fighter Group off at 1636 with a force composed of only twenty-seven Thunderbolts. Although there were no aborts, the mission's start was marred by two Jugs being damaged in a taxi accident as they moved out, and then an unidentified pilot crashed off base after becoming airborne. Apparently he was uninjured, but his P-47 was a write off. Arriving over Arnheim at 1755, the Group had another uneventful patrol and returned at 2007.

Major Gordon Baker was transferred to Headquarters 56th Fighter Group to replace Major Dade as Flying Executive Officer, as Dade had to return to the States on emergency leave. He was replaced by Capt. Donavan Smith as commanding officer of the 61st Fighter Squadron. One of the originals, Smith had been the youngest 2nd Lt. in the 61st FS when they went overseas. He would be promoted to Major on the 27th.

September 27: VIII FC FO 590. Bomber Command sent almost twelve hundred heavies to attack industrial targets in Germany. All Fighter Command groups were up on escort missions for them.

Capt. Donavon Smith led the mission off at 0741 with thirty-five Thunderbolts. RV was made over Appledorn at 0850 and escort was terminated west of Kassel at 0925. As the Group proceeded to St. Trond, ground control reported that several straggling bombers were under attack, so Capt. Smith took those P-47s that had sufficient fuel remaining back to assist them. Several of the heavies were then escorted out, but there was no sign of the Luftwaffe after RV with them was accomplished.

September 28: VIII FC FO 591. Again a thousand heavies were sent out to attack targets in Germany. The P-47 groups escorted the 2nd Bomb Division B-24s, while P-38s and P-51s escorted 1st and 3rd Bomb Division B-17s. Thirty-six German aircraft were knocked down by the bombers gunners and the P-38 and P-51 pilots, but all the P-47 pilots came up without a score.

Lt. Col. Schilling led forty-seven Thunderbolts off at 0937. The largest number of Jugs dispatched in quite a while. However, the number of effectives was reduced by eight aborts and one more early return that came back as an escort. They caught up with B-24s of the 3rd Air Task Force at Bruges and slow climbed up from underneath them to actually accomplish the RV at Koblenz. Escort was provided to north of Liege at 1330.

The mission was uneventful as far as escorting the Liberators was concerned, as no German fighters could be found. However, Schilling spotted a convoy forty-eight miles southwest of Koblenz, between Herforat and Speicher. He and his White Four, 2nd Lt. Walter Pitts, 63rd FS, went down to investigate. For some unknown reason Pitts never attempted to pull out of his dive and flew into the ground and was killed.

September 30: VIII FC FO 592. Back deep into Germany by Bomber Command under escort by Fighter Command. Over eight hundred heavies escorted by over seven hundred fighters, and for the first time in any large scale raid not a single claim by either a bomber crewman or a fighter pilot was made.

Major Baker led them off at 1155 to provide target and withdrawal support for the heavies attacking Munster. The thirty-six Thunderbolts, for the first time in a long time had no aborts. RV with the B-24s was made at Hamm at 1310 and broken at Ostend at 1456, and they landed, butt-sprung and bored at 1555.

September 1944 had been a good and bad month for the Wolfpack, but no one could deny that it had not been without interest and activity. The long suffering ground crews had been constantly at work on battle damaged aircraft that the pilots had brought home. For example, the 62nd Fighter Squadron had to change twelve entire wings and three engines on battle damaged Jugs. In the 61st FS, every P-47 but one suffered some degree of battle damage, and a total of eleven of their aircraft were lost to one form or another of enemy action. On September 5, the Group set a new record in destroying seventy-nine German aircraft, thirty on the morning's mission, and forty-nine in the afternoon. (Ten in the air, and sixty-nine on the ground). On September 18, the Group had sixteen pilots fail to return, and of the remaining twenty-three dispatched, sixteen more aircraft suffered battle damage in some form. (For this effort, the 56th Fighter Group received a Distinguished Unit Citation). As the month closed, the Group's roster showed that a total of seventeen pilots were missing in action, and time would show that many of these were killed.

The Republic Aircraft Corp. production line. Over 6,000 "bubble-top" Thunderbolts were built. (USAF)

Of the over 14,000 Jugs built, over 500 passed through the Wolfpack's inventory. They are shown here awaiting off-loading in England. (USAF)

October 1: Lt. Col. David Schilling was promoted to full Colonel today. By the end of the month Schilling had been credited with eighteen German aircraft destroyed in the air, and ten and a half on the ground. So far he had earned the Air Medal with five clusters, the Distinguished Flying Cross with five clusters, the Silver Star with two clusters, and our second highest award, the Distinguished Service Cross.

Capt, Paul Conger was transferred from the 61st Fighter Squadron to the 63rd FS to become their Operations Officer.

October 2: VIII FC FO 593. After weather prevented flying the previous day, Bomber Command sent twelve hundred heavies to Germany. Over seven hundred fighters went along, and once again they met no opposition from the Luftwaffe. No claims were made by either the bomber gunners or fighter pilots.

Major Comstock led the Group off at 0856 to provide penetration and withdrawal support for the heavies attacking Kassel and Hannover areas. RV was made near Limburg at 1032 with twelve Combat Wings of the 3rd Air Division. Just beyond the RV point the heavies were intercepted twice by flights of Fw 190s, but they were too far away to be encountered by the Wolfpack. The Fw's made quick and ineffectual passes on the bombers and dove away without inflicting any apparent (To the fighter pilots perception.) damage on the bombers. Escort continued to Dillenberg, where the fighters turned towards home to RTB at 1347. Two 63rd Fighter Squadron pilots were carried as NYR, 1st Lt. James Kyle and 2nd Lt. Frank

Ogden, but they had put down in friendly territory for fuel and returned later.

October 3: VIII FC FO 596. Once again over a thousand Big Friends and seven hundred fighters went in to bomb targets in Germany. And once again, the Luftwaffe did not make much of an attempt to stop the "Mighty Eighth." Only two German aircraft were destroyed by the fighters, and these were on the ground. Bomber gunners had no claims at all.

The strength and power of the 8th Air Force continued to change, also. On the previous day the 353rd Fighter Group had flown its first mission with P-51s after converting from P-47s. Today would be the last mission for the 479th FG with P-38s, and they too would be converting to Mustangs. Before much longer the 56th FG would be the only remaining P-47 group in the 8th Air Force.

Major Baker led the 56th Fighter Group off at 0947 with forty-eight Jugs as escort for heavies attacking the Lachen airdrome. Six would be forced to abort the mission, and one more returned as an escort for them. The B-24s of three Combat Wings of the 2nd Air Division were met east of World War I's Verdun battlefield at 1105. The bomber formation looked good, with two CW's hitting Lachen, but one Wing missed the target entirely. RTB time was 1420.

On this mission the Group got its first good look at a V-1 in flight near Saarbrucken. It was seen climbing up below them at a thirty degree angle and passing through 15,000 feet while they were at 24,000 feet. Visible for

The process of off-loading. Hardly the way to treat a lady. (USAF)

Now on the dock and awaiting transportation to the depot to be unpacked and reassembled before assignment to a unit. (USAF)

What made it all possible. The long-range belly tanks that extended the Thunderbolt's range into Germany's heartland. (USAF)

The remains of HV◉H 42-28834 that once belong to James Carter. It was torn up in a forced landing by Lt. Jack Hedke. Hedke was killed over Germany on January 14, 1945. (via Davis)

only eight seconds while it zipped by them, its contrail remained in the sky for a half-hour.

October 5: VIII FC FO 598. And again the heavies went back to targets in Germany, concentrating on airfields and railroads. Over a thousand bombers were dispatched, and only nine were lost. Again the Luftwaffe was hard to find. The bombers made no claims for fighters destroyed, and only one was shot down in the air, while fifteen were destroyed on the ground by the fighter pilots.

Col. Schilling led forty-eight Thunderbolts off at 0943. Once again seven P-47s had to abort for one reason or another. Escort was provided for B-24s of the 2nd Bomb Division attacking Paderborn, and RV was made near Lingen. Escort was broken just as the Liberators left their initial point on their bomb run to the target.

Turning for home, Schilling spotted 20-30 dummy aircraft and ten plus Me 110s parked on the Geseke airdrome.

With the 479th Fighter Group providing top cover, Schilling initially left the 61st Fighter Squadron high to provide additional cover and took the other two squadrons down to strafe. After silencing four flak emplacements, Schilling, leading the 62nd FS, destroyed three twin-engine Me 210s. Capt. John Eaves got an Fw 190. 1st Lt. Francis Nolan got a Ju 88. 2nd Lt. Roy Patterson got a Ju 88 and an Me 109. 1st Lt. Reigel Davis got a Ju 88, an Me 109 and damaged another. 2nd Lt. Robert Winters got an Me 109. Lt. George Choate destroyed an Me 110. Capt. William Wilkerson damaged an Me 109 and two He 111s.

Capt. Warren Kerr led the 63rd Fighter Squadron in to strafe, and 1st Lt.'s Charles Rotzler and James Kyle each got an Me 109 on the ground. 1st Lt. James Lister spotted two Me 109s in the air south of the field as he was completing his second strafing pass, so he went after them, closing to 300 yards before firing on one. Lister saw strikes on its right wing and left wingtip, and then lost sight of it as it dove through clouds smoking. Although entered as a kill, the claim was downgraded to a probable.

October 6: VIII FC FO 599. This time over twelve hundred B-17s and B-24s went to hit industrial targets in Germany. They were protected by almost eight hundred fighters. The Third Bomb Division B-17s knocked down three German fighters, while the Little Friends accounted for nineteen more in the air and thirty on the ground.

Major Baker led the mission. Off at 0923, RV was accomplished off Alte Mellum Island, a part of the Frisian Island chain, at 1120 with five Combat Wings of 2nd bomb Division B-24s. The heavies hit Wenzendorf airdrome, near Hamburg, while the Wolfpack orbited overhead, and then

were escorted out. An uneventful mission for the Group that RTB'd at 1423.

October 7: VIII FC FO 600. This day's effort included fourteen hundred B-17s and B-24s, along with nine hundred fighters on strikes against industrial targets in Germany. Even though five hundred fighters were not considered to be effective on the mission, the mission itself was the largest mounted so far.

Major Leslie Smith led the Group off Boxted at 0947 with forty-eight Thunderbolts. For the first time in a long time they had no aborts. RV was made near Osnabruck just before noon and broken off 2:25 later after their Big friends had hit Madgeburg. Again it was an uneventful mission for them and they RTB'd at 1515.

October 9: VIII FC FO 603. After taking a day off, two thousand bombers and fighters went to industrial targets in south and central Germany. This marked the last time the 9th Air Force fighters would fly with the 8th Air Force on heavy bomber missions. Once again the bombers had no claims at all, while the fighters got only one on the ground and one in the air.

Major Comstock led this mission. Off at 1251, the Group RV'd with the heavies near Namur at 1419 to provide withdrawal support for them returning from Mainz and Wiesbaden. Other than observing an unusual sort of Nazi aerial bomb at Koblenz the mission was uneventful and landed at 1641. The "flak phenomena" was a "rocket like flare whose path was traced by white smoke curving over at top on exploding released two orange colored bursts. Immediately afterwards numerous flak bursts appeared -20 plus in area."

October 10: Captain John B. Eaves, 62nd Fighter Squadron, was killed on a training flight that he was leading for replacement pilots. The engine of his Thunderbolt quit near Debden and he attempted to put his P-47 down in a field, but it struck an embankment running across the field with such force that it broke his aircraft in two just behind the cockpit. Eaves was the last of the original 62nd FS pilots that was still operational with the squadron and had just returned from the United States to start his second tour with them two weeks previously. He was buried with full honors at Cambridge.

October 11: VIII FC FO 1233A. The 8th Air Force sent a small force of B-17s to Wesseling and Koblenz. Only 135 Forts from the 1st Bomb Division. They were escorted by three P-47 groups, the 78th, 356th and the Wolfpack.

Major Baker led thirty-six Jugs off on the Ramrod at 0812 to provide penetration support for the heavies. Capt. Conger's 63rd Fighter Squadron covered the portion heading for Koblenz, while Baker led the other two squadrons that hit Wesseling. Baker's squadrons flew an uneventful mission.

Near Euskirchen, 2nd Lt. Julis DeMayo, Red Four on 1st Lt. Claude Chinn's wing, with the 63rd FS started a cross-over maneuver to position himself after RV with the bombers was accomplished. The completion of this maneuver would have placed DeMayo up-sun from Chinn, which would have made seeing him difficult against the sun's glare, and Chinn never saw him again. Someone from another squadron called, saying that a "Little Friend was going straight down." Attempts to contact DeMayo were fruitless, and he was declared as killed in action. It was suspected that his oxygen system had failed.

October 12: VIII FC FO 1235-A. Five hundred heavies to marshalling yards, airdromes and industrial targets in Germany. Five hundred Mustangs and Thunderbolts went out on Ramrods in support of the Big Friends.

Major Leslie Smith led the mission off Boxted at 0948. RV was made over the Zuider Zee at 1056 at 24,000 with one Combat Wing of the 1st Bomb Division. The heavies were escorted as far as Enschede, whereupon the MEW controller broke them off to intercept bogies seen on his "weapon" over Drummer Lake. The enemy aircraft were seen at 30,000 feet, and when the Luftwaffe saw the Wolfpack, they started to take unaggressive evasive action.

Capt. Conger's 63rd FS went after them, and they then "ran like hell." 1st Lt. James Lister went after an Fw 190 that was diving for the deck, and then attempted to hide in some low stratus clouds. So, Lister waited him out, and when the Fw 190 popped up back out of the clouds, Lister got on its tail and hammered it with his .50's. "The plane was smoking and the cockpit a ball of flame." It crashed. Flight Officer Eugene Andermatt chased an Me 109 down to 1,000 feet, where it was last seen smoking and heading straight down. He was credited with a probable.

October 14: VIII FC FO 1239-A. Over twelve hundred Big Friends went to Germany, of which over eleven hundred bombed effectively. They were escorted by over seven hundred Mustangs and Thunderbolts. Again there was no sign of the Luftwaffe and neither the fighters or the bomber gunners had a claim.

Major Baker led the Wolfpack off at 1025 with fifty-two P-47s, the largest force they had been able to put up in a long while. RV was made over Stadtkyll at 1215 with B-24s of the 2nd Air Division's 3rd and 4th Combat Wings heading for Cologne. The bombers were eighteen minutes late, and in poor formation, so it was good that the German's made no

Although the 62nd Fighter Squadron did not report any losses on October 11, 1944, someone came to grief on return from the Ramrod. (via Davis)

attempt to intercept them. The Ramrod was totally uneventful and escort was broken off over Chateau Dardenne to RTB at 1442.

October 15: VIII FC FO 1240-A. While almost eight hundred heavies went back to Cologne to hit industrial targets, the Wolfpack went out on a tactical mission.

Major Donovan Smith led them off at 0645, on the earliest morning mission in months. Smith, leading from the 61st Fighter Squadron, took that squadron to hit Guthersloh and Kassel. Strafing resulted in destroying four locomotives, six good cars, a truck and a barrage balloon. They also damaged two more locomotives and thirty-three goods cars, a flak position and other airdrome installations.

Capt. Townsed Parsons led the 62nd FS and they hit targets in the Hamm and Paderborn areas, getting a lot of rolling stock. 1st Lt. Lewis Brown damaged an Me 109 on the ground. Major Comstock's 63rd FS also hit Paderborn, along with Altenbecken, where results were considered poor. Lt.'s James Kyle, Thomas Saling, Russell Frederickson and Randel Murphy did get an Me 109 on the ground between them, however. On the way home, Lt. David Magel's, P-47 was hit in the aft section by a burst of heavy flak that cut all his control cables. A fire ensued that burned through his rudder trim tab cables and burned off his tail wheel. He got it back to Woodbridge for a belly landing and was recommended for a DFC for his skill in getting back to England.

October 17: VIII FC FO 1245-A. Over thirteen hundred heavies and eight hundred fighters went back to continue to paste the Cologne area. Things seemed to be getting almost to easy, as only four bombers and one fighter were lost. No claims were entered against the no-show Luftwaffe.

Col. Schilling led them off Boxted at 0810 with forty-eight Thunderbolts. Six had to abort, and two returned with them as escorts. RV was made over Liege at 0920 with five Combat Wings of 2nd Air Division B-24s. Escort was broken at Namur on the way out after a boring two hour escort with the only thing of interest observed being contrails of three V-2s headed for England.

October 18: VIII FC FO 1246A. Cologne remained the key target, but only six hundred heavies went out this day, escorted by six hundred fighters. Only five heavies were lost. The Luftwaffe remained out of sight.

Major Baker led the Ramrod off at 0927 with forty-five Jugs. Aborts continued to plague the effort, with five P-47s having to turn back, along with two as an escort for them.

(Many of these aborts were caused by a new manifold for the R-2800 engine that was designed by "Mr. Hitler." Constructed in two pieces and joined with a rubber seal, it was supposed to make maintenance easier for the ground crews. Yet the seal deteriorated after a few hours of use and then allowed oil and gas to be thrown all over the aircraft. It required six to eight hours effort to replace the seal).

RV with B-17s of the 1st Bomb Division was made fifty miles west of Cologne , and they were escorted to their target and out to Liege on the return. Uneventful.

October 19: VIII FC FO 1249A. The targets were shifted to other than Cologne for a change. Still, over a thousand heavies and seven hundred fighters penetrated and roamed Germany's skies almost at will. Six heavies were lost, but two of these were through a mid-air collision. Goering's vaunted fighters remained hidden from the 8th Air Force.

Major Comstock was in charge, leading the Wolfpack off at 1041 on a Ramrod to Mannheim. RV was made over the North Sea and escort provided through the target and out to east of St. Vith. RTB'd at 1449 after another milkrun.

October 22: VIII FC FO 1254-A. 8th Air Force Bomber Command sent over a thousand effective heavies to the Brunswick area to bomb through cloud cover. Again over seven hundred fighters went along as escorts, and

Colonel David Schilling in his "Hairless Joe" line up for takeoff. Wingman is Capt. George Bostick in "Ugly Duckling." (USAF)

again the Luftwaffe was a no-show. Only two bombers and one fighter were lost. Was the air war about over?

Col. Schilling led the 56th Fighter Group. Off at 1122, they swept ahead of the heavies to Madgeburg, where they patrolled the area for a period before turning to RV with 1st Bomb Division B-17s over Brunswick at 1402. Escort was broken at Enschede at 1500 and RTB was at 1640. Except for one P-47 being damaged by flak and another being struck by a bird, it was a totally boring mission.

October 24: VIII FC FO 1261. The Big Friends got the day off. Four hundred Mustangs and Thunderbolts went out to dive bomb and strafe, but Mother Nature got in the way of most of them.

Off at 1255 with Major Baker leading, the group proceeded to Neinberg, thence north to Breman, reversed course back to Neinberg, flew east to Celle and then out over Zwolle. The weather was solid undercast and few worthwhile targets for the fragmentation bombs could be found.

Boxted, the final home of the Wolfpack in England. It is now an apple orchard. (via Davis)

The 63rd Fighter Squadron jettisoned theirs in the North Sea on the way home. The 62nd FS found a few targets at the marshalling yard at Walsrode, but lost Lt. George Choate in the process. He just disappeared, and was later determined to have been killed.

Major Baker, leading from the 61st FS, ordered them to jettison their bombs into the Zuider Zee. Just after they got rid of their frags, 2nd Lt. William Osborne's P-47 was hit by flak. He pulled up, burning, rolled, and crashed into the water. He too was killed. The remainder of the squadron did some half-hearted strafing, claiming a locomotive destroyed and six box cars damaged.

October 25: VIII FC FO 1263-A. Hamburg was the main target, with twelve hundred effective B-17s and B-24s. Only two B-17s were lost. One P-51 was downed when an over eager B-24 gunner looked for something to shoot at, but the pilot was rescued.

Major L. C. Smith led the Ramrod off at 1118 with thirty-six Thunderbolts. RV was made over the Zuider Zee with four Combat Wings of 2nd Bomb Division B-24s at 1245. As the force approached Gelsenkirchen, Major Smith took the 62nd Fighter Squadron two miles off to the side of the others in an attempt to draw the flak away from the others. At first the flak came up between the two units, and then started to come up against "Platform" squadron (The 62nd FS's radio call sign). As Smith led the two apart, the flak continued to chase the fighters for two minutes before returning attention to the bombers and other fighters. Apparently the German gun laying radar still could not differentiate between the larger and smaller radar returns from the aircraft.

October 26: VIII FC FO 1264-A. Bomber Command went back to Western Germany to hit industrial and communication targets with eleven hundred effective B-17s and B-24s.

Col. Schilling led the Ramrod off at 1235. RV was made north of Zwolle at 1400 with four Combat Wings of the 2nd Air Division which were then escorted to Minden, and then brought them back out to Zwolle. Some bogies were reported, but could not be located, and one jet was seen down low, but could not be intercepted. Again, an uneventful mission.

The 63rd Fighter Squadron getting a little formation practice over England. (via Davis)

October 30: VIII FC FO 1273-A. Most of the Big friends were slated to attack German oil production target in the environs of Hamburg. B-17s of the 3rd Bomb Division were recalled because of the weather, and the 1st BD sought secondary targets. B-24s of the 2nd Bomb Division pressed on to Hamburg, but results were undetermined because of cloud cover.

Major Leslie Smith led this Ramrod off at 1044 as Col. Schilling had to abort. For the first time in months, the two "A" and "B" groups were dispatched, but their missions coincided. RV was made east of Lingen at 1222 at 24,000 feet. Two Combat Wings of 2nd Bomb Division B-24s were covered when they could be, as cirrus clouds separated the fighters from the bombers over Steinhuder Lake for a period. Again it did not matter, as the Luftwaffe was a no-show. RTB'd 1508.

Shocking news was received that evening. Colonel Zemke was missing in action. His P-51 had disappeared into clouds and no further word of him was forthcoming. His Mustang fell the victim of turbulence and had come apart on him. Thrown clear of the disintegrating aircraft, he became a POW.

In all, there was a lot of rain and mud to contend with at Boxted during the month, and only the eighteen missions could be flown. Nevertheless, the Wolfpack destroyed eighteen German aircraft and now had a total score of 724 -562 in the air and 162 on the ground, and led the 8th and 9th Air Forces in total kills.

November 1: VIII FC FO 1278-A. Fall weather with all its inherent problems continued to hamper operations. Only three hundred B-17s and B-24s flew effective sorties. They were covered by three hundred fighters.

The 56th Fighter Group put up only twenty-four Thunderbolts for this mission, a Ramrod. Off at 1205 with eight from each squadron, Major Comstock led them to RV with a single Combat Wing of 2nd Bomb Division B-24s over Egmond at 1320. This was unusual in itself, as on very few missions did the fighters and bombers join-up over England before setting course for the continent. The Liberators hit Gelsenkirchen, and the formation headed for home.

Approaching Enschede, the 62nd and 63rd Fighter Squadrons detached themselves to attempt to shoot down an Me 262 that was seen flying west and descending from 38,000 feet in a dive on the rear box of bombers.

The Group's mission report stated that only the one Me 262 was encountered, and that it was shot down by Lt. Walter Groce, 63rd Fighter Squadron, with assistance by Capt. Michael Jackson and 1st Lt. Francis Nolan, 62nd FS. This is indicative of just how confusing aerial combat can be, who did what, and how challenging the task was in interpretation of

OPPOSITE: "The Idaho Spud" and an obviously staged "last minute briefing."

combat claims and the awarding of the claim, itself. Three Fighter Groups had been involved in the shoot-down during the course of the combat. The 20th, 56th and 352nd, and a total of six pilots claimed credit The final assessment awarded the kill to Lt. Groce and Lt. William Gerbe, 486th Fighter Squadron.

After dodging in and out of heavy Mustang and Thunderbolt traffic to get into firing position, Groce had pulled his Thunderbolt's nose up to a seventy degree angle and fired with full deflection. The Me 262 flew through spray of .50 caliber fire and hits were seen on its right engine, which caught on fire. The Me 262 went into a flat spin and its pilot bailed out at 8,000 feet. Groce rolled over and followed the aircraft down, taking photographs and firing off a few more rounds. (It was also reported that a pair of unidentified P-51 pilots attempted to strafe the German pilot while he descended in his parachute).

November 2: VIII FC FO 1281-A. Another maximum effort day with over eleven hundred effective heavy bombers under escort by nine hundred fighters, including a group of 9th Air Force P-38s. Primary targets were synthetic oil production plants in Germany, with secondary's being rail targets. The Luftwaffe fought enforce for the first time in over a month, and paid dearly for their efforts. Bomber gunners claimed thirty-six destroyed and thirty-five probables. The Little Friends claimed 102 destroyed and five probables in the air, twenty-five more were destroyed on the ground. Forty bombers and sixteen fighters were lost.

The 56th Fighter Group set out on a Ramrod to Bielefeld at 1022 with their largest formation to date. Sixty-two P-47s behind Major Paul Conger. RV was accomplished over Zwolle at 1150 with B-24s of the 2nd Air Division.

At 1326, near Bielefeld, three Me 262s attacked Blue Flight of the 61st Fighter Squadron from behind. All three fired, and the P-47s of 1st Lt. Arthur Bux and 2nd Lt. Charles Woock were damaged. As the Me 262s tore through the Jug formation, Capt. Jackson's 62nd FS attempted to intercept them, but didn't have a chance with their comparatively lumbering Thunderbolts. Then, an Me 163 burst through them from behind and disappeared before they could even react to the threat. North of Munster two more Me 262s were seen, and Major Conger's 63rd FS turned into them. The Me 262s made a quick 180 degree turn and easily out distanced the Thunderbolts. With the jet encounters the complexity of the airwar had suddenly changed. The Group had no claims and RTB'd at 1423.

November 4: VIII FC FO 1286-A. The German oil industry continued to be the primary target. 1160 heavies went to Western Germany with almost nine hundred fighters on escort missions. Five bombers were lost, and only one German aircraft was damaged in the air.

Major Baker led the mission off at 1014 to provide penetration, target and withdrawal support to four Combat Wings of the 2nd Bomb Division. RV was made over Egmond at 1120, with the Big Friends again returning to Gelsenkirchen.

As the fighters approached the target they again attempted to decoy the flak gunners away from the heavies by flying across the bombers path at a forty-five degree angle and fifteen hundred feet above the bombers. Three such passes were made, and each time the flak followed the fighters instead of concentrating on the Big Friends. 2nd Lt. Wade Charlton, 63rd FS, picked up a bit of flak in the process and was forced to put down in friendly territory on the way back.

November 5: VIII FC FO 1288-A. 8th Air Force Bomber Command sent over twelve hundred effective heavies against rail targets in Germany. A dozen bombers were lost, along with six fighters, two of which belonged to the Wolfpack. Once again there was no sign of the Luftwaffe.

Major Leslie Smith led forty-eight Thunderbolts off Boxted at 0930 to fly an area patrol mission in support of the bombers. Arriving Durlach/Ludwigshaven, they patrolled for an hour ahead of the B-24s heading for Karisruhe, and then found a hole in the overcast near Mannheim and went down to strafe near Worms. The 62nd Fighter Squadron claimed four locomotives destroyed and twenty-five plus boxcars damaged.

The 63rd FS had the bad luck. 2nd Lt. Albert Henry, flying as Blue Two, was last seen near Bad Kreuenact making a strafing pass on a train. He was killed. On the way back, their Yellow Two, 2nd Lt. Robert Healy, bailed out into the North Sea off Orfordness, England. Air-Sea Rescue had a good fix on his location at the time, but he was never found. Presumably drowning due to exposure to the cold water.

November 6: VIII FC FO 1291-A. German petroleum industries in all forms continued to be the targets for the Big Friends. Almost eleven hundred heavies were effective on today's missions, and only five were lost. But five fighters were lost, too. Goering's "elite" Luftwaffe was a virtual no-show once again, as only four were downed by the fighter pilots, and none claimed by the bombers gunners. The frustration felt by the German fighter pilots must have been almost unbearable, to witness over two thousand Allied aircraft coming out of England on raids upon "The Fatherland" at a crack, and not being able to do anything about it.

Major Baker led the mission, to provide penetration, target and withdrawal support for four Combat Wings of B-24s. Off at 0853, RV was made at Turnhout at 1002, and broken off at Zwolle/Egmond on the return.

After breaking escort at Egmond, Capt. Michael Jackson's 62nd Fighter Squadron patrolled south of Arnhem. While doing so, they were fired upon by an unidentified type of German twin-engine fighter. Jackson turned and dove his Jug and was able to damage the interloper, but wasn't able to identify its type or get close enough upon it to inflict further damage.

November 8: VIII FC FO 1296-A. B-17s and B-24s went to Mersburg and oil industries along the Rhine River, respectively. The 3rd Bomb Division B-17s were recalled enroute, as the weather had gone sour on them. Thus, the fighters assigned to protect the 3rd BD joined with those covering the 1st BD. Eight hundred fighters flew effective missions, but only three hundred bombers did so.

For a change, the Wolfpack got to escort Flying Forts instead of the Libs they normally seemed to be assigned to. Off at 0905 with Col. Schilling leading, RV was made at Merseburg at 1055. One squadron of B-17s was on time over the target, so they were picked up by the 63rd Fighter Squadron and escorted out to Bad Frankenhausen, where upon the 63rd FS went strafing and tore up a train. The remainder of the bombers were fourteen minutes late, and they were picked up over Hanover and escorted as far as Hengelo by the 61st and 62nd FS's. On their way home, Major Leslie Smith's White Flight, 62nd FS, was jumped by a pair of P-51s that almost got Smith and wingman 2nd Lt. William Stovall.

Hanging a drop tank on Major Paul Conger's "Bernyce," a P-47M. (via Davis)

November 9: VIII FC FO 1299-A. The heavies went after tactical targets in the front lines areas, being escorted by Mustangs. The Thunderbolt groups went out on fighter-bomber missions.

Off at 0734 behind Major Leslie Smith, the Wolfpack went to the area around Aschaffenburg to bomb marshalling yards at Hiedenfeld, Trennfelz, Karlstadt and Lohr. Claims were sixteen locomotives destroyed and one damaged. Fifty-one freight cars and sixty trucks on flat cars were damaged, along with all sorts of other worthwhile targets. Capt. Robert Bradford, 63rd FS, was feared lost and declared MIA, but it turned out that he had put down at St. Omer for fuel. He returned the following day.

November 10: VIII FC FO 1301-A. The heavies went to attack Luftwaffe airdromes in Germany with P-51 escorts. The P-47s went Thunderbombing to other targets in Germany.

Major Conger led thirty-five Jugs off at 0843, but five had to abort. Arriving in the area of Ludwigslust at 1110, the Group spent fifteen minutes working over rail, road, and canal traffic with 100 pound GP bombs. Ten locomotives were destroyed, along with twenty-nine freight cars and sixty-six trucks on flat cars, along with miscellaneous other targets.

The 63rd Fighter Squadron lost 2nd Lt. Thomas Saling during the attack on the marshalling yard at Ludwigslust. He was last seen as he peeled off to start his dive bombing run when they arrived over the target. Yet, fifteen minutes later he called to say that he was setting course for home. Although there was light flak being thrown up at the time, the actual cause for Saling being killed remains a mystery.

November 11: VIII FC FO 1306-A. The heavies went back to oil and rail targets in Western Germany. It was almost a token effort in comparison to previous raids, as the three Bomb Divisions dispatched less than five hundred aircraft.

Major Donovan Smith led the Ramrod to provide penetration, target and withdrawal support for the B-24s of the 2nd Bomb Division attacking Bottop. Off at 0924, they arrived over the RV point early and had to orbit until the Big Friends got there. Escort was provided to Battop and out to the Zuider Zee. Uneventful, and RTB'd at 1320.

November 16: VIII FC FO 1314-A. As the winter season approached, so did the bad weather with low clouds and heavy precipitation. To a degree, the bombers could deal with this, if the cloud tops were low enough to permit them to formate before setting course for Europe. For the fighter it was another story. They could get higher before having to worry about getting into formation, but they lacked deicing equipment that would permit them to penetrate the clouds to begin with. The freezing level got lower each day, and airframe ice on a heavily loaded fighter was more of a threat than the Luftwaffe. An increase in strength and erratic upper wind patterns made navigation even more critical for a pilot that had to do it all – navigate, bomb, and shoot.

After five days of weather forced inactivity, Bomber Command sent out twelve hundred B-17s and B-24s to bomb along the front lines ahead of the planned ground offensive. B-17s of the 1st Bomb Division had to go it alone, as their slated fighters could not get airborne because of weather conditions over their bases. Little matter, as the weather and other factors kept the Luftwaffe grounded, also.

Col. Schilling led the Wolfpack off at 1005 to provide area support in the Aachen/Duren areas. They tookoff through a murky undercast and a solid layer of clouds, and arrived in the general target area at 1125. There was no sign of the 9th Air Force medium bombers they were supposed to cover, so they joined with B-17s that were looking for German gun emplacements to bomb. Except for sweating out the weather, the mission was uneventful for everyone but Lt. Arthur Gerow whose P-47 was damaged by a falling belly tank from another fighter.

November 18: VIII FC FO 1317-A. Bomber Command had the day off. Fighter Command went out on sweeps and had a pretty good time of it.

The Luftwaffe showed up and mixed it up with the fighter jocks for a change. Twenty-six German aircraft were destroyed in the air and sixty-nine on the ground. Seven Air Force fighter pilots became listed as MIA, with two of them from the Wolfpack.

Major Comstock led the Wolfpack off at 1017 to go Thunderbombing at Langenselbold. The target being an underground oil storage depot. Arriving there at 1200, the 61st Fighter Squadron went down to strafe. Capt. James Carter, who would discover that he was promoted to Major upon his return from this mission, led them down. On their first attack they destroyed five oil storage tanks and a locomotive.

As the squadron reformed they were attacked by a mixed formation of Fw 190s and Me 109s. Lt. Arthur Gerow, on his sixth combat mission, claimed two Me 109s, but one claim was downgraded to a probable. Capt. James Carter got an Fw 190, which did a wing-over, crashed and burned. This was his sixth and final kill. As a result of his leadership on this mission, Carter was awarded the Silver Star.

Carter: "I fired from about three hundred yards with small deflection and got a few meager hits. My K-14 didn't seem to be working so I switched to fixed (Reference to gyroscopic and "iron" gunsights.) and fired quite a long burst which blew pieces of the canopy off. The e/a crashed and burned. The parachute of the pilot was about ten yards to the right of the plane, unfolded but not open."

Was it rough? Note the bashed-in and holed drop tank. (via Davis)

Major Michael Jackson finished the war with 13.5 kills, of which eight were air-to-air. He joined the 62nd FS in June 1944 and finished his tour in May 1945. (USAF via Davis)

Capt.'s Benjamin Cathers and Withold Lanowski along with Lt.'s Charles Raymond, Robert Baughman and Russell Kyler all destroyed Fw 190s. 2nd Lt. William "Dewey" Clark claimed an Fw 190 destroyed that was downgraded to a probable, along with another as damaged. 2nd Lt. Robert Walker had a probable, and 2nd Lt. Luther Hines claimed a damaged.

During the course of the dogfight, which in a later war became probably more aptly named as a "furball," the 61st FS lost two pilots. 2nd Lt. Jack DeMars was seen under attack by an Fw 190 and was seen to bailout. What happened to him after this remains an unknown and he was declared killed in action. Capt. Gordon Blake was last seen heading out towards friendly territory and radio communication indicated that he was okay. At this time, Blake was only five miles from the front lines, but he didn't make it and became a POW.

The 62nd FS was led by Capt. Michael Jackson. After they worked over Langenselbold, Jackson led the squadron to Hanau where enemy aircraft were reported. Jackson shot down an Fw 190, as did Capt. William Wilkerson and Lt. John Ferguson. Lt. Norman Gould got an Me 109 whose pilot didn't like being chased by a Thunderbolt and he bailed out on his own volition.

Major Comstock, leading from the 63rd FS, had taken them down to strafe railroad tracks twenty miles southeast of Frankfurt, where Comstock destroyed a locomotive and others shot up the boxcars. Then Comstock spotted a heavily camouflaged airdrome bordered by woods at Gross Ostheim. After calling in the rest of the Wolfpack, Comstock went down to strafe and destroyed an He 111. At this point his propeller governor failed and Comstock headed for home by himself. 2nd Lt. Raymond Davis, Yellow Three, was in the process of strafing when he heard on the radio that there were bandits about. He looked up to see an aircraft crash, and then spotted an Fw 190 going in his direction, so he went after it. Davis closed on it and saw strikes, and the 190 pulled up, so Davis pulled up along side of it. He could see that it was on fire, and then its pilot bailed out. 1st Lt. Claude Chinn, Blue Three, got three Me 109s on the ground. Lt. Russell Frederickson, leading Red Flight, shared in the destruction of an unidentified type single-engine aircraft with his Red Three, 1st Lt. Robert Daniel. 2nd Lt. Randel Murphy destroyed an Fw 190. Several of these claims were challenged, however, and the 56th Fighter Group revised the claims to award Chinn with the three he claimed: Frederickson, Murphy and Daniel with damaging one Me 109 between them, and 2nd Lt. Willard Scherz with damaging an Me 109.

November 20: VIII FC FO 1320-A. Bomber Command sent a token force of 170 B-17s to hit the oil industries at Gelsenkirchen with an escort of 225 P-51s and P-47s. 325 other P-47s and P-51s went out on tactical missions.

Col. Schilling led forty-eight Thunderbombers off at 1001 to go bombing and strafing in the vicinity of Bonn. Because of the weather, their primary target could not be found, so Schilling led the Group down through a hole in the clouds to hit targets of opportunity southwest of Bonn. Their dropping 260 pound fragmentation bombs and strafing had only moderate results, damaging some worthwhile targets but actually destroying few. Between the weather, which prevented lining up on the targets properly, and heavy and intense flak that caused a lot of evasive action on the pilot's part and corresponding inaccuracy, it was not a good mission.

Capt. Robert Bradford, 63rd Fighter Squadron, White Three, and wingman Lt. Randel Murphy, encountered flak while letting down over Bonn at 6,000 feet. Bradford broke to the left, while Murphy turned right with the rest of the squadron.

"It looked as though he had broken for the deck from which there was a lot of light flak and 40mm. I called to him, but there was no reply," Murphy stated. Bradford was killed. The flak continued to take its toll. 2nd Lt. Luther Hines, 61st FS, crash landed in friendly territory on the way home with flak damage. Seven other P-47s suffered flak damage.

November 21: VIII FC FO 1323-A. It was back to a maximum effort type missions for both 8th Air Force commands. The three bomb divisions sent out almost thirteen hundred heavies to bomb synthetic oil plants that were covered by over nine hundred Thunderbolts and Mustangs. Bomber gunners only claimed 1-0-1 German fighters, but the fighter pilots claimed 68-7-22 in the air and destroyed five more on the ground. The Wolfpack missed out on all the action.

Major Baker led the escort mission off at 0947 with fifty-six Thunderbolts. RV with the last Combat Wing of 2nd Bomb Division B-24s was made at Nordholz at 1145. Escort was provided to the target, Hamburg, and out to Juist Island, uneventfully.

November 25: VIII FC FO 1333-A. After several days of weather enforced inactivity, Bomber Command sent seven hundred B-17s to Merseburg to hit oil plants while 271 B-24s went to a marshalling yard at Bingen. A third of the bomber force was damaged by flak, but the Luftwaffe was a no-show and there were no losses to enemy fighters; nor claims.

This Ramrod was off at 1017 with the fat P-47s again escorting the fatter B-24s, aka Milk Bottles and Pregnant Cows. The mission was flown with both "A" and "B" Groups, with Major Baker leading "A" Group and Major Conger leading "B" Group.

RV was made near Charleville at 1140 with two Combat Wings heading to Bingen where they were to bomb a Panzer division. Escort was provided to the target, along the Rhine River about forty-five miles southwest of Frankfurt, and then out to St. Frond. Another milk run that RTB'd at 1450.

November 26: VIII FC FO 529-B. Oil industries and transportation continued to be the focus of Bomber Command. Over eleven hundred heavies went out, with each Bomb Division having their forces split between the two type targets. The Luftwaffe had evidently marshalled their forces sufficiently to attempt to put up some resistance against the 8th Air Force. Bomber gunners claimed 16-11-11, while the fighter jocks claimed 114-3-31 in the air. Again it was a matter of being in the right place at the right time, as the 56th Fighter Group had no claims or losses to enemy action.

Major Carter led the Ramrod off at 0952. RV with the 2nd and 3rd Combat Wings of the 2nd Bomb Division B-24s was made over Meppel at 1129 at 26,000 feet. The initial RV turned out to be with the wrong bomber force, as the intended force was running late. The error was rectified and the correct bombers were picked up at Bielefeld a half hour later, covered to and over their targets at Bielefeld, and out over Ijmuiden at 1320. RTB time was 1420.

November 27: VIII FC FO 1343-A. A little over five hundred Big Friends went to attack marshalling yards in Germany. It was a good day for the heavies, as they had no losses. It was also a good day for the fighter pilots. Although fifteen AAF fighters were lost, they destroyed over a hundred German aircraft.

Major Comstock led the strafing mission off at 1016 with forty-eight P-47s, of which four had to abort. The Thunderbolts RV's with the 479th Fighter Group at Zwolle, and as the force overflew Drummer Lake, their ground controller, "Nuthouse" informed them of bandits to the south.

The Group turned south to go after the 60/80 contrails that came into sight. At this time the engine failed on 2nd Lt. Leo Czarnota's P-47, (Blue Two, 63rd Fighter Squadron.), and he was last seen in a circling descent. He bailed out at a lower altitude and became a POW.

The Luftwaffe was in a mixed formation at 25,000 feet and included some jet propelled fighters. While the 61st and 62nd Fighter Squadrons had no claims, and the 479th Fighter Group had but two, the 63rd FS got into it with some success.

1st Lt. Russell Frederickson, leading Red Flight, dove on a flight of Me 109s and they broke away to the left. But one broke to the right and Red Three and Four went after him. Red Three, 1st Lt. James Lister chased the Me 109 down to 3,000 feet before he could get into firing range. Lister fired and could see strikes all over it, and then had to witness the German pilot fighting the ensuing flames as he struggled out of the cockpit at only 200 feet. His parachute did not have time to open and he died only thirty yards from were his aircraft crashed.

Frederickson got into a Lufberry with two Me 109s and they made six circles before he could bring his gunsight to bear on the Number Two man. From 400 yards Frederickson saw numerous .50 caliber hits on its fuselage at the wingroots and then pieces started falling off the aircraft. He then shifted his gunfire to the Me 109 leader and repeated the same maneuver, firing from 400 yards. Again strikes were seen against the wingroots and pieces started falling off. It exploded as it hit the ground, and in neither case was the German pilot seen to be able to get out.

November 29: VIII FC FO 1346-A. Bomber Command's targets remained the same, oil and rail. Over a thousand heavies went out again this day after them. Only one B-24 was lost and there were no claims made by the 8th Air Force against the Luftwaffe.

Col. Schilling led this Rodeo out as an advance sweep ahead of 2nd Bomb Division B-24s. Off at 1000, the original intent of the mission had been to escort the Liberators to Paderborn as a Ramrod, but the mission orders were revised, and they met the returning B-24s over Neppel and escorted them out after making a patrol over western and northwestern Germany without any action.

Some P-47s were lost, however. 2nd Lt. Richard Hale, 62nd FS, crash landed on the continent after he ran out of fuel. 2nd Lt. William Stovall, 62nd FS, crashlanded at Halesworth due to mechanical problems that prevented him from being able to maintain altitude. 2nd Lt. Leo Ulfers, 61st FS, had to land on the continent for fuel and was considered a NYR for a period.

November 30: VIII FC FO 1354-A. Over twelve hundred heavies were effective against oil and rail targets in Germany. The Flying Forts went after the oil, while the B-24s concentrated on marshalling yards. Almost a thousand fighters were involved, including P-38s and P-51s borrowed from the 9th Air Force.

The 56th Fighter Group sent out both their "A" and "B" Groups for this mission. Major Baker led "A" Group off at 1031, while Major Comstock led "B" Group off at 1037. Thirty-six and twenty-four P-47s, respectively.

Baker's "A" Group made RV with four Combat Wings of B-24s over Verdun at 1145 and broke escort over Neukirchen at 1300. "Sweepstakes" radar reported bogies, and Capt. Regal Davis' 62nd Fighter Squadron went looking for them, but they were not found, so the squadron strafed the marshalling yard at Bickenback. Over Bickenback, Flight Officer Alben Calmes was hit by flak as he entered a cloud layer and was not seen again, although he told Lt. William Stovall he was okay. He was KIA.

The 63rd FS went down to strafe trains at Wurzburg, damaging sixty cars. Baker's 61st FS also went down to strafe, and destroyed four locomotives for the cost of two P-47s being written-off as a result of flak damage and being forced down on the continent. These were flown by Lt.'s David Mauldin and Edward Lightfoot.

Comstock's "B" Group had an uneventful escort. They RV with four Combat Wings of B-24s over Nancy at 1215 and escorted them through their target and out to Ostend. They RTB'd at 1451, fifty-five minutes ahead of "A" Group.

November had been a good and bad month for the Wolfpack. Several times they had been all set to go off on a mission, and then their orders were canceled. These sort of happenings took their tolls on everyone, as the pilots suited-up and psyched-up to fly off into the "clag" only to be let down, while the ground crews had to unbutton their aircraft and then secure them again, usually in rain or drizzle. They flew eighteen missions, but eight pilots were MIA. It could get awful lonely in a fighter's cockpit when its pilot was trying to figure the odds.

As December opened, Col. Schilling was the highest scoring fighter pilot in 8th Fighter Command still flying missions. His pending total was 34 1/2, of which twenty-four were air-to-air kills. December was another month of weather curtailed missions. Only seventeen were flown, although many more were briefed and then canceled at the last minute as weather factors caused the scrubbing of the effort. Still, it was a good month for the Wolfpack's hunts, as they ran up their score to exceed the eight hundred destroyed mark. In December they shot down sixty-two German aircraft, and destroyed twelve more on the ground. They closed out 1944 with a grand total of 809 1/2, of which 646 1/2 were air-to-air kills. Yet on the downside, eleven of their pilots were carried as MIA as a result of these combat missions.

December 23 was they best day for the 56th Fighter Group, and they established a new record for air-to-air action. They destroyed thirty-seven in the air, got one probable, and damaged fourteen. Of these, Schilling got five. On Christmas Day, they destroyed eight, and broke the eight hundred mark. Quite a gift.

December 2: VIII FC FO 533-B. The weather hampered Bomber Command operations. The 1st and 2nd Bomb Divisions went to attack rail targets successfully, but the 3rd Bomb Division was recalled from their primary target of Koblenz. Most of the Mustang groups were out on escort missions, while the remainder went on sweeps, as did the Thunderbolt groups.

Major Conger led the Wolfpack off at 1036 on a sweep and then had the intention of providing withdrawal escort to 2nd Bomb Division B-24s. They flew in ahead of the bombers to the Koblenz-Warburg area, and at 1220 they were advised by their ground controller, "Nuthouse," of bandits in the area.

With the Group between cloud layers at 20,000 feet, they were first radar vectored to the north, and then had their course reversed to south and Conger led them down through the cirrus layer.

As they broke free of the clouds, Major Conger spotted 20+ German aircraft in battle formation three miles in front of them. Tight line-abreast, in sections of eight aircraft, and stacked down, the Luftwaffe was heading for the last box of B-24s ahead of them.

Staying partially hidden by the cloud deck, Conger ordered Capt. Eugene Barnum's "Whippet" 61st Fighter Squadron to remain high as top cover for the 62nd FS, and led his 63rd FS in on the attack. Conger selected the lead Me 109 for himself, and not even having to "span" his K-14 gunsight, closed to 200 yards and commenced firing. After witnessing hits on its cockpit area, Conger saw its pilot bailout.

There was no evasive action being taken by the other Me 109s, so Conger closed on the next one in line and again fired from 200 yards. There were plenty of hits on its canopy and its coolant system let loose with a stream of glycol and pieces started flying off the aircraft. The right

P-47M 44-21187 as delivered to the Wolfpack. It was then assigned to the 61st Fighter Squadron and coded HV✪W. (via Davis)

side of its engine burst into flame and the Me went into a tight spin to the right. As it spun down, two small explosions occurred, and then it fell into a tight, inverted flat spin.

At this point, Conger, himself, came under attack by a pair of Me 109s while at 18,000 feet. He couldn't out climb them, or turn with them, so he had to dive away, finally escaping at 5,000 feet.

1st Lt. Pershing Trumble, 63rd FS, claimed one Me 109: "I observed strikes all over the canopy, wings and engine. His engine was on fire and he went into an uncontrollable spin to the left. The canopy was open, and the pilot slumped over in the cockpit . . ." This was Trumble's first kill.

Capt. John Fahringer, 63rd FS, claimed two. "As I opened fire, the 109 broke to the left and down. I followed him down, still shooting, until he burst into flames." The second one: "As I closed into range from astern the Me 109 flipped into a vertical bank to the left and I opened fire. The e/ a fell off into a spin and I followed him down in a vertical dive, still firing . . . Suddenly, the 109 lost all semblance of control and started to tumble . . . I zoomed back up to altitude, looked back down to see the 109 tumbling into the overcast at about 3,000 feet."

1st Lt. Russell Frederickson claimed one destroyed and one probable. On the probable he stated: "I followed him down and opened fire, but could see no hits. The 109 kept going straight down at over 350 mph until I saw him disappear into the overcast at 3,000 feet. The overcast was solid down to the ground, and I do not see how he could possibly have pulled out." On Frederickson's kill he stated: "One broke to the right and I went after him. We made a couple of circles down and then he went straight and flew on the deck. I followed and closed to 100 yards. I saw many strikes on the fuselage and wingroots. Parts started flying off – some of which came back and went through my engine. The canopy came off and the pilot bailed out. He was too low and his chute failed to open."

As the air battle continued it became even more complicated and involved. 1st Lt. Walter Groce, 63rd FS, Red Three, stated in his after mission report: "Red Leader, (1st Lt. Richard Anderson), started climbing for these four and I followed him. I was nearly in range when one 109 came in on my wingman's tail (2nd Lt. David Magel), so we broke. Then Lt. Anderson fired on one 109 and it spun. I followed it down, saw it pull out, so I went back up. Then I saw another Me at 12:00 O'clock to me and starting a turn to the right. I closed in and opened fire. My nose blanked out the e/ a except for the left wingtip. The pip (K-14 sight) was on my cowling in

line with the 109. I was turning inside of him and as he disappeared from my sight I looked down between my left wing and tail and saw pieces of an airplane which was disintegrated. This may have been the plane I shot at, but I do not know for sure as there was a mid-air collision in the same vicinity . . . The battle continued and there was an Me 109 above me with a P-47 after it. The 109 finally spun out and I followed him down. He finally straightened out and must have been clocking 400 mph. I nearly hit compressibility. Glancing at my airspeed indicator, I saw that I was doing nearly 500. The 109 continued down to the deck and into the clouds as I followed him. As I was closing, I lost him, so I went below the cloud layer. Pulling up above the clouds to the right, I spotted him again, went after him. Then it was a case of down and around, left and right. I finally got some good hits and he started smoking. He straightened out and I fired a couple more times. I closed in and had to pull up to avoid hitting him. I saw he was on fire. He then crashed into some trees, ending up in a little gully in a big ball of fire."

The mid-air collision that Groce reported was between Capt. Barnum, 61st FS, and Lt. Wyman Baker, 63rd FS. When Barnum saw a flight of P-47s from another squadron coming under attack, he took his "Whippet" White Flight down to intercept the Me 109s. Lt. Baker, not seeing Barnum, had the same thought and also dove into the fray. His Thunderbolt hit Barnum's from behind and both exploded. One P-47 was seen going down "with its wings badly torn." Another had a parachute entangled in its empennage.

There were ten parachutes seen in the air at this one time and nobody knew whose was who, but both of these pilots were killed. Barnum was on his second tour and was serving as his squadron's Operations Officer.

"Daily" (63rd FS) Red Flight continued to score. Anderson: "I fired, his plane flicked from the strikes and finally went into a flat spin. He spun approximately ten turns when one of his wings came off." Lt. Samuel Batson, Conger's wingman as White Two: "I opened fire at about 200 yards, seeing strikes all over his canopy and several large pieces fall off his fuselage. I then had to break off and pull up to avoid running into him . . . I glanced back over my shoulder and saw him roll over on his back, apparently very much out of control, with black smoke pouring from his plane." Lt. Paul Dawson claimed one Me 109 damaged.

From the 62nd FS, "Platform," only Capt. Reigel Davis was awarded claims, for two Me 109s destroyed. Major Robert Hall damaged another.

On their way home, Lt. Donald Allayaud said that he was low on fuel and was going to try and get down under the overcast to locate an airdrome where he could get some gas. It was believed that he encountered vertigo penetrating the clouds and that he spun-in and was killed.

December 4: VIII FC FO 1370-A. The concentration of Bomber Command remained fixed on rail transportation targets in Germany. Over eleven hundred heavies were effective against these targets, for the loss of only three. Fighter Command sent out over nine hundred P-47s and P-51s in support of the Big Friends, but the only German aircraft that could be found were on the ground.

Major Baker led the mission off at 0954 to provide a sweep ahead of the heavies, and then to assist in withdrawal support. The mission started off slightly confused, as the heavies were supposed to be met over the target, but the Nuthouse controller had trouble vectoring the Wolfpack to the proper Bomber Wing. As there was no sign of the Luftwaffe, Baker took the group down to look for targets of opportunity.

Neuburg airdrome was selected, and it turned out to be a virtually undefended gold mine of juicy targets. Over sixty German aircraft were just sitting there, including the Me 262s that were better faced on the ground than in the air. In all, the Group destroyed twelve and damaged fourteen German aircraft.

Comstock's 63rd Fighter squadron had the following claims: 1st Lt. Claude Chinn, destroyed two parked Me 262s and damaged another. 1st Lt. Walter Groce damaged what was believed to be an He 280. 2nd Lt. Randel Murphy damaged an Fw 190.

Baker's Red and Blue flights of the 61st FS strafed, too, but only 2nd Lt. Charles Woock had a claim, for a unidentified twin-engine type, although Lt. Charles Bond damaged another unidentified type twin. The 62nd FS had the highest number of claims. Capt. William Wilkerson destroyed an He 111. Capt. Francis Nolan destroyed one Fw 200 and damaged another. Capt. Michael Jackson destroyed an Me 262 and damaged another, along with a damaging an Fw 200. Lt. Norman Gould destroyed an Me

262. Lt. Eugene Beason destroyed an He 177 and an Fw 190. Lt. Andrew Chasko damaged four Me 262s. Other claims for damaged aircraft were shared by Lt.'s Henry, Ball and Daily. Additional strafing claims were against locomotives and rolling stock. Then came the real problem. Getting home. The weather briefers had missed alerting the pilots of extremely high winds out of the west, in excess of 100 mph. Coupled with the fuel expended on vectors looking for the Big Friends and then chasing after targets that turned out to be P-51s, the P-47s were hurting for fuel. Then they were informed that Boxted was fogged in. Most of the pilots either had to put down on the continent or seek other bases to land on in England. Many did not make it home. From the 62nd FS, nine out of their sixteen P-47s dispatched that morning didn't get home. Lt.'s James Elliott and Norman Gould bellied-in on Brittany Beach, returning two days later sans aircraft. 2nd Lt. Frank Aheron bellied in at St. Trond and got back December 7. 2nd Lt. Charles Carlson bellied-in near Abbeville and returned December 8. Major Robert Hall had to bailout over Brittany and broke his leg. Four more landed in Europe okay and came home over the next few days.

From the 63rd FS, Lt.'s Russell Campbell and Charles Clark bellied-in between Chaumont and Brienne okay. Seven P-47s written-off because of Mother Nature. There were a lot of empty hardstands at Boxted that night and ground crews sweating out the return of their pilots.

December 5: VIII FC FO 1374-A. Bomber Command's B-17s went to the "Big B," Berlin, while the B-24s went to Munster, with the B-24s still concentrating on rail targets. The Mustangs of Fighter Command had one of their best days of the war, destroying ninety-one German aircraft, getting probables on seven and damaging twenty-eight in the air and damaging two more on the ground. Thunderbolt pilots got zip!

Major James Carter led the mission from the 61st Fighter Squadron. Off at 0835, only thirty-three Thunderbolts and pilots were available after the previous day's debacle. RV was made over Meppel with four Combat wings of B-24s of the 2nd Bomb Division heading for Munster. Escort was broken at Stadtholn and they RTB'd at 1220 after an uneventful mission.

UN◇T of the 63rd FS was 42-19909 and named "Sugie." (Garrett via Davis)

December 10: VIII FC FO 1404-A. Although large scale missions were flown by both Fighter and Bomber Commands on December 6 and 9, the Wolfpack took the time off the regroup. On December 10 the Bomber Command sent five hundred heavies to Bingen, Koblenz and Lutzel to strike transportation targets.

Assigned to provide penetration, target and withdrawal support, the 56th Fighter Group got airborne from Boxted at 0827 behind Major Comstock. The B-24s were running late, so RV was not made until Malmedy at 1020. Escort was provided to Bingen, where Nuthouse vectored the Wolfpack off on targets that turned out to be P-51s. They RTB'd at 1250 after another uneventful mission.

December 11: VIII FC FO 1408-A. A maximum effort mission to Frankfurt and environs with fifteen hundred effective heavies escorted by eight hundred fighters. Of all this activity, only one German aircraft was damaged on the ground. Only five heavies and two fighters were lost.

Major Baker led the escort mission off at 0933. Landfall-in was over Dunkirk at 1037 and the Wolfpack flew the pre-briefed route in until they caught up with their proper boxes of Liberators, which were then escorted over Karlsruhe, their target, and out to east of Metz where escort was broken. Then, Nuthouse sent the Wolfpack off to escort some B-17s of the 1st Bomb Division, but when these were found they already had ample coverage by P-51s, so the Group headed for home. The weather once again interfered with their intentions and caused the pilots to seek alternate places to land, with most of them landing at Debden at 1415.

December 12: VIII FC FO 1412-A. The complexion of the war was certainly changing for the bomber crews over what it had been a year previously. Of nine hundred heavies sent out, only four were lost to enemy action. The targets remained mostly transportation this day. The fighters were all out on escort missions, but the Luftwaffe was grounded by the weather over Europe.

Major L. C. Smith led thirty-nine Wolfpack Thunderbolts out to provide penetration and withdrawal support for the Liberators. Five had to turn back with mechanical problems. The remainder RV'd with the first box of B-24s headed for Hanau at 1100, and escort was broken at Liege two and a half hours later after an uneventful mission.

December 14: No regular mission was scheduled, so Major Smith led a practice low-level mission with four more P-47s of the 62nd Fighter Squadron over the English Channel. During a turn, the Thunderbolt flown by 2nd Lt. Lowell Buschmiller drug its left wing tip into a wave. His P-47 cartwheeled, exploded and sank. Buschmiller was killed.

December 15: VIII FC FO 1422-A. A combined force of a thousand bombers and fighters went to Kassel and Hannover to hit a tank factory and marshalling yards. Seven B-17s were lost, but only one of these through enemy action. Two Mustangs were lost, neither through enemy action.

Major Baker led the penetration and withdrawal escort mission off at 0958 with forty-seven Thunderbolts. RV was made east of Egmond at 1120 with three Combat Wings of the 3rd Bomb Division enroute to Hannover. The flak was of heavy caliber, intense in firing, and totally inaccurate. Another milk run.

December 18: VIII FC FO 1430-A. Almost a thousand heavies were to attack communication and tactical targets in Germany, but weather forced the recall of the three hundred-fifty B-24s dispatched. Thus, only four hundred B-17s were effective.

Major Conger was in charge of this mission. Off at 1104, the forty-nine Jugs made landfall-in over Egmond at 1200 between cloud layers at 18,500 feet. The cloud layers ranged between 15,000 and 30,000 feet, thus all navigation had to be on instruments. There was no sign of the Luftwaffe, and the B-24s had been recalled, so they looked for B-17s headed for Mainz and Koln but they could not be located.

UN◉C belonged to Lt. Claude Chinn. 42-28741 was lost over Germany on December 2, 1944 with Lt. Wyman Baker. Baker was killed. (McBath via Crow/Davis)

In the vicinity of Oonsbruck, heavy and intense flak burst unexpectedly through the clouds and the Thunderbolt of 2nd Lt. Wilburn Haggard, 62nd Fighter Squadron, was hit. He reported going down, and spent the rest of the war as a POW. The sweep continued, and landfall out was over Ijmuiden by flights and elements between 1330 and 1400 to RTB at 1504.

December 23: VIII FC FO 1443-A. After a four-day stand-down enforced by Mother Nature via low clouds and precipitation, a relatively small force of four hundred effective Big Friends went to bomb communication and rail targets behind the German front lines. Six hundred fighters were effective, and had one of their better days. Fighter Command claimed 69-1-18 air-to-air kills against the Luftwaffe that was doing their best to support the German offensive known as "Operation Greif" by the Germans and officially as the Ardennes Counter-Offensive by Allied forces.

It is best known as The Battle of the Bulge today. It began on December 16, and the German attacks were intense and almost split the Allied lines that were thin at best and lacked any top cover, as low clouds and fog prevented air support by the 9th Air Force for several long, long days and nights endured by the beleaguered ground forces.

Col. Schilling led the mission, his first time at the helm in December, for what would be a most eventful area support mission under radar control. Off at 1006 with fifty-six P-47s, Schilling was also leading the Group's largest force for the month, unfortunately, eight pilots had to abort and their presence would be sorely missed.

In over Zeebrugge at 1055, they swept to Bonn where Nuthouse reported a large "gaggle" of enemy fighters. "Gaggle" was an understatement, as between 1145 and 1230 over three hundred-fifty German fighters were seen, of which two hundred-fifty were engaged by the Wolfpack. Overshadowing the interception of the mixed bag of Fw 190s and Me 109s was a "silver P-38 with black bands running fore and aft around the wings." The Luftwaffe pilots knew before hand that they were being hunted by the Wolfpack, and they were ready.

Schilling, leading from the 62nd Fighter Squadron, led the first engagement that took place over Euskirchen airdrome. They were at 26,500 feet, and the Me 109s were at 25,000, and Schilling ordered the squadron to spread into a simulated German formation and they then swung around them to come in on the rear of the German fighters as if they were more of the Luftwaffe joining the enemy formation. The tactic was successful and the 62nd FS knocked down nine of the German fighters at this point. Schilling claimed three Me 109s and two Fw 190s. Lt.'s Don Westover and Lloyd Geren shared an Fw 190. Lt.'s Andrew Chasko and William Daley each got an Me 109. Lt's Charles Carlson, Sanborn Ball, Norman Gould and Warren Lear got Fw 190s. Capt. Felix Williamson got an Me 109 and an Fw 190. (A total of fourteen claims are entered here, but not all of these were approved after assessment of the claims).

After reforming, Schilling headed the Wolfpack east to a point just south of Bonn where forty to fifty Fw 190s were seen headed northwest at 21,500 feet, with the 56th Fighter Group at 23,000 feet. The 61st FS, led by Capt. Benjamin Cathers, had the position of top cover for the Group at this point, and Cathers's led the pounce on the 150+ Focke-Wulf's. Capt. Joseph Perry claimed two destroyed and one damaged: Lt. John Frazier claimed two destroyed. Lt. Victor Bast claimed one destroyed. 1st Lt. Charles Woock, just promoted two days previously, claimed one probable and two damaged. Capt. William Bour, who had been promoted the previous week, claimed one damaged, and Lt. John Allen claimed one damaged. And then it was time to reform again and they returned to Euskirchen, over which Schilling believed the Luftwaffe was using as a rally point.

The air battle then moved to over Koblenz where the 63rd Fighter Squadron, led by Major Comstock, was able to become involved in the action. The 63rd FS ran into 120 German fighters, and Comstock stated that they were "very much aggressive." After being warned by the Nuthouse controller to expect them, they first spotted 60+ Fw 190s orbiting and climbing.

Comstock led the squadron in on their first pass with the sun behind them at their 4:00 O'clock position as they dove from 25,000 feet. As he stated in his after mission report, they "Made one pass through the middle of the formation of 190s and (Comstock) damaged one in the left wing. Pulling up, I turned head-on into the circle and one 190 turned out of the orbit to fire at me. We both started firing at a 1000 yards. His shots were below and when I hit him in the engine he stopped firing altogether . . . He jettisoned his canopy and jumped . . . I pulled up . . . under another 190 who could not see me. I stayed with him until he rolled out of the turn and then raised up right behind him. I opened fire at 22 yards.. strikes on the right side, pieces falling off. I then observed an Fw on the deck, pulled in behind him, observing a few strikes before my ammo ran out."

Flight Officer Melvin Hughes, 63rd FS, White Four, claimed 1-0-1. "After the second bounce I picked up four Fw 190s at 19,000 feet. I barrel-rolled to the tree-tops and was in a small valley when an Fw 190 made a pass at me as I turned left up the valley. He overshot me and as he tired to tighten the turn he flicked over and crashed in the side of a hill. I did not fire a shot. The second 190 was following me as I passed through a small village. I hit my left wingtip on something as I looked back at the 190, I saw him knock a portion of his left wingtip off, too (three feet of it). He staggered up slightly and up out of the valley. I came home on the deck."

2nd Lt. Randel Murphy, 63rd FS, Yellow Three, claimed 2-0-0. "I was chasing a long-nosed Fw 190 (Fw 190D "Dora"), which out ran me at 360 mph on the deck. While I was climbing back up, after breaking off, I saw another 190 chasing a 61st ship. I made a turn and dived down to get him off. The pilot of the 61st ship brought him back toward me and I had to make a head-on pass to get him . . . strikes from the cowl to the tail . . . The 190 went straight into the ground. As soon as I broke off my attack, and while making a climbing turn, another 190 made a pass at me. He followed me down as I dove for the deck. At about 500 feet off the deck I made a tight diving bank to the right, and, as the 190 tried to follow through, he stalled, snapped into the ground."

Other 63rd FS pilots scoring were Capt. Cameron Hart, two Fw 190s; Lt.'s Samuel Batson, Charles Clark, Robert Daniel, William Hoffman, and Willard Scherz were each credited with an Fw 190.

As may be expected, the Wolfpack did not come through this unscathed. As the 63rd FS made their initial attack over Koblenz, 2nd Lt. John Lewis was last seen diving into a cloud deck with an Fw 190 on his tail. He was not seen again and later was reported as killed. Lt. Charles Carlson, 62nd FS, was forced to bailout over Euskirchen, he was seen with a "good chute," and the circumstances surrounding his death are unknown. Lt. Lewis Brown, 62nd FS, had damaged two Fw 190s while in a Lufberry and then broke out of the circle to chase another. As he ran out of ammunition in pursuit of his quest, his P-47 was set on fire by another Fw 190 that had been sitting right on his tail. Brown bailed out and became a POW.

Lt. Robert Daniel, 63rd FS, had a busy twenty-four hours as a result of this mission. He had been slightly wounded by gunfire from a pursuing German aircraft, but managed to escape further damage, only to have his engine quit south of Paris and he had to bailout. He was picked up by Allied troops and taken to a hospital to have his wounds treated, and was awarded a Purple Heart on the spot. He returned to Boxted the following day, to the surprise of all who had thought that he had been either killed or captured. As also might be expected from such a conflict, the claims entered by all of the involved fighter pilots came under close scrutiny. The initial claims entered by the 62nd FS were for 10-0-4 Fw 190 and 9-0-0 Me 109s, but the 8th Air Force claims board only upheld claims for seven Fw 190s and three Me 109s by squadron pilots, and the five claimed by Col. Schilling from Headquarters 56th Fighter Group. The 63rd FS claimed 13-0-6, of which claims for a dozen were upheld. The 61st FS claimed five, and was awarded five. Thus of the thirty-seven claims entered, only thirty-two were upheld. Regardless, an 10.5 to one ratio for their losses was exemplary. Schilling would receive yet another Distinguished Service Cross for leading this mission.

December 24: VIII FC FO 1446-A. The 8th Air Force dispatched the strongest and largest aerial armada in history against targets in western Germany. Never before, or again would there be a force of almost three thousand bombers and fighters from the 8th Air Force with such a single-minded intent, to bring the war to a close. In addition, the Royal Air Force sent out 800 Halifax's and Lancasters. The US 9th Air Force sent 376 medium and light bombers, and their fighters flew 1,157 combat sorties. Over four thousand aircraft active at one time against one common foe! Only a dozen Big Friends were lost in combat during the day's events, but one of these was flown with B/Gen. Frederick Castle as co-pilot, and he would receive the MOH for his actions in permitting the crew to bail out after the B-17 had been hit by flak. Castle was the model for General Savage in the movie and novel *Twelve O'Clock High*.

Col. Schilling was back in the lead, with the Wolfpack out on a Free Lance support mission under the control of Nuthouse. Off at 1133 with fifty Thunderbolts, they made landfall-in at Knocke and were vectored to Koblenz where they were sent on fruitless chases against bogies that turned out to be Mustangs. Down to Frankfurt, and out again over Knocke, the mission turned out to be fruitless for the Group and they RTB'd at 1534.

December 25: VIII FC FO 1451-A. Christmas Day. Continuing fog over England and the previous day's maximum effort prevented a large-scale mission. However, a thousand heavies and fighters were able to get off to attack communication centers and rail targets within western Germany visually.

Major Baker led this mission, an area patrol. Off Boxted at 0925, they flew to Aachen under the control of Nuthouse, and then were vectored to Koblenz, where they found nothing but P-51s. Another vector showed them P-38s, and they were directed to north of Koln where they spotted thirty plus Me 109s that were actually intercepted directly over Cologne.

They were evidently headed for the Big Friends and using Air Force style formations and cross-over maneuvers, but the interception caused them to break formation and drop their belly tanks. "Some split and ran out; (the) main body stuck together and hit the deck."

Baker led the 63rd Fighter Squadron in on the intercept, and Capt. Cameron Hart claimed two (but was credited with one), while Lt. Samual Batson got another, for his third and last kill. From the 61st FS, Lt. William Clark was credited with his first and only kill.

The 62nd FS scored the best with Lt. William Daily getting two, Capt. Michael Jackson got one. Flight Officer Walter Sharbo got his first and second. All eight were Me 109s, and there were no losses incurred by the Wolfpack. A rather nice Christmas gift, in the fighter pilot's estimation.

December 26: VIII FC FO 1452-A. Adverse weather got in the way of heavy bomber operations and only seven bomb groups flew missions. Over three hundred fighters went out to either support the heavies as escorts or on fighter sweeps.

Major Leslie Smith led the Wolfpack off on an area patrol mission at 1235 with forty-eight Jugs. Landfall-in was over Ostend at 1330, whereupon they flew to Liege and took up vectors given by Nuthouse to Malmedy and then to the Cologne-Bonn area where some twenty plus German fighters were encountered. Major Conger's 63rd Fighter Squadron intentionally remained as top cover during the ensuing combat, while the 61st FS, Led by Capt. Joseph Perry, tired to get into an attacking position, but found themselves bounced by Fw 190s, so they broke contact with the German fighters, climbed and also provided top cover to the 62nd FS that took on the enemy fighters.

Major Smith took his "Daily" White Flight and dove on four Fw 190s that were covered by Me 109s at 23,000 feet and in the ensuing combat, Smith shot down one, while wingman Lt. Alfred Perry destroyed two. The Me 109s, having spotted the two other Wolfpack squadrons below them, for unknown reasons decided not to use their height advantage to attack, and had disappeared.

Upon return to England, Boxted was found to be totally fogged-in and the Group scattered to seek alternate landing fields. Some turned back to land on the continent, and all the rest put down where ever they could in the United Kingdom. It was not until the 30th of the month that all the pilots and aircraft were returned to Boxted, minus one that had nosed over on takeoff on the return flight.

December 27: VIII FC FO 1456-A. Ice fog continued to slow down offensive operations. Only 641 Big Friends got off on missions against rail targets. All fighter groups got off on missions but four and most of those going out were in support of the heavies.

Major Donovan Smith led this mission, A radar patrol under the control of Nuthouse. Those seventeen Jugs from the Wolfpack going out tookoff from the alternate Wartlesham Heath at 1150. Landfall-in was over Knocke at 1300 at 20,000 feet, and Nuthouse vectored them to Koln, where they received radar vectors to bogies, but none could be found. As they crossed-out over Ostend, Nuthouse advised Smith that Boxted was still fogged in, so once again they had to seek alternate airstrips to land at.

December 28: VIII FC FO 1458-A. An improvement in the weather permitted over twelve hundred heavies to attack rail and other transportation targets in Germany. All of the fighter groups also were able to get off in support of the Big Friends.

Col. Schilling led thirty Thunderbolts off Boxted at 1044 on an area patrol of the Koblenz area. In over Ostend, they arrived over Koblenz at 1215 at 28,000 feet. They orbited the area for an hour, but Nuthouse "had no business" for them and they RTB'd at 1428.

December 29: VIII FC FO 1463-A. This time the 8th Air Force Bomber Command concentrated on communications targets in Germany with almost eight hundred effective heavies. All but two fighter groups were out in support of them, including the 78th FG that was flying its first combat mission with P-51s after conversion from P-47s. The era of the Jug within the 8th AF, except for the Wolfpack, was just about over.

Major Donovan Smith led this mission. Off at 0800 with the more usual strength of forty-eight Thunderbolts, they went in over Knocke at 0900 at 20,000 to patrol the Koblenz area once again. They received one vector from Nuthouse, but the bogies turned out to be friendly, and after stooging around a little longer, they RTB'd at 1239.

December 30: VIII FC FO 1467-A. The weather had improved enough to permit Bomber Command to dispatch larger forces once again. Over thirteen hundred B-17s and B-24s went after both communications and transportation targets within Germany. Over five hundred fighters went out, too, but there was no sign of the Luftwaffe. Only four bombers and two fighters were lost.

Major Comstock led the mission. Off at 1005 on a Freelance-area patrol sweep, they crossed-in over Knocke at 1100, flew to Bonn-Koblenz, and again stooged around for an hour with little to do. RTB was at 1420.

December 31: VIII FC FO 1471-A. Bomber Command sent out 1327 Big Friends to attack strategic targets in Germany for the first time in two weeks, although communications targets were not ignored, either. All Fighter Command groups were also active. As was the Luftwaffe for a change. Bomber Command claimed 26-9-16, while Fighter Command claimed 61 1/2-2-5 in air-to-air combat.

Major Carter led this mission from the 61st Fighter Squadron. Off at 0857, they flew to Drummer Lake where they received vectors from Nuthouse to RV with 3rd Bomb Division B-17s headed for Misburg. Just after RV was accomplished, Nuthouse broke the 62nd Fighter Squadron away from the heavies to intercept some bogies over Quackenbruck. Capt. Felix Williamson, who had just returned to the 62nd FS and was leading the squadron on this mission, spotted two Me 109s down low, being covered by seven Fw 190s.

Williamson sent "Platform" Red Flight after the Me 109s and Blue Flight after the Fw 190s. The ensuing dogfight became a confusing mass of twisting and turning, diving and climbing aircraft. Flight Officer Leo Butiste shot down an Fw 190, damaged another, and also damaged an Me 109. Capt. Francis Nolan destroyed two Fw 190s. 2nd Lt. William Stovall is officially credited with shooting down two Fw 190s on this mission, and while the 62nd FS records credit him accordingly, the 56th Fighter Group records do not mention it at all. Regardless, Stovall was killed as he slid his P-47 into the line of fire of another while in pursuit of yet another Fw 190. The P-47 flown by 2nd Lt. Andrew Chasko was also seen to go down and explode, but it was not known whether flak or a German aircraft knocked him down. He survived as a POW.

January 1: VIII FC FO 1476-A. As the New Year's Day opened, the Luftwaffe launched their "Operation Hermann" against the RAF and 9th Air Force airfields on the Continent. Expecting to find the units in a lethargic state because of the traditional celebrations the previous night, they did not arrive over the Allied fields until between 0800 and 1000, which placed them directly into the face of the early morning tactical operations. Although surprised by the intensity of the German onslaught, recovery took place in a matter of seconds by the Allied pilots who were already airborne, and in minutes by those who were preparing to takeoff.

The German attacks, although effective to a degree, proved to be far more costly to the Luftwaffe than the Allied forces. Although the Luftwaffe destroyed 150 Allied aircraft, damaged fifty more severely and caused minor damage to many more, an estimated two hundred German aircraft were knocked down. Although the figures are comparative, most of the Allied aircraft were ruined on the ground, while the Luftwaffe lost theirs in the air, two-thirds of them to flak, and in the process they lost many of their remaining cadre of experienced pilots.

The 8th Air Force, meanwhile, sent 850 heavies against oil installations and transportation targets in western Germany. (As of this date, the Bomb Divisions were redesignated as Air Divisions.)

The Wolfpack was split into their "A" and "B" Groups for day's efforts. Major Donovan Smith led the "A" Group, while Major Leslie Smith led "B" Group. Each group was composed of twenty-four P-47s, and "A" Group got off at 1012, with "B" Group departing five minutes later. Both Groups were to provide penetration and withdrawal escort for four Combat Wings of the 3rd Air Division B-17s to Dollbergen, but as weather conditions had delayed their takeoff, RV was not accomplished until after the bombers had hit their targets and only withdrawal cover was given.

As the Luftwaffe concentrated on their own tactical raids, only 8th Air Force P-51s found themselves in any position to have any encounters with them, and they accounted for seventeen destroyed while the Mustangs were covering the 1st Air Division.

January 2: VIII FC FO 1479-A. Bomber Command sent a thousand heavies against tactical and communications targets in western Germany. Five hundred fighters went out on Ramrods to cover them.

"A" and "B" Groups again went out behind the two Major Smith's to provide penetration, target and withdrawal support. Major Donovan Smith led "A" Group off at 0944, while Major Leslie Smith led "B" Group off immediately after "A" cleared the traffic pattern. RV was made over Egmond with three Combat Wings of 2nd Air Division B-24s and escort for the most part was over a solid undercast. There was no sign of the Luftwaffe, and none were claimed by any 8th Air Force unit. RTB'd at 1350 after an uneventful mission.

January 3: VIII FC FO 1435-A. Twelve hundred Big Friends bombed effectively against rail and communications targets in western Germany. All of the Mustang fighter groups were out on escort missions for the heavies. The Wolfpack was assigned a free-lance sweep with their "A" and "B" Groups. Lt. Col. Dade led the "A" Group off at 0836, while Major Conger led "B" Group off ten minutes later. With radar vectors provided by

Nuthouse, the Groups swept Mannheim and Frankfurt on the east and to Trier on the west over a solid undercast that kept the Luftwaffe out of their way. A milkrun that returned at 1300.

January 5: VIII FC FO 1491-A. A thousand heavies went to Germany to bomb rail and airfield targets, while being covered by five hundred Mustangs.

The 56th Fighter Group tried something a different for a change, high level bombing while under the control of Nuthouse. Col. Schilling led the mission off at 1247 and they flew to Siegen to bomb a factory though the overcast. Each P-47 carried two 250 pound GP bombs, and the formation was flown in a tight diamond that was 450 yards long, 250 yards wide, and 300 yards in depth. On the first run over the target, Nuthouse sent them around because they were too far off course. On the second run, Nuthouse told them when to drop their bombs. The results could not be determined, as the bombs fell out of sight into the overcast. RTB'd at 1626.

This was the last mission for Major Donovan Smith, leading the 61st Fighter Squadron, as he completed his second tour of operations. Major James Carter became the final combat commander of the 61st FS.

January 6: VIII FC FO 1496-A. Bomber Command continued to concentrate on rail and communications targets in western Germany. This time only eight hundred heavies went out, covered by six hundred Mustangs. The only claims were for fourteen destroyed on the ground by P-51s.

This mission marked the second anniversary of the 56th Fighter Group's sailing from New York. Off at 0904, Major Leslie Smith led "A" Group with thirty-seven Thunderbombers back to Siegen with each carrying one 500 pound GP. Major Conger led "B" Group off ten minutes later with twenty-three Thunderbolts to provide a fighter escort of "A" Group.

"A" Group bombed on their first pass over Siegen on command from Nuthouse from 20,000 feet, but once again it was through an overcast and the results were not noted. Other than picking up some B-17s to escort home, the mission was uneventful and there was no sign of the Luftwaffe.

January 7: VIII FC FO 1499-A. Any and everything in western Germany was targeted by the eight hundred heavies dispatched during the course of the day's missions. Covered by seven hundred Mustangs, the Luftwaffe was not to be found, and only three heavies and one fighter were lost.

Lt. Col. Dade led the Wolfpack on a patrol under the control of Nuthouse at 0930. The forty Thunderbolts swept in over Aachen and were vectored to Cologne, where there was little to do but stooge around until fuel constraints dictated it was time to head for Boxted. The Group's 400th mission was uneventful and they RTB'd at 1358.

January 10: VIII FC FO 1503-A. A snow storm that swept over England the night before caused all sorts of headaches, incidents and accidents in attempting to get the missions off to strike airfields and transportation targets just thirty miles from the front lines. Nevertheless, nine hundred heavies were able to bomb effectively. Fighter Command sent out but three hundred P-51s and P-47s on a mixed-bag of missions.

Lt. Col. Dade was to lead the mission, but he had to abort right after the 0936 takeoff and command was passed to Capt. Michael Jackson of the 62nd Fighter Squadron. Right after Dade turned back, Flight Officer Walter Sharbo, 62nd FS, had to belly in at Clacton. He was uninjured, but the mission continued on a downhill trend, as there were a total of seventeen early returns out of the fifty-four P-47s attempting to compose the sweep over Koblenz.

As the Group passed over Cologne they were 7,000 feet below a force of B-17s that were in the process of bombing. Capt. Michael Gladych's 61st FS evaded the falling bombs, but then the German flak gunners concentrated their fire upon the P-47s instead of the Flying Forts, inflicting minor damage upon some of the Jugs and leaving the heavies Scot free. On return, two pilots had to put down on the continent and four more at Manston with flak damage, but no one was hurt.

January 13: VIII FC FO 1513-A. Ice, snow and low clouds continued to hamper combat operations. The Big Friends went to hit bridges and rail targets near the Rhine River with weather induced difficulties, while less than five hundred fighters were able to participate, mostly due to the weather creating problems getting off the ground.

Major Conger led the Wolfpack off at 0943 on a radar controlled sweep of the Koblenz area. After receiving several fruitless vectors on bogies by Nuthouse, they returned at 1327.

January 14: VIII FC FO 1515-A. Eight hundred fifty heavies were effective against German industries and road traffic in Germany. An equal number of fighters were active as either escorts for the heavies or on fighter sweeps. In clear skies over the United Kingdom and Europe, the action became hot and heavy as the Luftwaffe decided to interfere with the "Mighty Eighth." Bomber crews claimed 31-9-7 for the loss of seven heavies and five more being damaged beyond repair. Eighty B-24s were damaged, along with 213 B-17s. The fighter pilots "did themselves up proud," claiming 155-0-25 in the air and 3-0-5 on the ground for eleven lost and five having to be scrapped-out upon return.

Major Conger led thirty-nine Jugs of "A" Group off Boxted at 0943 on a Rodeo ahead of the bombers heading for Magdeburg. In over Schouwen Island, they flew to Ulzen and on to Schwerner Lake, then turned south to Standal (just north of Magdeburg), where they engaged a mixed gaggle of fifty to a hundred Fw 190s and Me 109s at 1215 hours that were already engaged with Mustangs of the 357th Fighter Group. (The 357th claimed 48 1/2 during this conflict).

Major Paul Conger was flying one of the recently received new P-47M-1s on this mission and he found that by pulling 78 inches of mercury he could out climb an Me 109 for the first time. Also that the "M" model Jug had a better rate of turn, yet the Me 109 still had a superior rate of roll. Regardless, Conger got on the tail of a 109 and shot it down along with damaging another. Also scoring from "Daily," the 63rd Fighter Squadron, was 1st Lt. Pershing B. Trumble who claimed two Me 109s, but only had one claim awarded. The 61st FS, led by Major Gladych, had but one opportunity on an Me 109, but it evaded their pursuit. These German pilot's were noted as "very aggressive."

Capt. Felix Williamson led the 62nd FS and they got in on the largest portion of the action near Berg. Williamson claimed a total of five destroyed, four Me 109s and an Fw 190, which ran his personal score to 10.5 and made him a double ace. He would receive the Distinguished Service Cross for his efforts on this mission.

Williamson: "As I neared these aircraft, I could see that most of them were Me 109s. A couple came down in front of the squadron so I picked one and gave chase. This one pulled up into the sun. I flew straight into the sun until I saw him come out on the left, when I fired a short burst at about eight hundred yards. The aircraft started to turn, and I turned with him, firing again as I closed up to about six hundred yards. This time I observed hits on the left wing and left side of the fuselage. The e/a began to smoke and the pilot bailed out.

"(Willie's second kill) began some of the most violent evasive action I have ever seen. This consisted of very fast rolls and vertical reverses. Every time I got into a position where I thought I could shoot, I was unable to find my sight. Finally we were both going straight down and the e/a was doing snap rolls. About this time I hit compressibility and could not control my a/c. I then concentrated on pulling out. As I began to do so, I passed the e/a about fifty feet out on to my right and he was still snapping. After I pulled out I observed a fire on the ground and Lt. Henley later informed me that the e/a continued to snap into the ground.

"(No. 3 was clobbered in a head-on pass) I observed many strikes on the nose and wings. The plane slipped off into a falling turn to his right and then started tumbling into the ground. {No. 4 was another head-on pass after which the canopy of the e/a came off and the pilot bailed out. At this time two more 109s came in after us. I called for my wingman to break and reefed my a/c hard to the left to try and get a shot. One e/a broke off and

pulled up to join about ten-plus above us. One e/a continued to press the attack and took a deflection shot at my wingman, Lieutenant Wither. I did not see any strikes but observed my wingman going straight down, smoking." (2nd Lt. James Wither was killed). " I did a wing-over and took a 45-degree deflection shot at this 109 and registered many hits on him. The e/a began to smoke badly, finally caught fire, and the pilot bailed out."

1st Lt. Donald Henley destroyed one Me 109 and shared another with 2nd Lt. Herschel Womack. 2nd Lt. Frank Aeron also shot down an Me 109.

Major Michael Jackson led "B" Group off with twenty-four P-47s five minutes behind "A" Group under the same Field Order and mission profile, only offset to the south. Their portion got off to an almost tragic start as 2nd Lt. Charles McBath lost his belly tank on the runway during his takeoff run. The skittering tank was then nicked by the P-47 of 2nd Lt. Russell Campbell and the tank exploded underneath his aircraft. With smoke and flame rising to 300 feet in the air, Campbell retracted his landing gear and bellied in on the end of the runway with his aircraft in flames. He escaped with minor burns.

Then, tragedy did strike as "B" Group headed across the English Channel, Jackson's wingman, 2nd Lt. Jack Hedke, 61st FS, had to bailout after having engine trouble twenty-five miles east of Clacton. An Air-Sea Rescue RAF Walrus located Hedke within fifteen minutes, but his body was floating face down and the water was too rough for the Walrus to land upon. A rescue launch was sent out to recover his body for burial.

"B" Group encountered three groups of Me 109s near Nienberg that numbered twenty plus. These Luftwaffe pilots were "startlingly aggressive and held their formations exceptionally well." "Yorker squadron," "B" Group's 63rd FS was led by 1st Lt. Charles Rotzler, who saw them first and alerted the rest of "B" Group and then dove into the fray.

Rotzler claimed one Me 109. Lt. Charles McBath, White Four, who had showed some degree of courage in continuing the mission without his belly tank, claimed two Me 109s. Lt. Ramon Davis claimed one Me 109. 1st Lt. Thomas Queen had his canopy shot off by Me 109 fire and was nicked in the neck by a fragment.

The 62nd FS acquitted themselves well. Major Jackson shot down an Me 109 and an Fw 190. Lt.'s William Daley and Kenneth Smith each destroyed an Me 109. The 61st FS had been continuing on course when the battle first started, so they had to turn back to join in. Down low, Lt. Robert Walker spotted one Me 109 preparing to land, only the German pilot decided to make a touch-and-go out of it instead, and Walker shot him down. Walker's kill was the last air-to-air victory for the 61st FS during the war. Lt. Russell Kyler found another in the area and shot it down, too.

However, as they say, bad things do come in threes. As all of the combats with the Luftwaffe were taking place near the Rhine River, one "B" Group pilot spotted what he took to be a pair of Fw 190s flying above a formation of Me 109s and Fw 190s at 15,000 feet. He dove on them and shot one down, witnessing its pilot making a successful bailout. It was a RAF Typhoon.

January 15: VIII FC FO 1519-A. Overcast skies over Europe limited bomber operations and for the first time in many months the 8th Air Force actually sent out more fighters than bombers. The 620 Big Friends hit rail targets in Germany, while most of the 730 fighters were up on escort missions. Only one heavy was lost to enemy action, and the Little Friends scored 14-0-19 for the loss of three aircraft.

(Now) Major Michael Jackson led the mission from the 62nd Fighter Squadron. Off at 1003, they were to provide top cover for three Combat wings of the 1st Air Division going to Brisach. RV was made over Nancy, and escort provided through the target and out to Charleroi before RTB at 1428. The weather was "very dense" and the mission was a milkrun for the Group that spent most of the time brushing up on their instrument work.

January 16: VIII FC FO 1521-A. Less than six hundred heavies were effective on missions against oil and industrial targets in Germany. Almost seven hundred fighters went along. Although the Luftwaffe did not show up, Mother Nature interceded with a heavy hand and created many problems for both the returning bombers and fighters. Half of the dispatched fighters had to land on the continent because they could not get home, and most of the bombers had to seek alternate airfields to return to in England.

Major Leslie Smith led fifty-four Thunderbolts off Boxted at 0837 on a Free Lance support mission ahead of the bombers. In to Drummer Lake, they swung north to Hannover on the instructions of Nuthouse, but there was no action to be found. While heading for Boxted on the way home they discovered that all of England had become fogbound. Most of the Group headed for Woodbridge, (39 aircraft), while others diverted to Martlesham Heath, (5), Bentwaters (4), and Framlingham (1).

Lt's Walter Groce and John Arnold, Blue Three and Four from the 63rd Fighter Squadron got stuck on top of the clouds and low on fuel, they elected to bailout instead of trying to penetrate into weather conditions they were not sure they could handle. One landed near Boxted and the other near Clacton, both successfully via the "nylon letdown."

January 17: VIII FC FO 1525-A. Seven hundred heavies went to oil and rail targets in Germany. 320 fighters went out as escorts for them. The Luftwaffe remained out of sight.

Major Jackson was at the helm again as forty-nine P-47s went out to escort 3rd Air Division B-17s going to Hamburg. Off at 1014, they picked up four boxes of Forts at 1126 and escorted them over the target and out to Fresian Island uneventfully.

January 21: VIII FC FO 1539-A. Although the 8th Air Force flew missions on January 18 and 20, the 56th Fighter Group did not participate in them. On January 21 the 8th AF went back to Germany to strike industrial and rail targets with nine hundred bombers and five hundred fighters.

Major Leslie Smith led the Group off at 0947 with thirty-two P-47s of the 62nd and 63rd Fighter Squadrons. (The 61st FS was standing down for conversion to P-47Ms). The takeoff was another one fraught with problems, as 2nd Lt. Robert Hall, Red Two, 63rd FS, aborted his takeoff without announcing it on the radio. The following element taking off, 1st Lt. Willard Scherz and 2nd Lt. James Davis over-ran Hall's still rolling aircraft and Scherz collided with it. The two aircraft burst into flames and while Scherz was fortunate to be able to escape from his, Hall perished. Hall was buried at Cambridge.

The Group proceeded in over Ostend and made RV near Metz with 2nd Air Division B-24s, but they were the wrong Big Friends, so Nuthouse gave a radar vector to the proper B-17 formation that were then escorted to their targets in the Strasbourg area. The heavies overflew the target and then made a 180 degree turn, apparently to make another run at the target, but the Wolfpack had to leave them at that point because their fuel had reached the "Bingo" level.

On the way home the 62nd Fighter Squadron went down to strafe targets of opportunity. Major Smith destroying a Ju 88 and sharing in the destruction of a Ju 52 with wingman 2nd Lt. Norman Gould.

At Boxted, meanwhile, 2nd Lt. Edward Lightfoot, 61st Fighter Squadron, had his share of excitement. While on a practice flight with a new P-47M, Lightfoot had an engine failure at 32,000 feet. He glided down for a belly landing and was uninjured. As the cause of the failure was discovered to be a breakdown of the high tension ignition leads, all of the 61st FS Thunderbolts were then grounded until the ignition harness's could be replaced. Also at Boxted, 2nd Lt. Max Dahl, 62nd FS, was killed while on a practice flight, but the circumstances of his death were unknown.

January 22: VIII FC FO 1544-A. Only two hundred B-17s went out on a mission to attack a synthetic oil factory at Sterkrade. Two hundred-sixty fighters were out, with most of these on fighter sweeps.

Major Jackson led thirty-six Thunderbolts from the 62nd and 63rd Fighter Squadrons off at 1108 to provide penetration, target and withdrawal support for the B-17s of the 1st Air Division. RV was made at landfall-in

over Egmond, but the Group had their force reduced by eleven that had to turn back with mechanical problems, part of this loss being made up by two spares from the 63rd FS. (The 62nd FS had nine of their eighteen P-47s launched abort). The escort was uneventful, as the Luftwaffe was apparently grounded because of the weather over Germany, and the mission returned at 1502.

January 27: Colonel David Schilling was transferred to 8th Air Force Headquarters as Assistant Director of Intelligence. He was replaced as commander of the 56th Fighter Group by Lt. Col. Lucian Dade. Major Leslie Smith replaced Dade as Deputy Group Commander. Capt. Felix Williamson filled the now vacant position of 62nd Fighter Squadron commander.

January 29: VIII FC FO 1566-A. Most of the 8th Air Force had been grounded during the intervening week because of the weather, although some missions had been flown on January 23 and 28 that the Wolfpack did not participate in. On the 29th, the heavies went to Central Germany to attack industrial and rail targets with eleven hundred heavies and seven hundred fighters.

During the course of the week of being non-operational, the 56th Fighter Group was briefed to expect a change in their mission to that of pure tactical interdiction. At this time, the Russian Army was 110 miles east of Berlin, and it was expected that the German Army would be attempting to move many of their forces from the Western Front to the Eastern Front to counteract the Russian movements.

Major Leslie Smith led a Ramrod to Altenbaken and Bielefeld to provide an escort for the 3rd Air Division on the way in, and then to strafe on their own on the way out. Thirty-seven P-47s tried to takeoff at 1040, but once again they had problems on the runway. First, one pilot from the 63rd Fighter Squadron aborted successfully, then 1st Lt. Pershing Trumble, Blue Three, started to abort and his P-47s went into a sideways drift across the runway. It was then struck by the Thunderbolt of his wingman, 2nd Lt. Wallace Knief. The pilots were uninjured, but both aircraft suffered major damage.

RV with the Big Friends was made just south of Meppel and they were shepherded to just west of Osnabruck before the Group broke away to descend to 10,000 feet to look for targets of opportunity. At Varel airdrome some fifteen Ju 88s were hidden in revetments, but the flak was too intense for the pilots liking, so they gave it a pass.

At Burge airdrome eight Me 410s were seen, and as the flak was lighter, the 63rd FS worked it over, with Capt. George Bostwick, their Operations Officer, destroying one on the ground. In the vicinity of Bagband a convoy of busses was spotted and the 62nd FS strafed it. A distasteful but necessary objective, and at least twenty German soldiers were killed as they ran for cover in the woods.

As January closed with two more days of bad flying weather, the ground crews continued to try and sort out the problems with the new P-47Ms coming into the Group. Although they had started to arrive in England in late December 1944 and had gone through depot checks, it was not until they had been run-in and flown for a period that the real problems began showing up. Even though they were some 20 mph faster "on the deck" than the P-47D-30 and had a faster rate of climb and higher critical altitude, they were not nearly as reliable. Primarily this was due to the aforementioned electrical problems. But the M's also had more electrical "automatic gadgets" that were difficult to keep working properly in the cold and humidity. Experimentation resulted in how to properly adjust the linkage between the throttle and the supercharger so that the engine could deliver its rated power, particularly at the altitudes that the M was supposed to be able to attain above that of the earlier D version.

Another problem was that the engine would not warm up properly, as the airflow through the cowling did not permit an even flow around the cylinder heads. This resulted in some cylinders running hot, while other were too cool, and resulted in rough running engines. It was solved by the locally installed baffles to reroute the air's flow. It was thought that these

The 61st Fighter Squadron climbs into the troposphere with their P-47Ms. This heavy version of the Jug was okay as a high altitude fighter, when everything was working right, but it excelled at low altitude work. (via Davis)

matters were now under control, but it was not to be, as the engines were further run and broken-in, further catastrophic engine failures would occur.

February 1945 was a dismal month for the 56th Fighter Group. Weather and other factors only permitted fourteen missions, of which most were boring escort sorties without any sign of the Luftwaffe. The expected interdiction missions to the Eastern Front did not materialize. Problems with the new aircraft had them on again, off again grounded. Two pilots were killed on training flights, and one lost in combat.

Still, the Group continued to run up their score against the Luftwaffe, knocking down nine German aircraft on February 3 and destroying two on

the ground on February 27. They finished February with a total of 847 1/2 German aircraft destroyed, 670 1/2 in the air and 177 on the ground, and continued as the premier 8th Air Force fighter group.

February 3: VIII FC FO 1586-A. An improvement in the winter weather permitted a large scale raid on Berlin by B-17s and on Magdeburg by B-24s in visual conditions. Nearly fourteen hundred heavies participated, along with nine hundred fighters. The Luftwaffe rose to the challenge. Twenty-five bombers and eight fighters were lost. No German aircraft were claimed by bomber gunners, but the fighters claimed 21-1-7 in the air and 17-0-11 on the ground.

Major Paul Conger led the longest Wolfpack mission so far. Off at 0827 they went on a sweep ahead of the B-17s to Berlin, and for the first time they had the range to overfly the city and proceed to the east for a period. After being briefed that the Russian Army was now but fifty miles from Berlin, the pilots were instructed on procedures to follow if they encountered Russian aircraft and recognition thereof. Also, in the event they encountered problems with their aircraft, to proceed eastward to bellyland on the grass on Russian held airstrips, as in all likelihood the runways were mined.

They arrived over Stendal at 28,000 feet at 1015, fifteen minutes ahead of the 1st Air Division. They then flew southeast for a few minutes before turning east and discovering many German aircraft above a wooded area southeast of Berlin. Major Conger ordered a 180 degree turn, and leaving Capt. Joseph "Jock" Perry, Operations Officer of the 61st Fighter Squadron and "Whippet" squadron as top cover, took the 62nd and his 63rd FS's down to attack.

By the time they had descended to 10,000 feet, the German aircraft had climbed to 3,000 feet and Conger's flights were in an ideal position for the attack on the fifteen plus Fw 190s. The Focke Wulf's broke left and started a defensive Lufberry, which took the furball back over Berlin where they all encountered light flak. Ignoring the flak, Conger selected an Fw 190 and fired, but had no success. As he overshot the German fighter, the Luftwaffe pilot turned his attention upon Blue Three, the P-47 flown by Lt.

The 62nd FS at Boxted with some of their gaudy camouflaged Jugs. All sorts of colors and patterns were attempted by the 56th FG to disguise their aircraft, but none accomplished more than adding forty pounds of weight and slowing the aircraft down. (via Davis)

Not all P-47s coded "S" belonged to Colonel Schilling. This UN❂S, 44-21118 belonged to Lt. Arthur Schupe. (via Davis)

David Magel, 63rd FS. Magel's Thunderbolt burst into flames and Magel bailed out. He was seen to delay his parachute opening until he was clear of the milling aircraft, and then had a good chute. Magel landed safely and ran into a wooded area. After the war it was found that he had died, but the cause was not known. Still, it was a shock to the Magel family at to have one son known to be a POW and the other listed MIA.

Conger then closed upon the same Fw 190 and fired. The Fw broke right, "went into a half roll, sliced off the roll, and then its right wing tore off and it crashed." Conger then damaged an Me 109 "that came out of nowhere in front of him, which was followed by another 109 that Conger and 2nd Lt. James Davis, Yellow Four, chased across Berlin until Conger caught him at 500 yards." Conger fired, "it broke left, hit some trees and crashed." (Davis was credited with a damaged upon it, Conger with the kill).

Capt. John Fahringer, the 63rd FS Assistant Operations Officer, was flying as Red One and he claimed one Me 109 destroyed and two damaged, along with damaging an Fw 190. Capt. Cameron Hart downed two Fw 190s, which made him an ace plus one and were his final kills. Lt.'s Frank Ogden and Phillip Kuhn each knocked down an Fw 190.

As the 63rd FS had this conflict under control, Capt. Felix Williamson led the 62nd FS down to overfly an unidentified airdrome southeast of Berlin. Williamson destroying an Fw 190 and an Me 109 and damaging an Fw 190 that had just taken off.

The twelve P-47s of the 61st FS that had remained as top cover were bounced at this time, too, by a dozen Spitfires, but no damage was inflicted. The mission returned at 1402 after a five and a half hour most eventful sweep.

February 4: No combat missions for the Wolfpack were flown, but training missions continued to take their toll. On the previous day, 2nd Lt. Richard Theyken, 61st FS, had made a forced landing in a malfunctioning P-47M. It was a write-off, but he was uninjured. On this day, 1st Lt. Kenneth Smith, 62nd FS, was killed on a training mission when his P-47M crashed near Tollesbury, England. The 62nd FS had just started to receive their "M's" that morning.

February 6: VIII FC FO 1595-A. A massive raid against oil and industrial targets within Germany was flown after a weather forced three day stand-down. Although planned as a visual raid, the weather forced bombing by electronic means by the thirteen hundred heavies that were covered by nine hundred fighters.

Major Carter led the mission to provide penetration, target and withdrawal support off at 0931. Only thirty-three P-47s could be made available for the mission. Nevertheless, RV with two Combat Wings of the 2nd Air Division B-24s headed for Magdeburg was made on schedule and an uneventful mission was flown, returning at 1432.

February 8: VIII FC FO ? A bomber force of four hundred was assembled, but recalled prior to leaving England. One B-17 from the force didn't hear the recall and courageously went on all by his lonesome to bomb Essen with three tons of bombs. He got home safely. The Wolfpack also got airborne, but was recalled while climbing through 7,000 feet, so they turned it into a formation training flight over England.

February 9: VIII FC FO 1605-A. Twenty-one hundred fighters and bombers flew a maximum effort mission against oil targets in Germany. The Luftwaffe showed up to counteract the effort and Mustang pilots claimed 24-3-8 in the air and 37-0-12 on the ground. Five Mustangs and eight heavies were lost. Capt. Felix Williamson led the escort mission off at 1039 with forty Thunderbolts of the 62nd and 63rd Fighter Squadrons. RV was made southwest of Liege with the 1st Combat Wing of the 2nd Air Division. A solid cloud deck from the surface to 2,000 feet prevented the Luftwaffe from getting through to the B-24s and the mission was uneventful.

February 14: VIII FC FO 1622-A. Back to oil and rail targets in Germany by Bomber Command with thirteen hundred heavies. Over nine hundred fighters went along as moral support.

The 1st Air Division, sent 311 effective B-17s to Dresden to support RAF operations against communications and rail targets. Lancasters bombed at night, and the Flying Forts by day. The destruction was complete, comparable to the devastation of Hamburg in July-August 1943. Although far more aircraft than the two B-29s that later struck Hiroshima and Nagasaki were involved, the casualties were comparable. 135,000 died at Dresden as a result of these missions, the largest number of casualties ever inflicted anywhere at any time in history. These missions, by the way, were conducted at the specific request of the USSR, as the other Allied forces had little interest in Dresden.

The Wolfpack split into their "A" and "B" Groups for this mission. Lt. Col. Dade led "A" off at 1037 with twenty-three Jugs from the 61st and 62nd Fighter Squadrons, with this being the first mission for the 61st FS and their new all-black P-47Ms. Major Conger led "B" Group off ten minutes later with twenty-six T-Bolts from the 62nd and 63rd FS's.

This flat black P-47M, HV◉J, belonged to Lt. Russell Kyler. It was serialed 44-21116. Note the protective hood over the gunsight and the two different methods of denoting Kyler's score. (Three air-to-air and seven ground kills). Garrett via Davis

"A" swept in ahead of the B-24s headed for Magdeburg, while "B" joined with the last Combat Wing of Liberators over Drummer Lake at 1200. Escort was provided out to Gifhorn fifty minutes later with only two German jets being seen, but they were not encountered.

February 15: VIII FC FO 1628-A. The weather continued to mess up operations. Eleven hundred heavies were sent to bomb strategic targets in Germany or tactical targets ahead of the Canadians and British forces heading for the Rhine River. The Liberators managed to bomb Magdeburg successfully, but most of the B-17s had to seek alternate targets.

Major Leslie smith led the mission, originally intended to provide penetration and target support for heavies attacking Wessel. However, the Group incurred a two hour weather delay and did not get airborne from Boxted until 1232, so they RV'd with the bombers over Wessel and provided withdrawal support instead. As there was a solid overcast over the continent there was no Luftwaffe opposition.

February 18: Again training missions over England proved to be as hazardous as combat. Until the price of aircraft started to run into today's millions, it was condoned to practice intercepts on any and all aircraft, as it was considered worthwhile to force aircrews to practice constant vigilance while in the air.

1st Lt. John Fraizer and 2nd Lt. Bryon Fisher, 61st Fighter Squadron, were up on a training flight when Fisher spotted six RAF Mustangs passing under them at 8,000 feet and they dove upon them from their altitude of 11,000 feet. Due to the glare and angle of the sun, at first the type was not identified, but after passing the first flight, both groups of pilots saw each other and the fight was on. The Number Three Mustang pilot apparently saw Fraizer and turned in behind him to join the mock battle, but apparently Fisher was also watching Fraizer, for the Mustang and the Thunderbolt collided with the P-51 being cut in two and the P-47 exploding in the air.

All of the P-47Ms were grounded once again as a result of the investigation into the cause of the forced landing on February 10 by 1st Lt.

Bradley, 61st FS. Electrical problems with cracked leads in the ignition harness again was the culprit.

February 19: VIII FC FO 1638-A. Bomber Command continued its relentless attacks on the German oil and transportation industries. Today's missions included eleven hundred effective Big Friends and over five hundred fighters.

The Wolfpack was tasked to provide penetration and withdrawal support to 2nd Air Division B-24s attacking Siegen ("Dr. Waldrick's Tool Factory") and Major Conger led the Ramrod off at 1205 with just thirty-two P-47s of the 61st and 63rd Fighter Squadrons. RV was made over Terschelling Island at 1315 with the last Combat Wing of Liberators. This was the same target that the Wolfpack had attacked January 5 and 6, and apparently they had not done so well, as now the heavies were hitting it. As there was a complete overcast over the continent, the bombing results by the heavies could not be observed, but it was noted that their formation was "sloppy."

February 20: VIII FC FO 1642-A. Nurnberg was the target for all three Air Divisions, but weather conditions caused a recall of 360 B-24s of the 2nd Air Division. Over eight hundred B-17s did get through to bomb effectively, however.

The Wolfpack went out on a fighter sweep ahead of the 2nd Air Division, launching at 1013 with thirty-two Jugs of the 61st and 63rd Fighter Squadrons. Major Carter led them off. They arrived over Nurnberg at 1210 and "stooged around uneventfully" until 1300. At this time Capt. Cameron Hart's 63rd FS picked up some bombers to escort out as far as Wurzburg, but since the Luftwaffe did not show up, the mission was logged as a milkrun.

February 21: VIII FC FO 1647-A. Twelve hundred heavies went back to Nurnberg. It was an exceptional mission for them, as they had no claims against the Luftwaffe, and no losses to any German activity. Only one B-17 was lost, over Allied territory on the way in, to an unknown cause.

"The Brat" belonged to Randall Murphy, 63rd FS. She was 44-21141. Murphy had two air kills, and nine on the ground. (via Davis)

Assigned to provide penetration, target and withdrawal support, Lt. Col. Smith led the Wolfpack off at 0912. Again the escort force was limited to thirty-seven Jugs of the 61st and 63rd Fighter Squadrons that were split into the "A" and "B" Groups for tactical purposes.

As the heavies were a half-hour late in arriving over Ostend, the Wolfpack went into an orbit for the duration, and finally set course at 0959. Arriving over Nurnberg the bombers were so bunched up that many of them had to circle to avoid congestion and make another bombing run on the target, but they got away with it without German interference.

The P-47M was appearing to be the main curse, as seven had to abort the mission on the way out, and four landed on the continent on the way home with mechanical problems that marred the otherwise uneventful mission.

February 22: VIII FC FO 1650-A. Operation Clarion was put into effect by Bomber Command. This operation called for bombing attacks to be made from the unusually low altitudes of between 6,000 and 10,000 feet, to increase bombing accuracy against pin point rail and road targets. Over fourteen hundred bombers and eight hundred fighters from the 8th Air Force participated. In total, the mission to ensnare the largest amount of German communications over the largest area included over 6,000 Allied aircraft that struck over the German noon hour for an hour and a half. It really must have been something to witness!

Major Conger led thirty-three Thunderbolts of the 61st and 63rd Fighter Squadrons off at 1027 to provide an escort to Halberstadt and Nordhausen for B-24s of the 2nd Air Division. RV was made east of the Zuider Zee and escort was provided to Drummer Lake by both squadrons. Over the lake the 61st FS broke away to strafe an oil storage depot at Oldendorf, but the results were negligible, as the tanks were apparently empty.

The 63rd FS broke escort over the Zuider Zee and also did some strafing along a highway, but with only moderate results.

February 23: VIII FC FO 1654-A. Operation Clarion continued with twelve hundred 8th Air Force bombers and seven hundred fighters. Only one B-17 was lost to enemy action, and only one German fighter was destroyed by a P-51 pilot.

Major Carter led the 56th Fighter Group on an escort mission off at 0920. Again they were composed of only thirty-three P-47s from the 61st and 63rd Fighter squadrons. RV was made with two Combat Wings of B-24s over Gottingen at 1115 and escort was broken off southwest of Drummer Lake at 1320. Due to a virtually solid undercast, the bombing results could not be seen and the mission was uneventful and returned at 1458.

Once again all of the recently cleared for flight P-47Ms were grounded. This time it was due to ruptured diaphragms in the carburetors. The Group, and particularly the 62nd FS were missing out on a lot of missions because of sick aircraft.

February 25: VIII FC FO 1662-A. Almost twelve hundred Big Friends went to Germany to attack transportation, oil, tank and aircraft factories. Bomber losses still remained unusually low with only eight being lost to direct enemy action. Three of these making it back to friendly airfields, but being damaged beyond repair. The 8th Air Force fighter pilots, finally, had some action, with twenty-one German aircraft being knocked down and thirteen more destroyed on the ground.

Major Paul Conger led the Group on his last mission. Off at 0816 with just nine P-47s from the 61st Fighter Squadron and twelve from the 63rd FS, they had three aborts. The mission was a sweep over the Giessen area under the control of Nuthouse. In over Knocke they headed for Koblenz, and were alerted to look for "rats," but none could be found, so they went strafing east of Schweinfurt.

While strafing some railroads "Daily Blue Flight" encountered more excitement than should be endured. Capt. Walter Flagg and 2nd Lt. Charles McBath went down to strafe fifteen railroad cars on a siding along side of a wooded area believed to contain an ammunition dump. The normal procedure was to strafe at a ninety degree angle to the tracks, as this reduced the vulnerability to antiaircraft fire, particularly if the train cars mounted guns, which they were often known to do.

McBath, for some reason, elected to strafe along the length of the cars, and "he found the train exploding in his face. He was totally engulfed in smoke and flames, putting him into complete darkness that was punctuated by flames. He thought that he had bellied-in the way his P-47 was reacting, and in the seconds after he broke out of the smoke he saw flames to 1,000 feet and cumulus type black clouds to 5,000 feet. As a result battle damage the right side of his engine was streaming oil, the left side smoking. His right wing was on fire, his left elevator had jumped out of its mounts and a foot of it was missing. He thought about jumping out, but Flagg stayed with him and directed him around flak barrages. "Fairbanks" said he was 20 minutes from friendly territory, but after 30 minutes he was still over occupied Germany with oil sloshing around in the cockpit so heavily that he couldn't keep his feet on the rudder pedals. Smoke was so thick he couldn't see out, or even his instruments. Flagg stuck with him and directed him to a blind, wheels-down landing at Verdun."

February 26: VIII FC FO 1665-A. Twelve hundred heavies went to Berlin escorted by seven hundred fighters. Bomber gunners made no claims, while Mustang pilots claimed four in the air and two on the ground.

Major Jackson led this escort mission off at 1022. This was Jackson's last mission of his extended tour. Twenty P-47s were dispatched and six had to abort. The 61st Fighter Squadron put up eight, and since the 62nd FS had not flown for awhile, they tried to put up twelve. Three of these were P-47Ds from storage, and nine more D models were borrowed from the 63rd FS, as the squadron P-47Ms could not be made operational. RV was made south of Meppel with the rear half of the 2nd box of B-24s from the 2nd Bomb Division. Over a solid undercast the mission was uneventful and escort was broken at Luneburg with RTB at 1606.

February 27: VIII FC FO 1670-A. Eleven hundred heavies went to attack rail and road traffic in Germany, mostly around Leipzig and Halle. Only three heavies were lost during this effort. Fighter Command sent out seven hundred fighters, and although they only shot down two, they destroyed eighty-one on the ground.

Lt. Col. Smith led the again limited Wolfpack off at 1030. They were only able to send out eighteen aircraft, and five of these were flown by 63rd Fighter Squadron rookie pilots flying with the other two squadrons for the experience. The mission was an escort as far as Saalfeld and then they dropped down through a hole in the undercast near Wiermar to look for targets of opportunity.

At Wiermar/Norha airdrome the 56th Fighter Group took over where the 4th FG left off, destroying four unidentified single-engine types and damaging three. Ground kills of two each being awarded to Lt. Col. Smith and wingman 1st Lt. Robert Baughman. (The 4th FG claimed forty-three destroyed during the course of their raid).

February 28: VIII FC FO ? Eleven hundred heavies went to attack rail targets in Germany. They were escorted by seven hundred P-51s, who then went strafing to destroy eighteen German aircraft on the ground.

The 56th Fighter Group again was forced to fly a mission with a limited number of aircraft. Twenty P-47s led by Major Carter were to provide an escort to Ruthen, but the Big Friends could not be found in the "clag," so they dropped down to fulfill the second part of the Field Order, dive bombing of Koblenz. But, they could not penetrate the weather and had to settle for dropping their 250 pound GP and external drop tanks that were fitted with igniters on an unknown industrial target near Offenbach. RTB'd 1730.

February had been a confusing mixture of weather problems and aircraft difficulties. The 61st Fighter Squadron had traded in most of their P-47Ds for Ms, and then all of the Ms were grounded because of carburetor problems. The 62nd FS had retained their Ds when they received their Ms, so their ground crews had between forty and fifty aircraft to maintain, including those borrowed by the 61st FS so they could fly missions. Although the Wolfpack flew a total of fourteen combat missions, the 61st and

63rd each got in thirteen, while the 62nd flew but eight. All were in limited strength with the overlap between the squadrons permitting what few operations there were.

March 2: VIII FC FO 1683-A. Twelve hundred effective B-17s and B-24s accompanied by seven hundred fighters struck synthetic oil plants at Bohlen, Magdeburg (along with a tank factory), and Ruhland. 110 German aircraft were destroyed, two thirds of them in the air by either aerial gunners or fighter pilots. Twenty-seven friendlies were lost.

Capt. Felix Williamson led twenty-two Thunderbolts off at 0808 as the P-47M hampered Wolfpack attempted to do their part on this escort mission. RV was made east of Meppel at 0940 with the 1st Combat Wing of 2nd Air Division B-24s. The Liberators were late arriving at the RV point, so the Jugs had to orbit over the Zuider Zee awaiting their charges. Although Nuthouse informed them of possible Luftwaffe activities, no bandits could be found, and the uneventful escort concluded northwest of Lingen at 1215.

March 3: VIII FC FO 1690-A. Eleven hundred heavies went to assorted targets in Germany. B-24s of the 2nd Air Division were split between Magdeburg and Nienburg. The B-17s of the 1st Air Division split between Hannover and Ruhland, while those from the 3rd AD hit Brunswick and nearby locales.

Lt. Col. Smith led the Ramrod to Nienburg off at 0700. The 63rd Fighter Squadron was only able to put up ten Jugs, while the 62nd FS furnished eleven. From this meager number each squadron had one abort.

RV was made east of Zwolle at 0835 with 1st Combat Wing of the 2nd Air Division, and then on the way into the target the B-24 formation split, with the second portion falling almost a mile behind the main portion. Conditions worsened, as the bombers attacked the target from three different directions in an attempt to find the target through holes in the undercast with little success. The heavies then proceeded south at Drummer Lake to attempt to find targets of opportunity. At this point, Smith had to advise Nuthouse that the Group was low on fuel and for Nuthouse to find them relief, as they had to turn for home. RTB'd at 1230 after a disgruntled effort.

March 4: VIII FC FO 1697-A. During the course of one of the more frustrating missions dispatched by Bomber Command, two towns in Switzerland were inadvertently bombed by two different bomb groups whose navigators misplaced Germany.

Although over a thousand heavies were sent out, only two-thirds of this number flew effective missions, with most of the remaining being recalled because of the weather.

Major Carter led the Group off at 0742. This time they were able to start with a more effective number, forty-one, but once again there were problems and fifteen had to abort for one frustrating reason or another. The RV was attempted at Friedburg at 0950, but it also was a messed-up affair. Intending to RV with B-24s, they found B-17s at the RV point, as, apparently there had been a massive problem over England in getting the initial formations established. Things got sorted out over St. Nicholas an hour later and the escort mission headed towards Stuttgart only to have to climb to 30,000 feet to get over a cloud front. Clearing the weather, the Wolfpack discovered bombers all over the place in small formations heading every which way. "Bombers most Snafued ever witnessed." The Ramrod continued to Aschaffenburg, where only eighteen B-24s bombed effectively, and escort was broken over Strasburg with a RTB time of 1231.

March 5: VIII FC FO 1704-A. Mother Nature continued to hamper operations and less than four hundred heavies flew effective sorties. The 1st and 3rd Air Divisions were only able to get four bomb groups off, each.

Capt. George Bostwick led the area support mission from the 63rd Fighter Squadron. Fifty-one Thunderbolts went out, with five aborts, and this was the first time in a month that all three squadrons were able to participate in a mission together. They reached Hamburg at 1008, five minutes ahead of the B-24s and were advised by Nuthouse that they were the only friendly aircraft in the area, so the 63rd FS chased a pair of unidentified aircraft from Hamburg to Parchim before they were identified as Mustangs. (On his way home after aborting over Europe an unidentified 62nd FS pilot had been chased by a silver, and unmarked Mustang that he had to evade by diving into cloud cover). Other than seeing a dozen possible Me 262s far above them in poor formation, the mission was uneventful and they RTB'd at 1312.

March 7: VIII FC FO 1715-A. Bomber Command again went after oil and communications targets in Germany. Of the twelve hundred aircraft sent out by both Fighter and Bomber Commands, not a single one was lost to enemy action. But one heavy crashed on takeoff, and another upon return. The survivability of bomber crews was certainly looking up.

Lt. Col. Dade led the escort mission off at 0829 with thirty-nine Thunderbolts, and for the first time in six weeks they had no aborts. RV was made over Meppel at 1003, with the B-24s being late again. Escort was provided over the target, Soest, and out to Liege. The milkrun returned at 1302.

March 9: VIII FC FO 1727-A. Bomber Command went back to Germany with a thousand effective heavies to strike rail and industrial targets. Seven heavies were lost and three more damaged beyond repair.

Major Carter led the 56th Fighter Group off at 0743, their earliest take off so far this year. Forty-seven P-47s went out, of which six aborted. On an Area Patrol mission, they arrived over Hangelo at 0908, overflew Drummer Lake and on to Munster and Arnham and out over Meppel at 24,000. Other than Lt. George Bradley, 61st Fighter Squadron, being shot at by friendly shore antiaircraft batteries as he aborted early on during the mission, it was another milkrun.

March 10: VIII FC FO 1735-A. Bomber Command sent thirteen hundred heavies into Germany to attack rail targets. Most of Fighter Command was detailed to support the Big Friends, but a few fighter groups were detailed to the 9th Air Force in support of their tactical operations.

The Wolfpack got a hurry-up order to dispatch as many of their aircraft as possible to assist in protecting the freshly captured Ludendorff railroad bridge over the Rhine River at Remagen. This bridge, captured intact after costly and heroic efforts by the 1st Army, would provide a funnel across the Rhine into Germany, itself, by the assault troops. The German forces were attempting to destroy the bridge through counterattacks and aerial bombardment, which the Allies could not afford to let happen under any circumstances.

Major Carter led twenty-three Thunderbolts from the 61st and 62nd Fighter Squadrons off at 1415 and they arrived over the bridge at 1520. Carter and the 61st FS took up a top cover position at 10,000 feet, while below them, and below an overcast, the 62nd FS under the lead of Capt. William Daley went into an orbit at 3,000 feet. As the 62nd rolled out of their first circle, Daley spotted two gaggles of enemy aircraft. Me 109s carrying bombs and Fw 190s providing top cover for them at 4,000 feet. The size of the bombs could not be determined, but they were larger than the normal Me 109 belly tank, and this was the first time that the Wolfpack had encountered Luftwaffe fighter-bombers.

The 62nd FS turned into the Luftwaffe and forced the Me 109s to jettison their bombs into an open field and the combat was joined. Lt. Norman Gould shot down one Me 109, while Lt.'s Donald Henely and Dennis Carroll shared an escorting Fw 190. Lt. David Ducey damaged an Me 109. The two aerial victories were the only two by the entire 8th Air Force this day.

March 11: VIII FC FO 1739-A. Twelve hundred effective heavies went to attack an oil refinery at Bremen and U-Boat pens at Hamburg. One B-17 and four Mustangs were lost, and no German aircraft were destroyed in the air.

Capt. Williamson led the Area Patrol mission to Kiel off at 1050 with forty-nine Thunderbolts. They arrived over Kiel at 1255 and Major Gladych took the 61st Fighter Squadron off to escort a Combat Wing of B-17s. With a solid undercast there was no sign of the Luftwaffe, but the squadrons that descended down through the clouds spotted several battleships and cruisers in the Borkum, Terschilling and Heligoland harbors. Apparently the Germans were recalling their fleets. RTB'd at 1550.

Lt. Charles McBath taxies out in "Dottie Dee," UN◉M, 44-21150. McBath joined the 63rd FS on November 10, 1944 and made 1st Lt. on April 8, 1945. (via Davis)

Flying out of Boxted while the mission was underway, 2nd Lt. Frank Aheron, 62nd Fighter Squadron, was killed when his P-47 crashed near Cranfield, Bedford, England.

March 12: VIII FC FO 1742-A. Thirteen hundred heavies went out to attack rail targets in Germany. Only one was MIA, and it went to Sweden. The fighters claimed four, for the loss of four.

Major Carter led them off Boxted at 0942 on a sweep ahead of the bombers to Hannover, Breman, Hamm, Kassel and Gottingen. Up to decent operational strength, fifty-one P-47s went out, but there were six early returns with mechanical problems.

The sweep was uneventful, although Nuthouse "Vectored all over Europe." On the way home, Lt. Alfred Bolender, 63rd Fighter Squadron, had to put down at Juvincourt, France with aircraft problems, otherwise it was another milkrun.

March 13: 1st Lt. Luther Hines and 2nd Lt. Richard Tuttle, 61st Fighter Squadron, were killed while conducting a training mission. While attempting a cross-over, the two aircraft collided and Tuttle's P-47 dove straight into the ground. Hines' Thunderbolt was cut in two behind the cockpit and he died the following day from injuries.

March 14: VIII FC FO 1752-A. For this day's efforts, Bomber Command sent out twelve hundred heavies to attack oil, rail and factories. Three Big Friends were lost and one written-off upon return. Fighter Command claimed seventeen German aircraft destroyed in the air for the loss of two, one of which was from the Wolfpack.

For the first time since the P-47M came on the scene the 56th Fighter Group sent out their "A" and "B" Groups. Capt. Williamson led "A" Group off at 1302 with thirty-six Jugs from the 62nd and 63rd Fighter Squadrons, while Major Joseph "Jock" Perry, Operations Officer of the 61st FS, led "B" Group off at 1307.

"B" Group made RV with the 3rd box of B-24s heading for Holzwickede (near Dortmund) at 1430 and escorted them 1555 near Siegen and then they RTB'd to land at 1804 after an uneventful mission.

"A" Group had picked up the Liberators at the same time, but they continued on with them until 1625 near Koblenz. At this time the 63rd FS broke off to head for home, only seeing five jets of an undetermined type that were not encountered. Williamson, meanwhile, took the 62nd FS to Frankfurt, back to Holzwickede, and then turned them south to discover two flights of the rare Arado 234 jet bombers.

Blue Flight, led by Lt. Sandborn Ball, started the chase, and Ball and his wingman, Lt. Warren Lear shared in the destruction of one. 1st Lt. Norman Gould, Red Three, knocked down another after closing and setting its right engine on fire, backing away, and then reclosing and firing again on it to set the other engine on fire. It spun in. This was Gould's fourth and last kill.

1st Lt. Sherman Pruitt, flying the mission as the spare for "Platform" squadron, chased down an Me 109 and forced its pilot to bailout. Pruitt then had to land on the continent because of an oil leak and had to phone in his claim. He returned to Boxted the next day with his gun camera film, but not his Jug. Two other pilots from the 62nd FS also had to land in Europe with mechanical problems.

While over Europe, 2nd Lt. Earl Townsted, 62nd FS, Thunderbolt developed an oil leak. He headed for home under escort by Capt. Robert Winters. But ten miles west of Knocke and over the Channel his engine gave out and Townsted had to bailout. Possibly he hit the tail of his aircraft, as his parachute did not open until he hit the water and he was killed.

March 15: VIII FC FO 1761-A. Thirteen hundred heavies and eight hundred fighters into Germany to attack tactical and strategic targets in the entire country.

Major Carter led the mission off at 1137 on what would be their longest one of the war. Six hours worth. Again, the Wolfpack was split between "A" and "B" Groups, with Carter leading "A," composed of the 61st and 62nd Fighter Squadrons, and Capt. Cameron Hart leading "B" made up completely from the 63rd FS. Intended to be a patrol over Berlin, the mission got off to a bad start when 1st Lt. Willard Scherz, White Three, 63rd FS, had his engine cut out just as he got his heavily loaded P-47 airborne. Scherz was killed when it crashed near the railroad station at Colchester.

Arriving south of Berlin at 1347, the two groups patrolled uneventfully until time to head for home, so they picked up three boxes of B-24s and took them as far as Madgeburg on the way out, breaking escort at 1445. Fatigued, they then found that the weather had turned sour at Boxted, and although all but four that landed at Raden, the rest got down safely at "homeplate," after "many go-arounds."

March 17: The key target and navigational checkpoint of Koblenz fell into Allied hands.

March 22: The Rhine River was crossed by the Third Army.

March 23: 1st Lt. Carl Bokina, 63rd Fighter Squadron, was killed while on a training flight.

March 24: VIII FC FO 1828-A. Operation Varsity was launched and the 8th Air Force was to provide tactical air support for the large scale parachute crossing of the Rhine River by the British 6th and United States 17th Airborne Divisions. Seventeen hundred bombers and thirteen hundred fighters were involved from the 8th Air Force. The 8th Air Force flew a total of 3,000 combat sorties, while the 9th Air Force flew 2,600. Over 3,500 German soldiers were taken prisoner on this one day as just one result of the airborne invasion.

After a nine day stand down/grounding, the Wolfpack was ready to get in on the action, and for the first time since the previous fall they flew two combat missions in one day.

Lt. Col. Dade led the first mission off at 0654 with twenty-four Thunderbolts from the 61st and 62nd Fighter Squadrons. Tasked with providing an area patrol over Drummer Lake, they arrived over the Lake at 0835 and patrolled uneventfully until 1040 in "CAVU" (Ceiling and visibility unlimited) skys. RTB time was 1202.

Lt. Col. Smith led the second mission. Off at 1500 with a dozen Thunderbolts from each squadron, they made RV with B-17s and B-24s of the 3rd and 2nd Air Divisions over Giessen at 1650. The intent of the Big Friends was to hit Luftwaffe airdromes to prevent the German fighters from becoming airborne and interfering with the parachute operations and they "really clobbered three airdromes." For the Wolfpack the mission was another boring milkrun, but the next day would be different.

March 25: VIII FC FO 1838-A. A thousand plane raid by the heavies had been planned against a tank factory and oil production plants, but the B-17 portion was scrubbed because of current and forecasted weather. The 2nd Air Division B-24s had an earlier takeoff time and proceeded with their portion of the scheduled events with four being lost and five written-off as a result of battle damage.

The Wolfpack were to escort the Liberators to Hitzacker. Major Williamson led them off at 0717 for an intended RV over Meppel at 0840, but the Big Friends were delayed and fuel consuming orbits had to take place until the bombers got there a half hour late.

Approaching the target area, and just before the Initial Point, six or seven Me 262s attacked from 18,000 feet between the first and second boxes of B-24s that were at 21,000 feet and sent two Liberators down in flames from the third box before diving off to the east. Only four parachutes were seen from the disabled bombers. One of the Me 262s was downed by a P-51.

Major George Bostwick, leading the 63rd Fighter Squadron for the second time as their squadron commander, took "Daily" Squadron off in pursuit. Although the jets soon outran the Jugs, Bostwick stooged the squad-

James Carter leads the "finger-four" formation in HV❂C. Major Carter was the last wartime commander of the 61st Fighter Squadron, from January 1945 on. (via Davis)

ron around for awhile trying to find where they might have gone to. He soon spotted the German airdrome at Parchim and circled the squadron over it at 12,000 feet for twenty minutes assessing the situation. There were between twenty and thirty jets parked there in plain sight, camouflaged in two-tone green with red and green stripes in front of their tails.

Bostwick's number four man, 2nd Lt. Edwin Crosthwait, called in a bogie and Bostwick ordered him after it. "It was an Me 262, and he led us back to the airdrome." (And Crosthwait shot it down).

Bostwick: "Upon reaching the airdrome, I spotted four more Me 262s milling around it, almost on the deck. I picked out one e/a who was flying parallel to the landing strip; as if he might be going to peel off to land. He did not, however, but flew straight down the runway. As he reached the end of the runway, he passed over a second e/a which was taking off and which was just breaking the ground. I pulled my nose through to get a shot at this e/a, but before I could he apparently saw me and made a tight turn to the left. His left wing dug into the ground and the plane cartwheeled . . . I then pulled back up to the right and picked up the e/a which I originally attacked. This one I damaged with several strikes."

Williamson, leading the Group from the 62nd FS, went after some jets after the bombers dropped their eggs on Hitzacker, but they were two

high, so they returned to the bombers and escorted them out as far as Quackenbruck before RTBing at 1257.

March 27: VIII FC FO 1551-A. The 8th Air Force Bomber Command did not fly missions this day. However, the 56th Fighter Group and two Mustang groups went out on a "Ramrod with Lance" escort mission for RAF Lancasters to Paderborn where the "Lancs" dropped "ten-ton Tessies."

Lt. Col. Smith led the Wolfpack off Boxted at 1530 with thirty-seven Thunderbolts. RV was accomplished north of Antwerp at 1640 with the Lancs that were operating in the usual RAF bomber stream, individual aircraft in-trail, style. Escort continued over the target and out to over Walcheren Island. Other than watching one Lancaster spin into the clouds at 18,000 feet near Gutersloh for no obvious reason, the mission was uneventful.

March 30: VIII FC FO 1863-A. Fourteen hundred heavies went out to curtail German U-Boat activities. Targets selected were the U-Boat pens, or construction sites at Breman, Hamburg and Wilhelmshafen, just inside Germany's northwest coast.

Lt. Col. Smith led the mission off at 1145 with fifty-three Thunderbolts. RV was made northeast of Leewarden, Holland at 1257 at 23,000 feet with two Combat Wings of B-24s headed to Wilhelmshafen. Escort continued until past the target and then Nuthouse diverted the Group to look for German jets, but none could be found, so escort to stragglers was attempted near Meppel, but none could be found, either, so the Group returned at 1614.

March 31: VIII FC FO 1874-A. Thirteen hundred Big Friends flew effective missions against miscellaneous targets in Germany. They were cover by over eight hundred fighters. Bomber gunners claimed three German aircraft, and the fighter pilots six, for a loss of an equal number of aircraft.

The Wolfpack once again sent their "A" and "B" Groups out. Lt. Col. Smith led "A" off at 0700, while Major Joseph Perry led "B" off eight minutes later on the same mission profile. "A" Group had thirty-three P-47s, while "B" had twenty. The fighter pilots had been briefed that they were to provide escort for B-24s of the 2nd Air Division to Hassel, but the bombers apparently hit either Hannover or Brunswick. They could not be sure, as there was a solid undercast, but someone's navigation was apparently off. In the target area an Me 262 came in and dove through the last box of the B-24s the 63rd Fighter Squadron was escorting. The 63rd FS chased it, but it easily out distanced them, only to make a 180 degree turn and come back at a straggling Liberator with two engines out. The German pilot missed and again evaded the fighters while the Lib continued its course for home. Near Hamburg, two B-17s were seen to be shot down by Me 262s and the 62nd FS went after them, but they were too far away and just too fast for the Jugs. The 61st FS had just a tad better luck, as between Hamburg and Steinhudder Lake, Red flight of "B" Group managed to get on the tail of a 262 and it was damaged by 1st Lt. Fred Barrett.

As March closed the Wolfpack would have its scoreboard showing 677 1/2 German aircraft destroyed in the air and 177 on the ground for a total of 854 1/2. The competition with the 4th Fighter Group was still close as to which was to be the higher scoring fighter group by the end of the war, which was certainly in sight, and there were a few 9th Air Force fighter groups in strong contention for the honor, also.

It, finally, appeared that the problems with the P-47M had been sorted out. It was believed that they had been improperly pickled prior to shipment from the States and that the cylinder heads suffered corrosion before they were delivered to the Group from the depot. It was decided that all engines with less than fifty hours on it would be replaced, as those engines that had passed this number of operating hours now seemed to be running satisfactorily.

Everyone believed that the Thunderbolt "is the finest propeller driven aircraft in the world." To get them to this point, the ground crews had to get up between three and five O'clock each morning to get their charges ready for flight. The alternative was the dreaded "Spam Can" P-51 Mustang that was sitting on their hardstands this very moment awaiting their chance to take the Wolfpack into combat. The P-51s had been brought in during March in the event that the P-47M problems could not be corrected. The ground crews dreaded the very idea of having to contend with in-line engines and glycol cooling systems, while the pilots had mixed emotions on the matter.

April 1: 1st Lt. John F. Frazier, 61st Fighter Squadron, was killed in a mid-air collision with another, unidentified, aircraft.

April 2: VIII FC FO 1882-A. 8th Air Force Bomber Command sent seven hundred heavies to bomb German airfields in Denmark, but the bombers were recalled over the North Sea because of weather conditions.

The Wolfpack dispatched both their "A" and "B" Groups on this escort mission. Lt. Col. Dade leading "A" Group and Major Williamson "B" Group. A total of fifty-two P-47s were sent out, but eleven had to either abort their takeoffs or return early. After a 1500 takeoff, RV was made at 1600 with three Combat Wings of B-24s. As the Jugs made landfall in over Nissum Fiord at 24,000 feet, the B-24s were seen to made a 180 degree turn and then they proceeded to jettison their bombs into the North Sea some fifty miles off the coast. RTB time was 1820.

April 4: VIII FC FO 1896-A. Fourteen hundred heavies went out to attack German airfields, but less than a thousand bombed effectively. Instructions were to bomb visually, and if unable to do so, retain the bombs, so as not to inadvertently hit the wrong people.

"A" Group was sent out behind Capt. Carter, while "B" Group was led by Capt. Bostwick. Off at 1730, "A" Group was composed of thirty-six P-47s of the 61st and 62nd Fighter Squadrons, while "B" Group was twenty-two Jugs from the 63rd FS. Both Groups were to escort two Combat Wings of B-24s, but the Liberators were late and off course in poor weather conditions.

"A" Group followed the bomber stream inbound to Perleberg, Germany and provided general escort to them until the proper formation could be located, over Luneberg. Yellow Flight of the 61st FS was intercepted by three Me 262s that attacked them from up-sun. 1st Lt. Russell Kyler claimed one Me 262 destroyed, but it was downgraded to a probable. Capt William "Dewey" Clark and Flight Officer John Kassap each claimed one damaged. 2nd Lt. Edmond Ellis was attacked by an Me 262, but managed to evade his fire. After this conflict, Lt.'s Ellis and Charles Raymond landed at Euskirchen, Germany to refuel. This airdrome had just been in Allied hands for two weeks, and marked the first intentional landing on German soil by Wolfpack pilots.

"B" Group RV'd over Norderney Island with three boxes of B-24s that were preceding a B-17 formation. They were to have escorted the 96th Combat Wing, but had difficulty in finding them, so they contented themselves with escorting the other "pregnant cows" in the meantime. Between Hamburg and Luneberg, Capt. Bostwick took two flights and went off in search of the 96th CW, and found them just as they were coming under attack by a pair of Me 262s. Capt. Charles Rotzler and Lt. Melvin Hughes went after one, chasing it to over Berlin, but never could close to firing range upon it.

April 5: VIII FC FO 1903-A. Ammo dumps, transportation railheads and airdromes were the targets selected by Bomber Command. Thirteen hundred heavies went out, but just over a thousand were considered effective.

Capt. Bostwick led the Wolfpack with fifty-three Thunderbolts off at 0830. Another Ramrod for the 2nd Air Division, this time going to Ingolstadt. The orders were specific, stay with the bombers, so although the 61st Fighter Squadron spotted twenty German twin-engine aircraft on the ground at Regensburg, thy had to leave them alone. However, north of Regensburg four Me 262s came in on an attack on some nearby B-17s and Blue Flight of the 63rd FS gave chase. Capt. John Fahringer, their Operations Officer, destroying one whose pilot bailed out. This was his fourth and last kill of the war. Lt.'s Donald Henley and Walter Sharbo, 62nd FS, shared in the damaging of another Me 262 that turned in front of them after making a pass on the B-17s.

April 6: VIII FC FO 1909-A. Over six hundred heavies were effective against targets in Germany. Most of these were in the area surrounding Leipzig.

Lt. Col. Dade led the thirty-nine Thunderbolts off at 0710 on a Ramrod to Halle (northwest of Liepzig). RV was made southwest of Marburg and escort provided over the target and out to Meiningen. With a solid undercast all the way, nothing could be seen and the mission was uneventful. RTB'd at 1225. Flight Officer Joseph Del Corso, 61st FS, dove into the ground while on a training flight. He was killed.

April 7: VIII FC FO 1914-A. With an improvement in the weather, over twelve hundred heavies were able to bomb effectively by visual means. The Luftwaffe was up in force, and the bomber gunners claimed 40-12-17. Fourteen B-17s and three B-24s were lost. Fighter Command did far better, claiming 64-1-15 for the loss of five Mustangs.

Major Carter led "A" Group with thirty-four P-47s, while Capt. Bostwick led "B" Group with twenty-one. Off at 1022, RV on the Ramrod to Duneburg and Krummel by 2nd Air Division B-24s was made at 1145. Soon thereafter, near Nienburg, an Me 262 made a pass on the bombers and was damaged by Capt. Bostwick . Then, near Celle, some Me 109s and Fw 190s "came up to fight." Bostwick knocked down two Me 109s for his seventh and eighth kills. Lt.'s Charles McBath and Frank Ogden each claimed one. (McBath's claim was approved, Ogden's downgraded to a probable).

Just before escort was terminated a single Me 109 was seen above the bombers, and then it dove through the bomber formation spraying ammunition everywhere. Capt. Robert Winters, 62nd FS, Blue Lead, and wingman Lt. Dennis Carroll gave chase, also courageously diving through the bomber formation. Although Winter's had his P-47s tail shotup by the bomber's gunners, he managed to catch the Me 109 down on the deck and shot it down.

April 8: VIII FC FO 1918-A. Eleven hundred bombers and eight hundred fighters went out, and there was no sign of the Luftwaffe. Nine bombers and one Mustang were lost.

The Wolfpack again sent out their two groups. Major Williamson leading "A" Group and Major Perry "B" Group. Off at 0907, they provided escort for two Combat Wings of B-24s to Halbersdorf in clear skies totally uneventfully and returned at 1458.

April 9: VIII FC FO 1929-A. Twelve hundred heavies went to targeted oil and ammunition dumps and German jet airfields almost uneventfully. Fighter Command sent out over eight hundred Mustangs that only claimed one German fighter in the air, but had a field day strafing. They destroyed eighty-four aircraft on the ground and damaged an additional fifty-six.

The Wolfpack flew a free-lance mission to Regensburg behind Lt. Col. Dade in the "Doublebolt," "Catagory E," a war-weary Thunderbolt that had been converted to a two-seater. Flying to first Wurzburg, then to Nurenburg, and on to Regensburg, they looked for worthwhile targets to strafe, but could not find a thing. The 61st Fighter Squadron historian stated that the mission was so boring that it "Looked like a Gertrude Stein poem on 'nil-ism." (sic).

April 10: VIII FC FO 1936A. Thirteen hundred heavies and nine hundred fighters off to attack Luftwaffe airdromes in clear skies. If the previous day's mission had been a bore, this day's effort was an exercise into the meaning of "labor intensive." Bomber gunners claimed 17-4-14, but eighteen B-17s and one B-24 were lost. Fighter pilots claimed but 2-0-2 in the air, yet scored a phenomenal 309-2-235 while attacking the German Air Force on the ground.

Major Carter led the Wolfpack off on their highest scoring mission to date, and what would prove to be their second highest scoring date of the war. Up to optimum strength for a change, sixty-two Thunderbolts went out, with only three aborts.

On a sweep ahead of the bombers, the P-47s went to Lubeck at 1415, and seeing nothing worthwhile went on to Muritz Lake at 1435. At this point Capt. William Wilkerson took part of the 62nd Fighter Squadron down to strafe. He destroyed a twin-engine unidentified twin-engine aircraft, while his wingman, Flight Officer Clinton Albright destroyed one and damaged another. The remainder of his squadron proceeded to New Ruppen airdrome where Lt. Leo Butsie destroyed an unidentified single-engine type and an He 111. Lt. Frank Koch destroyed two unidentified type twin-engine aircraft. Lt. Robert Jones and Herschell Womack each got an He 111. Lt.'s Donald Henely and William Stevenson each got a Ju 88. Lt. Walter Sharbo got two He 111s. Lt. Dennis Carroll got a "twofer," as he destroyed an unusual Ju 88/Me 109 "Mistel" piggy-back combination.

The 63rd Fighter Squadron split themselves into two squadrons with Capt. John Fahringer leading "A" and Capt. Bostwick "B." Since they

were running fifteen minutes ahead of the bombers heading for Brandenburg, Capt. Bostwick decided to go down and strafe the airdrome at Briest, but on the way he saw Mustangs working over the airdrome at Werder, and since there was no flak, he decided to bust in on their party. Bostwick destroyed two Ju 88s and a unidentified twin-engine type, along with damaging another "u/i-t/e" aircraft. Capt. Fahringer, meanwhile, had taken his "A" squadron to Stendal where he damaged three Fw 190s.

Neither the 56th Fighter Group nor the 63rd Fighter Squadron records specify exactly where the remaining ground claims took place, Werder or Stendal, but claims were awarded to the following pilots:

2nd Lt. James Naylor one Fw 190 and one unidentified single-engine type destroyed, along with damaging a Ju 88. Capt. Walter Flagg one Me 109 destroyed and one damaged, and two Do 217s destroyed. 1st Lt. John Arnold one Fw 190. 2nd Lt. Arthur Shupe one Fw 190 destroyed and two damaged. Lt. Thomas Smith one Ju 88 destroyed and one damaged. 1st Lt. William Hoffman destroyed two unidentified twin-engine types. Lt. Vernon Smith one Ju 88 destroyed and one damaged. Lt. Boss Vest one Ju 88 destroyed and one Me 109 damaged. 2nd Lt. Emmett Barrentine two Ju 88s destroyed and one damaged, along with damaging an He 177. Newly promoted 1st Lt. Charles McBath damaged a Ju 88.

Major Carter and the 61st Fighter Squadron worked over Rechlin airdrome and Muritz Lake. The flak was light and meager and the pilots strafed at will, believing that even more German aircraft would have been destroyed if they had fuel in their tanks, as the damaged aircraft just would not burn. 1st Lt. Fred Barrett claimed 2-0-3 Ju 88s. 1st Lt. Charles Raymond 1-0-5, all twin-engine unidentified types. 2nd Lt. Edmund Ellis destroyed a Do 217, an unidentified twin, and damaged four more unidentified twins. Capt. Charles Bond destroyed a Ju 88 at Rechlin and a unidentified type flying boat at Muritz, along with damaging a Do 217, a Ju 88 and a flying boat. Capt. Bond and 1st Lt. Phillip Clinton also shared in the destruction of an unidentified type. Lt. Clinton and Lt. Burton Blodgett also put in for a claim on an unidentified flying boat, but the final claim for it was awarded to Blodgett. Lt. Russell Kyler destroyed an unidentified twin-engine type and an Me 109, along with damaging a flying boat. Lt. Longfin Winski got both an unidentified twin-engine type and an unidentified flying boat, along with damaging two more twins. 2nd Lt. Richard Higgins destroyed a single-engine unidentified type, and then radioed that he had also damaged four unidentified twin-engine types. Capt. Charles Cole damaged a pair of Ju 88s. 2nd Lt. John Jones damaged a pair of flying boats and an unidentified multi-engine type. 2nd Lt. Edward Lightfoot damaged a flying boat.

With all of the air-to-ground action over with, the Wolfpack began to reform for the trip back to Boxted. The 63rd and 61st FS's RV'd with returning bombers south of Ulzen and escorted them to Drummer Lake before leaving them to other escorts and proceeding on course.

But on the way home the 62nd FS had another encounter with German jet fighters. Lt.'s Donald Henley and Walter Sharbo got an Me 262 after a lengthy chase, with final credit being given to 1st Lt. Sharbo. Capt. William Wilkerson shot down another Me 262 after chasing it to the deck from 22,000 feet. His only accredited kill. The German pilot managed to jettison his canopy, but failed to clear the aircraft before it crashed. Lt. Eugene Andermatt, 63rd FS, also got in on this action, damaging another Me 262.

On the way home two P-47s were lost. 2nd Lt. Clarence Tingen, 62nd FS, had to make an emergency landing at an RAF base on the continent after being hit by flak. He returned to Boxted the following day. 2nd Lt. Paul Stitt, 62nd FS, reported approaching an Allied landing strip also on the continent and that he was wounded. Details are unknown, and he died the next day. Thirteen additional P-47s were damaged by flak.

The competition with the 4th Fighter Group as to which was going to be the highest scoring 8th Air Force fighter group had been neck and neck until today. After claiming forty-four aircraft destroyed in the day's efforts, the close to tie score now stood at 914 for the Wolfpack and 893 for that "Fourth but First" outfit.

April 11: VIII FC FO 1944-A. Twenty-two hundred bombers and fighters went to strike any and everything in Germany. Only one B-17 was lost in combat. One B-17 and two B-24s were stricken off as a result of mission related incidents. Not a single fighter was lost.

The Wolfpack again was split into their "A" and "B" Groups for a Ramrod. Lt. Col. Dade led "A" Group, while Capt. Bostwick led "B." Off at 1043, they were to provide penetration, target and withdrawal support for two Combat Wings of B-24s to Amberg. Escort began over Aschaffenberg at 1445, and it was noted that the bombing was quite poor, with at least three bomber squadrons missing the target area entirely. The uneventful fighter mission returned at 1637.

April 12: 1st Lt. Edward Lightfoot, 61st Fighter Squadron, was killed in a mid-air collision with a P-51 while on a training flight.

President Roosevelt died and Vice President Harry Truman was sworn-in.

April 13: VIII FC FO 1964-A. Only 212 B-17s from two Combat Wings were sent on a strategic mission to Neumunster. Four hundred fighters went out either on escort for them or to fulfill other tasks. For the Wolfpack, the slated Free Lance trip to Eggebeck, Denmark would set a new record for any tactical mission in the "air-to-mud" role.

Marking their second anniversary in combat in the ETO, fifty-one Thunderbolts took off at 1325 behind Lt. Col. Dade on the Group's 458th combat mission. Two had to abort early on, Major Carter and 2nd Lt. John Panagiote, 61st Fighter Squadron, and they missed the whole show, being replaced by two spares and Capt. Victor Bast assumed the lead of the 61st FS.

Arriving over Eggebeck at 1510 they discovered that the airdrome held between 175 and 200 German aircraft parked under camouflage green netting. Dade took the 63rd FS down to 10,000 to look things over, and then he took his White and Blue Flights down to strafe any flak positions that might be active, making a pass from south to north over the field. No guns opened up, so Dade called down the rest of the squadron. As they came down, the flak guns opened up on them, so the 63rd concentrated their attention upon silencing the guns. Unfortunately, one German gunner managed to hit the P-47 flown by Lt. William Hoffman. He pulled up to 200 feet and bailed out over the airdrome, but his parachute failed to open in time and Hoffman was killed.

Lt. Randel Murphy, 63rd FS, set a new ETO record while working over the airdrome, ten enemy aircraft destroyed and five damaged: Five He 111s, one Fw 190, one Fw 200, one He 177, and two twin-engine unidentified types. Murphy damaged an Me 110 and four unidentified types. Murphy and most of the squadron were using the newly developed T-48 .50 caliber ammunition that had a higher muzzle velocity and incendiary strength than the older rounds, and it proved to be most effective. 1st Lt. Thomas Queen, who destroyed two Me 109s, three unidentified types, and damaged four unidentified types, said: "There was very little flak. We silenced three flak positions and started shooting up planes."

Other 63rd Fighter Squadron pilots scoring were as follows:

Pilot:	Destroyed	Damaged
1st Lt. Philip Kuhn	3 Me 110s, 1 U/I	1 U/I
Lt. Col. Lucian Dade	3 Me 110s	1 Me 110
2nd Lt. Thomas Hennessy	2 Me 110s	1 Me 110
1st Lt. Charles Clark	2 Me 110s	2 Me 110s
1st Lt. Robert Bailey	2 Me 110s	2 Me 110s
1st Lt. Charles McBath	1 Ju 88	1 Ju 88
2nd Lt. Vernon Smith	2 Ju 88s, 2 He 111s	2 Ju 88s, 2 U/I
1st Lt. John Arnold	1 He 111, 1 U/I	1 U/I
1st Lt. Edgar Huff	1 He 177, 1 U/I, 1 Me 210	2 U/I
Capt. Walter Flagg	1 Ju 88, 1 Fw 190	1 Fw 190s

2nd Lt. John Keeler	1 Ju 88, 1 Me 110	1 Me 410
2nd Lt. John Barrentine	1 Me 110	2 U/I
2nd Lt. Carter Taylor	1 He 111	1 Me 109, 2 Me 110s
Capt. Samual Stebelton	1 U/I	4 U/I

After the 63rd FS had made eight or nine passes and exhausted all of their ammunition, Lt. Col. Dade called down the 62nd FS to commence strafing and left the 61st FS as top cover for the moment. As the 62nd FS was strafing, the 364th Fighter Group showed up, but they soon saw that they were not wanted and "realizing situation was well in hand removed themselves as gentlemen should."

The 62nd FS had the following claims:

1st Lt. Donald Henley	2 He 111s, 1 Ju 87	3 He 111s
FO William Carrington	1 Ju 87	1 Do 217
2nd Lt. Irving Rich	1 Me 109	2 Me 109s
1st Lt. Donald Westover	2 Do 217s, 1 Fw 190	1 Me 109
Lt. Robert Jones	1 Fw 190, 1 He 111	1 Ju 88, 3 He 111s
Capt. Philip Flemming	4 He 111s	
1st Lt. Lloyd Geren	4 He 111s	3 He 111s
1st Lt. Virgil Elliott	2 He 111s	1 Ju 88
1st Lt. Sanborn Ball	3 1/2 He 111s	1 He 111
1st Lt. Donald Gunner	1 He 111	2 He 111s
1st Lt. Sherman Pruitt	1 He 111	
Lt. Col. Donald Renwick	1/2 He 111 (Shared with Lt. Ball).	
2nd Lt. William Stevenson		4 Ju 88s
1st Lt. Ralph Beeler		1 Fw 190, 1 He 111

Capt. Victor Bast brought the 61st FS down to finish up the job. "I never saw such a show before. Planes were just sitting around asking for it, and boy, we gave it to them. I kept shooting until my ammunition was gone." The squadron made a total of ninety-four individual passes on the field and fired 22, 243 rounds of .50 caliber ammunition. Claims were made by the following pilots:

1st Lt. Russell Kyler	4 Ju 88s, 1 Me 210	
Capt. Victor Bast	3 Ju 88s	3 Ju 88s, 2 U/I
Lt. Burton Blodgett	3 Ju 88s, 1 U/I	2 Ju 88s
2nd Lt. Ernest Treff	3 Ju 88s	5 Ju 88s
1st Lt. Franklin Rader	2 He 111s	1 He 111
1st Lt. William Bartle	2 Ju 88s	1 Ju 88, 1 Me 109
2nd Lt. Longfin Winski	2 Ju 88s	1 Ju 88, 1 Me 110
1st Lt. William Smith	1 Me 110	2 U/I
1st Lt. Charles Raymond	1 U/I	5 U/I
Capt. Charles Cole	1 U/I	2 U/I
1st Lt. Richard Higgins		2 Ju 88s
1st Lt. John Allen		2 U/I
1st Lt. Robert Hoeflein	1 Me 109	2 U/I
1st Lt. David Mauldin		1 Ju 88

The Wolfpack had totaled an hour and ten minutes over the airdrome as the 61st FS pulled away to head for home. They left 90+ fires burning behind them. The smoke had climbed to a thousand feet and leveled off into a solid cloud deck. The claims amounted to 95-0-95, for the death of one pilot. Even a barn full of hay and chickens had not gone without attention. The Wolfpack now totaled between 1002 1/2 and 1007 1/2, depending upon who was keeping the score. Regardless, the magic 1000 mark had been surpassed. Not too shabby for two years work and it was dedicated as a tribute to the President that had passed away the previous day.

April 16: VIII FC FO 1997-A. Twelve hundred bombers went out to attack rail targets in Germany and also to work over an isolated pocket of

The mission to Eggebek airdrome on April 13, 1945 resulted in claims of 95-0-95 German aircraft destroyed. The 56th FG attained the 1000 destroyed mark, too. The participating pilots are shown here. (USAF)

German resistance in the area of Bordeaux, France. This pocket would remain just that until the war ended, but it was no major factor to the closing of the war. Although bomber gunners made no claims, the fighter pilots got three in the air. Against ground-bound aircraft that the Luftwaffe had pulled back into Germany they did a little better. 724-0-373 was the claim for the day's efforts. Thirty Mustangs and one Wolfpack P-47 pilot was lost.

"A" Group was led by Major Carter with thirty P-47s, while Major Williamson led "B" Group with twenty. The mission was a Ramrod to Rosenheim and escort for three Combat wings of B-24s. Off at 1251, RV was south of Ludwigshaven at 1432 at 22,000 feet. After escort was terminated over Stuttgart at 1630, "A" Group headed home to land at 1822.

Williamson took "B" Group to look over the airdromes at Landshut, Pocking, Ingolstadt and Muhldorf. Mustangs were working over Landshut and Pocking, so Capt. John Fahringer took the nine P-47s of the 63rd Fighter Squadron to Ingolstadt where Fahringer damaged a Ju 88, and 2nd Lt. Boss Vest destroyed a another Ju 88.

At Muhldorf, a Mustang Group had just finished stirring up the proverbial hornet's nest of flak guns. They "had 20mm and .30 cal. coming from virtually all over the field, but particularly heavy concentration was in southwest portion. Fire from this area hit Capt. Appel forcing him into nearby hillside where plane hit, and caught on fire." Capt. Edward Appel, 62nd FS, "augured into a hill," but managed to survive the crash. He was one of the veteran bomber pilots that had signed-on for a tour as a fighter pilot after completing his tour in the Big Friends.

2nd Lt. Clarence Tingen, 62nd FS, destroyed an He 111. The 61st FS, Led by Major Gordon Baker managed to strafe the airdrome with some success, with Baker damaging a Ju 88 and 2nd Lt. David Mauldin damaging two Me 109s and an unidentified single-engine type.

Ground fire damaged four P-47s. Major Williamson and two of his squadron mates headed for St. Trond, Belgium where Williamson landed his Thunderbolt in flames after a fuel line ruptured as a result of battle damage. The other two got down okay at St. Trond while the fourth damaged aircraft returned to Boxted.

The two German aircraft destroyed were the last claims made by the Wolfpack during World War II. This mission turned out to be their last real

opportunity to get at the Luftwaffe. The 4th Fighter Group continued their own pursuit of the chance to become the top scoring fighter group. The 4th claimed 105 German aircraft destroyed in ground strafing attacks and surpassed the 1000 destroyed mark this day.

April 17: VIII FC FO 2007-A. Rail targets in southeast Germany and Czechoslovakia were the targets for Bomber Commands one thousand heavies that were sent out. A bomber gunner claimed one German fighter, while fighter pilots claimed thirteen destroyed in the air and 286 on the ground.

Lt. Col. Dade led the Wolfpack off at 1222 on a Ramrod to Beroun, near Munich. RV with two Combat Wings of B-24s was over Domhzlice and escort provided over the target and out to Cologne. The "Doublebolt" was along on the mission to look for worthwhile targets to strafe, but nothing could be found along the mission's track and they returned at 1814 after an uneventful flight.

April 18: VIII FC FO 2017-A. Just under eight hundred heavies went to attack German rail targets. Eight hundred fighters went along.

The Wolfpack was given a Free Lance mission. Just what they needed to ensure some kills to put themselves well out in front of the 4th Fighter Group. It was not to be. Off at 1040 with Lt. Col. Renwick in the lead, the 56th Fighter Group swept Lins, Salzburg and Munich, and saw absolutely nothing and RTB'd at 1647.

April 20: VIII FC FO 2039-A. Eight hundred heavies were effective against rail targets around Berlin and in Czechoslovakia. Only one bomber was lost. Over eight hundred fighters also went out, and claimed seven German aircraft destroyed in the air.

Major Carter led "A" Group off on the Ramrod to Muhlderf off at 0914. Capt. Bostwick led "B" Group off at 0920. "A" was composed of thirty-three P-47s from the 61st and 62nd Fighter Squadrons, while "B" was made up by twenty-two from the 63rd FS, on the same mission. They RV'd with the 3rd box of B-24s south of Frankfurt, took them over the target, and out to Strausberg. After terminating escort, "A" Group returned directly to Boxted while "B" Group went to look over Horaching and

Eferding airdromes. With nothing worthwhile to be found, they too headed for home and the milkrun mission was over at 1444.

April 21: VIII FC FO 2053-A. Bomber Command sent five hundred heavies out to attack rail targets and airdromes in southeastern Germany. Only two-thirds of the force was effective, because the B-24s of the 2nd Air Division were recalled, due to solid clouds obscuring the target area of Salzburg.

For the last time the 56th Fighter Group took to the air on a combat mission over Europe. Major Williamson led "A" Group off at 0831 with thirty-nine P-47s of 62nd and 63rd Fighter Squadrons. Major Joseph Perry led the eighteen Jugs that composed "B" Group from the 61st FS. Intended as a Ramrod for the B-24s, the Liberators were recalled while half way to their targets, so the two Group's swept a line from Linz to Laudshut and on to Inglestadt under a solid overcast. No German aircraft were to be found, and orders prohibiting ground strafing had come down from higher headquarters, so there was nothing to do but to return to Boxted. The last 56th Fighter Group P-47 landed from their last combat mission at 1435.

Although the 4th Fighter Group would fly one more mission after this date, they would do so without making any claims. At the termination of the war the initial box scores for the two groups would be 1003 for the 4th FG and 1,008 1/2 for the 56th FG. Pending claims and the reports from POW's would have to wait until the cessation of hostilities and the return of the prisoners. This obviously, would take some time, and history and conjecture on the "what ifs" still cast some doubt on exactly which was the highest scoring fighter group in the Air Force. For a period the 4th FG had been credited with 1,058 1/2, which was later reduced to 1,016. The Wolfpack wound up with credit for 1,006 1/2.

As a point of conjecture, however, is the way that the 9th Air Force handled their own claims. The 8th Air Force did continue processing claims after the war ended by interrogating returnees. The 9th AF terminated pro-

cessing theirs when the war ended. In addition, many of the records of the 9th AF were lost as their units moved so rapidly from one location to another within Europe, and through other factors.

There is some belief that a few 9th AF units may have out scored either the 4th or 56th FG's in air-to-air combat. The "Pioneer Mustang Group," the 354th FG, for example. The 354th claimed 701 enemy aircraft destroyed in the air, to the Wolfpack's 677 and the 4th FG's 539. (Which then placed the 4th FG in fourth position behind the 357th FG at 575). One will never know for sure exactly which was the top scoring outfit.

April 25: The last combat mission was flown by both 8th Air Force Fighter and Bomber Commands on this date. 589 heavies and 584 P-51s participated. The fighters claimed 1-1-0. Bomber Command would continue missions over Europe, however, until May 7, dropping surrender information leaflets and supplies to those on the ground.

May 1: 1st Lt. Albin Zychowski, 61st Fighter Squadron, was killed on a training mission. "He had been a part of a four-ship flight that was attempting a formation peel off break." The loss was considered to be a buzzing incident when his P-47 mushed into the ground near Tiverton, Devonshire. He had flown thirty-two combat missions.

May 2: Lt. Walter Hard, 61st Fighter Squadron, had to make a dead-stick landing at Bradwell Bay. Hard was on his first flight in England when the engine quit and he had to belly his P-47 in. The RAF did not appreciate him tearing up their runway.

May 3: Major James Carter, 61st Fighter Squadron Commanding Officer was transferred to Headquarters 56th Fighter Group, being designated the group and station operations officer. He was replaced by Major Gordon Baker as squadron commander.

Lt. Paul Dawson's P-47 painted up to commemorate Col. Zemke's contribution to the 56th FG. It was placed on display near the Eiffel Tower in Paris, and then scrapped. (USAF)

Lt. Colonel Lucian Dade, the last wartime commander of the Wolfpack.

May 8: It was official! The war in Europe was over. V-E Day had arrived. Actually, "the Word" had come down the previous day and all men, although confined to Boxted, were given May 7 and 8 off. Two Chaplains led the Group in prayer, and Lt. Col. Dade read congratulatory speeches from the "Head Shed" and one of his own. There was all the free beer that anyone could want, dispensed from the enlisted man's "Little Wheels" club.

May 10: With the war for the 56th Fighter Group over, the anticipated rumors concerning what was going to happen to the troops became reality. Physical training, inspections, and the other pain-in-the-ass things of that nature that go along with garrison duty began to manifest themselves. The men groused, but they had to be kept busy. Liberty passes were given as freely as possible. Many of the men took the opportunity to take part in Operation Trolley, where they were flown over Europe in B-17s and other aircraft to see just where their fighter pilots had been.

Headquarters sent down the requirements for rotation home, based upon a point system, with points being given for time overseas. Before the month ended, many of the 56th Fighter Group's original cadre were on their way home. They were transferred to Bomber Groups being returned to the United States, and were in turn replaced by enlisted men transferred in from those groups who lacked sufficient points for rotation.

This point system was a confusing situation for many, as those who had been overseas for "the duration," or had received awards, had dependents, etc. got to go home. The critical cut-off point number being 85. Those with less than this number were transferred into Occupation Forces, while those with few points packed their gear and prepared for a move half way around the world and assignment to units fighting Japan. The 56th Fighter Group was alerted for a move to Gablingen airdrome, near Augsburg, Germany for duty with the Occupation Forces.

May 22: 1st Lt. Franklyn Rader, 61st Fighter Squadron, was killed. Rader had previously been on detached service to the RAF at Catfoss since December 21, 1944 where he was serving as a gunnery officer. While flying a Typhoon, Rader got too low and mushed into the ground near Greatham Farm.

During the month the 56th Fighter Group got in the last batch of the new P-47Ms, now possessing virtually all that were built. With the point system having gone into effect, they gained everybody imaginable as replacement troops from ex dog trainers to motor boat drivers, and had to train these new people from scratch on how the care and feeding of a complex Thunderbolt was done. Every P-47 required an engine change. The poor discovered workmanship at Pratt & Whitney was creating a massive workload and problems for the inexperienced people to contend with. Everything from loose bolts to leaking gaskets was found wrong with the aircraft. They finally settled for disconnecting the water injection and limiting manifold pressure to 56" hg. to make them serviceable. It was no longer needed, anyhow.

Among the good news for the month was the return of many faces that were either known to be POW's or feared lost for good. Most knew that Col. Zemke, Lt. Col. Gabreski and Major Gerald Johnson had been POWs, but many of the lower graded officers status had been an unknown. Among those dropping in for a visit to the 62nd Fighter Squadron before returning to the States were Capt. Quirk, Lt. Reeder, Capt Morrill, Lt.'s Goldstein and Edens. 1st Lt. Hiram Bevins returned to the 61st FS and put in a claim for a Ju 88 destroyed Sept. 3, 1943 before he was shot down near Versailles. Unfortunately, there was no gun camera film, nor any witnesses still around to verify his claim, and after having a year and a half to think about it, the claim was rejected.

June 1945: There were no changes in command within the 56th Fighter Group during June. Lt. Col. Dade remained as Group Commander, while

Major's Baker, Williamson and Bostwick retained command of their respective 61st, 62nd and 63rd Fighter Squadrons.

The anniversary of D-Day was given the official status of a holiday, and everyone got the day off. The other big news was that the 56th Fighter group received their second Distinguished Unit Citation, for action on September 18, 1944 in support of the airborne invasion of Holland. The Wolfpack was the only 8th Air Force fighter unit to receive two such awards.

Operationally, the 56th FG was relieved from assignment to the 2nd Air Division (B-24s), and assigned to the 3rd Air Division (B-17s). This, obviously, mattered little to the troops. As of July 1, the Group carried 209 officers and 1054 enlisted men on their rosters. As the month closed, these numbers were reduced to 138 officers and 992 enlisted men. There was no change in the command structure, although many of the high-time combat pilots were transferred to the 70th Reinforcement Depot on July 18 for return to the Zone of Interior and possible movement to the Pacific Theater of Operations. An en masse transfer of the 450th Air Service Group, a part of the original cadre transferred to England in 1943, took place in July when these people rotated home to the United States.

One of the "neat" things the Group now had to play with was an Fw 190 that Major Williamson brought back from Germany. As the 61st Fighter Squadron already had an He 111, painted HV✪COW, the 62nd FS painted the Focke-Wulf up in their markings.

August 1945: Lt. Col. Lucian Dade was finally relieved of command of the Wolfpack and transferred to a staff position in Paris, France. He was replaced by Lt. Col. Donald Renwick. Major James Carter was Deputy Group Commander.

Army Air Forces Day was celebrated on August 1. Thirty-six P-47s were flown by the Wolfpack over France, Belgium, Germany and England "to show the flag." An open house was held at Boxted and the gates were open wide for the civilians to see where all the racket had come from and just how much work was involved in getting a fighter group off on a "show."

August 14: V-J Day and a holiday was celebrated once again, but this time none were restricted to Boxted. The war, with all its trials was over. No longer was there a threat of possible transfer of either the Group or individuals to the Pacific. Although few from the original Group still remained in England, those still there were eager enough to be ready to pack up and go home.

August 31: Lt. Charles Raymond, 61st Fighter Squadron, had a landing accident at Bury St. Edmunds. This was the last reported incident with a Wolfpack Thunderbolt in England.

September-October 1945. The men got their wish, orders were received to pack up their belongings and prepare to turn Boxted over to the RAF. First the RAF based a night-fighter Mosquito squadron there, and then 234 Squadron, flying Meteors. Boxted was shut down as a military base in August 1947, and today is an apple tree farm.

The P-47Ms had been pulled up close to the hangers for ease of maintenance and security, and then flown to Speke for inglorious scrapping. (Only one P-47M exists today, and it never served with a combat unit). The base then went into caretaker status.

On September 19 Lt. Col. Wilbur Watson, Headquarters 56th Fighter Group, several other officers and one fifth of the Group's enlisted men sailed for home on the maiden voyage of the *Europa* as a troopship.

On October 18, 1945 at 2359 hours the 56th Fighter Group and its associated squadrons and units were inactivated.

CHAPTER 3

POST-WORLD WAR II YEARS

May 1, 1946: The Strategic Air Command announced that the 56th Fighter Group would be reactivated at Selfridge Field, Mt. Clemens, Michigan. Named as the Commanding Officer of the Group was Colonel David C. Schilling. Selected as Deputy Commander was Lt. Col. William Banks, who became an ace with the 342nd Fighter Squadron and added four more confirmed kills while flying with the 348th Fighter Group in the South Pacific Theater. Both of these commanders were desirous of obtaining as many men from their original commands as possible. Thusly they intended upon forming an elite cadre of combat experienced personnel composed of people they knew of firsthand.

Col. Schilling had been given the choice of where he wanted to locate his new Group, and it was he who selected Selfridge Field. Schilling, being a Michigan native, made a choice that was not surprising. An advantage of Selfridge was that the base was geographically centrally located. Another advantage was that it was one of the oldest Air Force installations and was constructed with first rate buildings and hangers. The drawbacks were the known winter weather conditions for flying and the summer tourists. The tourist season always brought an increase in rent for off base dependent housing that was beyond what the average GI could pay to house their families. It took some arm-twisting on the part of the Air Force to partially resolve this problem.

The "new" 56th FG started with five officers and one enlisted man. By the end of the month the newly reformed fighter group had 116 officers and 305 enlisted men.

Initially, as the 56th Fighter Group was in the process of expansion, they were co-dependent upon the 146th Air Base Unit, BASUT, the tenant

unit at Selfridge for all administrative and logistical purposes. Also, during the months of May and June, the Group had no aircraft of their own and had to utilize those aircraft assigned to the BASUT for operational and pilot proficiency. The Group's maintenance section, under Major Francis Baker, an ex-Wolfpack Headquarters maintenance officer, handled all related aircraft maintenance functions for the Group, as none of the newly forming squadrons had a maintenance section of their own.

Selected as the first squadron Commanding Officers were: Major Donavan Smith, who regained his old 61st Fighter Squadron, Major Paul Conger, 62nd FS, and Major George Orr, 63rd FS. Smith and Conger being aces from the old Wolfpack, while Orr had four confirmed kills as a pilot with the 342nd FS. The new 56th FG Operations Officer was Lt. Col. William Dunham, a pilot with sixteen kills with the 342nd and 460th FS's. An impressive line-up for a fledgling unit. Also on the initial 56th FG roster were ten other veteran Wolfpack pilots. Yet, at this time none of the original enlisted men had made their way back to their old unit.

During July the 56th Fighter Group flew 1,188 hours in aircraft borrowed from the BASUT. Little of this flying time, however, was devoted to combat training. The majority of it was for proficiency flying, while the remainder was flown in conjunction with Army Air Force recruiting drives at airshows around the midwest. For these airshows, an unnamed acrobatic team was formed by Captain's James M. Jones, Howard Askelson and Clarence D. Christian. (Jones had three kills with the 62nd FS, Askelson had two with the 82nd FS). Shows were flown at Des Moines, Iowa; Milwaukee, Wisconsin; Saginaw, Michigan and Omaha, Nebraska using borrowed P-47s that were olive drab in color and featured the pre-World War

P-47N of the 146th BASUT/56th Fighter Group. The markings indicate that it was one of the Thunderbolts flown by the improvised aerobatic team. It bears a red vertical stabilizer with white and red horizontal stripes, and a blue vertical stripe. The aircraft serial number is yellow. (via Esposito)

Before the era of the Thunderbolt had ended, the Wolfpack had flown all of the major versions of the Jug. This one was a P-47N-5RE that actually belonged to the 146th BASUT at Selfridge Field, Michigan. (via Esposito)

II style red, white and blue tail stripes. The only major administrative change that took place during the month was the replacement Major Conger as Commanding Officer of the 62nd Fighter Squadron by another, higher ranking, ex Wolfpack pilot when Lt. Col. Gerald Johnson rejoined the Group. Also rejoining this month was Major George Bostwick, who became the Operations Officer of the 61st FS.

It should also be noted that one Colonel and three Lt. Colonels were graciously promoted by the Air Force to the rank of 1st Lieutenant during July. Schilling, Dunham, Banks and David McKnight. Twelve other officers were also promoted likewise, receiving permanent commissions in the Regular Army in lieu of Reserve commissions.

In August, the 56th Fighter Group flew 1137 hours with aircraft still borrowed from the BASUT. Major George Bostwick became the first officer to be transferred out of the Group when he was assigned to the Army Air Forces Institute of Technology at Wright Field, Ohio. He was replaced as Operations Officer, 61st Fighter Squadron, by Major George Perry. Perry having previously served as a Captain with the old 61st FS, where he had two kills. Major George Wilkerson, another of the "old heads," rejoined the Group in August, becoming assigned to the 62nd FS as their acting Operations Officer. A position he was rather familiar with, having served in this role in this squadron during the later months of the war.

The first Post War operational loss of a 56th FG pilot occurred during August when the borrowed P-51 flown by Lt. Sevarino Calderon crashed during an airshow at Bedford, Massachusetts. Calderon had been an experienced World War II combat pilot, having flown a tour out of England, where he earned the Distinguished Flying Cross. His P-51 was seen to roll out of control and crash into a wooded area and Calderon was killed.

Additional airshows were flown at Burlington, Iowa; Milwaukee, Wisconsin (again); Ionia and Selfridge Field, Michigan; Duluth, Minnesota; New Haven, Connecticut and Cleveland, Ohio, where the acrobatic team flew for the 1946 Cleveland Air Races. These shows were flown with between eight and twelve aircraft. The highlight, a crowd pleaser, was in that the .50 caliber machine guns were armed with blank ammunition that provided realistic sounds during the course of mock combat and air-to-ground strafing.

The 56th Fighter Group received its first inspection by the Air Inspector on August 27. Although not yet possessing any aircraft of their own, all units received a "Superior" rating for their present status.

During September, pilots were flown from Selfridge to Spokane Field, Washington in relays in a C-47 to begin picking up P-51H Mustangs from the depot where they had undergone winterization modifications after delivery from North American Aviation.

The Group maintenance sections, under Major Lawrence Pickett, had their hands full, as none of the previous 56th Fighter Group ground crews that his just rejoined their old unit, and few of the others had any experience with inline engines and radiator type cooling systems. Nevertheless, squadron maintenance sections were established and everyone looked forward to the arrival of their own aircraft.

Coinciding with the arrival of the "winterized" Mustangs came a Warning Order from Headquarters 15th Air Force, the parent unit for the Wolfpack. The original notice was to prepare for "an Arctic Experiment." Operation Arctic Calm. This experiment was to determine "the suitability of maintaining operational equipment in arctic regions." With the advent of the truly long-range strategic bomber in the form of the B-29 and the forthcomming B-36 Very Long Range bomber, it was recognized that geographical boundaries no longer existed. "The arctic was recognized as being the open gateway to any and all the great or potentially great nations of the world by air."

With the arrival of the first Mustangs, the 62nd Fighter Squadron was designated to be the first unit to participate in the Arctic Experiment, and they received priority in training and receiving the supplies they would need for a movement to the colder climate. One of the first changes to take place within the Group with the arrival of their own aircraft was to re-establish the "crew chief" maintenance system.

A pair of different "aces." Col. Francis Gabreski discusses the merits of the new P-51H Mustang with North American Aviation's premier test pilot, Bob Chilton. (USAF)

This method had been the standard system during World War II, but in the immediate Post War years, the system had been basically done away with. A lack of experienced personnel was one reason, another was the feeling by some elements within the Air Forces that a centralized maintenance system was more efficient and cost effective. The argument has continued for the decades since, and the program continues to wave back and forth.

There never has been any doubt in a pilots' or crew chiefs' mind that the crew chief system is far superior to any other. A crew chief "own's" the airplane and it is his name that goes upon its fuselage, and it is his name that goes on the dotted line certifying that the aircraft is safe and ready for flight.

It mattered little whether the aircraft was assigned to a pool for 2nd Lieutenants to fly or if it was the personal aircraft of a Lieutenant General, as the pilot was only permitted to "borrow" it for a period, and maybe add his name to its fuselage, if he had enough clout with the crew chief to begin with. This rapport is legendary.

The Wolfpack reached Technical Order and Equipment, TO&E, strength in October with a compliment of seventy-five P-51Hs. On October 24 Lt. Col. Banks and Captain Billy Edens, from the 62nd Fighter Squadron, departed for Ladd Field, Fairbanks, Alaska to make the final preparations for the arrival of the 62nd FS. The initial plans being to rotate the three squadrons through Ladd at two month intervals, with the 62nd FS going first.

Although the 412th Fighter Group had been the first P-51H unit, they only flew these Mustangs to a limited degree until they could re-equip with the new P-80As and became America's first jet unit. Thus the 56th Fighter Group was the first to become combat operational with this version of the Mustang. Already a year old when they got them, maintenance personnel discovered that there were many problems to be debugged and ironed out that should have been taken care of long before. As the Mustang production line had been shut down in November 1945, so was the pipeline of spare parts. Already there was a shortage of spares, and many of those available turned out to be faulty. More critically, it was discovered that the tail wheels were prone to collapse upon landing. This was found to be the caused by the improper installation of the restricters in the retracting mechanism. Whether they had been put in backwards at the factory or while the aircraft were undergoing the winterization modifications was unknown. Installing them properly cured the problem.

Since the purpose of the 56th Fighter Group was that of a Very Long-Range escort unit, the first escort mission was flown on October 13. General Carl Spaatz, the Air Forces' Chief of Staff, was due to speak in Milwaukee, so the Group RV'd with his personal B-17 over Selfridge Field and provided an escort for the Flying Fortress to the eastern shore of Lake Michigan. Escort was broken at this point, and while the B-17 flew across the Lake, the Mustangs flew the shoreline around to re-rendezvous with Spaatz's aircraft again near Milwaukee.

During the course of this mission Capt. Jack Wildberger, 63rd Fighter Squadron, had a propeller failure while approaching Milwaukee. The propeller went into a full high pitch, and Wildberger was seriously injured when he tried to make a forced landing with his Mustang. His back was broken and he lost an eye. A pressure screen in the propeller governor had ruptured and jammed the blades into an uncontrollable position. This resulted in all of the P-51H Mustangs being grounded until the screens could be modified.

Although the Wolfpack had flown several airshows during the summer as a part of the Army Air Force recruiting drive, one of the major non sequiturs of military life occurred in November. A "forced discharge of a number of officer personnel" took place. This act against a reforming unit resulted in the reduction of the 61st and 63rd Fighter Squadrons to "all but essential personnel," as the men were either lost to the Air Force or transferred to the 62nd FS to maintain its operational strength for the movement to Alaska.

Resultant to the grounding of the P-51H, flying time for the month of November was the minimum required by regulations. Each pilot got in his four hours for proficiency and flying pay in aircraft borrowed from the 146th BASUT. Capt. Frank Klibbe, Engineering Officer, 61st FS (Who had scored seven kills with the 61st FS during World War II.), was the Group technician that was working with Wright Field, Ohio to resolve the Mustang problems. Resolving the propeller problems was a major time consuming challenge that remained on-going. The problem with the tail wheels was slowly being rectified as the restricters were reversed in each aircraft, although not all could be changed before the Alaskan mission.

On November 20 the enlisted men and ground officers of the 62nd Fighter Squadron departed Selfridge Field for Ft. Lawton, Washington by train as the first part of the movement to Alaska. The air echelon remained scheduled for December, pending the release of the fighters for flight.

The policy of removing deemed surplus officers from the Air Force continued in December. Ninety officers at Selfridge Field, but not those assigned to the 56th Fighter Group, were effected by this program. Many of them were released from the service, while others were transferred from the base, and some were reassigned to the Wolfpack. Those joining the 56th Fighter Group were assigned to the 61st and 63rd Fighter Squadrons' to replace those previously transferred to the 62nd FS. Also, fifteen pilots from the 503rd Service Group were attached to the 56th FG for flying proficiency.

The grounding of the P-51H was lifted in mid-December and the flying schedule was packed with pilots trying to make up for time lost during the previous six weeks. In addition, many of the newly assigned pilots had to be checked out in the Mustang and, after a minimum of ten hours, permitted to start night flying. As many of these pilots were administrative "desk weenies" their flying proficiency was lacking and they required additional flying hours. This placed a heavy workload upon the ground crews, and a regular flying schedule had to be maintained during the Christmas holiday season in spite of an anticipated liberal leave policy that did not get to occur.

Arctic Cope, aka. Operation Deep Freeze, got off at 0930 on December 18. Twenty-eight P-51Hs and three B-29s were scheduled. One B-29 flew twenty minutes ahead of the fighters to ascertain weather conditions, another flew with them to verify navigation, while the third Superfortress was delayed because they could not get an engine started.

Fifteen minutes after takeoff the engine of 1st Lt. Charles Smoke's Mustang failed and he crash landed near Battle Creek, Michigan. It was a narrow escape type incident, as the weather at Battle Creek was down to a 500 foot ceiling with a visibility of only a mile and a half and Smoke

barely had time to break out of the clouds and select a field to land in before he ran out of altitude. Thirty minutes after takeoff Capt. Ray Dauphin had to abort the mission with an extremely high coolant temperature. He got back to Selfridge okay.

After passing Battle Creek the rest of the mission found clear skies that continued to their first refueling stop at Rapid City, South Dakota. Eighteen Mustangs then departed Rapid City on December 19, but had to turn back and land again after a short flight due to a previously unreported weather front that lay across their path. Many of these pilots reported extremely rough running engines while on this short flight, and as Lt. Col. Gerald Johnson and another pilot had a similar problem while preceding the mission into Great Falls, everyone stood-down until the causes could be identified. Lt. Smoke and Capt. Dauphin caught up with the rest of the 62nd FS at this point with spare aircraft.

The problem with the rough running engines was found to be caused by the engines running too cold. This caused the fuel to "fractionate" and create lead deposits that fouled the spark plugs. To bring the engines to a better operating temperature "gates" were installed behind the radiators in the coolant "doghouse" to restrict the airflow within the belly airscoop. They also fastened plates over the "cheese-hole" alternate carburetor intakes on the sides of the fighters noses, to keep cold air out of the engine nacelle.

At 1330 on December 21 twenty-seven Mustangs departed for Great Falls, Montana. One having to remain behind with a cracked coolant pump.

On December 23 the wayward P-51 arrived at Great Falls. All Mustangs were serviced and checked over. Preparations were made for a departure on December 24, and at 0820 the lead B-29 weather escort departed. The fighters followed, with the first off at 0855. The last B-29 landed after the fighters arrived at 1123 hours at Edmonton, Alberta. The Canadian air station was staffed by civilians who were "non-existent on the 25th and 26th due to the holidays." Thus the pilots and supporting ground company who had arrived on a C-47 had to keep their own company over Christmas.

Departure was scheduled for 0830 on the morning of December 27 on the next leg of the mission, to White Horse. It was a SNAFU affair. The fighters had been hangered because of the cold and a snow storm, yet of the two scheduled tug drivers, only one showed up, and he arrived late. As the Mustangs were pulled from the hangers and started, and while awaiting the others doing likewise, the plugs fouled on those first started.

This caused ten aborts and these aircraft all required a change of spark plugs before they could rejoin the effort. The first fighter departed at 0927, an hour behind schedule, and arrived at White Horse at 1408. As the airfield had only a single runway and no taxiway, each aircraft had to land singly and then taxi back the length of the runway before turning off. This delayed the landings considerably.

The first B-29 cleared White Horse at 0830 and the first P-51 at 0925 on the final leg to Ladd Field. The last P-51 landed at 1057. The contingent that had to be left behind at Edmonton departed at 0915 on December 29, but due to weather encountered enroute, had to land at Ft. St. John, Alberta instead of Ft. Nelson. After many further problems either with the weather or with the aircraft, they finally all were at Ladd Field by January 22, 1947.

The 65th Fighter Wing was reactivated at Selfridge Field in January 1947. Among the experienced Wolfpack pilots lost through transfer to the new wing was Major Ralph A. Johnson, who had three kills with the original 62nd Fighter Squadron and was presently serving as the Group Adjutant. With this activation another non sequitur of military life occurred. As a part of the reduction in force policy, the enlisted men in the lower four grades were informed that they could be discharged if they so desired. Of the forty-four eligible that had just flown to Alaska with the 62nd Fighter Squadron, thirty jumped at the chance and were flown back for discharge.

Operationally, flying at Selfridge was markedly reduced during the month, due either to prevailing winter weather conditions or packed ice and snow on the runways and taxiways. However, many of the Group pi-

A pair of P-51H-5NA's of the 56th Fighter Group on January 22, 1947. This was prior to the addition of the numbers on the vertical fins. (USAF)

The same formation in echelon right. The occasion was to provide an escort for Michigan Governor Kim Sigler on a visit to Selfridge Field. Note that the tail wheels were still all locked down at this time. (USAF)

lots were detailed in the meantime to ferry Mustangs and Thunderbolts from depots to various Air National Guard and Reserve units that were in the process of being formed and were receiving their first aircraft.

Col. Schilling, always looking for something new to do, and just having returned from accompanying the 62nd FS to Ladd Field, came up with another new idea. The P-51H featured a navigational instrument identified as an AN/ARA 8 Airborne Homing Adapter. Developed for use in the expanse of the Pacific Ocean, the ARA 8 worked like a Direction Finding system, only in reverse. A pilot requiring a DF navigational heading would transmit a radio tone for a steer from the ground station and the ground radio operator's equipment provided the pilot the direction to fly. With the ARA 8, the ground station would key the transmission, and the pilot's instrument would provide the proper navigational heading. It did not have

the problems with reciprocal headings being inadvertently issued by the ground controller that the DF stations did, and as it operated on VHF frequencies, it was not as prone to atmospheric interference as the standard Low frequency Automatic Direction Finding navigational equipment.

To Develop this program, Col. Schilling, Majors Orr and Smith, and two Captains flew to Smokey Hill Field, Kansas (Later renamed Schilling Air Force Base) to plot out how best to use the equipment. A mission was flown to San Antonio, Texas and then another fifteen hundred mile non stop flight from San Antonio to Selfridge with a B-29 making a radio transmissions and the fighters homing upon it enroute. It would have been a wonderful thing to have had over Europe, as then the fighters would have never had to worry about not being able to find their proper bombers to escort.

44-64315 was one of the P-51Hs assigned to the Wolfpack's aerobatic team. Lt. Severino Caldron was killed in this aircraft at Bedford, Massachusetts on May 8, 1947 while preforming in an airshow. (Robert O'Dell)

44-64319 was another P-51H assigned to the aerobatic team. It bore a yellow vertical stabilizer with red, white and blue tail stripes. Note the repeat of the "buzz number" under the port wing. (via Ralph Brown)

"Jet" was the word. It was announced during February that the 56th Fighter Group would soon be receiving the new P-80 Shooting Star. In the meantime, all restrictions upon the P-51H had been lifted and all aircraft were given 90 day/100 hour inspections. The 61st and 63rd Fighter Squadrons got in 900 hours flying time in their Mustangs in all required forms of flight, with emphasis on navigation and night flying, as their commitment remained as Very Long Range fighter escort for now.

There were two P-51H accidents at Selfridge involving snow and ice. Two additional accidents occurred at Ogden, Utah on February 6 and 9 with one of them also related to snow. Both of these latter accidents involving P-47Ns being ferried to the Air National Guard.

Lt. Col. Gerald Johnson reported back to Col. Schilling with some of his observations on flying in Alaska. As expected, the cold temperatures encountered had the most impact upon everything. There was at least twenty-three consecutive days where it was never warmer than -30 F. The average time between sunrise and sunset was six hours. (It had to be -20 F. or warmer in order to fly, as cockpit heat was inadequate and airframe coldsoak congealed oil, fuel and hydraulic fluid to much for the pumps and systems to operate properly if it was any colder). In spite of the obstacles, they did manage to fly over nine hundred hours in the later part of February when the average temperature was a balmy -15 F.

The Air Force just could not make up its mind who they needed and where. The rival 4th Fighter Group had been reactivated in September 1946, and somehow they still seemed to get their licks in on the Wolfpack. During March 1947 thirty-six experienced and desperately needed flightline men were lost from Selfridge to the 4th FG via transfers.

As Col. Schilling and Captain's Askelson and Scariano had just returned from Williams Field, Arizona where they had been checked out on the P-80, anticipation was high that the Mustangs would soon be replaced by the flying "blow-torches." The problem was that no one else within the Group had any experience with jet fighters at all. To solve this difficulty a Mobile Training Unit arrived from Chanute Field, Illinois to commence training everyone that would be effected by the change of mission aircraft.

The first of the P-80As arrived on March 8, and as the month ended they were a reality as twenty-three graced their flightline. Seventeen pilots were checked out and became rated as jet pilots. Fifty-five Mustangs remained at Selfridge, and twenty-seven additional were in Alaska with the 62nd FS. The Wolfpack still was carrying four P-47s, too, those that re-

mained under their care from the BASUT. But these conventional aircraft were all being given inspections prior to their transfer to other units.

Two Mustangs were lost, and one pilot, during the month of March. On March 2 Capt. Charles Riffle was killed west of Dayton, Ohio when his P-51H crashed in virtually zero-zero weather. A mechanical problem may have occurred that forced him down, or it may have been spacial disorientation. Riffle had previously been a member of the 494th Fighter Squadron and had .5 kill credited. Also, 2nd Lt. Anderson Atkinson made a forced landing near Thompson Station, Tennessee while also flying in adverse weather conditions. He was uninjured while belly landing in a corn field, but his Mustang was destroyed.

In the early part of April twenty-three Mustangs were flown to Kelly Field, Texas for storage. The ferry mission was led by Major Orr and pilots from the 63rd Fighter Squadron. By the end of the month the 56th Fighter Group was down to eighteen Mustangs, but now had seventy-one P-80s on hand. As this was more than the number of pilots available to fly them, and far exceeded the available maintenance crews, many of the new jets had to be "pickled" for a thirty day period, and then unpickled in time to meet applicable regulations. Due to a shortage of spare parts, several of these aircraft were also cannibalized while they were pickled. Mostly for their tires, fuel and hydraulic pumps, as the supply system could not keep up with the demand for spare parts.

On April 12 Lt. Col. Gerald Johnson returned with the 62nd Fighter Squadron, landing at 1700 with twenty-four P-51s. The ground echelon returned between April 22 and 24 after a combination of transportation, air, boat, and 65th Fighter Wing C-47s on their last leg from Seattle, Washington.

While at Ladd Field three Mustangs had been lost. One flown by Capt. Russell Westfall got literally thrown into the ground by the propwash from his element leader while landing. The other two were stricken-off as a result of a taxi accident. A snow plow operating upwind of the taxiway threw snow into their path that created a "white out" condition that blinded the pilots as they were running-up their engines and preparing to take the runway for takeoff.

The 62nd Fighter Squadron, upon its return, received further orders to fly an airshow at Manchester, New Hampshire on April 17 and then to land at Grenier Field. At this time these squadron personnel would be utilized as cadre to form the activating 82nd Fighter Group. This new group

A Mustang of the 62nd Fighter Squadron overflies the Crazy Horse Mountains of Alaska while the squadron was TDY to Ladd Field. The pilot is believed to be Lt. James Jones. (USAF)

would also be assigned to the Strategic Air Command as a Very Long Range fighter escort unit and would soon replace the 56th Fighter Group in this role. The first Commanding Officer of the 82nd FG, from reactivation on April 12, was Major Leland Raphun, but he was succeeded by Lt. Col. Gerald Johnson on June 2 when the 82nd became operational.

For two weeks the old 62nd Fighter Squadron existed only on paper, but on May 3 the first new officer personnel were assigned and by May 15 operational organization was completed. This move again required transfers of many of the men with in the Group: Lt. Col. John Goff was placed as Commanding Officer of the 61st Fighter Squadron while Major Donavan Smith became Operations Officer. Lt. Col. William Dunham was selected as the new Squadron Commander of the 62nd FS with Major Samuel Blair as Operations Officer. Dunham had sixteen kills in the Southwest Pacific

Theater while flying with the 348th Fighter Group, and Blair had destroyed seven Japanese aircraft while flying with the same group. Capt. Gardner Engel was the new Adjutant, and he had one kill with the 359th FS. Capt. Ray Dauphin was "A" Flight Leader. Thus the new squadron was equally balanced with the others with experienced combat pilots. The 63rd FS Squadron Commander, Major Orr, became their Operations Officer when a higher ranking officer came on board. Lt. Col. John Loisel was assigned the commander's position. Loisel had ten kills while flying with the 432nd Fighter Squadron, and got his eleventh while leading the 475th Fighter Group.

Also on May 15, the 61st Fighter Squadron moved to Oscoda Field, Michigan to commence a six week TDY assignment for gunnery training. This program would soon be expanded to include the other two squadrons

February 1947 was a hard month for Mustangs. This example was totaled when Capt. Lincivome undershot his approach during a night landing at Selfridge on the 21st. (USAF)

Lt. Cameron, 61st Fighter Squadron, hit a snowbank while landing on February 12, 1947. The cause was laid upon his inability to feel the amount of pressure he was applying to the rudder pedals, because of the heavy winter-wear flying boots he was wearing. (USAF)

The Wolfpack enters the jet era. The markings are factory fresh, before the application of the Group's designs. April 1947. (Esposito)

on rotational duty. At Oscoda there were facilities already constructed for both air-to-ground and air-to-air gunnery training for the new jets without having to contend with the aerial congestion found in the Detroit area that would have interfered with flying to and from the gunnery ranges for training.

By the end of May the Wolfpack was operational as a jet fighter unit. They had eighty-two F-80s, while holding on to fifteen Mustangs for use as hacks and proficiency training for those pilots not yet jet qualified. Although the supply problem for P-80 spare parts had not been cleared up, few operational problems were occurring. The most hazardous being the wing tiptanks. The low slung tanks did not clear the runway and taxiway light stanchions, so these all had to be lowered. Additional problems were that the tip tanks, made by the Weber Showcase Company, often did not feed properly. This would result in an off-balance fuel load that required the dropping of the expensive external tanks before the aircraft could be safely landed.

July 1947. Established on July 28 was the 56th Fighter Wing. The new Wing then became effectively organized on August 15 and was Head-

Colonel Schilling greets the delivery pilots of the first P-80As to Selfridge Field. Left to right, Schilling, Capt. Rudd, Lt. McKeever and Capt. Hunt. These were the first jet qualified pilots in the 56th Fighter Group. (USAF)

quartered at Selfridge Field. Its initial Commanding Officer was Colonel William Hudnell. Hudnell having previously been assigned to Headquarters Far East Air Force, and he had one accredited kill. The new "created" 56th Fighter Wing had no lineage of its own and was not entitled to any of the honors or to claim any of the history earned by the 56th Fighter Group. However, the new wing was permitted to use the insignia of the 56th Fighter Group. With one revision. The Group's motto "Beware of the Thunderbolt" was revised to "Ready and Waiting." for the Wing's use and was painted upon the right side of the nose of all the Group's P-80s. (The Beware of the Thunderbolt motto was later accepted as the Wing's own in April 1967).

This newly created Wing was an basically an administrative affair that controlled the operation of Selfridge Field. It originated under an experimental program, Wing-Base, where a combat wing was designated to replace the old BASUT in designation and in instances where the air field was dedicated to a specific role; ie, the home of a fighter-escort combat group. It would not be until the Korean War until Wing level personnel would have any true value to a combat unit, and then only in those units directly involved with fighting the "Forgotten War."

On September 18, 1947 the United States Air Force became an independent branch of military service. All air "Field's" were now designated as "Air Force Bases."

There is a massive, almost year-long gap in the history of the 56th Fighter Group between the fall of 1947 and the summer of 1948. Apparently all official records during this period were lost, but all unofficial contacts with the author have reported that nothing of significance occurred. Still, it is a shame that this sort of a thing was permitted to take place.

On June 11, 1948 the designation of aircraft were revised in many cases. Notably "P," as in Pursuit became "F," as in Fighter and the P-80 was now the F-80, a change that more accurately reflected its role.

On July 12 1948 Col. Schilling started the historical first Fox Able mission. This was a good will tour of Europe by pilots of the 56th Fighter Group and their P-80s. It was the supposed to have been the first enmasse overseas deployment of jet fighters by air but it was not quite to be. The Royal Air Force had a similar idea and was in the process of sending six Vampires Westbound. The RAF jets would land in Iceland, enroute, before the Wolfpack departed the United States.

The mission would demonstrate that an entire squadron could be rapidly and feasibly relocated from any base in the United States to anywhere in the World in a short period. It had both tactical and political ramifications. Tactically from the standpoint of the staging bases being able to

"Jackie" of the 62nd Fighter Squadron appears to be "rode hard and put away wet" after her return from Alaska in April 1947. The dual antenna masts behind the canopy are for the AN/ARA-8 Airborne Homing Adapter. (Robert O'Dell)

44-64204 also went to Alaska with the 62nd Fighter Squadron, and later with the 82nd Fighter Group. It too was transferred to the Ohio Air National Guard, this time to the 164th Fighter Squadron. It was destroyed in a flying accident in 1950. (Robert O'Dell)

logistically support the transit aircraft, that the air and ground crews could handle the deployment, and the new jet aircraft, themselves, were sturdy enough to withstand the stress of a rapid movement and be combat ready at their destination.

From a political standpoint it was a coup. The United States did not have any jet fighters in Europe at the time, and neither did Communist Russia who controlled Eastern Europe. In April Joseph Stalin had started around Berlin closing doors and windows on the citizens, and in June he locked the gates on the city. The Berlin Airlift had just started ten days prior to the 56th Fighter Group's deployment and before their arrival American fighter escort for the involved transports was limited to a single group of antiquated Thunderbolts.

Although the Russians were only flying Yak-9s and La-7s and really were doing little more than flying harassing buzzing flights with them against the transports supplying Berlin, the potential for a major conflict was in the offing. The faster jets would not only show further political resolve, but strengthen Allied air superiority. The 36th Fighter Group at Howard Air Base, Canal Zone, was alerted for a move to Germany with their P-80s as a reinforcement, but their transfer would be by ship and not arrive for months.

Schilling was sure that he could get there first and fastest by an airborne mission. And, since the 56th Fighter Group was already experienced with a staged deployment that he had participated in, he had a good idea of exactly what the mission would entail. They had charted the route beforehand, in April-May in a C-47. Schilling, with a survey team composed of Lt. Col.'s William "Dinghy" Dunham and Clay Tice, Major Donovan Smith, Capt.'s Frank Klibbe and Richard Ramsey flew the intended route, which was similar to the World War II ferry route across the North Atlantic Ocean.

Satisfied that the route would be adequate in all respects, mission planning got down to the logistics of the matter.

The first stop would be Dow Air Force Base at Bangor, Maine an earlier Port of Embarkation. The next stop would be Goose Bay, Labrador, the main jumping off point on the overseas ferry flight route during World War II, followed by stops at Bluie West 1 at Narsarssuak, Greenland; Keflavic, Iceland; Stornoway, in the Hebrides Islands off Scotland; Odiham, England and destination; Wiesbaden, Germany. The latter being the home of Headquarters USAFE. (United States Air Force in Europe, then under the command of General Curtis LeMay).

On July 7 the mission was launched and Dow was reached in 1:45 hours flying time. All but Klibbe and wingman Capt. Warren Patterson, continued on after a two hour refueling stop. Klibbe's trim tab motor having needed replacement. (They caught up with the flight at Goose Bay).

After delaying at Goose Bay for four days to meet with the westbound RAF pilots, and awaiting optimum weather conditions they proceeded to Bluie West 1, which proved to be an interesting and somewhat frightening experience to the jet pilots. The airfield is located at the end of one of a hundred fjords along the coastline and is one that is surrounded by high terrain. Thus the pilots had to find the proper fjord among the many in the area, and then fly its winding path to its source where the airfield was located.

The runway, itself, was short and ran up hill, and had a glacier at its end. A missed approach had to be made with sufficient altitude and started soon enough or else the aircraft would become a permanent monument on the landscape. Two more days were spent at Bluie West 1 waiting for the enroute weather to clear and having to change a buckled tailpipe on one F-80 before proceeding.

A lineup of P-51Hs of the 62nd Fighter Squadron prior to the mission to Alaska in December 1946. 44-64506 would make a second trip to Alaska with the 82nd Fighter Group in 1948, and was then transferred to Ohio's 166th Fighter Squadron. It was wrecked in a ground accident in 1950. (Col. William Dillard via Menard)

Col. Johnson's personal Mustang after he took over the command of the 82nd Fighter Group. His personal dedicated name remains, but the "kill" markings have been removed, and obviously the aircraft reassigned to another pilot, hence the higher group assignment number and single command stripe. (Peter Bowers)

Major Donovan Smith's Mustang at Selfridge. Smith had six air-to-air kills, three of them on one mission, during World War II. The battery door appears to be a replacement. (Robert O'Dell)

Finally, they moved on to Meeks Field, Iceland where they spent one night and then proceeded on to Stornoway for another night in primitive conditions, landing at Odiham on July 21. They moved on to Furstenfeldbruck on July 25.

Fox Able took two weeks to get to "Fursty," near Munich. Yet, flying time was a minimal 14:10. Col. Schilling had led the first flight of four P-80s, callsign "Catfish," with Major Donovon Smith and Capt.'s Frank Klibbe and Charles Bowers. The 61st Fighter Squadron, callsign "Charcoal," was led by Lt. Col. William Ritchie and included Capt.'s Russell Westfall and Harry Hunter, along with Lt. William Simpson. "Clipper" was the callsign of the 62nd FS, and they were led by Capt. Raymond Dauphin. Capt. Warren Patterson and Lt.'s Sherman Smith and John

Colonel Schilling and Gerald Johnson after Johnson brought the 62nd Fighter Squadron back to Selfridge Field in April 1947. Johnson appears happy to receive the news that he has just received command of his own fighter group. Note the "kill" markings on the fuselage. (USAF)

Col. David Schilling and his P-80 with Schilling's World War II scores well shown and differentiated between air-to-air and air-to-ground kills. (USAF)

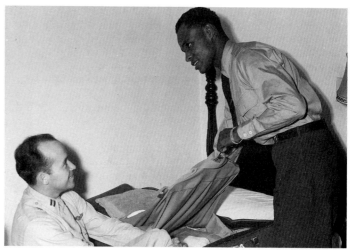

Integration came to the Air Force at the direction of President Truman. Here Lt. Col. Gabreski briefs a Naval exchange pilot, Lt. John Bauman, and Lt. Calvin Peterson, the first black pilot assigned to the Wolfpack. (USAF) Right: Lt. Calvin Peterson and Capt. Robert Dwan, 63rd FS, as Peterson settles into the BOQ at Selfridge. (USAF)

of that flight. Lt. Col. Clay Tice led the 63rd FS, callsign "Cobalt." Joining him were Capt. Heath Bottomly and Lt.'s Kenneth Millikin and Jerome Naleid. Lt. Robert Luedeka was the spare pilot who flew in the escorting B-17.

During the next two weeks the men flew seventy-nine sorties over Germany. Many of them while escorting B-29s in a show of force demonstrations. Also, buzzing was semi-legalized and the pilots were allowed to "flat hat" all over Germany so the people could see the new American jets. A mass formation was put together, too, with F-47s of the 86th Fighter Group that was composed of forty-eight Thunderbolts and the sixteen F-80s. They got good press, and Russian observers got their eyes full.

The return trip was started on August 15 via Stornoway, but there a weather delay was encountered. They finally departed Scotland on August

20 and got to Goose Bay the same day, chasing the sun and making rapid refueling stops in Iceland and Greenland enroute. They make the 2,196 miles in 4:50 hours flying time. The final hop returned them to Selfridge on August 21.

On August 1 the 56th Fighter Wing was "discontinued" and then "activated" the same day. Although it sounds confusing, there was some logic involved. The original Wing-Base experimental program that had been implemented a year previously had proven to be effective, so the experimental program was terminated per se and the Wing-Base program was placed in effect on a permanent basis. The Commanding Officer, Colonel William Hudnell, retained his position.

Colonel Schilling left the Wolfpack upon their return from Europe. He was selected to continue work upon developing the techniques of mass

At the start of the historic Fox Able mission to Europe, the mission pilots stopped at Bangor, Maine to refuel, and attracted quite a bit of attention on July 21, 1948. P-80 #19 was flown by Capt. Harry Hunter. (USAF)

Enroute to Germany, the Wolfpack contingent stopped at RAF Odihan to refuel and for protocol purposes. (USAF)

Under wraps at Furstenfeldbruck, Germany. The nearest F-80, #60, belonged to Lt. Col. Clay Tice. Tice had two kills in the Pacific Theater during World War II, and would later command the Fighter Weapons School at Nellis AFB. (Esposito)

over water deployments of jet aircraft, this time via in-flight aerial refueling of the fighters. The mission that Schilling and the Wolfpack had pioneered continued for years for those fighters not fitted with aerial refueling capabilities would continue to cross the Atlantic Ocean via the staging bases under the name of "High Tide," while those refueled in-flight after the development of aerial refueling capabilities for the fighters became known as "High Flight." Similar trans-ocean flights continue today under various tactical names.

Schilling was replaced as Group Commander by Lt. Col. Thomas DeJarnette. He had one kill with the 462nd Fighter Squadron, 506th Fighter Group. DeJarnette served as an interim commander until he was replaced by Lt. Col. Irwin Dregne. Dregne had become an ace while leading the 357th Fighter Group in Europe.

December 1948: A major change in the role of the Wolfpack took place on December 13 when the Group was transferred from SAC to the Continental Air Command and given the primary role of Air Defense. Inclement weather curtailed flying operations for much of the month December and into early 1949 and little training in their new role was able to take place. Most of the flying conducted being concentrated upon navigation and instrument flight work in an attempt at maintaining proficiency.

Some operational problems with the jet fighters continued, all within the normal scope of running a combat unit. On February 5, 1949 at Gunter Air Force Base, Alabama a F-80 making an emergency landing because of fuel exhaustion ran off the end of the 3,500 foot runway and collapsed the landing gear. Major damage was incurred.

February 21, 1949: The main bearing on a F-80's J-33 engine failed while at 32,000 feet while on a local training flight. The unidentified pilot attempted an air-start without success and made a belly landing in an open field. The aircraft was a writeoff.

On the same day another pilot landed hard at Oscoda AFB and collapsed the landing gear. Another writeoff.

February 23: A another unidentified pilot on an instrument flight lost control of his F-80 and had to bailout when it went into a high speed dive.

March 4: While landing at Williams Air Force Base, Arizona the landing gear collapsed on a F-80. It was a write-off.

March 11: While landing at Chanute AFB, Illinois a F-80 undershot his approach and hit a snowbank. Major damage was done to this aircraft.

At the end of March 1949 the 56th Fighter Group was only 36% combat operational according to the old Strategic Air Command criteria. Only 60.5% of the aircraft were considered in commission at any given time. Although three new aircraft were received from Eglin AFB in February, they did not make up for the attrition, and the Group was short five of the TO&E allotted F-80s.

April 1: The 62nd Fighter squadron moved to Oscoda AFB for training. They remained there until June 6, when they were replaced by the 61st FS. While the 62nd was at Oscoda the entire squadron complement of pilots became qualified in all phases of F-80 combat gunnery except rocket firing. (The lack of suitable rocket launching rails preventing this activity). Although it had been hoped that they would have been able to run two squadrons through Oscoda at a time during the summer months, in order to increase those squadrons qualifications, this could not take place. The Air National guard had selected the field for some of their own summer encampments, and there was not enough hanger or billeting facilities available for both operations.

Between April 4 and the 8 the 56th Fighter Group had an Operational Readiness Test where they flew twenty simulated combat missions. The missions were squadron and group level scrambles to test their air defense capability. Although twice the missions were hampered by the weather deteriorating to at or near landing minimums, all aircraft were recovered safely at Selfridge, to the evaluators satisfaction.

Major Ralph Johnson, Commanding Officer of the 61st Fighter Squadron, suffered injuries to his spinal column while on a local night navigation mission. His F-80 flamed out and Johnson was unable to get it restarted and had to bailout, striking his back against the ground as he landed in the dark. His injuries were severe enough that he was replaced by Major Albert Kelley as commander.

The 645th Aircraft Control Squadron (Later redesignated as Aircraft Control and Warning, AC&W.) became operational near Selfridge on May 2 and the 56th Fighter Group assigned the 61st Fighter Squadron to the task of bringing them to the state of readiness required far an adequate air defense organization. Designated "Blackjack," the 61st FS F-80s challenged the radar controllers every which way until June 6 when they moved to

Oscoda and then the 62nd FS took their place until June 21 when all F-80s were grounded. A total of 173 sorties were flown against the radar site.

While at Oscoda the 61st Fighter Squadron suffered an accident that could have been a tragedy. As one of their pilots was landing behind his element leader he got caught it its wake turbulence and was flipped over on his back. The pilot just managed to right the aircraft in time to smash into the trees at the end of the runway. The F-80 was demolished, but the pilot walked away from it.

On May 17 the 63rd Fighter Squadron moved to Eglin AFB, Florida to participate in training the radar controllers at their school. They remained there until June 21. On the way back one of their pilot's F-80 flamed out, but he bailed out successfully, albeit suffering minor injuries.

On May 25 the second Fox Able mission departed Selfridge for Furstenfeldbruck. The purpose of this particular mission was to expedite delivery of eleven new F-80Bs and four TF-80Cs (T-33s) to the 36th Fighter Wing. Fox Able 2 was the first actual mass delivery of jet fighters by air to an overseas location.

The 36th Fighter Wing, having moved to "Fursty" in July-August 1948 from Howard Field, Canal Zone via aircraft carrier showed that the transfer of aircraft and men via seapower was both slow and inefficient, at least as far as the Air Force was concerned. The time spent on and off loading aircraft on an aircraft carrier was time lost, not to mention the time wasted at sea. Another, and a major factor was aircraft corrosion from the salty sea air. Navy aircraft were built with corrosion preventative methods, but Air Force aircraft were not. As the future would soon show, those aircraft shipped via aircraft carrier to Korea would suffer massive corrosion problems and corresponding extensive delays in getting them combat ready because of the sea voyage.

The 56th Fighter Group, at the insistence of Lt. Col Dregne, was selected to see if a better and quicker way could be found for the transfer of aircraft, personnel and equipment.

As this was the second overseas mass movement of jet aircraft, the logistical support was strong. One C-54 was used to carry maintenance support equipment while two C-47s carried further equipment and ground crews. A RB-29 went along as a weather scout, and SB-17s were provided along the route for air-sea rescue, if required. The route flown would be similar to the previous Fox Able path, substituting RAF Kinross for Stornoway and RAF Manston for Odiham. Manston would be familiar to many, as it had been an emergency landing field for the 8th Air Force during the war.

The aircraft departed on schedule on and staged through Dow. The first major problem did not occur until the last aircraft landed at Bluie West 1. The runway was built with an upslope, and the particular aircraft was landed hard, bounced, and sheared the nose landing gear. It took three days to obtain a new nose wheel strut, as arrangements had not been made with the Military Air Transport Service to ship their supplies for them. Thus, a SB-17 had to be sent back to the States for the replacement strut. But this sort of problem was one of those they were looking for and would be resolved for the future hundreds of jet aircraft movements across the North Atlantic.

Additional problems noted were that the anti-exposure flying suits fit too tightly around the pilot's wrists and cut off circulation. Kinross needed an Automatic Direction Finding beacon for navigation, although their DF station was deemed adequate. The escorting B-29 should have a qualified

PREVIOUS: The ramp at Dow AFB, Bangor, Maine looks a little cleaner as the 56th Fighter Group stages through on their return on August 21, 1948. Note that the aircraft now bear the flags of the countries they visited. Capt. Ray Dauphin flew #42. This particular F-80 later went to the Oklahoma Air National Guard, and then the 169th Fighter Bomber Squadron, Illinois ANG. For years it languished in a park in Aurora, Illinois before being swapped for a F-105 and moved to Warner-Robbins AFB for restoration and display. (USAF)

jet pilot on board that was familiar with the route, and he should have the final say on whether the mission should proceed, or not.

Four pilots from the 56th Fighter Group participated: Lt. Col. Dregne led the mission with Major Samual Blair and, as expected, Col. Schilling wrangled himself free from Headquarters USAF and filled the remaining slot in the first element. Capt.'s Frank Klibbe and Clarence Haynes made up the other lead element. From the 61st Fighter Squadron were: Capt.'s Russell Westfall and Burt Rowen, 1st Lt.'s Thomas Smith, Mervin Reeves and Lee Stanley. Capt. William Schereffer, along with 1st Lt.'s Frederick Blesse and Gordon Humphrees from the 63rd FS. No pilots from the 62nd FS participated. Capt. John Quatannens was the spare, from Headquarters Squadron 56th Fighter Wing.

Upon delivery of the aircraft, the pilots and ground crews returned via C-54. Col. Schilling went back to developing his aerial refueling techniques, now being assisted by Major Klibbe who was designated as Project Officer on the F-84G/KB-29 program.

In July 1952 this program also bore fruit when Col. Schilling led the 31st Fighter Wing across the Pacific Ocean on the first trans Pacific jet fighter crossing, Fox Peter One. (Schilling had assumed command of the 31st Fw from his old friend and ex Wolfpack pilot, Lt. Col. Gerald Johnson on July 20, 1951). For their efforts, the 31st Fw won a Distinguished Unit Citation, the second one won by a unit under Schilling's leadership.

In late Spring Lt. Col. William Ritchie, 56th Fighter Group Operations Officer, was transferred to Operations and Plans Division Air Force Headquarters. Ritchie, who had two kills with the 386th Fighter Squadron, was replaced by Major Orr. Major Edward Popek, Commanding Officer of the 62nd Fighter Squadron, was temporarily replaced by Capt. Franklyn Moffitt. (Popek was credited with seven kills with the 342nd Fighter Squadron in the Southwest Pacific Theater). Major William Jacobsen remained as Commander of the 63rd FS.

June 1949: Lt. Col. David McKnight became the Commanding Officer of the 56th Fighter Wing. McKnight having been one of the initial cadre of the reforming 56th Fighter Group.

July 1949: Major Ralph Johnson was returned to flying status and assumed command of the 62nd Fighter Squadron. Major Popek was reassigned to Headquarters 10th Air Force, which was located at Selfridge and oversaw the operations of the Air Force Reserve and Air National Guard in the central United States.

One of the major problems with aircraft maintenance was the absolute shortage of qualified enlisted men. Many of the new men being transferred into the Group at this time were brand new troops with only a one year enlistment in front of them. Which was all that was required of them in the Post War years. Unskilled, the men had to be given OJT in their mandated specialties, but by the time they learned anything worthwhile, their enlistment was up and they were discharged. The time spent training them was totally wasted and would have been far better served in aircraft maintenance by the instructors to begin with. Such was the nature of policy and training Air Force wide at the time. As it was, again only 60% of the aircraft were in commission.

July was a rough month, too, as far as aircraft attrition was concerned. 2nd Lt. Henry French, 62nd Fighter Squadron, was killed after encountering a thunderstorm in Texas. 2nd Lt. Richard Glenn, 62nd FS, had an unusual incident over Sandusky, Ohio. His tip tanks collapsed and the aluminum shells wrapped over the leading edges of his wings rendering his F-80 uncontrollable. He belly landed in a field.

While at Oscoda AFB during their gunnery training program two pilots hit the towed targets, while another made a hard landing and tore off his F-80s tailpipe. (This customarily would cost him a bottle of his crew chief's favorite spirits). An additional pilot from the 81st Fighter Group that was attached to the Wolfpack for training in F-80s landed short at

After their return from Europe, the F-80s that had made the trip were in heavy demand for display at airshows. Lt.Col. William Ritchie's aircraft now carries practice bombs instead of drop tanks. Ritchie had two kills with the 386th Fighter Squadron in Europe. (Bachman via Esposito)

Selfridge AFB and blew a tire, causing the aircraft to slew and tear off the landing gear.

In August Major George Orr was transferred from Headquarters 56th Fighter Group to Oscoda AFB to become the Commanding officer of their 2476th BASUT. Major George Abel, Operations Officer of the 61st Fighter Squadron replaced Orr as Group Operations Officer. Abel, in turn, was replaced by one of the "Top Guns" when Capt. William Whisner took his place. Whisner had 15.5 air-to-air kills during WWII and would score 5.5 more in Korea in a few years. Whisner was later quoted as making one of the better remarks that personified the nature of a true fighter pilot. Referring to World War II, he had stated: "It wasn't much of a war, but it was the only one we had."

Captain Howard Askelson, who had been assigned as the Base Commander at Oscoda AFB returned to the Group, and then went TDY to the Tactical School. Major Henry Kirby, who had been the first Squadron Commander of Arkansas ANG 154th Fighter Squadron, and then their Senior Air Instructor, took over the position of Operations Officer of the 62nd FS from Capt. Franklyn Moffitt, who had temporally held the position. Kirby had one air-to-air kill, and four on the ground during the war.

On August 23 Colonel James Gunn replaced Lt. Col. McKnight as Commanding Officer of the 56th Fighter Wing. McKnight eventually wound up as Deputy Group Commander of the 4th Fighter Interceptor Wing in Korea.

The initial markings applied to the aircraft of the 56th Fighter Group were pretty plain. This example was one of the first received, and was assigned to the 62nd Fighter Squadron. Note that it still utilizes the original "PN" buzz letters. (Peter Bowers via Esposito)

The 62nd Fighter Squadron continued its string of bad luck through fatal accidents in August. 1st Lt. John Bylander was killed on his way back from Anchorage, Alaska in a F-51H that he was ferrying to an Air National Guard unit in Ohio. Near Whitehorse, Yukon Territory, Canada Bylander apparently tried to top some weather and succumbed to anoxia. Three more F-80s also suffered major damage in landing accidents. One by a pilot from the 62nd FS at Corpus Christi, Texas and one from each other squadron at Selfridge.

In September 1949 Lt. Col. Irwin Dregne was transferred to Okinawa. He would eventually become the Commanding Officer of the 51st Fighter Interceptor Group in Korea. Major Ralph Johnson took over the command of the 56th Fighter Group as a temporary assignment. Major William Jacobsen was assigned to Group Headquarters Deputy Group Commander. Major Charles Bowers assuming command of the 63rd Fighter Squadron vice Jacobsen.

During the 1949 Cleveland Air Races over Labor Day weekend the 61st Fighter Squadron furnished a team of four pilots to simulate divebombing for the airshow crowd. The demonstration proved to be so popular that General Hoyt Vandenberg sent his personal congratulations.

As a part of a general air defense training exercise, the 56th Fighter Group, along with all other units of the 1st, 9th and 10th Air Forces with mandated air defense duties in the northeastern United States were placed on simulated alert status. This exercise/position was run every Wednesday to challenge the radar Ground Control Intercept, GCI, sites within the control of the 26th Air Division.

On September 16 the 61st Fighter Squadron departed for Tyndall AFB, Florida to work with new radar controllers prior to their being assigned to specific GCI sites. This six week program gave the pilots both practical experience in making radar intercepts, along with giving them a first hand look at what went on in a radar control room. The squadron provided sixteen aircraft on a daily basis for the GCI controllers, and during bad weather, additional aircraft were flown to increase pilot experience. F-51Hs were utilized as high altitude targets, while A-26s flew the low altitude runs. Three missions were flown against the new B-50s between 25,000 and 30,000 feet. They made 405 flights, for a total of 670 sorties and 1102 successful interceptions.

As this was taking place, the 62nd FS was tasked with conversion training for members of Wisconsin's 126th Fighter Squadron that was switching from F-51Ds to F-80s. The 63rd FS, in the meantime, completed their proficiency training at Oscoda AFB.

The "big news" during October 1949 was the assignment of Lt. Col. Francis Gabreski as permanent Group commander, effective October 5. Gabreski had left the service for a year, and then rejoined. After a stint as a squadron commander, the USAF sent him to college, and he had just graduated. Supporting this came the assignment of Major Joseph Perry to Group Operations Officer. Perry being remembered as having scored two kills with the 61st Fighter Squadron during the war and being one of the first to rejoin the new 56th FG in July 1946.

Another major assignment was the transfer of Major Abel to Squadron Commander of the 62nd Fighter squadron when Major Ralph Johnson was transferred to the Wisconsin Air National guard as Senior Air Instructor.

The problems with the lack of qualified ground crews continued. Things got to the point where the pilots all had to do their own morning pre-flights on the aircraft, and then do their own refueling after they landed. As expected, there was little improvement in the aircraft in commission rate.

Still, the 61st Fighter Squadron, with only 60% of their authorized maintenance men broke the old record for F-80 flying hours during October. The old record, established by the 65th Fighter Squadron of the 57th Fighter Group in Alaska was 1180 hours, and the 61st flew 1311 in support of the GCI training program at Tyndall AFB.

The only major accident for the month resulted in the death of 1st Lt. William Bloyed, 63rd Fighter Squadron. Bloyed had attempted a night takeoff during a rainstorm at Selfridge AFB in a T-11 and lost control of the aircraft. (A T-11 was navigation trainer version of the C-45).

Major William "Hawkeye" Hawkins was named Squadron Commander of the 63rd FS. Hawkins having earned three kills in the China-Burma-India Theater.

On January 11, 1950 a F-80 was lost under unusual circumstances for a land based unit. During the morning hours 2nd Lt. Stanley Armstrong, 61st Fighter Squadron, was up on a routine training flight when apparently his Shooting Star went out of control. He was declared missing until Janu-

OPPOSITE: A pair of pilots from the 63rd Fighter Squadron indicate to each other via hand signals that they are ready to taxi. The nearest aircraft apparently has a replacement armament panel door. The white stripe on the glare panel also has a short length of string, which would indicate to the pilot, by slewing off to the side, if the aircraft was being yawed. (USAF)

The P-80 was an exceptionally "clean" aircraft for its day. Its lines just flowed, and those of us who remember it, recall its smoothness and grace in flight. (USAF)

When Monogram Models Inc. released their 1/48" scale model of the F-80 a decade ago, they used this example to depict. It was flown by Capt. Russell Westfall on the first Fox Able mission. (Esposito)

Lt. Kenneth Millikin flew this F-80 on the first Fox Able mission. It bears the standardized markings of the Group during the F-80 era. Just in front of the joining of the fuselage colored bands are the access panels for the engine and the plenum chamber doors. Above the four in the buzz numbers is the fuselage fuel tank refueling point. If the cap was not secure, fuel would siphon from the tank and flow back towards the plenum chamber, and if the doors were open the F-80 would become a fireball. The aft section of the fuselage was attached to the forward portion by just three bolts, and was joined just in front of the red turbine warning stripe. (USAF)

Just before the Wolfpack surrendered their F-80s for F-86s and were split-up between three Air Force bases, they went to Las Vegas AFB, now Nellis AFB, Nevada for the first annual USAF gunnery meet. The meet was won by the rival 4th Fighter Group. (USAF)

ary 20 and thereafter declared killed. Apparently he had gone down into either Lake Huron or into a heavily wooded area and the aircraft was never found.

On January 20, 1950 the 56th Fighter Wing, Group, and associated 61st, 62nd, and 63rd Fighter Squadrons were all redesignated as "Fighter Interceptor" Wing/Group/Squadron.

The continuing shuffle of squadron commanders placed Major Edwin Heller in charge of the 62nd Fighter Interceptor Squadron. Major Heller would later add to his fame by scoring 3.5 MiG-15 kills in Korea, which ran his total score as a fighter pilot to nine. (Including two one-half credits). Major Kirby was assigned to the U.S. Marine Corps as a part of the Inner-Service Exchange program. Six more officers were lost to the Group through the Air Force's reduction program. In six months they would be begging for these men to come back.

Preparations for participation in the annual Air Force Gunnery Meet, scheduled for March 28 at Las Vegas, Nevada got underway during January. To simulate the expected weather conditions and exercise areas, several of the pilots flew to Eglin AFB, Florida to practice, as the inclement winter weather continued to hamper flying out of Selfridge. Several other pilots also flew a dive bombing exhibition at Opa Locka, Florida during the middle of the month, participating in the Miami All American Air Maneuvers.

March 1950: The 56th Fighter Group sent twenty-one F-80s and one T-33 to Washington, DC to participate in the fly-over ceremony for the funeral of General Fairchild.

April 3: Lt. Col. Charles Parsons assumed command of the 62nd Fighter Interceptor Squadron. Parsons had previously been the Commanding Officer of the 74th Fighter Squadron on Guam.

June 1950: The change over from F-80s to F-86s was nearing completion. The 62nd Fighter Interceptor Squadron, which received their first F-86A-5 on April 25, now had twenty-five on board. On May 1 the Mobile Training Unit had arrived from Chanute AFB and by the 12th the first class of pilots had graduated. It was expected that 90% of the squadron would have finished the course before the squadron moved to Oscoda AFB on June 12 to commence gunnery training in the new Sabre's.

Administratively, Lt. Col. Charles King was moved from Group Operations Officer to Commanding Officer of the 63rd Fighter Interceptor Squadron. Major William Hawkins, the previous Commanding Officer was reassigned as squadron Operations Officer. Major George Jones, 63rd FIS Operations Officer, replaced Lt. Col. King as Group Operations Officer. King had been an ace with the 39th FIS during WWII. Major Jones would soon go to Korea, where he knocked down five MiG-15s and received three half credits while assisting in the destruction of three more.

On August 4, 1950 the 62nd Fighter interceptor Squadron was relocated to O'Hare Air Force Base, Illinois. At this time the 56th Fighter Interceptor Group/Wing ceased to be what could be considered as a cohesive fighter group in the traditional form of having its three operational squadrons co-located with the parent unit. The era of the true Wolfpack had come to an end.

APPENDIXES

APPENDIX I
WOLFPACK AIRCRAFT SPECIFICATIONS

The original P-47 version that was furnished to the 56th Fighter Group was the P-47B, the first production version of the Thunderbolt. Delivery of these aircraft commenced in June 1942, and the 56th FG continued to fly them until preparations commenced for the Group's move to England later that year. At this time the remaining aircraft were transferred to other units undergoing training in the United States. The attrition rate for these aircraft was extreme.

The P-47B differed from the prototype by having a Pratt & Whitney R-2800-21 engine that produced 2,000 horsepower, a sliding canopy and an antenna mast that was raked forward. Originally, the control surfaces were fabric covered, but most were retro-fitted with metal covered surfaces, except for the rudder, after many problems were encountered with the loss of the fabric in flight.

Span: 40' 9 5/16" Length: 35' 0" Weight: 12,085 pounds.
Takeoff/Military Power: 2,000 hp @ 2,700 rpm. Normal Power: 1,550 hp @ 2,550 rpm at Sea Level; 1,625 hp @ 2,550 rpm at 25,000 feet. Internal fuel: 205 US gallons. Range 830 miles at 10,000; 350 miles at 25,000 feet.

Upon arrival in England, the first P-47s received were the new P-47C. The "C" version differed externally from the "B" in length, having its accessory section lengthened 8", and by the installation of a vertical antenna mast. All control surfaces were now metal covered. An improved Pratt and Whitney engine was the R-2800-59. Gross weight was upped to 13,140 pounds. The P-47C-2 was equipped with the necessary mounting racks and fuel line plumbing to carry either a 200 US gallon ferry fuel tank or a 100 gallon combat tank. Internal fuel remained the same: 205 US gallons, of which 40 were reserve fuel, and the last fifteen gallon of this fuel could only be obtained by switching the selector switch to "Reserve."

The initial P-47Ds were identical in appearance to the P-47Cs, with the exception of two additional cowl flaps on each side of the engine cowling. The first P-47Ds were built under the designation of P-47D-1-RA, which indicated that they were built at the new Republic Aviation Corporation plant at Evansville, Indiana, while Republic's plant at Farmingdale, Long Island, New York produced the identical P-47D-1-RE. These early "D" models continued with the P&W R-2800-21 engine, but did feature additional pilot protection armor and refinements to the fuel, oxygen and exhaust systems. All-up weight and dimensions were similar to previous versions, as was the limited internal fuel capacity.

With the P-47D-5-RE and -6-RE came improvements desired by the fighter pilots. Although the Evansville versions, -3-RA and -4-RA were similar, they just were not quite as good. The D-5 had a General Electric

C-21 turbocharger and regulator and provisions for water injection, which increased War Emergency horsepower to 2,300 @ 27,000 feet. A further improvement to these aircraft came through the D-10-RE and D-11-RA that had an electrically driven water injection pump. Further improvements followed with the P-47D-15s and -16s that were built by both factories. Both of these modifications included the addition of the underwing bomb pylons and associated wiring and plumbing for carrying either external fuel or ordnance. The P-47D-20 and -21 had an improved General Electric ignition system, a slightly longer tail wheel strut and a few other internal modifications for the ease of maintenance. Another innovation was the use of ducted hot air from the engine to warm the machineguns, instead of electrical heating. One additional modification concluded the early series of P-47Ds. On the P-47D-22-RE and -23-RA came the Hamilton Standard or Curtiss Electric propellers, respectively, that were increased in diameter to 13' and improved high altitude performance.

For all these versions the wingspan remained at 40' 9"; while the length had extended to 36' 1" Height was 14' 8". Empty weight was 9,900, while the maximum weight was now up to 17,000 pounds. Although supposedly possessing a service ceiling of 40,000 feet, attaining anything above 32,000 feet in a combat environment remained an impossibility.

A major change to the Thunderbolt came with the introduction of the P-47D-25-RE and -26-RA through the introduction of the bubble canopy. Featured on these and subsequent models, the new canopy gave close to 360 degree visibility. Another major change was the installation of larger fuselage fuel cells, which increased capacity to 370 US gallons and extended combat duration by an additional thirty minutes. The P-47D-28 standardized the Curtiss Wright C542S propeller for all Thunderbolts. The next major improvement came through the P-47D-40-RA which added a dorsal fin to the vertical stabilizer (Which was retro-fitted to earlier "bubble-top" models.), to replace the lack of keel area given up through the canopy revision. The K-14 gyro gunsight replaced the previous reflector gunsight, along with the "iron sight."

The P-47D-40 now had increased in weight to 10,000 pounds empty and 17,500 pounds gross weight. Engine improvements had increased the horsepower to 2,430 hp at War Emergency setting. Although the service ceiling had been raised to 42,000 feet, attainable altitude in combat remained near 32,000 feet. Combat range was now 1,030 miles. The underwing "zero-length" rocket launching stubs introduced on the D-35 model became standard, also.

The P-47M was the last Thunderbolt version flown by the 56th Fighter Group. Externally similar to the P-47D-40, the "M" featured the Pratt & Whitney R-2800-57 engine that produced 2,800 hp under War Emergency conditions. It also had a larger capacity turbocharger, CH-4. With water-injection, the P-47M could attain 473 mph at 32,000 feet. And, when it was running right, it could catch a P-51, and when it wasn't, it could still out dive one. Although the exact figures are not available, it is estimated that over 500 Thunderbolts passed through the 56th FG's inventory during the war years. The P-47Ms were salvaged in England.

North American Aviation's P-51H was introduced to the 56th Fighter Group at Selfridge Field. The lightest operational version of the Mustang, the H model spanned 37', was 33' 4" long and had an empty weight of just 6,500 pounds. Gross weight was 11,500 pounds. Powered by a Rolls Royce, Packard built, Merlin V-1650 engine, this Mustang had a service ceiling of 42,000 and was capable of attaining 488 mph at 25,000 feet. It had an effective range of 1,600 miles. The Group had some seventy-five of these Mustangs, but were operational with them for less than a year. Most were passed on to the Air National Guard after the Group re-equipped with P-80s.

When the 56th Fighter Group entered the jet era they received Lockheed's P-80A. America's first operational jet fighter. They were the third fighter group to do so.

The P-80A spanned 39' 11" and was 34' 6" long. Empty weight was 7,920 pounds and takeoff weight was 14,500 pounds. Top speed was 558 mph and the service ceiling was 45,000 feet. Effective range was 540 miles. When the 56th FG re-equipped with F-86s in 1950 the P-80As were returned to the Lockheed Aircraft Corporation for refurbishing and upgrading to F-80C standards. Some then saw service in Korea, while the majority were reassigned to the Air National Guard.

APPENDIX II
AIRCRAFT MARKINGS

The original P-47Bs assigned to the 56th Fighter Group were painted in the factory standard application of olive drab top surfaces and neutral grey on the bottom. The last five digits of the aircraft's Serial Number was in yellow upon the vertical stabilizer. Soon after the aircraft were taken on board, the application of two digit numerals was added in white block style upon the fuselage in front of the inter cooler doors and upon the cowling. There was no corresponding relationship between these numbers and the aircraft's S/N. Some had popular names added to the cowling, but none had flamboyant artwork.

Upon receipt of the P-47C at King's Cliffe and Wittering, the new aircraft were individually identified by assigning them a three digit numeral code or a code letter and two digits, painted in white block style upon the fuselage. Immediately after the move to Horsham St. Faith the addition of white stripes was added to the vertical and horizontal stabilizers, and a white band was painted around the cowling to aid in identification of the P-47 over the Fw 190. At this time, also a revision to the national insignia came into being, by adding a yellow band around the national insignia. Also, it was standard to have the national insignia placed under the left wing, but as an identification enhancement, it was also placed under the right wing, usually these were beyond standard size. Many of the pilots and crew chiefs applied several coats of wax on their aircraft in an attempt to increase their speed. This resulted in a high-gloss finish that weared better than the normal paint.

In June 1943 the individual aircraft numerals gave way to standardized unit markings. The 61st Fighter Squadron was assigned "HV," the 62nd FS "LM," and the 63rd FS "UN." Each aircraft within a squadron was also given an individual code letter, and this usually corresponded to the first initial of the pilot's surname, if he was assigned a personal aircraft. As the standard compliment of aircraft, twenty-four to twenty-six aircraft per squadron approximated the number of pilots assigned to a squadron, this was a workable program. Then, as the number of aircraft available increased and the alphabet exceeded, the new aircraft were given their individual letter and differentiated by an underling white bar.

On June 29, 1943 the national insignia was revised to include a white rectangular bar on either side of the cockade and the entire insignia was banded in red. This insignia lasted until August 14 when the red portion was ordered changed to blue.

Commencing with the arrival of the P-47D-21 series that were in natural metal finish, NMF, the previous white tail bands were replaced with black stripes. Several of these aircraft, however, were then repainted in the traditional OD and neutral gray scheme, as there was no agreement as to which scheme was advantageous.

The "bubble top" P-47s were received in NMF, but again, many received a locally applied OD finish upon their fuselage and upper wing and empennage surfaces. Commencing in February 1944 the squadrons started painting the previously painted white portions of their aircraft's cowlings in their individually assigned squadron colors. The 61st Fighter Squadron used red, the 62nd FS yellow, while the 63rd FS retained white. The following month these colors were replaced by a twenty-four inch band around the cowling in red, identifying the 56th Fighter Group, while other 8th and

9th Air Force units used different colors or patterns. Coinciding with this, the 61st FS started to paint their aircraft's rudders red, and the 62nd FS did the same in yellow. The 63rd FS finally adapted medium blue for their individual color in September 1944 and started applying it to their rudders at that time.

Late in the day on June 5, 1944 the order was received to apply alternating black and white "invasion stripes" to the fuselages and wings of the fighters of the 8th and 9th Air Forces. Initially, these stripes circled the entire fuselage and banded both the lower and upper surfaces of the wings. As time progressed into the fall of 1944 these bands were either painted-out or removed from the tops of the wings and fuselages, and remained as such through the P-47D era within the Group. As this was taking place, experiments with various camouflage schemes commenced. No Technical Order for this is known, and it appears that the patterns were based upon the whim of the individual pilot. Most of these schemes were typical of those used by the Royal Air Force. Green and grey or light and dark grey in either shadow or mottle patterns. Some were all matt-black on their upper surfaces.

With the arrival of the P-47M in January 1945 the camouflaging reached new heights. The 61st FS P-47Ms were all painted in a flat black, with their individual aircraft code letters in white and, usually, outlined in red; along with red S/N's on the vertical fin. The 62nd FS went to a dark green and grey camouflage pattern with yellow codes and serial numbers. The 63rd FS utilized a dark blue to purple to sky blue camouflage pattern with NMF codes and serial numbers in blue. The rudder control surfaces were in the individual squadron colors.

P-51Hs assigned to the 56th Fighter Group at Selfridge Field (Later Air Force Base), Michigan bore standard markings for the Air Force during that period. In late 1945 the Army Air Force assigned each specific type of aircraft "buzz letters." The Mustang was identified as "PF" (Which was changed to "FF" when the P-51 was reidentified as the F-51.), and this included the last three numbers of the aircraft's serial number: ie: PF-506. These codes made it quite simple to identify an aircraft that was flying too low and nail the offending pilot. If he was low enough for an observer to read the code, he was too low. These buzz codes were painted in large black letters on the sides of the fuselage in front of the national insignia and below the canopy. On some, but not all Mustangs, they were repeated below the left wing, where "USAF" would later appear. Pilots were permitted to add their World War II scores to the side of their aircraft.

Squadron colors remained assigned, and the aircraft's spinners were painted accordingly, along with the tip of the vertical stabilizer. Black block-style two-digit numerals were added in early 1947 to the vertical stabilizer. These solely indicated the aircraft's corresponding parking spot on the 56th FG's ramp.

The exceptions to these markings was the addition of the pre-World War II style "tail stripes" that were placed upon the rudders of those borrowed P-47s and the P-51Hs of the 56th FG's acrobatic pilots aircraft for airshow purposes. These stripes alternated red and white horizontally and had a vertical blue stripe upon the rudder, while the vertical fin and dorsal spine were yellow.

When the P-80A arrived the 56th Fighter Group adopted more flamboyant markings. The noses of the aircraft were blazed in red, often outlined with a black stripe. The vertical fin was also painted with a horizontal band in the individual squadron color, red outlined in white for the 61st FS, yellow outlined in black for the 62nd FS and blue outlined in white for the 63rd FS. These bands also bore the number of the aircraft's parking location. The squadron insignia was painted on the left gunbay door, while the Group insignia appeared on the right door. The tip tanks were in the squadron color.

Initially, the P-80 was assigned the "buzz letters" "PN," but when the P-80 was redesignated as the F-80, this code was changed to first "FN," and then "FT." Corresponding with this came the addition of "U.S. Air Force" on the vertical fin and rudder between the tail band and the aircraft's serial number.

To indicate the status of the pilot normally assigned to a particular aircraft, colored bands were added to the fuselage and usually to the tip tanks. A flight leader had a single band, the squadron commander a double band, in the squadron's color. The Group commander's aircraft bore three bands, in the colors of all three squadrons. Below the canopy a blaze similar to Lockheed's Shooting Star design with a white star bore the name of the pilot normally assigned to the aircraft and the name of its crew chief. These were in the squadron's colors. During the first year the P-80A was in the 56th FG's inventory the aircraft continued to carry the pilot's score of World War II kills, but when Col. Schilling left the Group this practice was discontinued.

Appendix III
Aces of the 56th Fighter Group

Name	Air-to-Air	Air-to-Ground	Total	Notes
Schilling, David C.	22.5	10.5	33.5	
Gabreski, Francis	28	2.5	30.5	(Gabreski added six MiG-15s to his final score during the Korean War. The USAF now credits him with a total score of 34.5).
Johnson, Robert S.	27	-	27	
Zemke, Hubert	18	8.5	26.5	(15.25 w/56th FG, 2.5 w/479th FG)
Christensen, Fred	21.5	-	21.5	
Mahurin, Walker	21	-	21	(19.75 w/56th FG, 1 w/ 3rd CDO Sq. He then added 3.5 MiG-15s to this total during the Korean War. The USAF now credits him with a total score of 24.25).
Johnson, Gerald	16.5		16.5	(Includes one claim w/ 360th FS while on TDY)
Powers, Joseph	14.5	-	14.5	
Schreiber, Leroy	14	-	14	
Bostwick, George	8	6	14	
Jackson, Michael	8	5.5	13.5	
Williamson, Felix	13	-	13	
Murphy, Randel	2	11	13	
Quirk, Mitchel	12	5	1	
Dade, Lucian	6	6	12	
Conger, Paul	11.5	-	11.5	
Stewart, James	11.5	-	11.5	
Gladych, Michael	10	-	10	(Gladych also claimed 16+ while flying with the PAF, FAF and RAF, but the USAAF did not include credit for these as a matter of policy).
Morrill, Stanley	10	-	10	
Rankin, Robert	10	-	10	
Kyler, Russell	3	7	10	
Schlitz, Glenn	8	-	8	
Flagg, Walter	2	6	8	
Edens, Billy	7	-	7	
Klibbe, Frank	7	-	7	
Lamb, Robert	7	-	7	
Smith, Leslie	7	-	7	
Truluck, John	7	-	7	
Chinn, Claude	-	7	7	
Mosley, Mark	6.5	-	6.5	
Carter, James	6	-	6	
Cook, Walter	6	-	6	
Hall, George	6	-	6	
Hart, Cameron	6	-	6	
Keen, Robert	6	-	6	
Bennett, Joseph	5.5	-	8.5	(Bennett transferred to the 336th FS and had gained 3 more A-to-A with them).
McCauley, Frank	5.5	-	5.5	
Smith, Donovan	5.5	-	5.5	
Comstock, Harold	5	-	5	
Egan, Joseph	5	-	5	
Gerick, Stephan	5	-	5	
Gould, Norman	5	-	5	
Icard, Joseph	5	-	5	
McMinn, Evan	5	-	5	
Vogt, John	5	-	8	(Vogt transferred to the 360th FS and had gained 3 more A-to-A with them).
O'Neil, Eugene	5	-	5	
Blodgett, Burton	-	5	5	
Smith, Vernon	-	5	5	

APPENDIX IV
AIR-TO-AIR APPROVED CLAIMS
OF THE 56TH FIGHTER GROUP

The following roster of the 56th Fighter Group air-to-air claims is derived from USAF Historical Study #85, which gives the name, rank, serial number, date of credit and unit of assignment for the scoring pilot. The type of aircraft destroyed was taken from the 56th Fighter Group histories.

Headquarters

Zemke, Hubert Col.	Jun 13 43	Fw 190
Zemke, Hubert Col.	Jun 13 43	Fw 190
Zemke, Hubert Col.	Aug 17 43	Me 110
Zemke, Hubert Col.	Sep 3 43	Fw 190
Schilling, David C. Maj.	Oct 2 43	Me 109
Schilling, David C. Maj.	Oct 2 43	Fw 190
Zemke, Hubert Col.	Oct 2 43	Fw 190
Schilling, David C. Maj.	Oct 4 43	Me 110
Schilling, David C. Maj.	Oct 8 43	Fw 190
Schilling, David C. Maj.	Oct 10 43	Fw 190
Zemke, Hubert Col.	Oct 20 43	Fw 190
Zemke, Hubert Col.	Nov 5 43	Fw 190
Schilling, David C. Lt. Col.	Nov 26 43	Fw 190
Schilling, David C. Lt. Col.	Nov 26 43	Fw 190
Schilling, David C. Lt. Col.	Nov 26 43	.5 unidentified type and co-claimant.
Landry, Robert B. Col.	Dec 11 43	Me 109
Schilling, David C. Lt. Col.	Jan 11 44	Fw 190
Schilling, David C. Lt. Col.	Jan 29 44	Me 109
Johnson, Gerald W. Maj.	Feb 21 44	Fw 190
Zemke, Hubert Col.	Mar 6 44	Fw 190
Zemke, Hubert Col.	Mar 6 44	Me 109
Zemke, Hubert Col.	Mar 6 44	.25 Me 109 w/M.Becker, D. Peters, C. Reed (63rd FS)
Schilling, David C. Lt. Col.	Mar 29 44	Me 109
Schilling, David C. Lt. Col.	Apr 9 44	Fw 190
Schilling, David C. Lt. Col.	Apr 9 44	Fw 190
Schilling, David C. Lt. Col.	Apr 13 44	Me 109
Zemke, Hubert Col.	May 12 44	Me 109
Zemke, Hubert Col.	May 31 44	Fw 190
Zemke, Hubert Col.	May 31 44	Fw 190
Zemke, Hubert Col.	Jun 6 44	Fw 190
Zemke, Hubert Col.	Jun 7 44	Fw 190
Zemke, Hubert Col.	Jun 7 44	Fw 190
Schilling, David C. Col.	Aug 28 44	He 111
Schilling, David C. Col.	Sep 21 44	Fw 190
Schilling, David C. Col.	Sep 21 44	Fw 190
Schilling, David C. Col.	Sep 21 44	Fw 190
Schilling, David C. Col.	Dec 23 44	Me 109
Schilling, David C. Col.	Dec 23 44	Me 109
Schilling, David C. Col.	Dec 23 44	Me 109
Schilling, David C. Col.	Dec 23 44	Fw 190
Schilling, David C. Col.	Dec 23 44	Fw 190

61st Fighter Squadron

Johnson, Robert S. 2nd Lt.	Jun 13 43	Fw 190
Johnson, Gerald W. 1st Lt.	Jun 26 43	Fw 190
Powers, Joe H. 2nd Lt.	Jul 30 43	Me 109

Schreiber, Leroy A. Capt.	Jul 30 43	Me 109
Schreiber, Leroy A. Capt.	Jul 30 43	Me 109
Johnson, Gerald W. Capt.	Aug 17 43	Me 109
Johnson, Gerald W. Capt.	Aug 17 43	Me 109
Johnson, Gerald W. Capt.	Aug 17 43	.5 Me 109 w/F.McCauley
McCauley, Frank E. 1st Lt.	Aug 17 43	Fw 190
McCauley, Frank E. 1st Lt.	Aug 17 43	.5 Me 109 w/G.Johnson
Renwick, Donald D. Capt.	Aug 17 43	Me 109
Johnson, Gerald W. Capt.	Aug 19 43	Me 109
Johnson, Robert S. 1st Lt.	Aug 19 43	Me 109
Lamb, Robert A. Capt.	Aug 19 43	Fw 190
McCauley, Frank E. 1st Lt.	Aug 19 43	Me 109
McCauley, Frank E. 1st Lt.	Aug 19 43	Me 109
Gabreski, Francis S. Capt.	Aug 24 43	Fw 190
Gabreski, Francis S. Maj.	Sep 3 43	Fw 190
Marangello, William A. 2nd Lt.	Oct 4 43	Me 110
McCauley, Frank E. 1st Lt.	Oct 4 43	Me 110
Johnson, Robert S. 1st Lt.	Oct 8 43	Fw 190
Johnson, Gerald W. Capt.	Oct 10 43	Me 110
Johnson, Gerald W. Capt.	Oct 10 43	Me 210
Johnson, Robert S. 1st Lt.	Oct 10 43	Me 110
Johnson, Robert S. 1st Lt.	Oct 10 43	Fw 190
Brooks, Norman E. 1st Lt.	Oct 14 43	Me 110
Johnson, Gerald W. Capt.	Oct 14 43	Fw 190
McCauley, Frank E. 1st Lt.	Oct 14 43	Me 110
Stewart, James C. Major	Oct 18 43	.5 Me 210 w/M.Wood
Wood, Melvin C. 2nd Lt. 1/2	Oct 18 43	.5 Me 210 w/J.Stewart
Johnson, Robert S. 1st Lt.	Nov 3 43	Me 109
Barnum, Eugene E. 1st Lt.	Nov 5 43	Fw 190
Gabreski, Francis S. Major	Nov 5 43	Fw 190
Gabreski, Francis S. Major	Nov 26 43	Me 210
Gabreski, Francis S. Major	Nov 26 43	Me 210
Klibbe, Frank W. F/O	Nov 26 43	Me 109
Stewart, James C. Major	Nov 26 43	Do 217
Gabreski, Francis S. Major	Nov 29 43	Me 109
Gabreski, Francis S. Major	Nov 29 43	Me 109
Powers, Joe H. 1st Lt.	Nov 29 43	Me 109
Foster, Justus D. 1st Lt.	Dec 1 43	Fw 190
Mudge, Dick H. 1st Lt.	Dec 1 43	Me 109
Aggers, William R. F/O	Dec 11 43	.5 Fw 190 w/D.Smith
Conger, Paul A. 1st Lt.	Dec 11 43	Me 109
Conger, Paul A. 1st Lt.	Dec 11 43	Me 109
Conger, Paul A. 1st Lt.	Dec 11 43	Ju 88
Gabreski, Francis A. Major	Dec 11 43	Me 110
Lamb, Robert A. Capt.	Dec 11 43	Me 110
Lamb, Robert A. Capt.	Dec 11 43	Me 110
Lamb, Robert A. Capt.	Dec 11 43	Me 110
Powers, Joe H. 1st Lt.	Dec 11 43	Me 110
Powers, Joe H. 1st Lt.	Dec 11 43	Me 109
Roberts, Robill W. 1st Lt.	Dec 11 43	Me 110
Roberts, Robill W. 1st Lt.	Dec 11 43	Ju 88
Smith, Donovan F. 1st Lt.	Dec 11 43	Me 110
Smith, Donovan F. 1st Lt.	Dec 11 43	Me 110
Smith, Donovan F. 1st Lt.	Dec 11 43	.5 Fw 190 w/W.Aggers
Bennett, Joseph H. Capt.	Dec 20 43	Me 110

Name	Date	Aircraft		Name	Date	Aircraft
Johnson, Robert S. 1st Lt.	Dec 22 43	Me 109		Johnson, Robert S. 1st Lt.	Mar 15 44	Fw 190
Powers, Joe H. 1st Lt.	Dec 20 43	Me 109		Johnson, Robert S. 1st Lt.	Mar 15 44	Fw 190
Johnson, Robert S. 1st Lt.	Dec 30 43	Fw 190		Johnson, Robert S. 1st Lt.	Mar 15 44	Me 109
Johnson, Robert S. 1st Lt.	Dec 31 43	Fw 190		Klibbe, Frank 2nd Lt.	Mar 15 44	Fw 190
Johnson, Robert S. 1st Lt.	Dec 31 43	Fw 190		Powers, Joe H. 1st Lt.	Mar 15 44	Fw 190
Johnson, Robert S. 1st Lt.	Jan 5 44	Fw 190		Powers, Joe H. 1st Lt.	Mar 15 44	Me 109
Stewart, James C. Major	Jan 5 44	Fw 190		Rankin, Robert J. 1st Lt.	Mar 15 44	Me 109
Carter, James R. Capt.	Jan 11 44	Me 109		Rankin, Robert J. 1st Lt.	Mar 15 44	Me 109
Foster, Justus D. 1st Lt.	Jan 11 44	Me 109		Smith, Leslie C. Capt.	Mar 15 44	Me 109
Johnson, Robert S. 1st Lt.	Jan 21 44	Fw 190		Gabreski, Francis S. Lt. Col.	Mar 16 44	Fw 190
Bennett, Joseph H. Capt.	Jan 29 44	Me 110		Gabreski, Francis S. Lt. Col.	Mar 16 44	Fw 190
Bennett, Joseph H. Capt.	Jan 29 44	.5 Me 110 w/P.Neyland		McMinn, Evan D. F/O	Mar 16 44	Fw 190
Gabreski, Francis S. Lt. Col.	Jan 29 44	Me 210		Powers, Joe H. 1st Lt.	Mar 16 44	Me 109
Neyland, Praeger 2nd Lt.	Jan 29 44	.5 w/J.Bennett		Powers, Joe H. 1st Lt.	Mar 18 44	Fw 190
Wood, Melvin C. 2nd Lt.	Jan 29 44	Me 210		Stream, Dale E. 2nd Lt.	Mar 18 44	Fw 190
Barnum, Eugene E. 1st Lt.	Jan 30 44	Me 210		Stewart, James C. Major	Mar 20 44	Me 109
Carter, James R. Capt.	Jan 30 44	Fw 190		Stewart, James C. Major	Mar 20 44	Me 109
Gabreski, Francis S. Lt. Col.	Jan 30 44	Me 210		Stream, Dale E. 2nd Lt.	Mar 20 44	Me 109
Gabreski, Francis S. Lt. Col.	Jan 30 44	Me 109		Gabreski, Francis S. Lt. Col.	Mar 27 44	Me 109
Johnson, Robert S. 1st Lt.	Jan 30 44	Me 210		Gabreski, Francis S. Lt. Col.	Mar 27 44	Me 109
Johnson, Robert S. 1st Lt.	Jan 30 44	Me 109		Gladych, Michael FLT.	Mar 27 44	Me 109
Klibbe, Frank W. 2nd Lt.	Jan 30 44	Me 109		Rankin, Robert J. 1st Lt.	Mar 29 44	Me 109
Powers, Joe H. 1st Lt.	Jan 30 44	Fw 190		Andersz, Tadeusz FLT.	Apr 9 44	Me 109
Hamilton, Samuel D. 1st Lt.	Feb 6 44	Me 109		Hamilton, Samuel D. 1st Lt.	Apr 9 44	Fw 190
Lamb, Robert A. Capt.	Feb 6 44	Me 109		Johnson, Robert S. Capt.	Apr 9 44	Fw 190
Powers, Joe H. 1st Lt.	Feb 6 44	Me 109		Smith, Leslie C. Capt.	Apr 9 44	Me 109
Rankin, Robert J. 2nd Lt.	Feb 6 44	Me 109		Johnson, Robert S. Capt.	Apr 13 44	Fw 190
Stewart, James C. Major	Feb 11 44	Fw 190		Johnson, Robert S. Capt.	Apr 13 44	Fw 190
Carter, James R. Capt.	Feb 20 44	Me 110		Conger, Paul A. Capt.	Apr 15 44	Fw 190
Gabreski, Francis S. Lt. Col.	Feb 20 44	Me 210		Gabreski, Francis S. Lt. Col.	May 8 44	Me 109
Gabreski, Francis S. Lt. Col.	Feb 20 44	Me 210		Klibbe, Frank W. 2nd Lt.	May 8 44	Me 109
Johnson, Robert S. 1st Lt.	Feb 20 44	Me 210		Klibbe, Frank W. 2nd Lt.	May 8 44	Fw 190
Johnson, Robert S. 1st Lt.	Feb 20 44	Me 210		Conger, Paul A. Capt.	May 12 44	Fw 190
Lamb, Robert A. Capt.	Feb 20 44	Ju 88		Conger, Paul A. Capt.	May 12 44	Fw 190
Smith, Donovan F. 1st Lt.	Feb 20 44	Me 110		Maul, Arthur C. 2nd Lt.	May 12 44	Me 109
Smith, Donovan F. 1st Lt.	Feb 20 44	Me 110		Rankin, Robert J. 1st Lt.	May 12 44	Me 109
Funcheon, Donald M. 1st Lt.	Feb 21 44	Me 109		Rankin, Robert J. 1st Lt.	May 12 44	Me 109
Gladych, Michael FLT.	Feb 21 44	Me 109		Rankin, Robert J. 1st Lt.	May 12 44	Fw 190
Gladych, Michael FLT.	Feb 21 44	Me 109		Rankin, Robert J. 1st Lt.	May 12 44	Fw 190
Klibbe, Frank W. 2nd Lt.	Feb 21 44	Me 109		Thomton, Cleon C. 1st Lt.	May 12 44	Me 109
McMinn, Evan D. F/O	Feb 21 44	Me 109		Jure, James M. 2nd Lt.	May 13 44	Fw 190
Mussey, Claud E. 2nd Lt.	Feb 21 44	Me 109		Keen, Robert J. 1st Lt.	May 13 44	Fw 190
Gabreski, Francis S. Lt. Col.	Feb 22 44	Fw 190		Keen, Robert J. 1st Lt.	May 13 44	Fw 190
McMinn, Evan D. F/O	Feb 22 44	Fw 190		Keen, Robert J. 1st Lt.	May 13 44	Fw 190
Smith, Donovan F. 1st Lt.	Feb 22 44	Fw 190		Heineman, Richard M. 2nd Lt.	May 19 44	Fw 190
Smith, Leslie C. Capt.	Feb 22 44	Fw 190		Smith, Leslie C. Major	May 19 44	Fw 190
Smith, Leslie C. Capt.	Feb 22 44	Fw 190		Smith, Leslie C. Major	May 19 44	Fw 190
Stewart, James C. Major	Feb 22 44	Me 109		Carter, James R. Capt.	May 22 44	Fw 190
Blake, Gordon J. 1st Lt.	Feb 24 44	Fw 190		Clark, James J. 2nd Lt.	May 22 44	Fw 190
Funcheon, Donald M. 1st Lt.	Feb 24 44	Fw 190		Gabreski, Francis S. Lt. Col.	May 22 44	Fw 190
Powers, Joe H. 1st Lt.	Feb 24 44	Fw 190		Gabreski, Francis S. Lt. Col.	May 22 44	Fw 190
Stewart, James C. Major	Feb 24 44	Fw 190		Gabreski, Francis S. Lt. Col.	May 22 44	Fw 190
Funcheon, Donald M. 1st Lt.	Feb 25 44	Me 109		Heineman, Richard M. 2nd Lt.	May 22 44	Fw 190
Lamb, Robert A. Capt.	Feb 25 44	Me 109		Heineman, Richard M. 2nd Lt.	May 22 44	Fw 190
Johnson, Robert S. 1st Lt.	Mar 6 44	Fw 190		Herin, Reginald A. 2nd Lt.	May 22 44	Fw 190
Stewart, James C. Major	Mar 6 44	Fw 190		Landwski, Witold F/O	May 22 44	Fw 190
Stewart, James C. Major	Mar 6 44	Fw 190		McMinn, Evan D. F/O	May 22 44	Fw 190
Bennett, Joseph H. Capt.	Mar 8 44	Fw 190		McMinn, Evan D. F/O	May 22 44	Fw 190
Bennett, Joseph H. Capt.	Mar 8 44	Me 109		Neyland, Praeger 2nd Lt.	May 22 44	Fw 190
Bennett, Joseph H. Capt.	Mar 8 44	Me 109		Gladych, Michael FLT.	Jun 6 44	Me 109
Blake, Gordon J. 1st Lt.	Mar 8 44	Fw 190		Gabreski, Francis S. Lt. Col.	Jun 7 44	Me 109
Brooks, Norman E. 1st Lt.	Mar 8 44	? Brooks is not mentioned in either squadron or group records as participating in this day's missions.		Gabreski, Francis S. Lt. Col.	Jun 7 44	Fw 190
				Gerick, Steven F/O	Jun 7 44	Me 109
				Gladych, Michael FLT.	Jun 7 44	Me 109
				Popplewell, Joel I. 2nd Lt.	Jun 7 44	Me 109
Gladych, Michael FLT.	Mar 8 44	Fw 190		Rankin, Robert J. 1st Lt.	Jun 7 44	Me 109
Johnson, Robert S. 1st Lt.	Mar 8 44	Me 109		Belk, Oscar M. 1st Lt.	Jun 12 44	Me 109
Johnson, Robert S. 1st Lt.	Mar 8 44	Me 109		Gabreski, Francis S. Lt. Col.	Jun 12 44	Me 109
Klibbe, Frank W. 2nd Lt.	Mar 8 44	Fw 190		Gabreski, Francis S. Lt. Col.	Jun 12 44	Me 109
Mussey, Claude E. 2nd Lt.	Mar 8 44	Me 109		Gerick, Steven F/O	Jun 12 44	Me 109
Stewart, James C. Major	Mar 8 44	Me 110		Gerick, Steven F/O	Jun 12 44	Me 109
Stewart, James C. Major	Mar 8 44	Fw 190		Gerick, Steven F/O	Jun 16 44	Me 109
Gerick, Steven F/O	Mar 15 44	Me 109		Gabreski, Francis S. Lt. Col.	Jun 27 44	Me 109

Name	Date	Aircraft
Jure, James M. 2nd Lt.	Jun 27 44	Me 109
Lanowski, Witold FLT.	Jun 27 44	Me 109
Patterson, Warren S. 1st Lt.	Jun 27 44	Me 109
Carter, James R. Capt.	Jul 4 44	Me 109
Sisson, Edward A. 1st Lt.	Jul 4 44	Me 109 Credited by the AAF, but not mentioned in either squadron or group records as participating in this day's missions.
Gabreski, Francis S. Lt. Col.	Jul 5 44	Me 109
Gladych, Michael SL.	Jul 5 44	Me 109
Keen, Robert J. 1st Lt.	Jul 5 44	Me 109
Keen, Robert J. 1st Lt.	Jul 5 44	Me 109
Keen, Robert J. 1st Lt.	Jul 5 44	Me 109
Landwski, Witold FLT.	Jul 5 44	Me 109
Gladych, Michael SL.	Aug 12 44	Ju 88
Conger, Paul A. Capt.	Aug 28 44	.5 He 111 w/J.Jure
Jure, James M. 2nd Lt.	Aug 28 44	.5 He 111 w/P.Conger
Clark, James J. 1st Lt.	Sep 12 44	Me 109
Jure, James M. 2nd Lt.	Sep 12 44	Me 109
Getz, Stuart H. 1st Lt.	Sep 21 44	.5 Fw 190 w/W.Osborne
Gladych, Michael SL.	Sep 21 44	Fw 190
Gladych, Michael SL.	Sep 21 44	Fw 190
Kyler, Russell S. 2nd Lt.	Sep 21 44	Fw 190
Osborne, William J. 2nd Lt.	Sep 21 44	.5 Fw 190 w/S.Getz
Baughman, Robert A. 1st Lt.	Nov 18 44	Fw 190
Carter, James R. Capt	Nov 18 44	Me 109
Cathers, Benjamin E. Capt.	Nov 18 44	Fw 190
Gerow, Arthur H. 2nd Lt.	Nov 18 44	Fw 190
Kyler, Russell S. 2nd Lt.	Nov 18 44	Fw 190
Lanowski, Witold FLT.	Nov 18 44	Fw 190
Raymond, Charles J. 2nd Lt.	Nov 18 44	Fw 190
Bast, Victor E. 1st Lt.	Dec 23 44	Fw 190
Frazier, John F. 2nd Lt.	Dec 23 44	Fw 190
Frazier, John F. 2nd Lt.	Dec 23 44	Fw 190
Perry, Joseph H. Capt.	Dec 23 44	Fw 190
Perry, Joseph H. Capt.	Dec 23 44	Fw 190
Clark, William D. 1st Lt.	Dec 25 44	Fw 190
Kyler, Russell S. 1st Lt.	Jan 14 45	Me 109
Walker, Robert E. 1st Lt.	Jan 14 45	Me 109

62nd Fighter Squadron

Name	Date	Aircraft
Cook, Walter V. Capt.	Jun 12 43	Fw 190
Harrison, Charles R. 1st Lt.	Jun 26 43	Fw 190
Harrison, Charles R. 1st Lt.	Aug 17 43	Me 110
Reeder, Caleb L. 2nd Lt.	Aug 17 43	Me 110
Quirk, Michael J. 1st Lt.	Aug 19 43	Fw 190
Jones, James M. 1st Lt.	Aug 24 43	Fw 190
Schreiber, Leroy A. Capt.	Aug 24 43	Fw 190
Carcione, Anthony R. 1st Lt.	Sep 7 43	Me 109
Johnson, Ralph A. 1st Lt.	Sep 7 43	Me 109
Goldstein, George G. 1st Lt.	Sep 16 43	Me 109
Taylor, Robert B. 1st Lt.	Sep 16 43	Fw 190
Coronios, Harry 1st Lt.	Oct 8 43	Fw 190
Quirk, Michael J. 1st Lt.	Oct 8 43	Fw 190
Schreiber, Leroy A. Capt.	Oct 8 43	Fw 190
Carcione, Anthony B. 1st Lt.	Oct 10 43	Me 109
Cook, Walter V. Capt.	Oct 10 43	Me 210
Eaves, John B. 1st Lt.	Oct 10 43	Me 109
Jones, James M. 1st Lt.	Oct 10 43	Fw 190
Taylor, Robert B. 1st Lt.	Oct 10 43	Fw 190
Cook, Walter V. Capt.	Nov 11 43	Fw 190
Cook, Walter V. Capt.	Nov 11 43	Fw 190
Goldstein, George G. 1st Lt.	Nov 11 43	Fw 190
Icard, Joe W. F/O	Nov 11 43	Fw 190
O'Neill, Eugene W. Capt.	Nov 11 43	Fw 190
Boyle, Mark K. 2nd Lt.	Nov 26 43	.5 Me 109 w/E.O'Neill
Bryant, John P. 1st Lt.	Nov 26 43	Me 110
Carcione, Anthony R. 1st Lt.	Nov 26 43	Me 210
Christensen, Fred J. 2nd Lt.	Nov 26 43	Me 110
Cook, Walter V. Capt.	Nov 26 43	Me 110
Cook, Walter V. Capt.	Nov 26 43	Me 110
Johnson, Ralph A. Capt.	Nov 26 43	Me 110
Johnson, Ralph A. Capt.	Nov 26 43	Me 110
Morrill, Stanley R. 1st Lt.	Nov 26 43	Me 109
O'Neill, Eugene W. Capt.	Nov 26 43	Fw 190
O'Neill, Eugene W. Capt.	Nov 26 43	.5 Me 110 w/M.Boyle
Valenta, Irvin E. F/O	Nov 26 43	Me 110
Valenta, Irvin E. F/O	Nov 26 43	Me 110
Prudden, Harry M. 2nd Lt.	Nov 29 43	.5 Me 210 w/L. Schreiber
Schreiber, Leroy A. Capt.	Nov 29 43	.5 Me 210 w/H. Prudden
Williamson, Felix D. 1st Lt.	Nov 29 43	.5 Fw 190 w/D.Schilling
Christensen, Fred J. 2nd Lt.	Dec 1 43	Me 109
Morrill, Stanley B. 1st Lt.	Dec 11 43	Me 109
Craig, Horace C. Major	Dec 20 43	Do 217
O'Neill, Eugene W. Capt.	Dec 20 43	Me 109
Quirk, Michael J. 1st Lt.	Dec 20 43	Me 109
Williamson, Felix D. 1st Lt.	Dec 22 43	Me 109
Quirk, Michael J. 1st Lt.	Jan 4 44	Fw 190
Christensen, Fred J. 2nd Lt.	Jan 5 44	Fw 190
Morrill, Stanley B. 1st Lt.	Jan 5 44	Me 109
Morrill, Stanley B. 1st Lt.	Jan 11 44	Me 109
Carcione, Anthony R. 1st Lt.	Jan 30 44	.5 Ju 88 w/S. Morrill
Morrill, Stanley B. 1st Lt.	Jan 30 44	.5 Ju 88 w/A.Carcione
Quirk, Michael J. 1st Lt.	Jan 30 44	Me 109
Christensen, Fred J. 1st Lt.	Feb 4 44	Fw 190
Fields, James F. 2nd Lt.	Feb 4 44	Fw 190
Quirk, Michael J. Capt.	Feb 4 44	Fw 190
Quirk, Michael J. Capt.	Feb 4 44	Unidentified twin-engined type
O'Neill, Eugene W. Capt.	Feb 6 44	Fw 190
Icard, Joe W. 2nd Lt.	Feb 8 44	Me 109
Morrill, Stanley R. 1st Lt.	Feb 11 44	Me 109
Christensen, Fred J. 1st Lt.	Feb 20 44	Ju 88
Christensen, Fred J. 1st Lt.	Feb 20 44	.5 Do 217 w/S.Morrill
Morrill, Stanley B. 1st Lt.	Feb 20 44	Me 110
Morrill, Stanley B. 1st Lt.	Feb 20 44	.5 Do 217 w/F.Christensen
Schreiber, Leroy A. Capt.	Feb 20 44	Me 109
Schreiber, Leroy A. Capt.	Feb 20 44	Me 109
Schreiber, Leroy A. Capt.	Feb 20 44	Me 109
Bluhm, Roy B. 2nd Lt.	Feb 21 44	Me 109
Harrison, Charles R. 1st Lt.	Feb 21 44	Me 109
Icard, Joe W. 2nd Lt.	Feb 21 44	Fw 190
Fields, James E. 2nd Lt.	Feb 22 44	.5 Fw 190 w/M.Quirk
Fields, James E. 2nd Lt.	Feb 22 44	.5 Me 109 w/L.Schreiber
Quirk, Michael J. Capt.	Feb 22 44	Fw 190
Quirk, Michael J. Capt.	Feb 22 44	.5 Fw 190 w/J.Fields
Roy, Frederick L. 2nd Lt.	Feb 22 44	Fw 190
Schreiber, Leroy A. Capt.	Feb 22 44	.5 Me 109 w/J.Fields
Gordon, William P. 1st Lt.	Feb 24 44	Fw 190
Morrill, Stanley B. 1st Lt.	Feb 24 44	Me 109
Quirk, Michael J. Capt.	Feb 25 44	Fw 190
Christensen, Fred J. 1st Lt.	Mar 6 44	Fw 190
Icard, Joe W. 2nd Lt.	Mar 6 44	Fw 190
Cherry, Robert C. 1st Lt.	Mar 8 44	Fw 190
Eaves, John B. 1st Lt.	Mar 8 44	.5 Fw 190 w/M.Quirk
Fields, James E. 2nd Lt.	Mar 8 44	Fw 190
Moseley, Mark L. 1st Lt.	Mar 8 44	Fw 190
Quirk, Michael J. Capt.	Mar 8 44	.5 Fw 190 w/J.Eaves
Schreiber, Leroy A. Capt.	Mar 8 44	Fw 190
Schreiber, Leroy A. Capt.	Mar 8 44	Me 109
Williamson, Felix D. 1st Lt.	Mar 8 44	Fw 190
Bryant, John P. 1st Lt.	Mar 15 44	Fw 190
Christensen, Fred J. 1st Lt.	Mar 15 44	Fw 190
Christensen, Fred J. 1st Lt.	Mar 15 44	Fw 190
Fields, James F. 2nd Lt.	Mar 15 44	Fw 190
Jones, James M. 1st Lt.	Mar 15 44	Fw 190
Moseley, Mark L. 1st Lt.	Mar 15 44	Fw 190
Quirk, Michael J. Capt.	Mar 15 44	Fw 190
Buszko, Thaddeus S. 1st Lt.	Mar 16 44	Fw 190
Canizares, Arlington W. 2nd Lt	Mar 16 44	.5 Fw 190 w/L.Schreiber
Christensen, Fred J. 1st Lt.	Mar 16 44	Fw 190
Christensen, Fred J. 1st Lt.	Mar 16 44	Fw 190
Morrill, Stanley B. 1st Lt.	Mar 16 44	Fw 190
Schreiber, Leroy A. Capt.	Mar 16 44	Me 109
Schreiber, Leroy A. Capt.	Mar 16 44	.5 Fw 190 w/A.Canizares

Williamson, Felix D. 1st Lt.	Mar 16 44	Fw 190	McMahan, Darrel F. 1st Lt.	Sep 12 44	Me 109
Canizares, Arlington W. 1st Lt.	Apr 9 44	.5 Me 109 w/L.Schreiber	Brown, Lewis R. 2nd Lt.	Sep 21 44	Fw 190
Powers, Joseph H. Capt.	Apr 9 44	Me 109	Henley, Donald 2nd Lt.	Sep 21 44	Fw 190
Schreiber, Leroy A. Major	Apr 9 44	.5 Me 109 w/A.Canizares	Jackson, Michael J. Capt.	Sep 21 44	Fw 190
Boyle, Mark K. 1st Lt.	Apr 13 44	Me 109	Patterson, Roy L. 2nd Lt.	Sep 21 44	Fw 190
Chattaway, William P. 1st Lt.	Apr 15 44	Fw 190	Winters, Robert E. 2nd Lt.	Sep 21 44	Fw 190
Christensen, Fred J. Capt.	Apr 15 44	Me 109	Ferguson, John W. 1st Lt.	Nov 18 44	Fw 190
Christensen, Fred J. Capt.	Apr 15 44	Fw 190	Gould, Norman D. 2nd Lt.	Nov 18 44	Me 109
McClure, Wendell A. 1st Lt.	Apr 20 44	.5 Ju 88 w/F.Williamson	Jackson, Michael J. Capt.	Nov 18 44	Fw 190
Williamson, Felix D. Capt.	Apr 20 44	.5 Ju 88 w/W.McClure	Wilkerson, William F. Capt.	Nov 18 44	Fw 190
Bennett, Eugene E. 2nd Lt.	May 4 44	.5 Fw 190 w/R.Cherry	Davis, Riegel W. Capt.	Dec 2 44	Me 109
Cherry, Robert C. 1st Lt.	May 4 44	.5 Fw 190 w/E.Bennett	Davis, Riegel W. Capt.	Dec 2 44	Me 109
Cherry, Robert C. 1st Lt.	May 4 44	Me 410	Ball, Sanborn N. 1st Lt.	Dec 23 44	Fw 190
Powers, Joe H. Capt.	May 4 44	Me 109	Beason, Eugene M. 1st Lt.	Dec 23 44	Me 109
Johnson, Robert S. Capt.	May 8 44	Me 109	Daley, William C. 1st Lt.	Dec 23 44	Me 109
Johnson, Robert S. Capt.	May 8 44	Fw 190	Geren, Lloyd F. 2nd Lt.	Dec 23 44	.5 Fw 190 w/D.Westover
Lewis, Gordon H. 2nd Lt.	May 8 44	Fw 190	Gould, Norman D. 2nd Lt.	Dec 23 44	Fw 190
Greene, Jack E. 1st Lt.	May 12 44	Me 109	Lear, Warren S. 1st Lt.	Dec 23 44	Fw 190
King, Herman E. 1st Lt.	May 12 44	Me 109	Perry, Alfred O. 2nd Lt.	Dec 23 44	Fw 190
Powers, Joe H. Capt.	May 12 44	.5 Me 109 w/J.Vitale	Perry, Alfred O. 2nd Lt.	Dec 23 44	Fw 190
Vitale, Joseph F/O	May 12 44	.5 Me 109 w/J.Powers	Westover, Don A. 2nd Lt.	Dec 23 44	.5 Fw 190 w/L.Geren
Dade, Lucien A. Major	May 13 44	Fw 190	Williamson, Felix D. Capt.	Dec 23 44	Me 109
Eaves, John B. Capt.	May 19 44	Fw 190	Williamson, Felix D. Capt.	Dec 23 44	Fw 190
Eaves, John B. Capt.	May 19 44	Fw 190	Daley, William C. 1st Lt.	Dec 25 44	Me 109
McClure, Wendell A. 1st Lt.	May 31 44	Fw 190	Daley, William C. 1st Lt.	Dec 25 44	Me 109
Tucker, Charles F. Capt.	May 31 44	Fw 190	Jackson, Michael J. Capt.	Dec 25 44	Me 109
McElhare, William W. 1st Lt.	Jun 6 44	Fw 190	Sharbo, Walter J. F/O	Dec 25 44	Me 109
Bostwick, George F. 1st Lt.	Jun 7 44	Me 109	Sharbo, Walter J. F/O	Dec 25 44	Me 109
Moseley, Mark L. 1st Lt.	Jun 7 44	.5 Ju 88 w/J.Pierce	Perry, Alfred O. 2nd Lt.	Dec 26 44	Fw 190
Pierce, Jack W. 2nd Lt.	Jun 7 44	.5 Ju 88 w/M.Moseley	Perry, Alfred O. 2nd Lt.	Dec 26 44	Fw 190
Butler, George H. 2nd Lt.	Jun 8 44	Me 109	Smith, Leslie C. Major	Dec 26 44	Fw 190
Edens, Billy G. 2nd Lt.	Jun 8 44	Me 109	Butiste, Leo F. F/O	Dec 31 44	Fw 190
Edens, Billy G. 2nd Lt.	Jun 8 44	Fw 190	Nolan, Francis A. Capt.	Dec 31 44	Fw 190
Moseley, Mark L. 1st Lt.	Jun 8 44	Fw 190	Nolan, Francis A. Capt.	Dec 31 44	Fw 190
Moseley, Mark L. 1st Lt.	Jun 8 44	Fw 190	Stovall, William H. 2nd Lt.	Dec 31 44	Fw 190
Van Noy, George H. 2nd Lt.	Jun 8 44	Me 109	Stovall, William H. 2nd Lt.	Dec 31 44	Fw 190
Cherry, Robert C. 1st Lt.	Jun 27 44	Me 109	Daley, William C. 1st Lt.	Jan 14 45	Me 109
Christensen, Fred J. Capt.	Jun 27 44	Me 109	Henley, Donald 1st Lt.	Jan 14 45	.5 Me 109 w/H.Womack
Baker, Gordon E. Major	Jul 4 44	Me 109	Henley, Donald 1st Lt.	Jan 14 45	Me 109
Bostwick, George E. 1st Lt.	Jul 4 44	Me 109	Jackson, Michael J. Major	Jan 14 45	Me 109
Bostwick, George E. 1st Lt.	Jul 4 44	Me 109	Jackson, Michael J. Major	Jan 14 45	Fw 190
Bostwick, George E. 1st Lt.	Jul 4 44	Me 109	Smith, Kenneth L. 1st Lt.	Jan 14 45	Me 109
Dade, Lucien A. Major	Jul 4 44	Me 109	Williamson, Felix D. Capt.	Jan 14 45	Fw 190
Dade, Lucien A. Major	Jul 4 44	Me 109	Williamson, Felix D. Capt.	Jan 14 45	Me 109
Jackson, Michael J. Capt.	Jul 4 44	Me 109	Williamson, Felix D. Capt.	Jan 14 45	Me 109
Knafelz, Albert P. 1st Lt.	Jul 4 44	Me 109	Williamson, Felix D. Capt.	Jan 14 45	Me 109
Knox, Baird W. 1st Lt.	Jul 4 44	Me 109	Williamson, Felix D. Capt.	Jan 14 45	Me 109
McElhare, William W. 1st Lt.	Jul 4 44	Me 109	Womak, Herschell O. 2nd Lt.	Jan 14 45	.5 Me 109 w/D.Henley
McMahan, Darrel E. 2nd Lt.	Jul 4 44	.5 Me 109 w/F.Newell	Williamson, Felix D. Capt.	Feb 3 45	Fw 190
Merrill, Wiley H. 1st Lt.	Jul 4 44	Me 109	Williamson, Felix D. Capt.	Feb 3 45	Me 109
Merrill, Wiley H. 1st Lt.	Jul 4 44	Me 109	Carroll, Dennis A. 2nd Lt.	Mar 10 45	.5 Fw 190 w/D.Henley
Newell, Frank C. 1st Lt.	Jul 4 44	.5 Me 109 w/D.McMahan	Gould, Norman D. 1st Lt.	Mar 10 45	Me 109
Moseley, Mark L. Capt.	Jul 4 44	Me 109	Henley, Donald 1st Lt.	Mar 10 45	.5 Fw 190 w/D.Carroll
Sheridan, Dayton C. 1st Lt.	Jul 4 44	Me 109	Ball, Sanborn N. 1st Lt.	Mar 14 45	.5 Ar 234 w/W.Lear
Butler, George H. 1st Lt.	Jul 5 44	Fw 190	Gould, Norman D. 1st Lt.	Mar 14 45	Ar 234
Cherry, Robert C. 1st Lt.	Jul 5 44	Fw 190	Lear, Warren S. 1st Lt.	Mar 14 45	.5 Ar 234 w/S.Ball
Christensen, Fred J. Capt.	Jul 5 44	Fw 190	Pruitt, Sherman 1st Lt.	Mar 14 45	Me 109
Edens, Billy G. 2nd Lt.	Jul 5 44	Fw 190	Winters, Robert E. Capt.	Apr 7 45	Me 109
Pierce, Jack W. 1st Lt.	Jul 5 44	Fw 190	Sharbo, Walter J. 2nd Lt.	Apr 10 45	Me 262
Bostwick, George E. 1st Lt.	Jul 6 44	Me 109			
Moseley, Mark L. Capt.	Jul 6 44	Me 109			
Christensen, Fred J. Capt.	Jul 7 44	Ju 52			
Christensen, Fred J. Capt.	Jul 7 44	Ju 52			

63rd Fighter Squadron

Christensen, Fred J. Capt.	Jul 7 44	Ju 52	Comstock, Harold E. 1st Lt.	Aug 17 43	Me 109
Christensen, Fred J. Capt.	Jul 7 44	Ju 52	Mahurin, Walker M. Capt.	Aug 17 43	Fw 190
Christensen, Fred J. Capt.	Jul 7 44	Ju 52	Mahurin, Walker M. Capt.	Aug 17 43	Fw 190
Edens, Billy G. Capt.	Jul 7 44	Ju 52	Schlitz, Glen D. 1st Lt.	Aug 17 43	Fw 190
Edens, Billy G. Capt.	Jul 7 44	Ju 52	Schlitz, Glen D. 1st Lt.	Aug 17 43	Fw 190
Edens, Billy G. Capt.	Jul 7 44	Ju 52	Schlitz, Glen D. 1st Lt.	Aug 17 43	Fw 190
Jackson, Michael J. Capt.	Jul 7 44	Ju 52	Truluck, John H. 2nd Lt.	Aug 17 43	Fw 190
Jackson, Michael J. Capt.	Aug 28 44	Ju 88	Whitley, Edgar D.1st Lt.	Aug 17 43	Me 110
Butler, George H. 1st Lt.	Sep 5 44	Fw 44	Egan, Joseph L. 1st Lt.	Aug 19 43	Fw 190
			Vogt, John W. 1st Lt.	Aug 19 43	Me 109
			Whitley, Edgar D. 1st Lt.	Aug 19 43	Me 109

Name	Date	Aircraft
Adrianse, Lyle A. Capt.	Sep 3 43	Fw 190
Goodfleisch, Don M. Capt.	Sep 3 43	Fw 190
Mahurin, Walker M. Capt.	Sep 9 43	Fw 190
Coenen, John E. 1st Lt.	Sep 27 43	Fw 190
Coenen, John E. 1st Lt.	Sep 27 43	Fw 190
O'Connor, Wayne J. 1st Lt.	Sep 27 43	Me 109
Truluck, John H. 1st Lt.	Sep 27 43	Fw 190
Truluck, John H. 1st Lt.	Sep 27 43	Me 109
Brown, Jack D. 1st Lt.	Oct 4 43	Me 110
Comstock, Harold E. 1st Lt.	Oct 4 43	Me 110
Goodfeisch, Don M. Capt.	Oct 4 43	Me 110
Ludwig, Vance P. 1st Lt.	Oct 4 43	Me 110
Ludwig, Vance P. 1st Lt.	Oct 4 43	Me 110
Ludwig, Vance P. 1st Lt.	Oct 4 43	Me 110
Mahurin, Walker M. Capt.	Oct 4 43	Me 110
Mahurin, Walker M. Capt.	Oct 4 43	Me 110
Mahurin, Walker M. Capt.	Oct 4 43	Me 110
Schlitz, Glen D. 1st Lt.	Oct 4 43	Me 110
Smith, Benard R. 2nd Lt.	Oct 4 43	Me 110
Vogt, John W. 1st Lt.	Oct 4 43	Me 110
Wilson, John D. 1st Lt.	Oct 4 43	Me 110
Vogt, John W. 1st Lt.	Oct 20 43	Fw 190
Mahurin, Walker M. Capt.	Nov 3 43	Me 110
Mahurin, Walker M. Capt.	Nov 3 43	.5 Me 109 w/J.O'Connor
O'Connor, Wayne J. 1st Lt.	Nov 3 43	.5 Me 109 w/W.Mahurin
Hall, George F. 1st Lt.	Nov 5 43	Me 210
Reed, Charles W. 2nd Lt.	Nov 5 43	Fw 190
Wilson, John D. 1st Lt.	Nov 5 43	Fw 190
Burke, Sylvester V. Capt.	Nov 11 43	Me 109
Comstock, Harold E. 1st Lt.	Nov 26 43	Me 110
Mahurin, Walker M. Capt.	Nov 26 43	Me 110
Mahurin, Walker M. Capt.	Nov 26 43	Me 110
Mahurin, Walker M. Capt.	Nov 26 43	Me 110
Truluck, John H. 1st Lt.	Nov 26 43	Fw 190
Mahurin, Walker M. Capt.	Nov 29 43	Me 109
Schlitz, Glen D. 1st Lt.	Dec 11 43	Me 210
Mahurin, Walker M. Capt.	Dec 22 43	Me 109
Mahurin, Walker M. Capt.	Dec 22 43	Me 109
Burke, Sylvester V. Major	Jan 11 44	Me 109
Robey, Archie H. 2nd Lt.	Jan 11 44	Me 109
Schlitz, Glen D. 1st Lt.	Jan 11 44	Me 109
Schlitz, Glen D. 1st Lt.	Jan 11 44	Me 109
Schlitz, Glen D. 1st Lt.	Jan 11 44	Me 109
Smith, Benard R. 2nd Lt.	Jan 11 44	Fw 190
Cavallo, Anthony S. 2nd Lt.	Jan 29 44	Me 210
Egan, Joseph L. 1st Lt.	Jan 30 44	Me 210
Hall, George F. 1st Lt.	Jan 30 44	Me 109
Hall, George F. 1st Lt.	Jan 30 44	Me 109
Langdon, Lloyd M. 2nd Lt.	Jan 30 44	Me 109
Langdon, Lloyd M. 2nd Lt.	Jan 30 44	Me 109
Mahurin, Walker M. Capt.	Jan 30 44	Ju 88
Mahurin, Walker M. Capt.	Feb 3 44	Me 109
Reed, Charles W. 1st Lt.	Feb 3 44	Me 109
Burke, Sylvester V. Major	Feb 11 44	Me 109
Egan, Joseph L. 1st Lt.	Feb 21 44	Me 109
Vogt, John W. Capt.	Feb 21 44	Me 110
Adrainse, Lyle A. Capt.	Feb 22 44	Me 110
Egan, Joseph L. 1st Lt.	Feb 22 44	Me 109
Hall, George F. 1st Lt.	Feb 22 44	Me 110
Hall, George F. 1st Lt.	Feb 22 44	Me 110
Vogt, John W. Capt.	Feb 22 44	Me 110
Johnson, Gerald W. Major	Feb 24 44	Fw 190
Truluck, John H. 1st Lt.	Feb 24 44	Fw 190
Johnson, Gerald W. Major	Feb 29 44	Ju 52
Johnson, Gerald W. Major	Mar 2 44	Me 109
Becker, Marvin H. 2nd Lt.	Mar 6 44	.25 Me 109 w/D.Peters, C.Reed, H. Zemke
Hall, George F. 1st Lt.	Mar 6 44	Fw 190
Mahurin, Walker M. Capt.	Mar 6 44	Fw 190
Peters, Donald V. 2nd Lt.	Mar 6 44	.25 Me 109 w/M.Becker, C.Reed, H.Zemke
Reed, Charles W. 1st Lt.	Mar 6 44	.25 Me 109 w/M.Becker, D.Peters, H.Zemke
Becker, Marvin H. 2nd Lt.	Mar 8 44	Me 109
Johnson, Gerald W. Major	Mar 8 44	Me 109
Johnson, Gerald W. Major	Mar 8 44	Me 109
Mahurin, Walker M. Capt.	Mar 8 44	Ju 88
Mahurin, Walker M. Capt.	Mar 8 44	Fw 190
Mahurin, Walker M. Capt.	Mar 8 44	Fw 190
Robey, Archie H. 1st Lt.	Mar 8 44	Me 109
Smith, Benard R. 1st Lt.	Mar 8 44	Me 110
Trulock, John H. 1st Lt.	Mar 8 44	Me 109
Egan, Joseph L. 1st Lt.	Mar 15 44	Fw 190
Johnson, Gerald W. Major	Mar 15 44	Me 109
Johnson, Gerald W. Major	Mar 15 44	Me 109
Peters, Donald V. 1st Lt.	Mar 15 44	Me 109
Robey, Archie H. 1st Lt.	Mar 15 44	Fw 190
Robey, Archie H. 1st Lt.	Mar 15 44	Fw 190
Trulock, John H. 1st Lt.	Mar 15 44	Fw 190
Johnson, Willard D. 2nd Lt.	Mar 27 44	.25 Do 217 w/S.Lowman, W.Mahurin, I.Porowski
Lowman, Samuel J. F/O	Mar 27 44	.25 Do 217 w/W.Johnson, W.Mahurin, I.Porowski
Mahurin, Walker M. Major	Mar 27 44	.25 Do 217 w/W.Johnson, S.Lowman, I.Porowski
Porowski, Isadore D. 2nd Lt.	Mar 27 44	.25 Do 217 w/W.Johnson, S.Lowman, W.Mahurin
Johnson, Willard D. 2nd Lt.	Apr 15 44	.5 Fw 190 w/S.Stamps
Stamps, Samuel O. 1st Lt.	Apr 15 44	.5 Fw 190 w. W.Johnson
Cavallo, Anthony S. 1st Lt.	May 12 44	Fw 190
Cavallo, Anthony S. 1st Lt.	May 12 44	Fw 190
Wakefield, J. Carroll 1st Lt.	May 12 44	Me 109
Wakefield, J. Carroll 1st Lt.	May 12 44	Me 109
Peters, Donald V. 1st Lt.	May 31 44	Fw 190
Becker, Marvin H. 1st Lt.	Jun 7 44	.5 Fw 190 w/S.Dale
Curtis, Joseph R. 1st Lt.	Jun 7 44	Fw 190
Dale, Sam B. 2nd Lt.	Jun 7 44	.5 Fw 190 w/M.Becker
Becker, Marvin H. 1st Lt.	Jun 30 44	Ju 88
Curtis, Joseph R. 1st Lt.	Jul 4 44	Me 109
Curtis, Joseph R. 1st Lt.	Jul 4 44	.5 Me 109 w/W.Frederick
Frederick, Walter R. 1st Lt.	Jul 4 44	.5 Me 109 w/J.Curtis
Magel, Robert W. F/O	Jul 4 44	Me 109
Flagg, Walter L. 2nd Lt.	Jul 5 44	Me 109
Casteel, Barney P. 1st Lt.	Jul 6 44	Fw 190
Curtis, Joseph R. 1st Lt.	Jul 6 44	Me 109
Guerrero, Thomas 1st Lt.	Jul 6 44	Fw 190
Anderson, Richard P. 2nd Lt.	Aug 3 44	Fw 190
Fling, Roy T. Capt.	Aug 12 44	Me 109
Albright, Edward M. 1st Lt.	Aug 28 44	He 111
Flagg, Walter L. 1st Lt.	Aug 28 44	Me 109
Grace, Walter R. 2nd Lt.	Aug 28 44	He 111
Anderson, Richard B. 2nd Lt.	Sep 5 44	Me 109
Anderson, Richard B. 2nd Lt.	Sep 5 44	Me 109
Daniel, Robert J. 2nd Lt.	Sep 5 44	Me 109
Hart, Cameron M. 2nd Lt.	Sep 5 44	Me 109
Kyle, James A. 1st Lt.	Sep 5 44	Me 109
Timony, Eugene J. 1st Lt.	Sep 5 44	Fw 190
Warboys, Richard T. 1st Lt.	Sep 5 44	Me 109
Grace, Walter R. 2nd Lt.	Sep 21 44	Fw 190
Pitts, Walter H. 2nd Lt.	Sep 21 44	Fw 190
Pitts, Walter H. 2nd Lt.	Sep 21 44	Fw 190
Lister, James E. 2nd Lt.	Oct 12 44	Fw 190
Grace, Walter R. 1st Lt.	Nov 1 44	.5 Me 262 w/W.Gerbe (486th FS)
Davis, Ramon R. 1st Lt.	Nov 18 44	Fw 190
Frederickson, Russell 1st Lt.	Nov 27 44	Me 109
Frederickson, Russell 1st Lt.	Nov 27 44	Me 109
Lister, James F. 1st Lt.	Nov 27 44	Me 109
Anderson, Richard B. 1st Lt.	Dec 2 44	Me 109
Batson, Samuel K. 2nd Lt.	Dec 2 44	Me 109
Conger, Paul A. Major	Dec 2 44	Me 109
Conger, Paul A. Major	Dec 2 44	Me 109
Fahringer, John C. Capt.	Dec 2 44	Me 109
Fahringer, John C. Capt.	Dec 2 44	Me 109
Frederickson, Russell 1st Lt.	Dec 2 44	Me 109
Grace, Walter R. 1st Lt.	Dec 2 44	Me 109
Trumble, Pershing B. 1st Lt.	Dec 2 44	Me 109
Batson, Samuel K. 2nd Lt.	Dec 23 44	Fw 190

Clark, Charles R. 2nd Lt.	Dec 23 44	Fw 190		McBath, Charles T. 2nd Lt.	Jan 14 45	Me 109
Comstock, Harold E. Major	Dec 23 44	Fw 190		Rotzler, Charles M. 1st Lt.	Jan 14 45	Me 109
Comstock, Harold E. Major	Dec 23 44	Fw 190		Trumble, Pershing R. 1st Lt.	Jan 14 45	Me 109
Daniel, Robert J. 1st Lt.	Dec 23 44	Fw 190		Conger, Paul A. Major	Feb 3 45	Fw 190
Hart, Cameron M. Capt.	Dec 23 44	Fw 190		Conger, Paul A. Major	Feb 3 45	Me 109
Hoffman, William R. 2nd Lt.	Dec 23 44	Fw 190		Fahringer, John C. Capt.	Feb 3 45	Me 109
Hughes, Melvin J. F/O	Dec 23 44	Fw 190		Hart, Cameron M. Capt.	Feb 3 45	Fw 190
Murphy, Randel L. 2nd Lt.	Dec 23 44	Fw 190		Hart, Cameron M. Capt.	Feb 3 45	Fw 190
Murphy, Randel L. 2nd Lt.	Dec 23 44	Fw 190		Kuhn, Philip G. 2nd Lt.	Feb 3 45	Fw 190
Schertz, Willard C. 2nd Lt.	Dec 23 44	Fw 190		Ogden, Frank M. 1st Lt.	Feb 3 45	Fw 190
Batson, Samuel K. 2nd Lt.	Dec 25 44	Me 109		Bostwick, George E. Major	Mar 25 45	Me 262
Hart, Cameron M. Capt.	Dec 25 44	Me 109		Crosthwait, Edwin C. Capt.	Mar 25 45	Me 262
Conger, Paul A. Major	Jan 14 45	Me 109		Fahringer, John C. Capt.	Apr 5 45	Me 262
Davis, Ramon R. 1st Lt.	Jan 14 45	Me 109		Bostwick, George E. Major	Apr 7 45	Me 109
McBath, Charles T. 2nd Lt.	Jan 14 45	Me 109		Bostwick, George E. Major	Apr 7 45	Me 109
				McBath, Charles T. 2nd Lt.	Apr 7 45	Me 109

APPENDIX V
EVADERS

Appel, Edward H.
Barnes, William H.
Bennett, Eugene
Grosvenor, William
McLure, Wendell A.
Mahurin, Walker
Sheehan, Robert
Vitale, Joseph

APPENDIX VI
PRISONERS-OF-WAR

Bevins, Hiram
Blake, Gordon
Brown, Cleve
Brown, Lewis
Chasko, Andrew
Czarnota, Leo
Edens, Billy
Fields, James
Frye, Chester
Gabreski, Francis
Garth, Winston
Goldstein, George
Greene, Jack
Haggard, Wilburn
Hertile, Earl
Hodges, Glen
Johnson, Gerald
Johnson, Willard
Kelley, Robert
Kozey, John
Lewis, Gordon
Magel, Robert
Marcotte, John
McClure, John
McElhare, William
Morrill, Bryon
Mudge, Dick
Piper, Preston
Quirk, Michael
Reeder, Caleb
Rougeau, Edward
Spanely, George
Steele, Robert
Van Able, Wilfred
Wood, Melvin
Zemke, Hubert

GLOSSARY

"Ajax": Tactical identification of VIII Fighter Command.

Bandit: An aircraft identified as an enemy.

Bingo: The fuel state reached at the limit of a fighter mission indicating that it was time to head for the "homeplate."

Bogie: An unidentified type aircraft.

Circus: An early term for a bomber escort mission.

Chattanooga: Air-to-ground attacks against German rail transportation.

"Daily": Tactical radio callsign "A" squadron, 63rd FS, "B" squadron was "Yorker", while based at Boxted.

"Darkey": the direction finding, DF, control center in England from which a pilot could obtain a radio steer to his home base or an emergency landing field.

"Dogday": Tactical radio callsign of Boxted.

ETO: European Theatre of Operations.

"Fairbanks": Tactical radio callsign of headquarters 56th Fighter Group "A" squadron; "B" squadron was "Subway", and "C" squadron was "Pantrie."

Field Order: Identification of the mission as to role and time.

FLAK: An adopted German term (FLug-Abwehr-Kanone) to identify anti-aircraft fire. Identified as light, medium and heavy in intensity and caliber. ie; Heavy medium flak would indicate a high concentration of 88mm fire, etc.

Fullhouse: A local air patrol over a given location in enemy territory.

GP: General purpose bombs, ranged from 100 to 1000 pounds.

Homeplate: A pilots' home airfield.

Jackpot: Air-to-ground attacks against German airdromes.

"Keyworth": The tactical callsign of "A" squadron, 61st FS until April 22, 1944. "B" squadron was "Halsted."

KIA: Killed in Action.

MEW: Microwave Early Warning, aka, radar (Radio detection and ranging).

"Noball": Missions against V-1 and V-2 sites.

Pancake: To land, sometimes used to indicate that a pilot would have to land wheels-up.

Pathfinder: Aka, PFF. An H2X radar equipped bomber used to locate the target.

"Platform": Tactical radio callsign of "A" squadron, 62nd FS, "B" squadron was "Icejug", while based at Boxted.

"Postgate": Tactical callsign of "A" squadron, 63rd FS until April 22, 1944. "B" squadron was "Northgrove."

POW: Prisoner of War.

Ramrod: Early term for a bomber escort mission.

Rodeo: Early term for a mission intended to force the Luftwaffe into a fight.

"Royalflush": MEW directed missions designed to "flush-up" Luftwaffe fighters.

RTB: Return to base (to land) or time of landing.

Rhubarb: A low altitude sweep over enemy territory.

RV: Rendezvous (Point of).

Scoring: Claims were made, as example, as 6-2-1, which indicated six were claimed as destroyed, two probables, and one damaged.

Stud: A divebombing mission.

"Sturdy": Tactical callsign for Halesworth.

Type 16: MEW missions (radar) under tactical control of the 65th Fighter Wing, identified via the tactical radio callsign "Tackline" until early 1944, and then "Colgate." Other signs worked with were "Nuthouse" and "Sweepstakes."

Whippet": Tactical radio callsign of "A" squadron, 61st FS until April 22, 1944. "B" squadron was "Household", while based at Boxted.

WIA: Wounded in Action.

"Woodfire": Tactical callsign of "A" squadron, 62nd FS until April 22, 1944. "B" squadron was "Groundhog."

"Yardstick": Tactical callsign for Headquarters 56th Fighter Group until April 22, 1944. "B" squadron was "Ashland."

BIBLIOGRAPHY

Cadin, Martin, *Black Thursday*, New York: Dell Pub. Co., 1960

Carter, Kit C., and Mueller, Robert, *Combat Chronology 1941-1945*, Washington, Center for Air Force history, 1991.

Davis, Albert H., Russell J. Coffin and Robert B. Woodward, ed., *The 56th Fighter Group in World War II*, Washington: Infantry Journal Press. 1946

Davis, Larry, *56th Fighter Group*, Carrollton: Squadron/Signal, 1991

Freeman, Roger A., *The Mighty Eighth*, Garden City, New York: Doubleday and Co., 1970

– *Mighty Eighth War Diary*, London: Janes. 1981

– *Mighty Eighth War Maunual*, London: Janes. 1984

Fry, Gary L. and Ethell, Jeffrey L., *Escort to Berlin*, New York: Arco Publishing Ltd., 1980

Gabreski, Francis and Carl Molesworth, *Gabby: A Fighter Pilot's Life*, New York: Orion Books, 1991

Hess, William N., *Zempke's Wolfpack*, Osceola: Motorbooks, 1992

Infield, Glenn, *Big Week*, New York: Pinnacle, 1974

Jablonski, Edward, *Double Strike*, New York: Doubleday, 1974

Johnson, Robert S. with Martin Caidin, *Thunderbolt*, New York: Ballantine Books. 1958

Klibbe, Frank W., "Fox Able One-The First Transalantic Jet Deployment," *Air Force Magazine*, October 1980, 72-80.

Mahurin, Walker "Bud.", *Honest John*, New York: Van Rees Press, 1962

McCrary, John R. and David E. Scherman, *First Of The Many*, New York: Simon and Schuster. 1944

Sims, Edward H., *The Aces Talk*, New York: Ballantine Books. 1972

Stafford, Gene, "Blow Torch Across The Atlantic," *Wings*, February 1973, 60-67.

Zemke, Hubert and Roger A. Freeman, *Zemke's Wolfpack*, New York: Orion Books, 1988

– *Zempke's Stalag*, Washington: Smithsonian Institution, 1991

Original copies of the official 56th Fighter Group history are in the archives at Maxwell Air Force Base, Montgomery, AL. This material is also available on microfilm reels BO 151 and BO 152 for the 56th FG, itself, and reels AO 746 and AO 747 for the war years concerning the 61st, 62nd and 63rd fighter squadrons.

INDEX

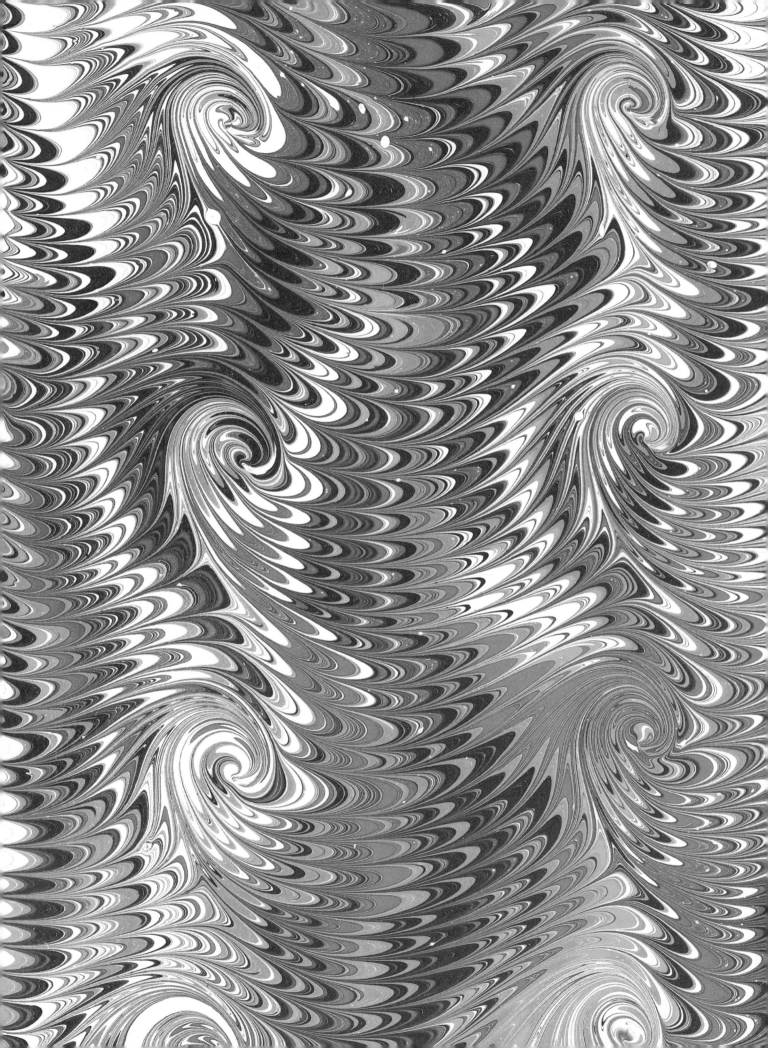